TEXTILES

TEXTILES

Third Edition

Norma Hollen and Jane Saddler

IOWA STATE UNIVERSITY

Drawings by Harriet Allen and Donna Danielson

IOWA STATE UNIVERSITY

Photographs by Lou Facto

IOWA STATE UNIVERSITY

The Macmillan Company, New York/Collier-Macmillan Limited, London

Third Printing, 1969

Earlier editions © copyright 1955 and 1964 by The Macmillan Company.

Some of section on fabrics © 1952 by Norma Hollen and Jane Saddler in *Modern Textiles*.

Library of Congress catalog card number: 68–10814

The Macmillan Company
Collier-Macmillan Canada, Ltd., Toronto, Ontario

Printed in the United States of America

Preface to the Third Edition

In updating and revising *Textiles* for its third edition, we have attempted to incorporate the new developments in fiber, yarns, fabric construction, and finishes. The information on fibers has been organized so the student can see the relationships between fibers, and in each chapter the new developments are discussed separately. As in the previous edition, the sections on fabric construction are presented in detail, and information has been added on stretch fabrics, nonwovens, durable press, multi-component fabrics, and other topics that have attained increased importance since the publication of the second edition.

A comprehensive view of past and present textile development is presented, and the student is thereby encouraged to evaluate the newest products in terms of past accomplishments, current demands, and future possibilities.

Special attention has been devoted to the selection of illustrations, more than one third of which are new in this edition. We hope that the numerous charts, line drawings, and photographs will prove especially valuable. Throughout the text, visual elements have been positioned in strict accordance with relating textual explanations, so that full and effective use may be made of all illustrations.

Norma Hollen
Jane Saddler

Fig. A. An easy way to prepare fabric swatches.

Preface

This book has been written for a first college course in textiles. Concepts, principles, and facts about fibers, yarns, fabric constructions, and finishes are presented in technical terms. An explanation of physical and chemical terminology is given so that chemistry need not be a prerequisite for understanding the text.

The primary objective is to give enough information about fabrics so the student can intelligently select and care for textile products. Illustrations, written and visual, relate to both apparel and household textiles, but the text is not oriented to specific end-uses, since textile principles can be applied to any end-use. We hope both students and teachers will be able to make these applications.

A good overview of the textile industry is included so that students will understand production as well as consumer problems and will have a greater appreciation for past developments as well as a broad concept of future possibilities in the field.

Textiles is a rapidly changing field. It is impossible for one to "keep up-to-date" without reading about, experimenting with, and evaluating new products as they come on the market. So that new developments can be related to or classified with the basic understandings learned in a textile course, much emphasis has been placed on classification of information.

Fibers are organized according to the Textile Fiber Products Identification Act of 1960. Fiber blends are discussed. New yarn developments as well as traditional spinning techniques are included, with emphasis on yarn properties. Basic fabrics are discussed in the unit on fabric constructions; other fabrics are described in the Glossary. New developments in construction and in finishing are presented with the emphasis on the effect produced.

There is little repetition in the text, but facts, concepts, and principles are interrelated, so that it is necessary to recall or refer to other sections when studying. The book is cross-indexed for easy reference.

In studying textiles, students must handle and examine fabrics. It is usually the teacher's responsibility to select and prepare the fabrics. We have found that cutting or tearing fabrics into strips, stacking them in units, stapling at intervals, and cutting between staples is an easy way to prepare swatches. (See Figure A.)

We wish to express our appreciation to Mrs. Harriet Lewis for her constructive criticism and valuable suggestions and to the students at Iowa State University, for whom the first book was written and by whom we have been guided in testing the effectiveness of this revision.

Norma Hollen
Jane Saddler

vii

Contents

x   **Contents**

TEXTILES

Introduction

The study of textiles is concerned with fabrics and the materials from which they are made. Asleep or awake, at work or play, sick or well, rich or poor, everyone uses textiles.[1] People wear clothing for various reasons: for warmth, for protection from the elements or hazards connected with their jobs, to make themselves more attractive, for status, for identification (armed forces, religious orders, and so on), and in some cases to conform to, or defy, the current social custom.

Textiles are widely used in the home. Floors are carpeted with textiles, sofas and chairs are upholstered, windows are draped, and beds are outfitted with textiles from mattress ticking to the bedspread with many different textile layers in between. Towels are used for drying purposes as well as for decoration in bathrooms and kitchens. Table linens are used to provide an attractive background for the table service, for absorbing sound, and for protection of wood surfaces.

In industry, textiles have many uses; for example, conveyer belts, tapes, bagging, and pads to absorb sound. The automotive industry uses many textile products. Tires have a fabric or tire cord base, seats are upholstered, and floors carpeted with textiles.

Textiles are used for special purposes, such as to provide protection or ensure the proper living environment for air-space travel. There are more than 1,800 military uses for textile products.

Textiles are important in the world's economy. All emerging countries develop a textile industry. When compared with 27 major industries in the United States, the textile industry ranks second in size, fourth in total number of manufacturing units, first in total number of employees, second in dollar wages paid, and third (steel and food rank higher) in total value added to raw materials.[2]

In the United States, about 15 million people receive their livelihood from textiles. In 1966, there were 7,500 textile plants in 42 states. The textile industry has made major contributions to the development of civilization. Animal husbandry, particularly the domestication and breeding of sheep, and the planting of seeds and growing of

---

[1] American Textile Manufacturers Institute, Inc., "Textiles for You." Booklet.

[2] George S. Linton, "Raw Material, Construction, Color, Finish," *Applied Basic Textiles*. Sloan and Pearce, 1966.

crops were in the beginning equally important for both food and fiber. The change from hand processes to machine processes, from home industry to the factory system, sparked the Industrial Revolution. The Jacquard loom, which operates from punch cards, was, perhaps, the start of automation. The development of man-made fibers has been a major contribution to the economy of all countries. They have made it possible to provide all kinds of fabrics in all price ranges so that consumers can buy a "fashion look" at low cost. The discovery that fibers could be synthesized from simple organic substances (nylon was the first fiber to be so prepared) ranks with the discovery of the wheel in its importance.

Some of the interesting textile developments in recent years are:

1. Disposable textiles, important in sanitary and surgical end-uses. Used in fashion-fabrics in the late 1960's.
2. Man-made leather-like fabrics, important in apparel, home furnishings accessories, and luggage.
3. Man-made fur-like fabrics, important in apparel.
4. Indoor-outdoor carpeting.
5. Stretch fabrics, important for comfort as well as support garments.
6. Durable press, important in apparel and home furnishings.

Because of the many changes in textiles, consumers need to know more about fabrics than ever before in order to make satisfactory choices. Desirable properties in clothing textiles are protection, esthetic appeal, durability, and ease of care. The relative importance of these properties depends on the specific end-use.

Different consumers want different properties for the same use. One person may place a high value on easy-care and will only buy garments that can be washed, dried, and worn without ironing; another person who likes crisp smooth textures will willingly give more time and energy to caring for garments. Some consumers want to care for their own garments; others depend on service organizations for reconditioning.

It is true of all fabrics that the performance and care required are determined by a combination of factors; namely, *the fiber content*, *the yarn structure*, *the method of construction*, and *the fabric finish*. For example, a blouse or shirt may be of cotton, wool, a man-made fiber, or a blend of fibers. The fiber or fibers used will determine whether it is hand washable, machine washable, or dry cleanable; whether it will wrinkle or be resilient; whether it will pill or shrink; whether it will be absorbent or water-repellent. The yarns in the garment may be absorbent or water-repellent, smooth or fuzzy, very fine or coarse, and have high twist or low twist. The structure of the yarn will contribute to resiliency, absorbency, shrinkage, and so on. The fabric in the blouse or shirt may be woven or knitted, which will determine its resiliency, absorbency, or shrinkage potential. The finish on the fabric may be durable or nondurable, and it may be visible or nonvisible. Different finishes give color, body, or surface beauty to the fabric, and they also may be used to compensate for lack of resiliency of fiber, yarn, or fabric construction, or to stabilize the fabric because of inherent shrinkage of the fibers or imposed shrinkage due to yarn and fabric construction.

The performance of garments is also dependent on trimmings, linings, and the like. The consumer should be aware that poor performance is not always due to the fabric itself but may be due to lack of compatibility of fabrics used together in a garment. For example, the cotton fabric of a blouse can be ironed with a hot iron, but trim of nylon lace is heat-sensitive and will melt or fuse at the touch of a hot iron.

Consumers must have basic information about fibers, yarns, fabric construction, and finishes if they are to select and care for textile products intelligently.

1 Textile Fibers

Fibers are pliable hair-like substances that are very small in diameter in relation to their length. They are the fundamental units used in the making of textile yarns and fabrics.

Until the twentieth century, all fibers were obtained from natural sources. Only four fibers—cotton, wool, flax, and silk—were commonly used. Because wool and flax were easy to spin, they were used more than the others when spinning and weaving were hand processes. After the Industrial Revolution, cotton became the most widely used fiber. Silk has always been expensive because its production has been dependent on hand labor. In the past 60 years, 17 different generic groups of man-made fibers have been produced. A *generic name* is the name of a family of fibers of similar chemical composition. Cotton, wool, flax, and silk are generic names for the natural fibers. The *generic names* for all the fibers are given in the table on page 4.

Many fibers exist in nature but are not used for textile fabrics because they lack the properties that make a fiber spinnable—length, pliability, strength, and cohesiveness. For example, kapok and milk-weed fibers are too brittle to spin into yarns. Silk is a long continuous filament and does not need to be cohesive, but it is strong and pliable. To be suitable economically for use, fibers must be inexpensive, readily available, and constant in supply.

One advantage of man-made fibers is that they can be produced the year round; whereas cotton and wool, for example, are all obtained during one short period each year and must be stored during the remainder of the year. Storage is expensive and uses up much building space. Natural fibers are subject to *lack of uniformity* due to weather conditions, nutrition or soil fertility, insects, and disease. Quality of natural fibers varies for the above reasons and also because they are produced in several varieties (cotton) and breeds (wool). Man-made fibers are uniform in quality because it is possible to control the entire production process. The size, shape, luster, length, and other properties of man-made fibers can be varied by changes in the production process.

The major textile fibers are listed by generic name in the table on page 4. Trade names—the names used by man-made fiber producers to identify their fibers—are not included. A list of United States fiber producers and their trade names can be found in Appendix C.

TEXTILE FIBERS

Natural Fibers	Man-Made Fibers*
Wool	Rayon
Silk	Acetate
Specialty hair fibers	Nylon
Cotton	Acrylic
Flax	Modacrylic
Jute	Polyester
Hemp	Olefin
Pineapple	Spandex
Abaca	Saran
Sisal	Glass
Kapok	Vinal
Asbestos	Vinyon
	Azlon†
	Metallic
	Lastrile
	Nytril†

* The man-made fiber generic names were established in 1958 by the Federal Trade Commission when the Textile Fiber Products Identification Act was passed. (See page 38.)
† Not produced in the United States.

The amounts and kinds of fiber used are ever-changing because of economic conditions, end-use requirements, research and development of fibers, and marketing and promotion. In the table below, notice that more man-made fibers are being used each year.

FIBER CONSUMPTION IN THE UNITED STATES

	(% on a weight basis)				
	1925	1935	1945	1955	1965
Cotton	86	79	76	65	51
Wool	10	12	11	6	4
Silk	2	2	—	—	—
Rayon and acetate	1.6	7	13	23	19
Nylon	—	—	0.5	6	11
Acrylics, polyester	—	—	—	—	15
Estimated per capita consumption in pounds	29	30	38	39	42
Total number of pounds (millions)	2,550	3,550	6,000	6,600	8,200

SOURCE: Adapted from *Textile Organon*, 1967.

Fabric properties, the primary concern of the consumer, are due to the combination of fiber properties, yarn properties, fabric construction, and finish properties. All these properties are interdependent; for example, a fiber's dye affinity determines the kind of dye to be used.

To analyze a fabric for expected performance, one usually starts with the fiber content. Some knowledge of a fiber's properties will help one to anticipate the performance contribution that the fiber will make to a fabric. For example, if a fiber has low absorbency, its contributions will be as shown below. Some are desirable; some are not.

Low-Absorbency Fiber

1. Static build-up
2. Quick drying
3. Difficult for dyer to color
4. Poor skin-comfort—clammy
5. Prevents evaporation of perspiration
6. Dimensionally stable to water
7. Good wrinkle recovery when laundered
8. Waterborne stains do not penetrate
9. Resin finishes are not absorbed

Fiber Structure

Fiber structure includes the external structure, the internal structure, and the chemical composition and structure.

External Structure

The external structure consists of length, diameter, cross-sectional shape, surface contour, crimps or twists, and distinctive parts.

Length. Fibers are obtained from the fiber producer in the following forms.

Filament	Staple
Natural filament	Natural staple
Monofilament	Man-made staple
Multifilament	Filament tow

Filaments are long continuous strands. Silk is the only natural filament fiber. Yarns made from filaments are of two types: monofilament and multifilament. *Monofilament* yarns are made of a single fiber of high strength and smoothness. Very sheer hosiery is made from a very fine monofilament. Sheer blouses, veils, and gowns are other examples of monofilament used in apparel. Large monofilaments are used in car seat covers, screenings, furniture webbing, and so on. *Multifilament* yarns are made of a number of tiny filaments with or without twist. The size and number of the filaments may vary. These yarns give a soft pleasant surface texture, luster, and luxurious drape. They are used in silk-type dresses, blouses, shirts, lingerie, and the like. Filament yarns are shown in Figure 1-1.

Staple fibers, either natural or man-made, are short in length and are measured in inches. They range from $\frac{1}{2}$ inch to 24 inches in length. Figure 1-2 shows staple fibers. All the natural fibers except silk are staple. Man-made staple and filament are spun by different equipment, often in different factories.

Filament tow is a collection of many parallel filaments with crimp but without twist and grouped together in rope form. (See Figure 1-3.) These filaments are later cut or broken into staple fibers. Several different lengths of cut staple are shown in Figure 1-4.

Diameter, Size, or Denier. Man-made fibers can be made uniform in diameter, can be varied in diameter shape, and can be made thick-and-thin at regular intervals throughout their length. (Additional information is given in the discussion of each individual fiber.) Natural fibers are subject to growth irregularities and therefore are not uniform in size or in development. The finer the diameter of a fiber,

the more pliable it is and the softer it feels. The thicker the fiber, the more body and stiffness it has and the more it will resist crushing—in carpets for example.

In natural fibers, fineness is a major factor in determining quality. Fineness is measured in microns (1/1000 of a millimeter).

DIAMETER RANGE FOR
NATURAL FIBERS

Cotton	16 to 20 microns
Flax	12 to 16 microns
Wool	10 to 70 microns
Silk	11 to 12 microns

In man-made fibers, diameter is controlled by the size of the spinneret holes and by stretching during or after spinning. The fineness of man-made fibers is measured in *denier*. Denier is determined by weighing 9,000 meters of yarn (or fiber). It is the weight in grams of this unit length. Staple fiber is sold by denier and fiber length, whereas filaments are sold by denier of the yarn or tow and the number of filaments in the yarn or tow. To determine the filament size, the yarn denier can be divided by the number of filaments.

$$\frac{40 \text{ denier yarn}}{20 \text{ filaments}} = 2 \text{ denier for each filament}$$

Clothing fibers range from one to seven denier. The same denier fiber is not suitable for all use. Clothing fibers do not make good carpets and vice

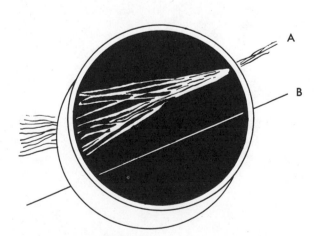

Fig. 1–1. Types of filament fiber yarns. A. Multifilament yarn. B. Monofilament yarn. (Courtesy of E. I. du Pont de Nemours & Company.)

Fig. 1–2. Staple from man-made fibers after the uniformly cut lengths have been fluffed. (Courtesy of E. I. du Pont de Nemours & Company.)

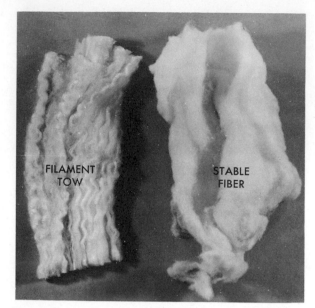

Fig. 1–3. Section of a filament tow or rope, showing thousands of filaments from which it is made.

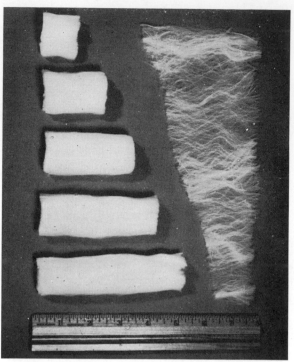

Fig. 1–4. Filament rope or tow cut into uniform lengths as required by the ultimate use in fabrics and garments. (Courtesy of E. I. du Pont de Nemours & Company.)

Fig. 1–5. Carpet wool on the left; carpet rayon on the right. (Courtesy of Bigelow-Sanford.)

versa. One of the early mistakes made by the carpet industry was using clothing fibers for carpets. They were too soft and pliable, and the carpets did not have good crush resistance. Rayon carpet fiber, introduced in 1953, was the first fiber especially made for carpets.

Carpet fibers range in denier from 15 to 24. Carpet wools are usually a mixture of fibers of different deniers. Except for denier size, carpet fibers have the same characteristics as the other fibers in the family to which they belong. For example, neither carpet wools nor clothing wools are very flammable and both have good resiliency. Further information about carpet fibers is given with the discussion of the individual fibers. Figure 1–5 shows some carpet fibers.

Cross-sectional Shape. Fiber shape of man-made fibers is controlled by the spinneret. Shapes vary from round to flat and straw-like and are important because they help determine the texture of fabrics. For a silk-like texture, trilobal fibers, which resemble silk in size and cross section, are made. Shape is also important in luster, bulk, and body and helps determine the *hand* or feel of the fabric. The natural fibers derive their shape from the way (1) the cellulose is built up during the plant growth; or (2) the shape of the orifice through which the silk fiber is extruded; or (3) the shape of the hair follicle and the

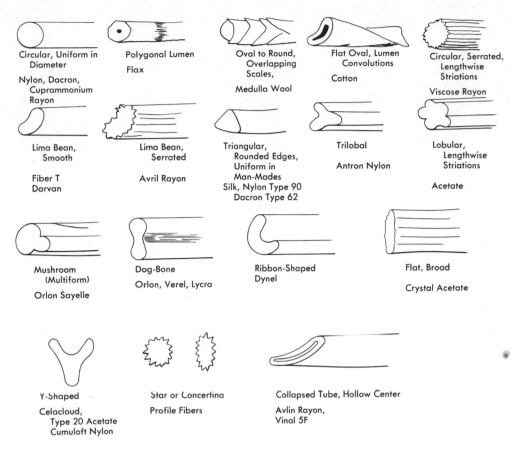

Fig. 1–6. Typical cross-sectional shapes and fiber contour.

formation of protein substances in animals. Figure 1–6 shows typical cross sections.

Surface Contour. Surface contour may be smooth serrated, lobular, or rough. The surface contour is defined as the surface of the fiber along its shaft. Some of the differences in the surface contour of the different fibers are shown in Figure 1–6. Surface contour is important in the hand and texture of the fabric.

Crimp. Crimp refers to the waves, bends, or twists that occur along the length of the fiber. Fiber crimp should not be confused with weave crimp, which results from the interlacing of yarns in the fabric, nor with molecular crimp, which results from the way molecular chains are built up. Fiber crimp increases cohesiveness, resiliency, resistance to abrasion, and gives increased bulk and warmth to fabrics. It helps fabrics to maintain their loft or thickness, increases absorbency and skin-contact comfort, but reduces luster.

A fiber may have one of three kinds of crimp, namely: mechanical crimp, natural or inherent crimp, or latent (chemical) crimp. *Mechanical crimp* is imparted to fibers by passing them through fluted rollers to produce a two-dimensional, saw-tooth crimp. The bends are angular in contrast to the rounded waves of a natural crimp. If the fluted rolls are heated, the crimp will be permanent in the thermoplastic or synthetic fibers. Figure 1–7 shows mechanical crimping gears. Texturizing processes to give loft, bulk, or stretch are done on filament (sometimes staple fiber) yarns by dropping the yarns into a stuffing box, or running them through a

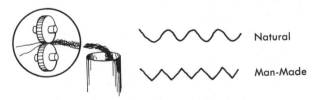

Fig. 1–7. Mechanical crimping gears.

false twister or subjecting them to a curling process. (See "Textured Yarns," page 105.) *Natural* or *inherent* crimp occurs in cotton and wool. Cotton has a two-dimensional twist called convolutions. (See page 32.) Wool has three-dimensional crimp.

The third type of crimp, *latent or chemical*, exists in the fiber in an undeveloped state until the finished garment is either (1) immersed in a suitable solvent, or (2) given a heat treatment to develop the crimp. This kind of crimp occurs in fibers that have been modified in the spinning solution or in the extrusion process. The modification produces a fiber that will shrink more on one side than it does on the other. High shrinkage of one side forces the fiber to curl.

Distinctive Parts. The natural fibers, except for silk, usually have three distinct parts: an outer covering called a skin or cuticle, an inner area, and a central core that may be hollow. Diagrams on pages 19 and 31 show the structural arrangement of the wool and cotton fibers. Parts of the man-made fibers are not as complex as those of the natural fibers and there are usually just two: the skin and a solid core.

Internal Structure

The internal structure of fibers is described in these terms: degree of polymerization, oriented, amorphous, crystallinity, cross links, and molecular bonds.

Fibers are composed of millions of molecular chains held together by cross links or molecular bonds. The length of the chains vary just as the length of fibers vary. The chain length is described as *degree of polymerization* (D.P.). Polymerization is the process of joining molecules together and if many molecules are joined together to make a chain, the fiber has a high degree of polymerization. Cotton, for example, has 10,000± molecules in a chain, whereas rayon has 350± molecules in the chain. Rayon, therefore, has a relatively low D.P.

Molecular chains are held together by *cross links* or bridges between the chains or by attractive forces called *hydrogen bonds* and *Van der Waals forces*. The attractive forces are similar to that of a magnet for a piece of iron. The closer the magnet gets to the iron, the more attraction. Hydrogen bonding is the attraction of hydrogen atoms (which have a positive force) of one chain and oxygen or nitrogen atoms (which have a negative force) of an adjacent chain. The closer the chains are together,

the stronger the bonds. Van der Waals forces are similar but weaker bonds.

Molecular chains lie in various configurations in the fiber.[1] (See Figure 1–8.) The representation (a)

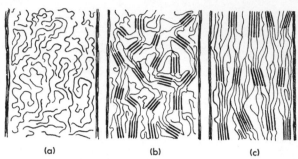

(a) (b) (c)

Fig. 1–8. (a) Unoriented, noncrystalline polymer. (b) Unoriented, crystalline polymer. (c) Oriented, crystalline polymer.

shows molecular chains in a random or unoriented arrangement, which is called *amorphous*. The drawing (c) shows molecular chains in an orderly or *oriented* arrangement. The arrangement of molecules in a fiber resembles the arrangement of fibers in a yarn. Strong yarns have long molecular chains parallel to the fiber axis and to each other. When man-made fibers are extruded from the spinneret, most of the molecules are in random orientation. The molecules on the surface are somewhat regular due to the frictional resistance of the solution to the sides of the spinneret holes. Stretching or drawing increases the orientation of the fiber, reduces the diameter, and packs the molecules closer together. (See Figure 1–9.)

Unstretched or Undrawn   Stretched or Drawn

Fig. 1–9. Before and after drawing the fiber.

Crystalline areas in a fiber are those in which the molecular chains are parallel to each other and close together. It is in the crystalline areas that hydrogen bonding and Van der Waals forces occur. Notice in drawing (b) that a fiber may have crystallites but not be oriented; that the molecular chains, while parallel to each other, are not necessarily parallel to the

[1] T. Alfrey, *Mechanical Behavior of High Polymers.* New York: Interscience Publishers, 1948, p. 344.

fiber axis. Crystallites are built up by nature in the natural fibers; and in the man-made fibers they occur during the coagulation or solidification of the filaments as they are spun. Stretching of the man-made fibers induces crystallinity.

Chemical Composition

The chemical composition of fibers is the factor that makes one fiber family (generic group) different from another. It is the basis for classifying fibers as cellulose, protein, acrylic, and so on. Some fibers are *homopolymers*—composed of like chemical structures—whereas others are *copolymers*—composed of two different substances. Some fibers have reactive groups; whereas others have no reactive groups, thus making them inert chemically.

Fiber Properties

Fiber properties are due to the structure of the fiber and contribute to fabric properties. This relationship is outlined in the following chart. Charts giving specific data and comparisons of fibers for each *starred* (*) property are in the Appendix. Discussions of the individual fiber properties are in those fiber chapters.

FIBER PROPERTIES VS FABRIC PROPERTIES

Fiber Property	Is Due to	Contributes to Fabric Property
Abrasion resistance is the ability of a fiber to withstand the rubbing or abrasion it gets in everyday use.	Tough outer layer, scales or skin Fiber toughness* Flexible molecular chains	Durability Abrasion resistance Resistance to splitting
Absorbency is the ability of a fiber to take up moisture and is expressed in terms of moisture regain*, which is the percentage of moisture that a bone-dry fiber will absorb from the air under standard conditions of temperature and moisture.	Chemical structure—hydroxyl groups Molecular structure, amorphous areas, low crystallinity	Comfort—warmth, water repellency, absorbency, static build-up Dyeability Spotting Wrinkle resistance and crease recovery Shrinkage Tear strength
Ageing resistance	Chemical structure	Storing of fabrics
Chemical reactivity is the effect of acids, alkali, oxidizing agents, solvents.	Chemical structure—polar groups	Helps determine care required during cleaning—bleaching, ability to take acid or alkali finishes
Cover is the ability to occupy space for the purpose of concealment or protection.	Crimp, curl, or twist Cross-sectional shape	Warmth in fabric Cost—less fiber needed
Cohesiveness is the ability of fibers to cling together during spinning. This is an important property in staple but not in filament.	Crimp or twists	Resistance to ravel
Creep is delayed elasticity. The fiber does not recover immediately from strain but will recover gradually.	Molecular structure—lack of side chains, cross links, strong bonds; poor orientation	Streaky dyeing and shiners in fabric
Density—see *Specific Gravity*		

Fiber Property	Is Due to	Contributes to Fabric Property
Dyeability is the ability of fibers to be dyed.	Chemical structure—reactive groups—dye sites Molecular structure: orientation crystallinity cross linkages H-bonds Fiber diameter	Ability to be dyed or printed
Elastic recovery★ is the ability of fibers to recover from strain. *Elasticity* is the ability of a stretched material to return immediately to its original size. Fibers usually have high elasticity for low stretches and high elasticity for high stretches.	Molecular structure: side chains cross-linkages strong bonds	Processability of fabrics Resiliency Delayed elasticity or creep
Electrical conductivity is the ability to transfer electrical charges.	Chemical structure—polar groups	Poor conductivity causes fabric to cling to machinery during fabric and garment production; clinging of fabric to person in cold, dry atmospheres; electric shocks
Elongation★ is the ability to be stretched, extended, or lengthened. For production of yarns and fabrics a minimum of 10 per cent elongation is desirable. Elongations vary at different temperatures and when wet or dry.	Fiber crimp Molecular structure: molecular crimp orientation	Facilitates textile working Increases tear strength Reduces brittleness Provides "give" and stretchiness
Feltability is ability of fibers to mat together.	Scale structure of wool	Ability to make fabrics directly from fibers Special care required during washing
Flammability is the ability to ignite and burn.	Chemical composition	Flammability of fabric
Hand is the way a fiber feels when handled—silky, harsh, soft, crisp, dry tactile.	External structure: diameter cross-sectional shape crimp length	Hand of fabric
Heat conductivity is the ability to conduct heat away from the body.	External structure: crimp cross-sectional shape uniformity of cross section	Warmth
Heat sensitivity★ is the ability to soften, melt, or shrink when subjected to heat.	Inner structure: fewer intermolecular attractive forces no cross links Heat causes molecules to vibrate	Determine safe washing and ironing temperatures Makes heat setting possible Makes certain fabric finishes possible

Fiber Property	Is Due to	Contributes to Fabric Property
Hydrophobic, hydrophilic, hygroscopic	*See* Absorbency	

Luster is the light reflected from a surface. It differs from shine in that it is more subdued, since the light rays striking the surface are broken up.	External structure:
	  fiber length
	  crimp
	  cross-sectional shape
		Luster

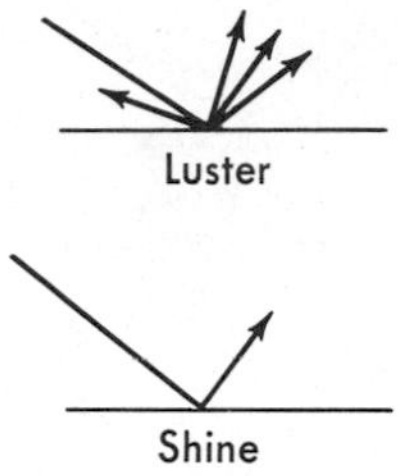

Fig. 1–10. Reflection of light from the fabric surface.

Fiber Property	Is Due to	Contributes to Fabric Property
Loft or compressional resiliency, refers to the ability of a fiber, yarn, or fabric to spring back to its original thickness after being compressed.	Fiber crimp	Springiness, good cover Resistance to flattening
Moth resistance	Chemical composition—no sulfur present	Care during storage
Mildew resistance	Chemical composition	Care during storage; selection of fabrics for damp humid climate
Pilling is the balling up of fiber ends on the surface of fabrics.	Fiber strength*	Pilling
Specific Gravity and *Density* are measures of the weight of a fiber. Density is the weight in grams per cubic centimeter, and specific gravity is the ratio of the mass of the fiber to an equal volume of water at 4° C.	Chemical composition	Warmth without weight Loftiness—full and light Buoyancy to fabric
Stability is the retention of size, shape, or form.	Chemical composition Strong molecular bonds	Resistance to shrinkage
Stiffness or *rigidity* is the opposite of flexibility. It is the resistance to bending or creasing.		Body of fabric
The *strength* of a fiber is defined as the ability to resist stress and is expressed as tensile strength (pounds per square inch) or as tenacity* (grams per denier).	Molecular structure—D.P., orientation, crystallinity	Durability, tear strength, sagging, pilling, fabric weight
Sunlight resistance is the ability to withstand degradation from direct sunlight.	Chemical composition	Durability of curtains and draperies, outdoor furniture, outdoor carpeting

Fig. 1–11. Identifying fibers by the burning test.

Fiber Identification

The procedure for identification of the fiber content of a fabric depends upon the nature of the sample, the experience of the analyst, and the facilities available. Since there are laws that require the fiber content of apparel and household textiles to be indicated on the label, the consumer may need to look for identification labels only. If he wishes to confirm or check the information on the label, the burning test and some simple solubility tests may be used.

Visual Inspection

Visual inspection of a fabric for appearance and hand (feel) is always the first step in fiber identification. It is no longer possible to make an identification of the fiber content by the appearance and hand alone because man-made fibers can be made to resemble the natural fibers. However, observation of the following characteristics is helpful.

1. Length of fiber. Untwist the yarn to determine length. Any fiber can be made in staple length but not all fibers can be filament. For example, cotton and wool are always staple.

2. Luster or lack of luster.
3. Body, texture, hand—soft-to-hard, rough-to-smooth, warm-to-cool, or stiff-to-flexible.

Burning Test

The burning test can be used to identify the chemical composition such as cellulose, protein, mineral, or chemical and thus identify the group to which a fiber belongs. *Blends cannot be identified by the burning test.* If visual inspection is used along with the burning test, fiber identification can be carried further. For example, if the sample is cellulose and also filament, it is rayon; but if it is staple, a positive identification cannot be made.

General directions for the burning test:

1. Ravel out and test several yarns from each side of the fabric to see if they have the same fiber content. Differences in luster, twist, and color will indicate that there might be two or more kinds of fibers in the fabric.
2. Hold the yarn horizontally, as shown in Figure 1–11. Use tweezers if desired. Feed the yarns slowly into the edge of the flame from the alcohol lamp and observe what happens. Repeat this several times to check results.

See the chart on page 13 for identification of fiber groups.

The Microscope Test

A knowledge of fiber structure, obtained by seeing the fibers in the microscope and observing some of the differences among fibers in each group, is of help in understanding fibers and fabric behavior.

Positive identification of most of the natural fibers can be made by using this test. The man-made fibers are more difficult to identify because some of them look alike and their appearance may be changed by variations in the manufacturing process. Positive identification of the man-made fibers by this means is rather limited. Cross-sectional appearance is helpful if more careful examination is desired.

Longitudinal and cross-sectional photomicrographs of individual fibers are included in the fiber chapters and these may be used for reference when checking unknown fibers.

IDENTIFICATION BY BURNING

Fibers	When Approaching Flame	When in Flame	After Removal from Flame	Ash	Odor
Cellulose Cotton Flax Rayon	Does not fuse or shrink from flame	Burns	Afterglow	Grey feathery smooth edge	Burning paper
Protein Silk Wool	Fuses and curls away from flame	Burns slowly	Sometimes self-extinguishing	Crushable black ash	Burning hair
Acetate	Fuses away from flame	Burns with melting	Continues to burn and melt	Brittle black hard bead	———
Acrylic	Fuses away from flame	Burns with melting	Continues to burn and melt	Brittle black hard bead	———
Modacrylic	Fuses away from flame	Burns very slowly with melting	Self-extinguishing	Brittle black hard bead	———
Nylon	Fuses and shrinks away from flame	Burns slowly with melting	Usually self-extinguishing	Hard grey bead	Celery-like
Olefin	Fuses and shrinks away from flame	Burns with melting	Continues self-extinguishing	Hard tan bead	———
Polyester	Fuses and shrinks away from flame	Burns slowly with melting; black smoke	Usually self-extinguishing	Hard black bead	Sweetish odor
Saran	Fuses and shrinks away from flame	Burns very slowly with melting	Self-extinguishing	Hard black bead	———
Spandex	Fuses but does not shrink from flame	Burns with melting	Continues to burn with melting	Soft black ash	———

Directions for using the microscope:

1. Clean the lens, slide, and cover glass.
2. Place a drop of water on the slide.
3. Untwist a yarn and place the loosened fibers on the slide. Cover with the cover glass and press down to eliminate air bubbles.
4. Place the slide on the stage of the microscope, and then focus with low power first. If the fibers have not been well loosened, it will be difficult to focus on a single fiber.
5. If a fabric contains more than one kind of fiber, test each. Be sure to check both the warp and filling yarns.

Solubility Tests

Solubility tests are used to identify the man-made fibers by generic class and to confirm identification of natural fibers. Two household tests, the acetone test for acetate and the alkali test for wool, are described on pages 54 and 21 respectively.

In using the following tests the specimen is placed in the liquid in the order listed below. The specimen is stirred for 5 minutes and the effect noted. Fiber, yarns, or small pieces of fabric may be used. The liquids are hazardous and should be handled with care. Chemical laboratory exhaust hoods, gloves, aprons, and goggles should be used.

SOLUBILITY TESTS

Solvent	Fiber Solubility
1. Acetic acid-glacial, 75° F	Acetate
2. Hydrochloric acid, 20% concentration, 1.096 density, 75° F	Nylon
3. Sodium hypochlorite solution (ph 11), 75° F	Silk and wool (silk dissolves in hydrochloric acid at 75° F)
4. Xylene (meta), 282° F (boil)	Olefin and saran (saran dissolves in 1.4 dioxane at 200° F). Olefin is not soluble.
5. Ammonium thiocyanate, 70% concentration, 266° F (boil)	Acrylic
6. Butyrolactone, 70° F	Modacrylic, acetate
7. Dimethyl formamide, 200° F	Spandex, modacrylic, acrylic, acetate
8. Sulfuric acid, 75% concentration, 1.065 density, 75° F	Cotton, flax, rayon, nylon, acetate
9. Cresol (meta), 200° F	Polyester, nylon, acetate

2 *Protein Fibers*

All protein fibers contain the chemical elements *carbon*, *hydrogen*, *oxygen*, and *nitrogen*. Wool also contains *sulfur*, which gives it some properties different from those of silk. Natural protein fibers are products of animal growth. Man-made protein fibers (regenerated) are made by dissolving and resolidifying protein from animals or plants.

The protein of the wool fiber is called *keratin* and that of the silk fiber is *fibroin*. The basic units of the protein molecule of both fibers are amino acids joined together in linear *polypeptide* chains. A simple formula is:

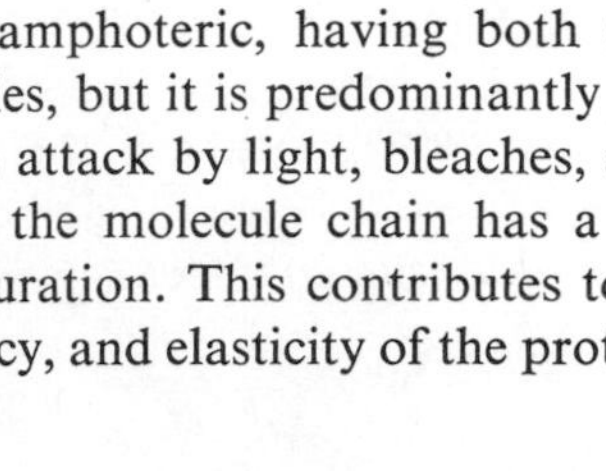

$$
\begin{array}{c}
\text{R} \\
|\\
\text{CH} \qquad \text{O} \\
\diagup \quad \diagdown \ \| \\
\text{NH}_2 \qquad \text{C OH}
\end{array}
$$

Amino   Carboxyl
group   group
(basic)   (acidic)

Protein is amphoteric, having both acidic and basic properties, but it is predominantly basic. It is susceptible to attack by light, bleaches, and alkali. Observe that the molecule chain has a somewhat folded configuration. This contributes to the flexibility, resiliency, and elasticity of the protein fibers.

PROPERTIES COMMON TO ALL PROTEIN FIBERS

Properties	Importance to the Consumer
Resiliency	Resists wrinkling. Wrinkles hang out between wearings. Fabrics tend to hold their shape.
Hygroscopic	Comfortable in cool damp climate. Moisture prevents brittleness in carpets.
Weaker when wet	Handle carefully during washing. Wool loses about 40% of its strength and silk loses about 15%.
Specific gravity	Fabrics feel lighter than cellulosics of the same thickness.
Harmed by alkali	Use neutral or slightly alkaline soap or detergent. Perspiration weakens the fiber.
Harmed by oxidizing agents	Chlorine bleaches damage fiber so should not be used. Sunlight causes white fabrics to turn yellowish.
Harmed by dry heat	Wool becomes harsh and brittle and scorches easily with dry heat. Use steam! White silk and wool turn yellow.
Flame resistance	Do not burn readily, are self-extinguishing, have odor of burning hair, and form a black crushable ash.

COMPARISON OF WOOL AND SILK

Wool	Silk
Staple only	Filament and staple
Cell structure	Solid fiber
Elliptical cross section	Triangular cross section
Three-dimensional fiber crimp	No fiber crimp
Bicomponent	Single component
Double molecule chain	Single molecule chain
Molecular crimp	Molecular crimp
Cross-links	No cross-links

All protein fibers have some common properties. These are given in the table on page 15.

Wool

Wool is one of the oldest and most universally used textile fibers. Written records indicate that it was probably used in the Near East about 600 B.C. and it is possible that its use dates back even farther. A woolen rug which was found, preserved by natural refrigeration, in a frozen burial mound in the Altai mountains on the border of Siberia and Outer Mongolia is said to be the oldest known article made of wool that is still in existence in the world.[1] It dates back to the period between 500 and 300 B.C. and is now kept in the USSR State Hermitage Museum in Leningrad.

Sheep were probably the first animals domesticated by man. The covering of primitive sheep consisted of two parts; a long hairy outer coat that was used primarily for rugs and felt, and a light downy undercoat that was very desirable for clothing. The fleece of present-day domesticated sheep contains primarily a soft undercoat. It is thought that cross-breeding of sheep to increase the amount of undercoat began about 100 A.D. By 1400 A.D., the Spanish had developed the merino, a breed of sheep that was the forerunner of all the breeds of sheep that produce fine wool. The wool of the merino contains no hair or kemp fiber. Kemp is a coarse, brittle,

[1] "Frozen Tombs of the Scythians," M. I. Artamonov, *Scientific American* **212**: 100 (May, 1965).

dead-white fiber found in the fleece of primitive sheep and still found in the wools from all breeds of sheep except the merino. Merino sheep produce the most valuable wool, which makes up about 30 per cent of the world production. Of this about 66 per cent comes from Australia.

Sheep were not known to the American Indians. The Navajo sheep are descendants of an unimproved long-hair breed brought over from Spain. The only carpet wool now produced in the United States comes from these sheep. The sheep are quite small with an undercoat of fibers 3 to 4 inches long and an outer coat 4 to 6 inches long. Carpet wools are made up of a mixture of fine fibers, long hairy fibers, and kemp. Most of the world's supply of coarse carpet wools come from nomadic flocks grown in Asia, Argentina, New Zealand, and Scotland.

Kinds of Wool

The term "wool" as used (legally) in the textile industry includes hair fibers from the Angora goat, Cashmere goat, camel, alpaca, llama, and vicuna. True wool is the fleece of the sheep. It comes from several sources—it is sheared from wool-type sheep, pulled from the pelts of meat-type sheep, and reclaimed from used clothing and manufacturers' cutters scraps. This reclaimed wool formerly was sold as new wool. Wool is one of the more expensive fibers and it is often blended with less expensive fibers to reduce the cost of the fabric or to extend its use. To protect consumers as well as the producers, manufacturers, and distributors from unrevealed presence of substitutes or mixtures and to inform the consumer of the source of the wool fiber, Congress passed the Wool Products Labeling Act in 1939. The law requires that a label or tag giving the fiber content in terms of percentage and also giving the source of the wool must be firmly attached to any product containing wool.

Terms that describe wool fibers according to their source have been set up by the Federal Trade Commission. They are:

1. *Wool* refers to new wool or wool fibers reclaimed from knit scraps, broken threads, and noils. (Noils are the short fibers that are combed out in the making of worsted yarns.)
2. *Reprocessed wool* is obtained from scraps of new woven or felted fabrics which have been

garnetted (shredded) back to the fibrous state and used again in the manufacture of woolens.

3. *Reused wool*, sometimes called shoddy, is obtained from rags and old clothing which have been used or worn. The rags are cleaned and sorted and shredded into fibers. Reused wool is often blended with new wool before being respun. It is usually used in utility fabrics—mackinaw-type fabric, which is thick and boardy, and interlinings.

Reused and reprocessed wool are important in the textile industry. These fibers, however, lose some of the desirable properties of new wool during the garnetting process, because the fibers are not only broken by the mechanical action of the garnetting but are also damaged by wear. The fibers are not as resilient or strong and durable as new wool.

The Wool Products Labeling Act does NOT tell the consumer anything about the *quality* of the wool fabric. The consumer must rely on feel and texture to determine quality. The term "virgin" on the label does not necessarily mean good quality and the term is not defined by law. However, a Federal Trade Commission ruling has defined virgin wool as wool that has never been processed in anyway before its complete manufacture into the finished garment. This eliminates knit clips and broken threads from being labeled virgin wool.

Fineness, color, crimp, strength, length, and elasticity are wool fiber characteristics that vary with the breed of the sheep. (See Figure 2–1.) There are about 30 breeds of improved sheep in the world. Lamb's wool comes from animals less than seven months old and it is softer and finer than the fiber from older animals. The term "lamb's wool" usually appears on the label when that fiber is present in a garment. The *length* of wool fibers ranges from 1 to 14 inches depending on the kind of sheep. The length of true wool is determined somewhat by the length of time between shearings. Long wool fibers are used for worsted yarns and the shorter fibers are used in woolen fabrics. The *diameter* of wool fibers varies from 10 to 50 microns. A micron is 1/20,000 inch. Merino lamb's wool may average 15 microns in diameter.

Grading and sorting are two marketing operations that put wools of like character together. In *grading*, the whole fleece is judged for fineness and length. Fine combing wools measure 2.5 inches or more

Fig. 2–1. Photo showing length of wool fiber and crimp. (Courtesy of the Wool Bureau.)

in length. French combing wools are 1.5 to 2.5 inches long. The coarser clothing wools are around 1.5 inches. *Sorting* breaks up the individual fleece into various qualities. The best quality comes from the sides and shoulders; the poorest from the lower legs.

The quality of apparel wool is based on its fineness and length. High quality does not necessarily imply durability, since fine fibers are not as durable as coarse fibers. In 1964, the Wool Bureau—an organization that promotes the use of wool and sponsors wool research—adopted the Woolmark as a symbol of quality to be used on all merchandise that meets the Wool Bureau's specifications for quality. A testing program is used to check the quality of items bearing the Woolmark symbol. (See Figure 2–2.)

Physical Structure and Related Properties

A knowledge of the physical structure and chemical nature of the fiber contributes to an understand-

PURE VIRGIN WOOL

Fig. 2–2. The Woolmark symbol of quality. (Courtesy of the Wool Bureau, Inc.)

ing of performance and care. Wool's excellent properties are pointed up by the following quotation (*Textile Industries Magazine*, April, 1964):

Wool Wet but Useable. A cargo of South African wool which has been lying in about 160 feet of water 50 miles off Nantucket Island, Mass., for 22 years will be salvaged and used, a Boston firm reports. The wool—14,000 bales of it—is in the freighter *Oregon*, which sank after a collision during World War II. Divers report that the wool, worth $5½ million, is in good condition except for a quantity near the point of impact, which is saturated with bunker oil.

Physical Structure. The wool fiber is made up of two or three layers—an outer layer of scales called the cuticle, a middle area called the cortex, and a central core called the medulla that is usually absent in fine wool. The photomicrographs of the fiber in Figure 2–3 show the scale covering.

The *medulla* is a honeycomb-like core containing air spaces that increase the insulating power of the fiber. It appears as a dark area when seen through the microscope and is helpful in fiber identification but does not influence the color of the fiber.

The *cuticle* or scale layer is a horny nonfibrous keratin consisting of an epicuticle, exocuticle and endocuticle. The epicuticle is a very thin protective film on the outside. It contributes to the water-repellent nature of wool and is damaged by alkalies in laundering or scouring and by wear.[2] The exocuticle is the main part of the scale layer. In fine wools, the scales completely encircle the shaft, and each scale overlaps the bottom of the preceding scale, like parts of a telescope. In medium and coarse wools, the scale arrangement resembles that of shingles on a roof or scales on a fish. The free edges of the scales project outward and point toward the tip of the fiber. They cause skin irritation for some people. The thickness and shape of the scales vary with the kind of animal. The scale covering gives wool good abrasion resistance.

The free edges of the scales are a factor in *felting*. Felting is a unique and important property of wool and is of a purely physical nature. Under mechanical action such as agitation, friction, and pressure in the presence of heat and moisture, the wool fiber tends to move rootward, and the edges of the scales interlock preventing the fiber from returning to its

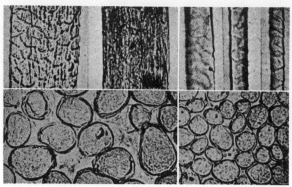

Fig. 2–3. Photomicrographs of wool fiber, showing longitudinal views above and cross-sectional views below. (From Werner von Bergen and Walter Krauss, *Textile Fiber Atlas.* Copyright 1949 by Textile Book Publishers, Inc.)

original position with the result that the fabric becomes thicker and smaller—that is, shrinks or felts.

Movement of the fibers is speeded up and felting occurs more rapidly under extreme or severe conditions. A wool garment may be shrunk down to half its original size. Lamb's wool felts more readily than other wools. In soft fluffy fabrics, the fibers are not held firmly in position and are free to move, so that these fabrics are more susceptible to felting than the firmly woven fabrics. Felting should not be confused with *fulling*, a manufacturing process. (See page 22.)

The felting property is both an advantage and a disadvantage. It is utilized to advantage in making fabric directly from fibers without first spinning or weaving. It is a disadvantage because it makes the washing of wool fabrics more difficult than the washing of fabrics of other fiber contents and it causes boardy places in wool garments during wear. Treatments to prevent felting shrinkage are based on the principle of smoothing off the rough edges of the scales. (See page 197.)

The *cortex* is the main part of the fiber. It is made up of long, slightly flattened, cigar-shaped cortical cells with a nucleus near the center, shown in Figure 2–4. In natural-colored wools, the cortical cells contain colored pigments. Each cortical cell can be broken down into fibrils, microfibrils, and protofibrils. Each microfibril is made up of eleven protofibrils, which in turn contain three parallel *coiled* polypeptide molecular chains.[3]

[2] O. J. Onions, *Wool: An Introduction to Its Properties, Varieties, Uses and Production.* New York: Interscience Publishers, 1962.

[3] A. R. B. Skertchly, "The Lure of the Golden Fleece," *Textile Institute and Industry* (June, 1965), p. 140.

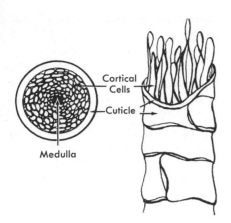

Fig. 2–4. Physical structure of wool fibers. (Courtesy of Werner von Bergen. Reprinted by permission of *Industrial & Engineering Chemistry*.)

The cortex also contains a disorderly matrix of polypeptide chains in which the orderly microfibrils are embedded.

The natural crimp of the wool fiber is due to the presence of two kinds of cortical cells—the paracortical and the orthocortical cells. They occur on different sides of the fiber and are unevenly arranged along the fiber, thus causing the bends and turns that give wool fibers a natural three-dimensional crimp. (See Figure 2–5.) The orthocortex has greater absorption than the paracortex, and it swells when wet causing a decrease in the crimp of the fiber. When the fiber dries, the crimp returns. Wool is called a bicomponent fiber because of the difference in the two sides. It is the only natural bicomponent fiber. Orlon Sayelle and nylon Cantrece are two man-made bicomponent fibers.

Physical Properties The wool fiber has been described as a giant molecular coilspring with outstanding elasticity. Wool's elasticity, resilience, and

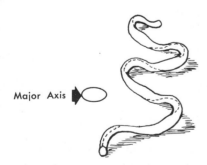

Fig. 2–5. Three-dimensional crimp of wool fiber. (From Giles E. Hopkins, *Wool as an Apparel Fiber*. Copyright by Rinehart & Company, Inc.)

flexibility (as well as the scale structure and natural crimp) contribute to fabric properties such as durability, wrinkle recovery, bulk, lofty hand, warmth, and abrasion resistance.

The *outstanding elasticity* of the wool fiber is the result of the coiled molecule structure and the waves and bends in the fiber. When stress is applied, the coils, waves, and bends straighten out and allow the fiber to stretch as much as 30 per cent of the original length before it breaks. When stress is removed, the fiber returns to its original length. Recovery takes place more slowly when the fiber is dry. Steam, humidity, and water hasten recovery. Wool is said to have perfect elasticity in water.

Wool's *resiliency* is excellent when the fiber is dry and poor when it is wet. If a dry fabric is crushed in the hand, it tends to spring back to its original position when the hand is opened. This crease-recovery property is important to the manufacturer because it permits energetic mechanical treatments in finishing woolens and worsteds. It is important to the consumer because it minimizes the amount of pressing needed between dry cleanings. Fabrics made of wool fibers are not all equally resilient. Some of this difference is due to fiber variation, the kind of yarn, and the construction and finish of the fabric.

Resiliency is important in the *warmth* properties of the fabric. Wool fibers do not pack well in yarns because of the crimp and the scales, and this makes wool fabrics porous and capable of incorporating much air. Still air is one of the best insulators because it keeps body heat close to the body. Wool maintains its thickness and lightness because the resilience of the fibers enables them to recover from crushing. Although wool is a *poor conductor* of heat, this is not an important factor in warmth.

The *flexibility* of wool is excellent. Wool fibers can be bent back on themselves 20,000 times without breaking as compared to Sea Island cotton, which breaks after 3,000 flexings, and rayon, which breaks after 75. Atmospheric moisture helps wool to retain its flexibility. Wool carpets, for example, will become brittle if the air is too dry.

Molecular Structure, Chemical Nature, and Related Properties

Wool, as it comes from the sheep, contains a grease that makes up 10 to 25 per cent of the fiber weight. This grease is recovered during the cleaning process and is sold as lanolin for use in cosmetics and medicines. The fiber itself is a protein called

Fig. 2–8. Wool cloth before (left) and after (right) fulling.

solution will completely destroy wool. As wool disintegrates, it turns yellow, becomes slick, and turns to a jelly-like mass and then goes into solution. To make a 5 per cent alkali solution, add 1 tablespoon of lye to 1 pint of water and heat to boiling.

If a fabric is a blend or combination of wool and other fibers, the wool in the blend will disintegrate leaving only the other fibers. Mild alkalies are used in scouring wool fibers to remove the grease and dirt in preparation for spinning and also for *fulling* of cloth. Fulling, also called *milling*, is a cloth-finishing process in which the cloth is washed in a thick soap solution and squeezed by wooden rollers to shrink the cloth and close up the weave by bringing the yarns closer together.[7] After fulling, the cloth has more body and cover, as shown in Figure 2–8. The shrinking is dependent on the action of heat and moisture on the molecule structure and also on the scale structure. Fulling, the process, should not be confused with felting, the property.

Acid Damage. Acid damage occurs less often in wool. In the manufacture of fabrics, acids are used to remove any cellulose impurities that are still in the fabric after weaving. This treatment is called *carbonizing* and is discussed on page 189. Acids are also used to activate the salt-linkages and make the dye sites available to the dye.

Flammability. Since wool burns very slowly

and is self-extinguishing, it creates *no fire hazard*. The burning test (page 13) can be used to distinguish protein from cellulose or thermoplastic fibers, but it will not distinguish between wool and silk.

Care of Wool Fabrics

Wool also undergoes chemical changes in use. Minor modifications of the cystine linkage resulting from ironing and steaming have a beneficial effect while those from careless washing and exposure to light have a detrimental effect. It would no doubt be advantageous to give younger generations of housewives scientifically based advice on these points.[8]

Mild alkalies, soaps, and detergents used in home laundry cause little if any damage, if heat and agitation are kept at a minimum. Wool does not soil readily and soil removal is no problem. Grease and oils do not spot wool fabrics as readily as they do fabrics of other fiber contents. Wool in its natural state is about 25 per cent grease.

Hydrogen peroxide is used for *bleaching*, which should be very carefully controlled. The common household chlorine bleach should not be used because of the damage it causes. (Wool is often used in its natural creamy white state because of its sensitivity to bleaches.)

Overexposure to sunlight and heat causes white wool to turn yellow. Dry cleaning solvents do not harm wool, and this method of cleaning is usually preferable because it creates less wrinkling, fuzzing, and shrinkage. A good brush is essential in caring for wool garments, which should be brushed after each wearing. Care should be given to the under

[7] R. Nason Hoyt, "Fulling, Past and Present," *American Dyestuff Reporter* **54** (November 22, 1965).

[8] *Ciba Review*, 1965/5–6, p. 35.

collars and inside of cuffs on coats and trousers. A firm, soft brush not only removes dust but it gently lifts the fibers back to their natural springiness. Damp fabrics should be allowed to dry before brushing. Garments should have a period of rest between wearings to recover from deformations. Baggy elbows and skirt seats will become less baggy as the garment rests. Hanging the garment over a tub of hot steamy water or spraying a fine mist of water on the cloth will speed up recovery.

Unless *mothproofed*, wool fabrics should be stored so that they will not be accessible to moth. The sulfur of the cystine linkage seems to be palatable to the clothes moth. Moth will also eat, but not digest, any other fiber that is blended with wool. Mothproofing (page 192) consists of chemically breaking and reforming the cystine crosslinks of the wool molecule.

Specialty Hair Fibers

Specialty wools are obtained from the goat family and the camel family.

Goat Family	Camel Family	Others
Angora goat— mohair	Camel's hair Llama	Angora rabbit— angora
Cashmere goat— cashmere	Alpaca Vicuna Guanaco	Fur fibers

Because specialty wools are available in less quantity than sheep's wool, they are usually more expensive. Like all natural fibers, they vary in quality. The fibers obtained from these animals are of two kinds, the coarse, long outer hair and the fine, soft undercoat. The coarse fibers are used for interlinings, upholstery, and some coatings, whereas the very fine fibers are used in the luxury coatings, sweaters, shawls, suit and dress fabrics.

Mohair, the fiber from the Angora goat, is raised in Turkey, South Africa, and the United States. Texas is the largest producer of mohair in the United States.

Mohair is our most resilient fiber and has none of the crimp found in sheep's wool, giving it a smoother surface that is more resistant to dust and more lustrous than wool. Mohair is very strong and has a good affinity for dye. The washed fleece is a lustrous white.

Cashmere comes from a small goat raised in Kashmir, China, Tibet, and Mongolia. The fibers vary in color from white to gray to brownish-gray. The hair is combed by hand from the animal during the moulting season. Only a small part of the fleece is the very fine fiber, probably not more than one-half pound per goat.

Camel's hair is obtained from the two-hump Bactrian camel of Mongolia and Tibet. It is said to have the best insulation of any of the wool fibers, since it keeps the camel comfortable under extreme conditions of temperature during a day's journey through the cold mountain passes and the hot valleys. The hair is collected by a "trailer" who follows the camel caravan and picks up the hair as it is shed and places it in a basket carried by the last camel. He also gathers the hair in the morning, at the spot where the camels lay down for the night.

Because the camel's hair gives warmth without weight, the finer fibers are much prized for clothing fabrics. They are often used in blends with sheep's wool, which is dyed the tan color of the camel's hair.

There are so many qualities of cashmere and camel's hair that care should be taken by the consumer to determine the quality of fiber he is buying. The best way to judge the quality is by the feel. Consumers should be guided by the reputation of the manufacturer or retailer.

The *llama and the alpaca* are domesticated animals of the South American branch of the camel family. The fiber is 8 to 12 inches in length and is noted for its softness, fineness, and luster. The natural colors are white, light fawn, light brown, dark brown, gray, black, and piebald.

Vicuna and guanaco are wild animals of the South American camel family. They are very rare, and the animals must be killed to obtain the fiber. Vicuna is the softest, finest, rarest, and most expensive of all textile fibers. The fiber is short, very lustrous, and a light cinnamon color.

Angora is the hair of the Angora rabbit and is raised in France and in small amounts in the United States. Each rabbit produces only a few ounces of fiber, which is very fine, fluffy, soft, slippery, and fairly long. It is pure white in color.

Silk

Silk is often referred to as the "Queen of the Fibers." Chinese legends tell us that silk was discovered in 2640 B.C. by a Chinese empress. The Chinese carefully guarded their secret of the silk cocoon for 3,000 years. They wove beautiful fabrics and sold them to Eastern traders, who carried them back to their own countries where they were prized very highly. Thus, a very great demand for silk was created. In A.D. 300 refugees from China took cocoons to Korea and started raising silkworms. Japan learned about silk production from the Koreans. The industry spread through central Asia into Europe, and by the twelfth century, Italy was the silk center of Europe. This leadership was taken over by France in the seventeenth century. Weaving of silk became important in England when many Huguenot weavers emigrated from France to England in 1685.

Sporadic attempts to cultivate silk have been made in the United States. The charters of the various colonies stipulated that a silk industry must be started. Because of climatic conditions, the North was not able to grow mulberry trees; and in the South, growing cotton, which was also needed by the mother country, was much more profitable.

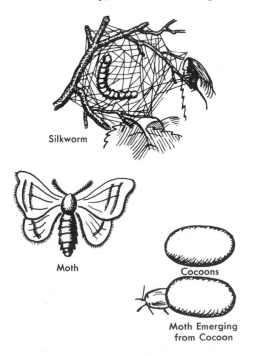

Fig. 2–9. Silkworm, moth, and cocoon.

Silkworm

Moth

Cocoons

Moth Emerging
from Cocoon

But as late as 1933, some manufacturers of silk fabrics tried raising silkworms.

During World War II, the government froze the import and production of silk in this country. The existing fibers were reserved for use by the armed forces. Our supplies from Japan and China were cut off, and for the decade from 1939 to 1949, we were without silk.

The introduction of nylon for hosiery took away much of Japan's market for silk. Another threat facing the silk industry today is a labor shortage due to technological progress. The industry has relied in the past on women from farm families for its labor force. With agricultural prosperity and industrialization in Japan, it is no longer necessary for women to do this work to maintain minimum survival for their families. Silk production has largely been a household operation, and for production to survive, it will be necessary to combine and systematize these small operations—to develop organizations similar to the cooperatives in the United States. Unless these changes are made in the industry, it is predicted that silk will be so expensive that it will become a luxury fiber like vicuna.

Silk can be produced in any temperate climate, but it has only been successfully produced where there is a cheap source of labor. Silk is a continuous filament protein fiber produced by the silkworm. (See Figure 2–9.) *Cultivated silk* is obtained by a carefully controlled process in which the silkworm lives a coddled and artificial life especially for the purpose of producing fibers. *Wild silk* production is not controlled; instead, these silkworms feed on oak leaves and spin cocoons under natural conditions.

Production and Processing

Sericulture is the name given to the production of cultivated silk. The sericulture process begins with the silk moth, which lays eggs on specially prepared paper. The eggs are kept in cold storage until they are needed for hatching. Hatching takes place continuously throughout the mulberry growing season, making it possible to keep labor and equipment at a minimum. The eggs are hatched into caterpillars, which are put on special mats and fed fresh, young mulberry leaves.

When the silkworm is grown, it spins a fiber cocoon around itself. The bulk of the silk moths are killed inside the cocoons by heat, and only those needed for reproduction are allowed to emerge. The pierced cocoons are used for staple fiber.

Since it is possible to control the fineness, uniformity, and strength of the silk fiber by selective breeding, better silk is resulting from research in this area.

Processing Silk—From Fiber to Yarn. *Reeling* or unwinding the filaments from the cocoon is done in an establishment called a filature. Until 50 years ago, reeling was done by hand. The conventional system of reeling described below still requires much hand labor. In conventional reeling, a number of filaments from several cocoons are gathered together onto an aluminum reel. (See Figure 2–10.) One operator can handle a basin of 20 spindles (five to eight cocoons to one spindle). The operator determines the denier of the yarn solely by eyesight.

The silk is rewound, twisted into a skein, and packaged for shipping. (See Figure 2–11.) The skeins are packaged into books (30 skeins to a book) weighing 4.5 pounds, and 20 to 30 books are formed into bales for shipment. When the silk arrives at the mill, it is opened, bunched, soaked, dried, and wound on bobbins.

In automatic reeling, the silk fibers are laced from the cocoon through a guide to a chemical bath, which softens the thread. The filaments go around a revolving horizontal roller, which dries and winds them onto a spool or cone ready for weaving on delivery. Silk in this form has a high import duty. In addition to speeding up the process of winding the filament, the automatic reeler also has a cocoon finding-feeding mechanism, which regulates the size and uniformity of the yarn. Uniform yarns are more suitable for weaving on

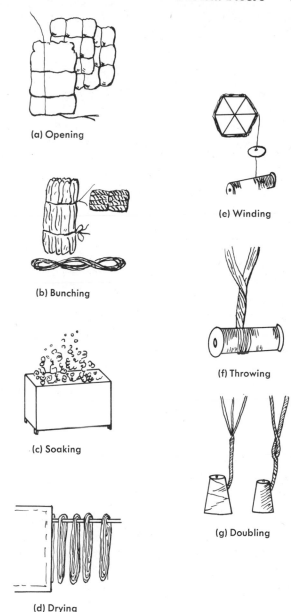

(a) Opening

(b) Bunching

(c) Soaking

(d) Drying

(e) Winding

(f) Throwing

(g) Doubling

Fig. 2–11. Processing silk in the mill.

Fig. 2–10. Winding silk filaments on a reel.

high-speed looms than are hand-reeled silk yarns, which slow up the weaving process. This machine increases production three or four times and cuts labor by 70 per cent, since one operator can manage 400 to 600 spindles. Reelers who have mechanized account for less than half of the silk production.

Types of Silk

Silk refers to cultivated silk.

Wild or *tussah* silk is a tan-colored fiber from the uncultivated silkworm, which feeds on scrub oak.

As the cocoons are always pierced, the fibers are shorter than reeled silk. Shantung, pongee, and honan are fabrics made from wild silk.

Duppioni silk comes from two silkworms who spin their cocoons together. The yarn is uneven, irregular, and large in diameter.

Raw silk refers to cultivated silk-in-the-gum. Raw silk varies in color from gray-white to canary yellow, but since the color is in the sericin, boiled-off silk is white. The term is often incorrectly used to describe spun silk.

Reeled silk is the long continuous filament, 300 to 1,800 yards in length.

Spun silk refers to yarns made from staple fiber from pierced cocoons and waste silk.

Waste silk is comprised of the tangled mass of silk on the outside of the cocoon and the fiber from pierced cocoons.

Properties

Silk is universally accepted as a luxury fiber. The slogan "only silk is silk" emphasizes its uniqueness. Good quality silk fabrics have a desirable hand and draping quality, which serve as a standard by which to measure silk-like man-made fibers.

Physical Structure. Silk is the only natural filament. It is a solid fiber; but unlike the man-made fibers it is not uniform in size. (See Figure 2–12.) The filaments are 300 to 1,800 yards long. In cross section, the fibers are like triangles with rounded corners. The rod-like, almost circular fibers are responsible for the luster and smoothness of silk. The diameter of silk fibers ranges from 2 to 5 microns, making it the finest of the natural fibers. The approximate average denier per filament is 1.2.[9]

The silk fiber is a double strand held together by a gum or sericin, a water-soluble substance secreted by the silkworm. This sericin is a very important part of the silk fiber. It serves as a warp sizing for the silk yarns as they are threaded on the loom and woven into the "gray goods" cloth. Because of the sericin, the silk yarns can be used without twist (zero twist). When the sericin is removed from the fiber in the degumming process (about 25 per cent weight loss), the fabric structure becomes more mobile. The low twist and the mobile structure are major factors in the "dry" tactile hand and the liveliness, suppleness, and drape of silk fabrics.

[9] Du Pont Bulletin X-156, "Multi-fiber."

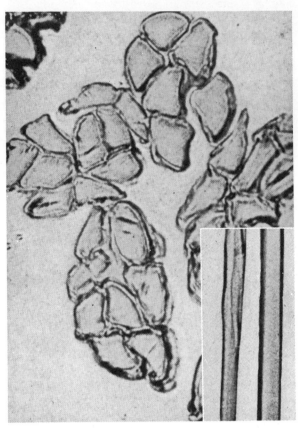

Fig. 2–12. Photomicrograph of silk fiber; longitudinal and cross-sectional view. (From Werner von Bergen and Walter Krauss, *Textile Fiber Atlas*. Copyright 1949 by Textile Book Publishers, Inc.)

Zero twist yarns are important in the good covering power exhibited by silk.

Molecular Structure. Silk contains the elements carbon, hydrogen, oxygen, and nitrogen, which are joined together in wavy or crimped molecular chains. Unlike wool, the chains are single rather than double. This structure gives silk an elasticity of 15 to 20 per cent.

Silk is a high-to-medium strength fiber that loses some strength when wet. Filament silk can be made into very sheer fabrics.

Chemical Properties. Silk is harmed by direct sunlight to a greater extent than any other fiber. It is harmed by strong alkalies and oxidizing agents.

Silk takes dyes well, and it seems to have a depth

of color or jewel-like tone not found in the man-made fibers that look like silk. Fast colors are available, but many converters need to be educated to use them. Brilliant colors are often not fast to washing.

Silk is sold and usually woven "in-the-gum." The sericin makes up about one-fourth of the fiber weight and is removed by degumming. It is washed in hot water and soap or synthetic detergent for two to four hours, then rinsed one to three hours in clean hot water. Sericin must be completely removed to develop the inherent fiber properties.

Care

The care of silk garments depends more on the kind of dye used and the yarn structure than on the fiber content. If fast colors are used and the yarns are not creped, silk may be washed and ironed. Mild soaps and detergents should be used.

Water spotting, caused by migration of weighting agents to the outer edge of the spot, was one of the early problems of silk. Most manufacturers are now using a waterspot-resistant finish.

Wash-and-wear silk and silk with durable pleats are now made by application of resin finishes.

3 Cellulose Fibers

Cellulose is an example of a single chemical compound that will yield a large variety of fibers. Natural cellulose fibers, such as cotton, flax, jute, hemp, and ramie, are built up by nature during the growth of the plant and come from the seed, the stem, or the leaves. Man-made or regenerated cellulose fibers, such as rayon, are made by dissolving and resolidifying natural cellulose. An understanding of the nature of cellulose is basic to the study of these fibers.

Molecular Structure

The basic unit of the cellulose molecule is the *glucose unit* and it is the same for both natural and regenerated fibers. The glucose unit is made up of the chemical elements carbon, hydrogen, and oxygen.

The formula in Figure 3–1 shows how these elements are arranged in the glucose unit. It also shows two glucose units joined together to form the cellobiose unit characteristic of cellulose.

The cellulose molecule is a long linear chain of glucose units. (See Figure 3–2.) The number of

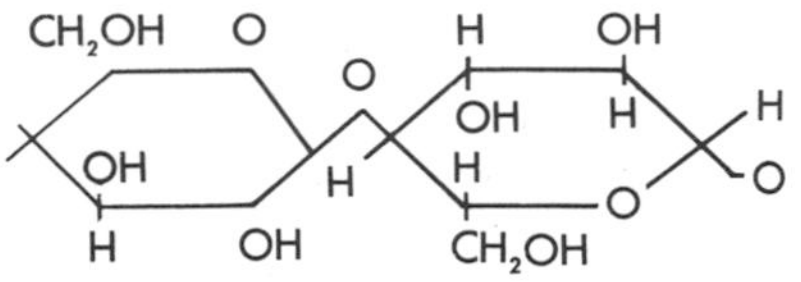

Fig. 3–1. The cellulose molecule.

units in the chain depends on the origin of the cellulose. Natural and regenerated cellulose differ in the length of the molecule chain. Fibers with long molecular chains are stronger than those with short molecular chains. Rayon fibers are not as strong as the natural cellulose fibers for two reasons:

1. Rayon is made from pine tree cellulose (some from cotton linters), which has a shorter chain length than cotton.
2. The molecular chain is broken into shorter lengths during manufacture.

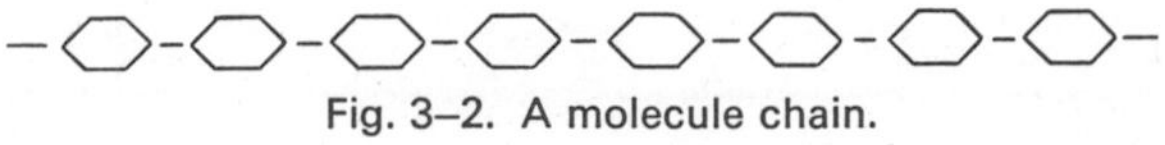

Fig. 3–2. A molecule chain.

PROPERTIES COMMON TO ALL CELLULOSE FIBERS

Property	Importance to Consumer
Good absorbency	Comfortable for summer wear Good for towels, diapers, and handkerchiefs
Good conductor of heat	Sheer fabrics cool for summer wear
Can withstand high temperature	Fabrics can be boiled to sterilize No special precautions in ironing
Low resiliency	Fabrics wrinkle badly unless finished for recovery
Lacks loft. Packs well into compact yarns	Yarns can be creped. Tight, high-count fabrics can be made Makes wind-resistant fabrics
Good conductor of electricity	Does not build up static
High density (1.5 ±)	Fabrics feel heavier than comparable fabrics of other fiber content
Harmed by mineral acids, but little affected by organic acids	Fruit stains should be removed immediately from a garment to prevent setting
Resistant to moths	Storage problem is simplified
Attacked by mildew	Soiled garments should not be put away damp
Flammability	Cellulose fibers ignite quickly, burn freely, have an afterglow, and gray feathery ash. Filmy or loosely constructed garments should not be worn near an open flame
Moderate resistance to sunlight	Draperies should be lined

Polymerization is the process of joining small units together. The large unit is then called a *polymer*. Therefore, all fibers are the polymer of some fiber-forming substance. (Definitions of the man-made fibers, set up by the Federal Trade Commission, use this term.) The *degree* of polymerization (D.P.) refers to the number of units that have been joined to make the molecular chain. Notice the difference in D.P. of the materials listed in the table following.

DIFFERENCES IN DEGREE OF POLYMERIZATION

Cellulose Source	Degree of Polymerization* (Length of Chain)
Cotton	2,000 (+)
Pine tree cellulose	700 to 800
Regular rayon	300 to 450
High-wet-modulus rayon	450 to 600
High-wet-modulus polynosic rayon	550 to 750

* Frank R. Charles, "Cellulose Chemistry in Relation to Fibre Property," *Canadian Textile Journal* **83**: 16 (August 5, 1966).

Chemical Nature

The chemical reactivity of cellulose is related to the three hydroxyl groups (OH groups) of the glucose unit. These groups react readily with moisture, dyes, and special finishes. Chemicals such as bleaches that cause a breakdown of the molecule chain of the cellulose usually attack the oxygen atom and cause a rupture there.

All cellulose fibers have common properties that are based on the chemical composition and the molecular structure. Some of the important properties are given in the chart at the left.

Cotton

Cotton is the generic name for a fiber that grows from the seed of the cotton plant—a seed-hair fiber. Cotton is a short fiber ranging from 0.5 to 2 inches depending on the variety. Long-staple cottons are the most valuable, the most difficult to produce, and the least abundant. Research is continually in process to develop better varieties of cotton. Older varieties lose out to new ones that show promise. The longest, finest fiber—Sea Island cotton—which was grown in the islands off the coast of Georgia is no longer of commercial importance. Instead, the finest varieties are from the Pima strain, which was developed by crossbreeding the American cotton grown by the Pima Indians with Egyptian cotton. Common varieties are given in the following chart.

VARIETIES OF COTTON

Long-staple (over 1⅛ inches)
    Pima—California, Arizona, New Mexico
    Supima—California, Arizona, New Mexico
Short-staple (under 1⅛ inches)
    Deltapine—Midsouth, Far West
    Acala—Far West
    Coker—Southeast
    Lankart—Southwest

History

Cotton dates back to ancient times when, from 1500 B.C. to A.D. 1500, India was the center of the cotton industry. The cotton industry developed in Egypt at about the same time. Some of the best long-staple cotton is grown in the Nile valley. In the United States, the Pima Indians were growing cotton when the Spaniards came to this country. One of the items that Columbus took back to Queen Isabella was a hank of cotton yarn. In 1769, England became the center of cotton manufacture with the invention of the spinning jenny and the spinning frame by Arkwright and Hargreaves. In the American colonies, New England was the cotton manufacturing center. After World War II, manufacturing costs and competition from foreign imports caused the spinning and weaving industries to move to the South, particularly to North and South Carolina where the climate was milder, wages and taxes were lower, and there were fewer labor restrictions. New modern plants made it possible to change to continuous processing with more automation. Cotton growing shifted to the Southwest and Far West where cotton could be irrigated and fiber quality was affected less by changing weather conditions.

Production

Cotton is the most widely used fiber in the world. This wide use of cotton has been the result of four revolutionary developments: (1) early machine inventions, which made mass production possible; (2) mercerization, which made cotton more silk-like; (3) compressive shrinkage, which gave guaranteed size to garments; and (4) durable-press, wash-and-wear finishes, which improved resiliency.

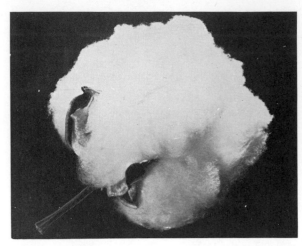

Fig. 3–3. An opened cotton boll. (Courtesy of the National Cotton Council of America.)

Cotton grows in any part of the world where the growing season is long. The United States, China, and Russia lead in cotton production. The area of growth is a major factor affecting the quality.

Cotton grows on bushes three to four feet high. The blossom appears, falls off, and the *boll* begins its growth. Inside the boll are seeds from which the fibers grow. When the boll is ripe, it splits open, and the fluffy white fibers stand out like a powder puff. (See Figure 3–3.) Cotton is picked either by hand or by machine. Mechanization and weed control have reduced the number of man-hours required to produce one bale of cotton. After picking, the cotton is taken to a *gin* to remove the fibers from the seeds. Figure 3–4 shows a saw gin, in which the

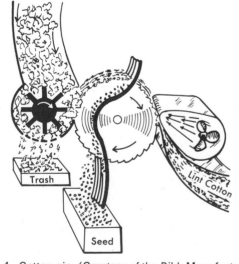

Fig. 3–4. Cotton gin. (Courtesy of the Bibb Manufacturing Company.)

whirling saws pick up the fiber and carry it to a knife-like comb, which blocks the seeds and permits the fiber to be carried through.

The fibers, called *lint*, are pressed into bales weighing 100 pounds, ready for sale to a spinning-mill. The average yield is 2.5 bales per acre. However, Arizona, the state with the largest production per acre, has produced as much as five bales per acre. The seeds, after ginning, look like the buds of the pussywillow. They are covered with very short fibers—$\frac{1}{8}$ inch—called *linters*. The linters are removed from the seeds and are used to a limited extent as raw material for the making of rayon and acetate. The seeds are crushed to obtain cottonseed oil and meal.

Physical Structure

Raw cotton is creamy white in color. The fiber is a single cell which, during growth, pushes out of the seed as a hollow cylindrical tube over 1,000 times as long as it is thick. The cross-sectional shape varies with the maturity of the fiber. Immature fibers tend to be U-shaped and the cell wall is thinner while mature fibers are more nearly circular with a very small central canal.

The cotton fiber is made up of a cuticle, primary wall, secondary wall, and lumen. (See Figure 3–6.)

The *cuticle* is a wax-like film covering the primary or outer wall.

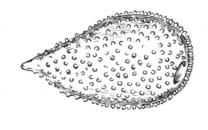

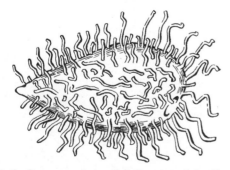

Fig. 3–5. Cotton seed showing the start of the fibers. Top, as lumps. Bottom, as they become seed hairs.

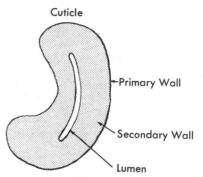

Fig. 3–6. Cross section of mature cotton fiber.

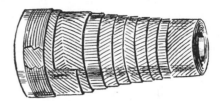

Fig. 3–7. Schematic diagram showing layers of cellulose.

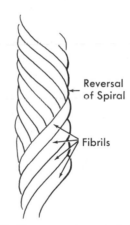

Fig. 3–8. Reverse cotton spirals in cotton.

The *secondary wall* contains successive layers of cellulose similar to the growth rings in a tree. One layer is laid down each day of the 20 to 30 days of growth. (See Figure 3–7.) Each layer is built up of fibrils—bundles of molecular chains—which are laid down in a spiral arrangement. The diagram in Figure 3–8 shows one fibril bundle in its spiral path around the fiber. At intervals, the spirals *reverse direction*. These reversals of spirals are an important factor in the twist, elastic recovery, and elongation of the fiber, as well as in yarn strength.

The *lumen* is the central canal through which the nourishment travels during growth. In the mature fiber, the dried nutrients in the lumen give the characteristic dark areas that can be seen under a microscope.

Convolutions or ribbon-like twists characterize the cotton fibers. As the fiber matures, the lumen collapses and the reverse spirals cause the fiber to twist. The twist forms a natural crimp that enables the fibers to cohere to one another, so that despite its short length, cotton is one of our most spinnable fibers. Convolutions can be a disadvantage, since dirt collects in the twists and must be removed by vigorous washing.

The *quality* of cotton depends on the staple length, the number of convolutions, and the brightness of the fiber. Long-staple cotton has about 300 convolutions per inch, while short-staple has less than 200. Cotton fibers vary from 16 to 20 microns in diameter. Notice in the photomicrograph (Figure 3–9) the difference in size and shape.

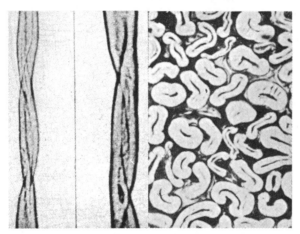

Fig. 3–9. Photomicrograph of cotton fiber showing longitudinal (left) and cross-sectional views. (From Werner von Bergen and Walter Krauss, *Textile Fiber Atlas.* Copyright 1949 by Textile Book Publishers, Inc.)

Properties

A general discussion of the cellulose molecule of cotton and other cellulose fibers is given on page 28.

The general properties of cotton are similar to those of the other cellulose fibers. (See chart, page 29). Cotton has a unique combination of *low cost, easy washability,* and *comfort characteristics* that have made it superior to other fibers for use in such things as summer clothes, work clothes, sheets, and towels. When cotton is blended with other fibers, the cotton "look" is maintained because consumers like the clean, fresh, somewhat dull appearance of cotton fabrics.

The *dry strength* of the cotton fiber is medium (3.8 grams/denier) but its wet strength is approximately 30 per cent greater, which means that it can be handled quite roughly during cleaning—rubbed to remove soil, twisted to remove moisture, boiled to sterilize, and so on.

The *low resiliency* of cotton has been improved by durable-press finishes, but the finish lowers the strength of the cotton fabric. Blends with polyester and nylon fibers have given better performance than 100 per cent cotton fabrics, but a continuing research program is developing finishes and finishing procedures that cause less degradation of the fiber. The National Cotton Council, an organization supported by the cotton growers, sponsors a great deal of this research. Research programs are designed also to improve the warmth, soiling, and strength properties of cotton.

Luster has been improved by mercerization, but it is effective only on long-staple cotton. Blending cotton with high-wet-modulus rayon and synthetics of about 1.5-inch staple improves the luster. Rayon adds softness and good hand to the blend.

Mercerized cotton differs physically from regular cotton. In mercerization, cotton yarns or cloth is treated with caustic soda (sodium hydroxide, an alkali) either in a stretched or relaxed state. The treatment causes the fibers to swell and some of the convolutions are straightened out, making the fiber almost rod-like in shape. (See Figure 3–10.) The swelling causes a molecule rearrangement that makes the hydroxyl groups more accessible so that the fiber is more absorbent, takes and holds dyes more readily and permanently than unmercerized cotton. If the treatment is carried out under tension, the yarns or cloth are more lustrous. *Slack mercerization* is used to produce stretch fabrics of 100 per cent cotton. In this process, woven cotton cloth is treated in a loose or slack tension state; and as the cotton fibers swell and become shorter, they cause the yarn to crimp.

Identification of Cotton

The burning test identifies cellulose fibers. They burn quickly, give off a white smoke, have an afterglow, and smell like burning paper or leaves. The afterglow is as important as the flame, since, if allowed to smolder, it may start a fire. The burning test does not distinguish cotton from the other cellulose fibers. Cotton can be identified specifically by the microscope test. The staple form of the fiber

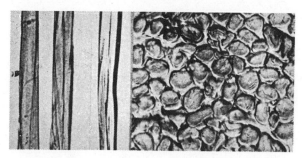

Fig. 3–10. Photomicrograph of mercerized cotton showing longitudinal and cross-sectional views. (From Werner von Bergen and Walter Krauss, *Textile Fiber Atlas*. Copyright 1949 by Textile Book Publishers, Inc.)

helps in identification. If a filament fiber burns like cellulose, it is not cotton because cotton is always a staple fiber.

Flax

The history of flax dates back over 10,000 years. Linen fabrics found in the Swiss lake dwellings show that Neolithic man was skilled in the production of flax. In ancient times, Egypt was called the "land of linen." In the seventeenth century, Ireland became the center of the manufacture of linen, when a group of skilled Huguenot weavers, fleeing persecution in France, settled there. The word "linen" comes from the Celtic word "llin." The flax industry in the United States dates from the early 1800's, when many Irish weavers emigrated to this country.

Production

Russia leads the world in flax production. Germany, the Baltic states, and Argentina are also large producers of flax. Flax is an important crop in Canada, both for fiber and for seed. Research programs sponsored by the Canadian industry have resulted in improved production processes there. The best quality flax is produced in Belgium.

Because work involved in the processing of flax has always been extremely laborious, production has flourished in countries where labor is cheap. Mechanization has been slow, and complete mechanization is still to be achieved.

Harvesting is done by pulling the flax plants either by hand or machine.

The bast fibers lie in bundles in the stem of the plant just under the outer covering or bark. They are sealed together by a substance composed of pectins, waxes, and gums. To loosen the fibers so that they can be removed from the stalk, the pectins must be dissolved by bacterial rotting called *retting*, and the woody portion of the stem broken away.

Retting is one of the most important steps in flax preparation. It is done in fields as dew-retting, in streams, or in large retting tanks where the bacterial count and temperature can be carefully controlled. If flax is dew-retted, the plants are laid out in orderly rows in the field as they are pulled. If it is to be stream- or tank-retted, the plants are tied in bundles. After the flax is removed from the retting tanks, the bundles are dried in the fields. The seeds are removed at the mill by passing the seed and the plant through a deseeding machine. If the flax is dew-retted, a machine pulls the seeds from the plants the first time the swaths are turned.

Breaking or *scutching* removes the woody portion of the flax stem. The fibers are passed between fluted rollers to break up the stem and the woody part is removed by agitation.

Hackling or *combing* separates the fiber bundles and removes short fibers by drawing the fibers through a series of combs. The individual fibers tend to cling together and some are broken. This process gives the characteristic thick-and-thin yarn, which produces the uneven "linen-like" texture of the fabric.

Hackling helps determine the length and fineness of the fibers by separating the short broken fibers called *tow* from the long combed fibers called *line*. The line fibers are ready for spinning into yarn. Notice in Figure 3–11 how much the combed strands resemble combed hair.

The long-line fibers are used in better quality linen fabrics and contribute to the luster that is typical of good quality.

The short, broken tow fibers must be carded to prepare them for spinning into yarn. They are used in less expensive linens.

Further separation of the fibers takes place during spinning, weaving, and finishing.

Physical and Molecular Structure

Flax is unlike other natural fibers in that the length and fineness dimensions are not clearly definable. The primary fibers, which average 0.5 to

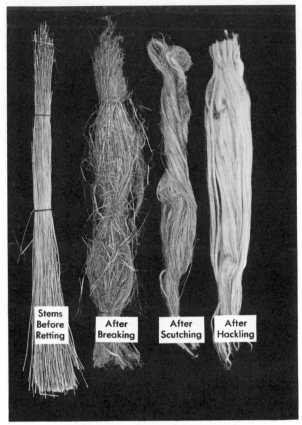

Fig. 3–11. Flax fiber at different stages of processing.

2.15 inches in length and a few microns in diameter, are bound together in fiber bundles and are never completely separated into individual fibers. Flax fiber, as commonly used, is made up of many primary fibers.

Flax fibers can be identified under the microscope by crosswise markings called nodes or joints. These are shown in Figure 3–12.

The markings on flax have been attributed either to cracks or breaks during harvesting or to irregularity in growth. The fibers may appear slightly swollen at the nodes and resemble somewhat the joints in a stalk of corn. They have a small central canal similar to the lumen in cotton. The cross section (see Figure 3–13) is several-sided or polygonal with rounded edges.

Flax fibers are grayish in color when dew-retted and yellowish in color when water-retted. Flax has a more highly oriented molecular structure than cotton, and is, therefore, stronger than the cotton fiber.

Properties and End-Uses

Flax is a prestige fiber due to its limited production and relatively high cost, The term "linen" refers to cloth made from flax. This term is, however, often misused today in referring to fabrics that

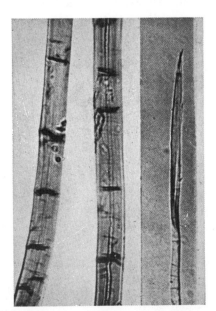

Fig. 3–12. Photomicrograph of flax showing nodes or joints. (From Werner von Bergen and Walter Krauss, *Textile Fiber Atlas*. Copyright 1949 by Textile Book Publishers, Inc.)

Fig. 3–13. Photomicrograph of flax showing cross section of fiber bundles. (From Werner von Bergen and Walter Krauss, *Textile Fiber Atlas*. Copyright 1949 by Textile Book Publishers, Inc.)

look like linen—fabrics that have thick-and-thin yarns and are fairly heavy or crisp. The term "Irish linen" always refers to fabrics made from flax.

The unique and desirable characteristics of flax are its body, strength, and thick-and-thin fiber bundles, which give texture to fabrics. (See Figure 3–14.)

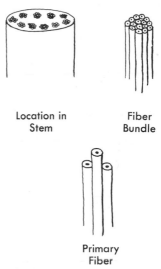

Location in
Stem

Fiber
Bundle

Primary
Fiber

Fig. 3–14. Flax fibers before and after being removed from the stem of the plant.

Flax is twice as strong as cotton and is also stronger when wet. Linen thread is still used to stitch shoe soles. Flax has poor flex-abrasion resistance, however; and for this reason, it is better to roll table linens or hang them over hangers rather than to fold them in sharp creases.

Spots and stains are easier to remove from linen fabrics than from cotton, but linen is more readily weakened by bleaches. Linen is also more resistant to bacterial action and mildew than cotton.

Linens wrinkle badly in laundering, and should be ironed while quite damp. The dampness makes it possible to set the iron at a higher temperature for linen than for cotton although they have the same resistance to heat. Ironing on the right side will increase the luster.

The main disadvantages of flax are low resiliency and lack of elasticity. Crease-resistant finishes on dress and suiting linens are quite satisfactory, but they reduce the durability of the fabric.

Table linens usually are not treated because they often are white and, until recently, resin-treated fabrics turned yellow when bleached.

Quality

Since flax is a natural fiber, it varies in quality. In judging linen fabrics, long, fine fibers, smooth yarns, and a high count are indicative of good quality. A new process for treating flax makes it possible to deliver the fiber to spinners fully bleached and consistent in quality. Modern finishes, such as durable press, are easier to achieve.

Ramie

Ramie or grasscloth has been used for several thousand years in China. It is grown in countries that have a hot humid climate. In the United States, ramie is grown in the everglades region of Florida.

The plant is harvested by cutting. After cutting, a new growth starts immediately. Three crops a year may be harvested.

The ramie fiber bundles are removed by a decorticating machine. This machine strips the stalks as it pulls them through a series of rollers, which remove all of the woody portion. After decortication, the fiber must be degummed by a mild chemical bath. The ramie fibers are longer than any of the other fibers in the bast fiber group. They range from one to twelve inches and are usually cut into desired staple length before spinning.

Much of the raw fiber is exported to Japan where it is spun into yarns and woven into fabrics. The Japanese are the largest producers of ramie yarns and fabrics in the world. Germany ranks second, and France is third.

When seen under the microscope, ramie is very similar to flax fiber. It is pure white. It is one of the strongest fibers known and its strength increases when it is wet. It has silk-like luster. Ramie also has a very high resistance to rotting, mildew, and other organisms.

Ramie also has some disadvantages. It is stiff and low in resiliency, hence it wrinkles very easily. Ramie has the most highly crystalline molecular structure of any of the cellulose fibers, creating its high strength as well as its lack of resiliency. Ramie is low in elasticity; it is brittle, and breaks if folded repeatedly in the same place.

Ramie is used in fabrics resembling linen, such as suitings, shirtings, table cloths, napkins, and handkerchiefs.

Hemp

The history of hemp is as old as that of flax. Because hemp lacks the fineness of the better quality flax, it has never been able to compete in the clothing field. Some varieties of hemp are, however, very difficult to distinguish from flax.

Hemp production and manufacture are very similar to that of flax. In 1942, the government sponsored a hemp-growing program in the United States to supply war needs. Its high strength and light weight made it particularly suitable for twine, cordage, and thread for stitching the soles on soldiers' shoes. After the war, the demand for hemp declined; it is now one of the less important fibers.

Jute

Jute was known as a fiber in Biblical times. India, the largest producer of jute, has 112 jute mills as compared to 113 for cotton. Jute is the cheapest textile fiber and is the second most widely used vegetable fiber, ranking next to cotton. The individual fibers in the jute bundle are shorter than those of the other bast fibers. It is the weakest of the cellulose fibers.

The greater part of the jute production goes into bagging for sugar, coffee, and so forth, or is used in carpet backing, rope, cordage, and twine. The olefin fibers are now competing with jute in these areas.

1939 - nylon

4 Introduction to Man-Made Fibers

As early as 1754, scientists were experimenting with ways to produce a fiber that resembled the natural fiber silk but that would be easier and cheaper to produce. The first successful fiber was made by Count Hilaire de Chardonnet, a Frenchman, in 1884. After he studied the silkworm as it digested mulberry leaves, he succeeded in making a nitro-cellulose solution that could be forced through a nozzle into a chemical bath to solidify the fiber by coagulation. Fabrics made from this fiber, called "artificial silk," were exhibited at the World's Fair in 1890. Viscose rayon and acetate were developed at about the same time. In the early 1900's, the research emphasis was on improving these new fibers.

In the 1940's and 1950's research turned to production of many new kinds of fibers. Nylon, polyesters, acrylics, and others were developed. By the 1960's interest had shifted to the modification of existing fibers for wider end-use applications.

The production program for a new fiber is long and expensive and a producer has to invest millions in research and development before any profit can be realized. A patent on the process gives the producer 17 years of exclusive rights to the use of the process—time to recover the initial cost and make a profit. The price per pound of the fiber during this time is high, but it will drop later. The owner of the patent can license other producers to use the process and the licensee pays a royalty.

A fiber must be converted into a successful fabric that will please the consumer if it is to compete in the market. To ensure that his fiber will appear in quality fabrics, the producer institutes a *Fabric Quality Program* and licenses his trade name. The Federal Trademark Act[1] requires anyone who licenses a trademark to control "the nature and quality of the product to which the trademark refers" or lose his rights. The *quality* of a fabric is a realistic value and does not mean "best on the market." It is a level of performance that will be satisfactory to most consumers in the mass market. Fabric Quality Control programs are closely supervised. Company representatives check retail stores. Fabric performances such as shrinkage, color fastness, resistance to pilling, resistance to wrinkling, and so forth, are checked regularly in a quality-controlled laboratory. In 1964 the Celanese

[1] Daniel Powderly, "Trademark Licensing," *Modern Textiles Magazine* **45**:61 (March 1964).

Corporation had 14 licensed trademarks and issued 90 million tags and labels. These tags are valuable to the company because they are recognized by the consumer.

Legislation

Previous to 1950, two laws had been enacted by Congress, one to control the labeling of wool products and one to control the labeling of furs. A third law relating to flammability of fabrics was enacted in 1954. With fewer fibers fewer laws were needed. As the number of fibers grew and as each fiber family continued to expand, the number of names on labels caused a great deal of confusion for the consumer. In 1959, Congress passed the *Textile Fiber Products Identification Act*, which covers the entire field of textile fiber content labeling and advertising *except* as already covered by the Wool Products Labeling Act and with specific exceptions. (Advertising rules and exceptions are not discussed here.) The purpose of the Act is to afford protection to the consumer through the enforcement of ethical practices. It also protects producers of textile products from unfair competition resulting from the unrevealed presence of substitute materials in textile products. The following information is required on the labels of apparel items.

1. The *per cent* of each natural or man-made fiber present must be listed in the order of predominance by weight. Fibers representing less than 5 per cent cannot be named unless they have some constructive value.
2. The *name* of the manufacturer or his registered *identification* number. (Trademarks may serve as identification, but they are not required information.)
3. The first time a trademark appears in the *required* information, it must appear in immediate conjunction with the generic name and in type or lettering of equal size and conspicuousness. When the trademark is used elsewhere on the label, the generic name shall accompany it in legible and conspicuous type the *first* time it appears.

Although the law was passed in 1958, it did not become effective until 1960. During this interval, the Federal Trade Commission held hearings in regard to inequalities or injustices that the law might cause. Then it established rules and regulations to be observed in enforcing the law. The following list of man-made fiber generic names was established by the Federal Trade Commission in cooperation with the fiber producers. A *generic name* is the name of a family of fibers all having similar chemical composition. The Federal Trade Commission definitions for these generic names are included in the discussions of each generic fiber.

Cellulosic	*Noncellulosics (synthetics)*		*Mineral*
Acetate	Acrylic	Polyester	Glass
(Triacetate)	Azlon*	Rubber	Metallic
Rayon	Lastrile†	Saran	
	Modacrylic	Spandex†	
	Nylon	Vinal*	
	Nytril*	Vinyon	
	Olefin		

* Not made in the United States.
† Discussed in Chapter 12.

There are several stages in the production of a new fiber. First a fundamental research program is planned to discover a new material and a way of making it into a fiber. When this phase of the program is successful, a pilot plant is built so that laboratory procedures can be scaled up to prepare for commercial production and to produce enough experimental fiber to support a fiber evaluation and fabric development program. The qualities and performance of the fiber are evaluated in an applied research and development center. The end-uses for the fiber are determined here also. Burlington Industries, the largest spinner and weaver of man-made yarns and fabrics, has worked with the fiber producers in developing fabrics from many of the new fibers. When the fiber is ready to be offered to the consumer, a commercial plant is built.

Fiber producers must find many uses for a fiber if the company is to prosper and grow. A continuing research program is needed to develop a *family* of fibers, each of which has properties specifically designed to meet some consumer need. Each member of this fiber family is referred to as a *modification*, *variant*, *type*, or *second-generation* fiber. Nylon 420 is a good example of a fiber modification that was developed to fill a need—a reinforcement fiber for blending with cotton.

Naming the Fibers

While the fiber is in the experimental stage, it is referred to by a number, for example, M-27 or

X-51. Later it is given a trade name (trademark). A trade name is a name chosen by a company to identify a particular fiber sold by that company and to distinguish it from fibers of the same generic class produced or sold by others. Because it is a very definite selling tool, the choice is an important one. It should be pleasant in both sight and sound and preferably two syllables in length. If it starts with an "A" it will have the advantage of coming first in any alphabetical listing. The endings "on," "an," and "el" are popular for fiber names. Some fibers are named for the company and some for the chemical composition. All trade names should be capitalized.

Promotion

It has been said that even the best fiber could not succeed without an intensive promotional program. The fiber producer must assume responsibility for promotion that will sell his fiber not only to his own customers—the manufacturers and retailers—but also to his customer's customer—the consumer. The fiber is usually introduced on the market in an

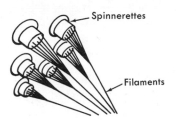

Fig. 4–1. Spinnerets. (Courtesy of the FMC Corporation, American Viscose Division.)

end-use where it shows outstanding performance and where existing fibers have weaknesses. For example, Orlon was first promoted in soft, lightweight sweaters because they did not shrink and required no blocking as wool did. Also, a new fiber is often introduced as a higher-priced luxury item to give it a desirable image and later the item works its way down to the mass market.

Manufacture

Three fiber spinning methods are used—*wet* spinning, *dry or solvent* spinning, and *melt* spinning.

FIBER SPINNING PROCESSES			
Wet Spinning	**Dry or Solvent Spinning**	**Melt Spinning**	

Wet Spinning		Dry or Solvent Spinning		Melt Spinning	
Rayon	Acrilan acrylic	Acetate	Orlon acrylic	Nylon	Polyester
Creslan acrylic	Zefran acrylic	Vinyon	Modacrylic	Saran	Olefins

Wet Spinning
1. Raw material is dissolved by chemicals.
2. Fiber is spun into acid bath.

Fiber Spinning Process

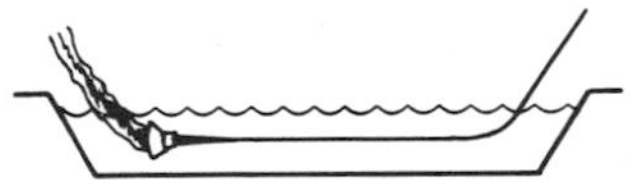

Fig. 4–2a.

3. Fiber solidifies when coagulated by acid.

Oldest process
Most complex
Weak fibers until dry
Washing, bleaching, etc., required before use

Dry or Solvent Spinning
1. Resin solids are dissolved by solvent.
2. Fiber is spun out into warm air.
3. Fiber solidifies by evaporation of solvent.

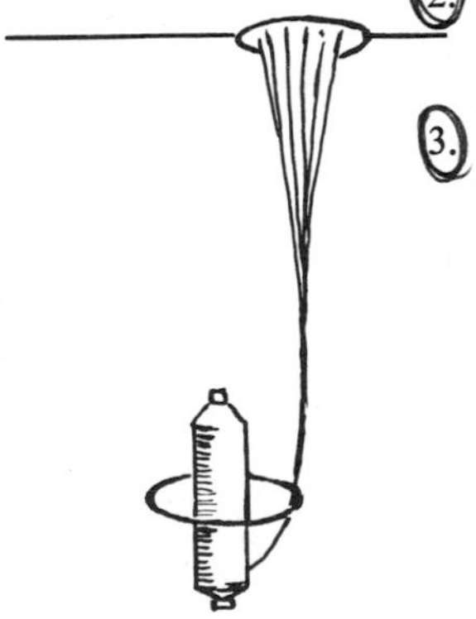

Fig. 4–2b.

Direct process
Solvent required
Solvent recovery required
No washing, etc., required

Melt Spinning
1. Resin solids are melted in autoclave.
2. Fiber is spun out into air.
3. Fiber solidifies on cooling.

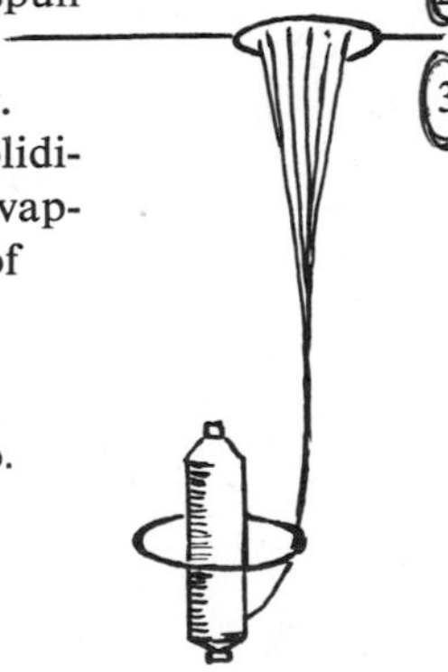

Fig. 4–2c.

Least expensive
Direct process
High spinning speeds
No solvent, washing, etc., required
Fibers shaped like spinneret hole

These are discussed in detail in later chapters but a brief comparison is given in the table on page 39. All the processes are based on these three general steps:

1. Dissolving the raw material to make a solution.
2. Extruding the solution through a spinneret to form a fiber.
3. Solidifying the fiber by coagulation, evaporation, or cooling.

The spinneret, a small thimble-like nozzle, is one of the most important parts of the spinning equipment. The holes can be made smaller than the diameter of a human hair and, although usually circular, can be almost any shape. They are made of platinum or a similar metal that will be resistant to acids and the effects of wear by the spinning solution as it flows through. Figure 4–1 shows some spinnerets.

A comparison of the three spinning processes is given in the chart and in Figure 4–2 (page 39).

Fiber Forms and Common Production Modifications

Fiber Forms

Man-made fibers are produced in three *forms*: filament, filament tow, and staple.

Filament fibers are spun from spinnerets with 350 holes or less as determined by the size of the yarn to be made. The number of holes in the spinneret determines the number of filaments in the yarn. As the individual fibers emerge from the spinneret holes and are solidified, they are immediately brought together, with or without a small amount of twist, to form a continuous filament yarn. The term "yarn" is used by the fiber producer to refer to continuous filament yarn. (Filament yarns are discussed on page 917.)

Staple fibers are made from filaments spun from large spinnerets with as many as 3,000 holes. The product of 100 or more spinnerets is collected, as illustrated in Figure 4–3, into a large rope of fibers called *tow*. This rope or tow is crimped and then made into staple by cutting (or breaking). The length of the staple is determined by the use to which it will be put. The staple fiber or tow is packaged in cardboard packages (bales) and shipped to a yarn

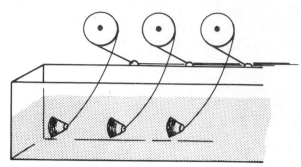

Fig. 4–3. Collecting fibers from several spinnerets for cutting into staple.

spinning mill to be made into *spun* yarns. (Spun yarns are discussed on page 90.)

One of the advantages of the man-made fibers is the control it is possible to exercise over each step of the production process. Fibers can be tailored to fit a wide variety of end-uses that require physical or chemical properties not found in the parent fiber or in the natural fibers. For example, the suit that astronauts will wear on the moon will be made of man-made fibers that will protect them from the heat of the +220°F lunar day and the cold of the −250°F lunar night. The suit must be light and pliable enough to enable the astronauts to perform necessary tasks. Chemical and physical modifications of the man-made fibers can be accomplished by:

1. Adding substances to the polymer or to the spinning solution.
2. Changing the size and shape of the spinneret holes.
3. Varying the conditions of extrusion and solidification.
4. After-treating the solidified fiber.

Modifying the Spinning Solution or the Polymer

The following fiber modifications or variants are made by the addition of some substance to the spinning solution or to the polymer.

Delustering is a process in which titanium dioxide, a white pigment, is added to the fiber spinning solution before the fiber is extruded. In some cases it is mixed in at an earlier stage—while the resin polymer is being formed. The particles of pigment prevent the reflection of light from the surface of the fiber. Variation in the amount of pigment will control the degree of luster to produce *semidull* or *dull* fibers. Fibers that have not been delustered are referred to as bright fibers. Delustered fibers

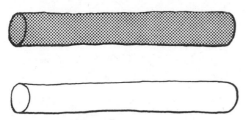

Fig. 4–4. Diagram showing a bright fiber (left) and a delustered fiber (right) as they would look under a microscope.

can be identified under the microscope by the presence of what appears to be peppery black dots as shown in Figure 4–4. The photograph in Figure 4–5 shows three cones of yarn of different lusters.

Fibers with high luster are limited to use in silk-like garments, decorative fabrics, and to fabrics that will be exposed to sunlight for periods of time. Bright fibers are more resistant to sunlight than are dull fibers. Absorbed light causes more degradation or "tendering" than does reflected light. The initial strength of a delustered fiber is also less than that of a bright fiber. Rayon, for example, is 3 to 5 per cent weaker when it is delustered.

Solution dyeing is the addition of colored pigments or certain dyes to the spinning solution or to the resin polymer. It is also called spun-dyeing or dope-dyeing. The fibers are sometimes referred to as producer-colored. The process was developed originally as a remedy for gas-fading of green, gray, or blue colors used in dyeing acetate fiber. (See page 54.) Black is usually the first color to be used, and then other colors are produced as suitable fast-color pigments are developed.

Solution-dyed fibers cost more per pound than uncolored fibers. This difference is offset later by the cost of dyeing yarns and fabrics. The fastness of the color is excellent. The colored fibers have been used in automotive upholstery, curtains, and in swim suits that will be exposed to chlorine and/or salt water. One disadvantage of the fibers from the manufacturer's standpoint is that he must carry a large inventory to be able to fill orders quickly. He is also less able to adjust to fashion changes in color, because it is not possible to strip the color from these fibers and redye them.

Whitening agents such as fluorescent whitening compounds (dyes) can be added to make whiter fibers or fibers that resist yellowing. Du Pont describes its Type 91 as containing an optical bleach additive. Eastman's Kodel IV has a built-in optical brightener. American Enka's Blanc de Blanc is spun with an optical bleach additive in the melt. These whiteners are permanent to washing and dry cleaning. They are an advantage in foundation garments because they eliminate the necessity for bleaching. The fibers are used in white shirts, blouses, and the like.

Cross-dyeable fibers are common. Some fibers are nondyeable and must have the basic polymer altered to make them receptive to dyes. Some fibers are acid-dyeable or basic-dyeable or both. By the proper selection of dyes it is possible to mix these fibers in a blend and dye one of the fibers of the blend while the other remains white, or to blend fibers of different dye-receptivity and achieve a two-color effect. Enkrome rayon, Type 82 Dacron, and Orlon Type 72 are examples of basic dyeable fibers. Antron Type 815 nylon is an example of a fiber that is available in different dye index levels—light, medium, and heavy shades.

Heat-resistant fibers have a heat stabilizer added to the polymer.

Light-resistant fibers have a light stabilizer and also delustering pigments added to the polymer.

Changing Size and Shape of Spinneret Holes

Fiber modifications made by changing the size and shape of the spinneret holes are:

1. Carpet fibers: heavy denier from 15 to 24 denier
2. Trilobal fibers: silk-like
3. Flat fibers: straw-like or high luster
4. Multilobal fibers: bulk

Varying Conditions of Extrusion and Solidification

Fiber modifications made by varying the conditions of extrusion and solidification are:

Fig. 4–5. Bright and dull rayon yarns. (Courtesy of the American Viscose Corporation.)

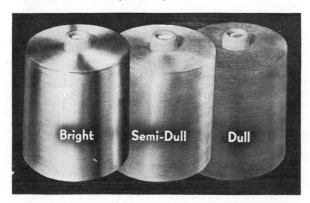

Bright   Semi-Dull   Dull

1. Thick-and-thin: slub yarns and multicolor effects
2. Hollow filaments

After-Treatments

Fiber modifications by after-treatments are:

High-tenacity fibers are produced by drawing or spinning either during or after spinning. The drawing may be done while the fiber is hot or cold depending on the individual fiber. Strength may be as high as 13 gram/denier. Stretching organizes the molecular chains into a more orderly pattern and permits the bonding forces to hold the chains together more tightly thus increasing the strength. High-strength fibers are used in clothing and household items, but most higher tenacity fibers are used in industrial items such as tire cords.

Nonpilling fibers are made with lower strength and elongation so that the fibers will break and pills will not accumulate on the surface of the cloth. Strong fibers resist breaking and pills accumulate.

Crimped Fibers

Crimped fibers are the result of more than one of the above changes in the spinning process. They may be crimped by:

1. Crimping gears after spinning.
2. Cooling one side of a melt-spun fiber faster than the other side.
3. Using two different polymer components to spin a fiber that has one component on one side and the other component on the other side; bicomponent fiber.
4. Heating one side of a melt-spun fiber after spinning

Heat-Sensitive Fibers

All the man-made fibers *except rayon* have some degree of heat-sensitivity. *Heat-sensitivity* is the resistance of a fiber to melting or glazing when exposed to high temperatures. It is important in everyday use and care of fabrics and also in various manufacturing processes. Heat is encountered in washing, ironing, pressing, during sewing and garment alteration and in dry cleaning. Dyeing, scouring, singeing, and so on are examples

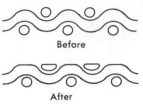

Before

After

Fig. 4–6. Heat and pressure cause permanent flattening of the yarns—glazing.

of fabric-finishing processes that are done with heat. The heat-sensitive fibers differ in their level of heat resistance. Safe ironing temperatures are given in a table on page 216.

Ironing is the highest temperature to which a garment is normally exposed in home use. Precautions should be taken to adjust the iron setting so that it is within safety limits for fiber content of the garment to be ironed. If the iron is too hot, the fibers will soften enough to be flattened by the pressure of the iron, or the fabric will melt. Flattening of the surface is called *glazing*. (See Figure 4–6.) Use of a soft press pad that will permit the edges and seams to sink down into the pad when pressure is applied will prevent glazing. Garment alteration is difficult because creases are hard to press in or out, particularly in nylon, and top-stitching may be needed to hold sharp creases and edges. (The acrylic fibers are quite different from the nylons and polyesters in their response to pressing. This difference is discussed in the section on acrylics.) Fullness cannot always be shrunk out of sleeve caps or other sections, and so patterns may have to be changed in the areas where fullness is usually controlled by shrinkage.

Heat-settability is the property of a fiber that enables it to take and hold a "set" shape or size under conditions of intended use. It is both an advantage and a disadvantage to the consumer.

Advantages	Disadvantages
Embossed designs are permanent.	"Set" creases and wrinkles are hard to remove in
Pleats and shape are permanent.	ironing or in garment alteration.
Size is stabilized.	Care must be taken in washing or ironing to prevent
Pile is crush-resistant.	ing or ironing to prevent
Knits do not need to be blocked.	the formation of set wrinkles.
Clothing resists wrinkling during wear.	

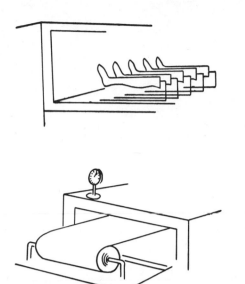

Fig. 4–7. Heat setting nylon hosiery and yard goods. (Courtesy of E. I. du Pont de Nemours & Company.)

Heat-setting is a treatment—a factory process—that is more or less a baking or steaming cloth finish. Its purpose is to stabilize the size or shape of the fabric or garment. It may be done at any stage of construction or finishing depending on the level of heat resistance of the fiber and other qualities. The temperatures for heat-setting range from 375° to 445° F. The heat is just high enough to bring the fiber *almost* to the melting point that is specific for that fiber and then it is cooled. Injection of steam is the usual practice. Uniform heat application is necessary to ensure a quality product. There should not be any strain on the fiber while it is in the softened state. The heat-setting process must be adapted to the thickness and texture of the fabric, the diameter of the fiber, and the thickness of the yarn. Heat-setting with steam usually takes place in an autoclave. The diagram in Figure 4–7 shows the preboarding of nylon hosiery. Hot calender rolls or air are used for dry heat-setting.

5 Man-Made Cellulosic Fibers

Rayon and acetate are both manufactured from cellulose obtained from natural sources such as cotton linters and wood pulp. The cellulose in rayon, *regenerated cellulose*, is physically changed by the fiber spinning process but it is still chemically the same as natural cellulose. Acetate, on the other hand, is the result of a chemical change. The cellulose combines chemically with acetic compounds to form cellulose acetate, a *cellulose derivative*, with properties that are quite different from those of rayon. However, the source of both fibers is still cellulose and so they are classified as cellulosic fibers. The table at the right gives some of the differences.

Both natural and man-made cellulose fibers are low-cost in price per pound and compete with one another in the textile market. The price of cotton fluctuates more than that of the others. If the price of cotton goes higher than the price of rayon, mills now tend to use rayon instead of cotton in end-uses that are suited to regular rayon or any of the modified types.

Filament costs more than staple and comes from the fiber producer as a *yarn*, whereas staple fiber must go through the costly operations of mechanical yarn spinning. Prices differ also for variations in denier, crimp, color, and so on. Producer-colored fibers are more expensive than uncolored fibers. Some typical prices are given in the table below.

Major Differences Between Rayon and Acetate

Rayon	Acetate
Cellulose physically changed	Cellulose chemically and physically changed
Scorches with too much heat	*Melts* with too much heat
Does NOT dissolve in acetone	Dissolves in acetone
High absorbency	Fair absorbency
No static	Static
Wrinkles unless resin treated	Resilient when *dry*
Most versatile fiber Cotton-like, wool-like, linen-like, silk-like	Much use in silk-like garments at lower cost

TYPICAL PRICES PER POUND FOR CELLULOSE FIBERS

Fiber	Staple, Uncolored	Filament, Uncolored	Filament, Colored
	(in dollars)		
Cotton*	0.35–0.36		
Rayon, regular	0.30(±)	0.80(±)	1.35(±)
Rayon, high-wet-modulus	0.37(±)		
Diacetate	0.40(±)	0.97(±)	1.27(±)
Triacetate	0.48(±)	1.26(±)	1.63(±)

SOURCE: *Modern Textiles Magazine* (March, 1967).
* Range in price from 1960 to 1966. *Textile Organon* 37: 175 (October, 1966).

Rayon *Wet spun*

Rayon is a manufactured fiber composed of regenerated cellulose, as well as a manufactured fiber composed of regenerated cellulose in which substituents have replaced not more than 15% of the hydrogens of the hydroxyl groups.

Federal Trade Commission

Rayon is the oldest and most widely used man-made fiber. It is the most versatile of *all* fibers, and only cotton is used in larger quantities. Observation of the silkworm spinning a cocoon and of the spider spinning a web led man to experiment with various solutions and spinning processes in an attempt to make a silk-like filament. By the last half of the nineteenth century, three different processes were developed for converting solid cellulose into a solution, and spinnerets had been made for extrusion of the fiber. The cuprammonium process was developed in Germany in 1857; the nitrocellulose process in France in 1884; and the viscose process in England in 1892. The viscose process is widely used today, the cuprammonium process is used by only one company, and the nitrocellulose process is no longer in use.

Commercial production of viscose rayon in the United States started in 1910 and the fiber was sold as artificial silk until the name "rayon" was adopted in 1924. Viscose filament fiber, the first form of the fiber to be made, was a very bright lustrous fiber. Because it had very low strength, it was used in the crosswise direction of the cloth, whereas the lengthwise yarns were of silk, which was strong enough to withstand the tension of the loom. The double Godet wheel, invented in 1926, made it possible to stretch the filaments to give them strength. Delustering agents, which were added to the spinning solution, made it possible to have dull as well as bright fibers. By 1932, machinery had been designed especially for staple fiber. Large spinnerets with ten times as many holes were used and the fibers from several spinnerets were collected as a large rope called "tow," which was then crimped and cut. Figure 5–1 shows crimped staple.

Perhaps the most important factor in rayon's success as a textile fiber was that it could be produced at a low cost so that people at every economic level could buy fabrics that had the beauty, hand, and color of wool, silk, and linen. Rayon's first uses were in the clothing field, and its first success was in crepe and linen-like fabrics. Rayon's *low resiliency* restricted its use in competition with wool and silk until the late 1930's when resin finishes for wrinkle recovery were developed. Rayon's uses in cotton-like fabrics were limited by poor laundering stability and by inability to be mercerized with caustic soda or to be Sanforized for shrinkage control. This defect not only restricted its use in washable items of 100 per cent rayon but meant that it was unsuitable for blends with cotton, since cotton is routinely treated with caustic soda as a part of the cloth-finishing processes.

After high-tenacity tire cord and heavy denier carpet fiber were developed in 1937, 65 per cent of

Fig. 5–1. Crimp in rayon staple.

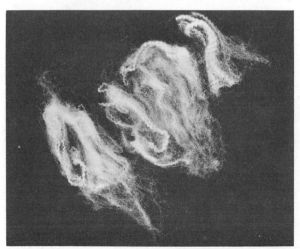

the rayon produced went into industrial and household uses and less went into apparel. The development of the high-wet-modulus rayon in the late 1950's (see page 48) made it possible for rayon to be (1) used in washable fabrics for dresses, sheets, and towels, and (2) in blends with cotton. This gave new stimulus to the use of rayon in apparel. The wide variety of end-uses for rayon is given below.

MAJOR USES FOR RAYON FIBERS

Apparel	Household	Industrial
Silk-like fabrics especially crepes, brocades, shantung, faille, and velvet	Rugs and carpets (alone or in blends) Upholstery and slip-covers Curtains and draperies	Tire cord
Blends for a cotton-like, wool-like, linen-like hand	Tableclothes, bedspreads, blankets Sheets and towels	

Viscose rayon, including the modified fibers such as high-wet-modulus rayon and others, has about 37 per cent of the total market for man-made fibers while cuprammonium accounts for approximately 0.5 per cent. Fibers are produced more economically by the viscose process. Fine filament yarns and novelty yarns are produced by the cuprammonium process, while almost equal amounts of filament, staple, and tow in a wide range of fiber types are produced by the viscose process.

Manufacture of Rayon Fiber

All rayon is made from cellulose obtained by purifying cotton linters or wood pulp. The production processes differ in the chemicals that are used to put the cellulose into solution; in the kind of ingredients added to the solution and the length of time it is aged; in the concentration, temperature, and ingredients in the coagulation bath; and in the mechanical treatments during and after spinning. The processes are given in the chart on page 47.

Physical Structure

The length, diameter, and cross-sectional shapes of rayon are important in that they help to determine the structure and the appearance of the fabric. Cuprammonium is a fine round rod-like fiber. (See Figure 5–3.) Viscose is characterized by lengthwise lines called *striations*. These are the result of "wrinkles" that form when liquid is lost from the fiber during coagulation. The cross section shows a serrated, circular shape. (See Figure 5–3.) Cross-sectional shapes of some of the modified rayons are shown later.

Fibers can be of any length and any diameter. Staple fibers and tow have a diameter range from

Fig. 5–2. Photomicrograph of cuprammonium rayon showing cross section of the fiber. (Courtesy of American Bemberg.)

Fig. 5–3. Photomicrograph of longitudinal and cross-sectional views of viscose rayon fiber. (Courtesy of E. I. du Pont de Nemours & Company.)

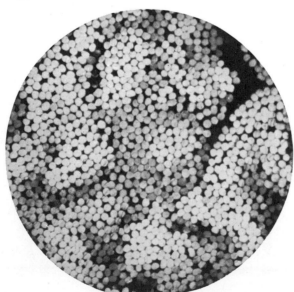

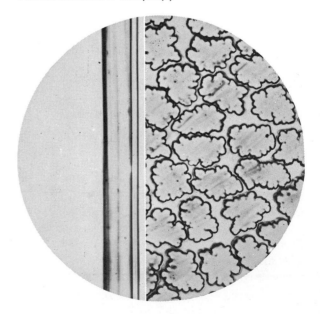

SPINNING RAYON FIBER

Cuprammonium	Regular Viscose	High-Wet-Modulus Viscose

I. Dissolve Blotter-like Sheets of Purified Cellulose

Moisten cellulose.	Soak in caustic soda (sodium hydroxide) (1 hour).	Use weaker caustic soda.
Dissolve in Sweitzer's reagent, a solution of ammoniacal copper sulfate.	Shred into crumbs.	Same as for viscose.
	Age 2 hours.	No ageing.
Use low temperature.	Treat with carbon disulfide	Same.
Filter.	(Crumbs turn orange)	
Age.	Xanthation.	
Delusterants and pigments may be added.	Dissolve in dilute caustic soda.	Use less caustic soda.
	Delusterants and pigments may be added here.	Same.
	Filter and age to ripen.	No ageing.

II. Extrude Through Spinneret and Coagulate
(Each hole in the spinneret forms one fiber. Together the fibers form a yarn.)

Pumped through spinneret with *large holes* into a glass spinning funnel.	Extrude into acid bath.	Process is similar to that of regular viscose except for slower spinning speeds, more dilute acid bath, and per cent of stretch.
Water flows in from the top. Flow of the water and pull of take-up reel stretches the fibers—"Stretch spinning."	Acid causes fibers to coagulate.	
	Fibers are drawn out of bath and around two Godet wheels where they are stretched.	
Fibers pass through a dilute acid to complete coagulation.	Fibers are washed, bleached, softened, and dried.	

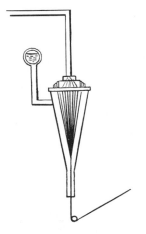

Fig. 5–4a.

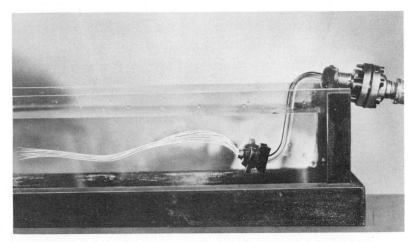

Fig. 5–4b.

Process favors the production of fine fibers and of thick-and-thin fibers for novelty yarns. (Thick-and-thin filaments are made by altering the drive of the spinning pump.)	Cheaper to produce than cuprammonium rayon.	There is less breakdown of molecule chains so fibers swell less and can be treated with alkalies.
	Tougher and stronger than cuprammonium rayon.[1]	Can be used where 100% cotton can be used.
	Inorganic materials like silicates may be dissolved in the alkaline dope to produce ceramic fibers.	

[1] Richard H. Braunlich, "New Developments in Rayon," *American Dyestuff Reporter* **54**:38 (March 1, 1695).

1.5 to 15 denier and filament yarns vary from 40 to 5,000 denier with from 10 to 980 filaments per yarn. Staple fibers are usually given a mechanical crimp.

Rayon can be delustered or solution-dyed. Both types have trade names that help identify them. For example, Dul-tone is a delustered fiber and Coloray is a producer-colored fiber.

Molecular Structure and Properties

The rayons are regenerated cellulose and the length of the molecule chains depends on the kind of natural cellulose that was used and on the spinning process. Regular (basic) rayon has a much shorter chain length than cotton as well as lower crystallinity and less orientation of the molecules. Its core is highly amorphous and its skin is somewhat oriented. The molecular structure and the chemical composition are responsible for most of the fiber properties.

Rayon fibers vary in *strength* as shown below.

Regular rayon	0.73 to 2.6 g/d
Intermediate tenacity rayon	2.4 to 3.2 g/d
High-tenacity rayon	3.0 to 5.7 g/d
High-wet-modulus rayon	3.4 to 10 g/d

Regular rayon loses approximately 50 per cent of its strength when wet. The high-wet-modulus rayon was developed to furnish a type of rayon that would retain more of its strength when wet. While viscose is somewhat stronger than cuprammonium neither fiber is very resistant to *abrasion*.

The *absorbancy* of rayon is dependent on the inner structure of regenerated cellulose, which is highly amorphous; thus it can be penetrated easily by water and other aqueous solutions. This property is advantageous in several respects: easy dyeability, acceptance of resins for durable press or wrinkle recovery, ability to absorb perspiration so that skin-contact garments are comfortable not clammy, and reduction of static build-up in rayon/synthetic blends. As water enters the fiber, it breaks the hydrogen bonds between the molecular chains, pushes them apart, and causes the fiber to swell. In this swollen state the fibers are about 50 per cent weaker and are more easily distorted. Garments have a tendency to shrink and clothes to dry more slowly.

Rayon, like all cellulose fibers, has very low *resiliency* because of the weak hydrogen bonds.

Fabrics wrinkle badly unless given a resin finish for wash-and-wear or durable press. Rayon suffers less loss of strength in resin finishing than cotton does.

The *heat reactivity* of rayon is the same as that of cotton. If the temperature is too high rayon *scorches*, then *burns*. Rayon cannot be distinguished from the other cellulose fibers by burning. However, if the fabric is made of filament fibers rather than staple fibers, it can be identified as rayon because *rayon is the only filament cellulose fiber*. See chart, page 13.

The care of rayon is relatively simple. Regular rayon can be washed but it retains a much better appearance if it is dry-cleaned. It is also less apt to fade if dry-cleaned. High-wet-modulus rayons wash like cotton. The rayons are not damaged by ordinary bleaches and household chemicals if they are properly used. They can be washed in hot water and ironed like cotton.

Special Viscose Modifications

Fiber modifications are called *types*, *variants*, or *second-generation* fibers. They are the product of a company's continuing research program to explore the potential of its fibers and develop properties in them that are suitable for new end-uses. Fiber modifications are made by changes in the spinning solution, the techniques of extrusion, or in the coagulation of the fiber. Viscose rayon has been on the market longer than any of the other fibers and during this time a number of types have been developed:

Solution-dyed	Cross-dyeable
Delustered	Ceramic
High-tenacity	Bacteriostatic
Carpet fiber	Self-crimping
High-wet-modulus	Bicomponent
Multicellular	Tire cord
Cross-linked	Acetylated (Avron XL)

High-Wet-Modulus Rayon

This fiber modification, the product of a research program designed to improve the washability of rayon, is one of the most outstanding developments in rayon research. The first high-wet-modulus fiber, Toramomen, was made in Japan in 1938. Little interest was shown in the fiber by American producers until a series of articles appeared in *Modern Textiles Magazine* in 1955. However, in Europe a group of fiber producers became interested in the Japanese fiber and obtained an option on the process and adapted it for commercial production. A license was granted to them in 1958 and they began production of a fiber called Zantrel Polynosic. (*Poly* means many and *nosic* means fibrils.) In 1960, the Hartford Company[2] began production of Zantrel in the United States. The Federal Trade Commission ruled that it should be called Zantrel Polynosic Rayon. An appeal was made requesting permission to use the generic name "polynosic" rather than "rayon," but the request was denied. Meanwhile research in the United States had resulted in the development of other high-wet-modulus rayon fibers.

There are two types of high-wet-modulus rayon: (1) the modifier or zinc-based, and (2) the polynosic or non-zinc-based. In the modifier type, amino compounds are added to the spinning solution. All high-wet-modulus rayon spinning processes maintain maximum molecular chain length and fibril structure regularity by preventing, insofar as possible, the breakdown of the natural molecular structure, which occurs in regular rayon. Some of the differences between the manufacturing processes of high-wet-modulus rayon and regular rayon are presented on page 47.

High-wet-modulus fibers have *lower elongation* and *higher wet and dry strength* than regular rayon. Fabrics have relatively high *stiffness* when they are wet, and, like cotton, they resist deformation when wet. Drapery fabrics of high-wet-modulus rayon do not exhibit the "elevator effect" of regular rayon draperies, which lengthen when a high moisture content of the atmosphere increases the weight of the drapery fabric, and then as the air dries, shorten again. Fabrics made of high-wet-modulus rayon have the following advantages:

1. Stability equal to cotton.
2. Can be Sanforized.
3. Can be mercerized.
4. Can be plisséd.

2 Now owned by American Enka Corporation.

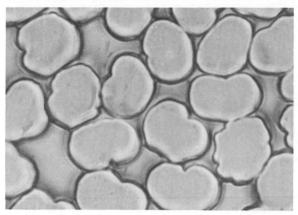

Fig. 5–5. High-wet-modulus rayon, Avril. (Courtesy of the FMC Corporation, American Viscose Division.)

5. Have hand more like cotton.
6. Strength is close to that of cotton.

The shape of the high-wet-modulus rayon differs from that of regular viscose. Figure 5–5 shows a cross section of Fiber 40 (Avril).

A comparison of some of the properties of cotton, high-wet-modulus rayon, and regular rayon is presented in the following table.

COMPARISON OF COTTON, REGULAR RAYON, AND HIGH-WET-MODULUS RAYON*

Properties	Cotton	Regular Rayon	High-Wet-Modulus Rayon
Fibrils	Yes	No	Yes
Molecular chain length	800+	250±	500±
Swelling in water	6%	26%	18%
Average Stiffness	57–60	6–50	28–75
Tenacity, g/d			
dry	3.8	2.0	3.4
wet	4.8	1.0	2.7
Breaking elongation†	12%	11%	30%

* High-wet-modulus is a measure of the wet breaking strength divided by the breaking elongation.
† Elongation with a lead of 0.5 g/d.

Most of the high-wet-modulus fibers are sold under a *fabric quality control* program. The fiber is sold by type letter or number and the finished fabric may carry the trade name if it meets the fiber producers' fabric testing requirements. Fiber types and trade names are given in the following chart.

Modifier Type	Polynosic Type
Avril (Fiber 40)	Zantrel (Fiber HM)
American Viscose Co.	American Enka Corp
Zantrel 700 (Enka 700)	Lirelle (W-63)
American Enka Corp.	Courtaulds North America
Xena (Fiber B)	
Beaunit	
Nupron	
Industrial Rayon Corp.	

Multicellular Viscose Rayon

Multicellular rayon fibers have a unique, thin-walled, broad, flat cross section, which imparts

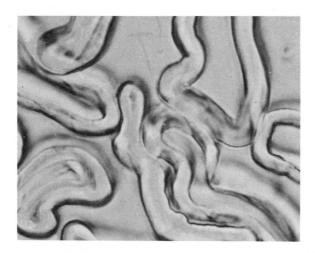

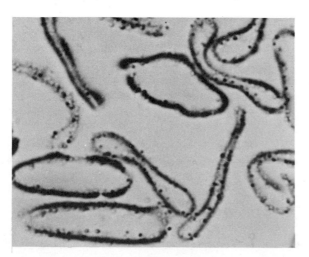

Fig. 5–6. Multicellular viscose rayon. Top, 1.5 dull RD-100 Avlin; bottom, 3.0 RD-100 Avlin. (Courtesy of the FMC Corporation, American Viscose Division.)

crispness and luster or, in dark shades, a glitter to the fabric. The wet fibers will bond to one another or to other kinds of fibers as they dry. No adhesive is necessary. The flat surface of the fiber permits larger areas of contact between adjacent fibers. The bonds can be broken by mechanical action during wear but new bonds will form when the fabric is rewetted and dried. The shape of the fibers permits them to intertwine and restricts the movement of other fibers in a blend to prevent packing and thus give a linen-like hand (Figure 5–6). The name Avlin was at first designated for this fiber by the American Viscose Corporation, but in 1967 it was reassigned to their new polyester fiber. This type of fiber is made by inflating the fiber with dispersed gas at the jet face. Avlin is the trademark of the American Viscose Company, the only producer. Uses are in fabrics with linen-like texture. A resin finish is needed for crease resistance.

High-Tenacity (Strength) Viscose Rayon

High-tenacity rayon refers to a rayon fiber with a tensile strength of three or more gram/denier. The table gives figures for the tensile strength of the cellulose fibers.

Fiber	Tenacity in Gram/denier
Flax	6.0
Cotton	3.8
Rayon, regular	0.7–2.6
High-tenacity rayon	3.0–5.7

High-tenacity rayon is made from a normal spinning solution. It is the result of modifications in the spinning techniques—stretching—and the coagulating bath—higher temperature and addition of zinc salts. In 1926 the double Godet wheel was introduced; one wheel revolves faster than the other and thus stretches the fiber as much as 25 per cent and increases the strength by about 1 g/d. In 1935 it was discovered that one night foreman was keeping the doors and windows of the factory closed and thereby raising the temperature of the spinning bath so that the fiber was being stretched at a higher temperature and was a stronger fiber than that produced by the day foreman. In 1911 it was discovered that the addition of 1 per cent zinc sulfate to the spinning bath improved coagulation.

In regular rayon, the spinning speed is quite high and the coagulation and regeneration occur almost

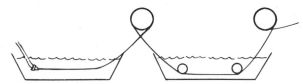

Fig. 5–7. Double Godet stretching in hot water bath to increase strength.

simultaneously. This results in a skin that is oriented and a core that is amorphous. In high-tenacity rayon, the spinning speed is reduced and a flexible, semipermeable skin is formed. This plus the high temperature makes it possible to develop more uniform orientation and crystallinity when the fiber is stretched.

After the fiber leaves the coagulating bath, it is run through a 90° C hot water bath (100° C is boiling) between two Godet wheels, which revolve

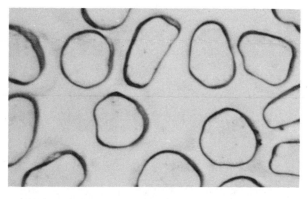

Fig. 5–8. Cross section of high-tenacity rayon fibers. Top, 1.5 XL, Avron; bottom, 8.0 denier bright, Super L. (Courtesy of the FMC Corporation, American Viscose Division.)

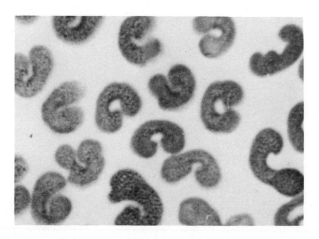

at different speeds and stretch the fibers just short of the breaking point, 75 to 100 per cent. (See Figure 5–7.)

High-tenacity rayon is used in tire cords and for other industrial purposes. Tyrex and Dynacor are trade names.

High-strength apparel fiber was developed for use with other high-elongation fibers such as nylon and the polyesters. It can also be used in washable sheers. It has good abrasion resistance and can be resin-treated for crease resistance. Avron is the trademark for articles made from the American Viscose high-tenacity fiber Avisco XL and Avisco XL II. (See Figure 5–8.) Comiso is the trademark for Beaunit's high-strength staple and tow.

Self-crimping Viscose Rayon

Self-crimping viscose fibers (latent crimp) are produced by a modification that results in a difference in the two sides of the fiber. Under the influence of moisture, one side of the fiber will swell more than the other and cause the fiber to curl. This curling action can be demonstrated by wetting one side of a piece of paper. The wet side of the paper will swell, and the edge will curl in toward the dry side. Curling is the result of differences in surface tension.

Self-crimping viscose is produced by two different methods. In the first method, the acidity of the coagulating bath is lowered and the salt content is raised. This causes a skin to form around the fiber as it solidifies. This skin bursts and a new and thinner skin forms over the ruptured area. The difference in the thickness of the skin causes the difference in the surface tension that causes the fiber to curl. *Avicron* is a self-crimping fiber produced by the American Viscose Corporation. It is produced in heavy denier for use in pile fabrics or as tow to make direct spun yarns for worsted-type fabrics. (See page 102.) Figure 5–9 is a photomicrograph of Avicron. Notice the difference in the "skin" on the two sides of the fiber. Figure 5–10 shows Avicron before and after crimping. The crimp is permanent.

The second method consists of spinning an aged solution and an unaged solution side by side through the same spinneret. The aged solution develops a thick skin and the unaged solution develops a thin skin. The fiber swells more on the thin side. Procedures for this kind of fiber (conjugate fiber or bicomponent fiber) were developed by the American

Fig. 5–9. Cross section of Avicron rayon. Note the difference in thickness on the skin on the two sides. (Courtesy of the FMC Corporation, American Viscose Division.)

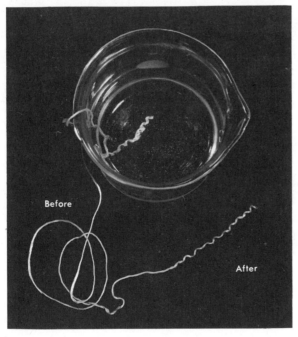

Before

After

Fig. 5–10. Avicron self-crimping fiber curls when immersed in water.

Viscose Company in 1949. Turn to pages 63 and 76 for a discussion of nylon and acrylic bicomponent fibers.

Cross-linked Viscose Rayon Fibers

Cross-linked rayons are made by adding a cross-linking agent (resins) to the spinning solution before the extrusion of the fiber. (They should not be confused with the rayons that are given a resin fabric finish, that is, crease-resistant rayons.) The cross-linking reaction of the resin and the cellulose molecular chains is similar to that which occurs when resin is used as a fabric finish for rayon and cotton. (See page 202 of Chapter 24.) Corval, produced by Courtaulds in Canada, is the only fiber of this type. It has not been completely satisfactory in that cross-links have broken with repeated laundering and white fabrics have sometimes picked up chlorine.

Acetylation of Rayon Fibers. This process consists of treating the fiber with a catalyst and then exposing it to the vapors of acetic anhydride at relatively high temperatures. The fibers have impressive strengths and are quite similar chemically to the acetate fibers. They can be heat-set and are insoluble in the solvents that dissolve acetate.

Cross-dyeable Fibers. In 1967, American Enka introduced the fiber Enkrome,[1] a chemically altered fiber that will accept acid dyes without changing its dyeability by direct dyes. It was developed to meet the need for multicolor effects. Dyeing can be done in one dyebath and takes a heavier shade. Physical properties are the same.

Ceramic Viscose Rayon Fibers. Ceramic fibers are made by dissolving inorganic substances like sodium silicate in the spinning solution. They will withstand extremely high temperatures.

Bateriostatic Viscose Rayon. These fibers are in the experimental stage. They would be used for sanitary, disposable products.

Acetate

Acetate is a manufactured fiber in which the fiber forming substance is cellulose acetate. Where not less than 92% of the hydroxyl groups are acetylated the term triacetate may also be used as a generic description of the fiber.

Federal Trade Commission

The history of the acetate fiber as a separate fiber family began in 1952 when the Federal Trade Commission issued a regulation that separated acetate

[1] H. L. Reed, "Cross-Dyeable Rayon," *Modern Textiles* **48**:51 (January, 1967).

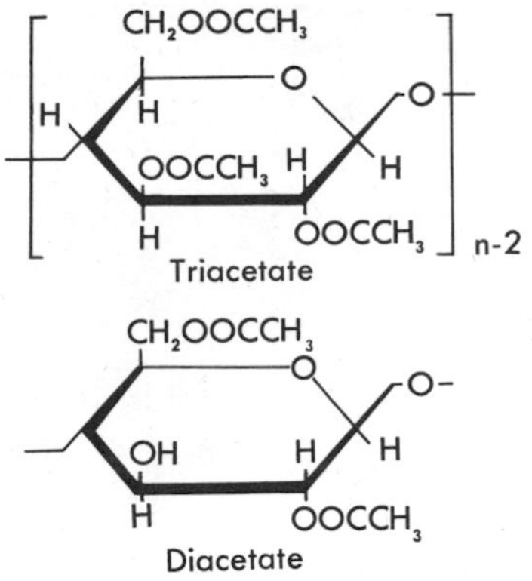

CH₂OOCCH₃

Triacetate

Diacetate

Fig. 5–11. Diacetate and triacetate molecules.

from the rayon family to which it had belonged since the 1924 ruling that designated all cellulose-base fibers as rayon. Acetate fiber producers had been unhappy about the 1924 ruling because they felt that acetate was different enough in chemical composition and properties to merit a generic name of its own. Their protests led to the 1952 ruling. A promotional program introduced the "new" fiber to the public under the slogan "The Beauty Fiber." Consumers did not know that they had been using this fiber under the name "rayon" and a great deal of confusion resulted at first.

Two kinds of acetate fibers are manufactured.[2] Triacetate was made experimentally in 1914, but because no suitable solvent or dyes were available at that time, it was not commercially produced until 1953 when the Celanese Corporation introduced it under the trade name Arnel. Diacetate—usually called just acetate—was the first acetate produced commercially in 1919 by the Lustron Corporation, which later merged with the Celanese Corporation, now the largest producer of acetate. A method discovered during World War II for recovering the solvent acetone was responsible for making the acetate spinning process economically successful.

Acetate is an *ester* of cellulose that differs both physically and chemically from pure or regenerated cellulose. The ester is formed by treating cellulose (an alcohol) with glacial acetic acid, sulfuric acid, and acetic anhydride. In this reaction, called *acetylation*, some of the hydroxyl groups of cellulose are replaced by acetyl groups. Diacetate has fewer hydroxyl groups that have reacted with the acetic acid than has triacetate. (See Figure 5–11.)

[2] Fortisan rayon, a saponified acetate, was discontinued in 1967.

Manufacture

Both fibers are produced as filament and staple by the following process: Purified cellulose from cotton linters or wood pulp is mixed with glacial acetic acid and then allowed to stand until a clear solution forms. Water is added; the solution is aged and hydrolyzed to a cellulose acetate. This is then precipitated as acetate resin flakes. The flakes are dissolved in *acetone* to make the spinning solution. The solution is extruded into a column of warm air and the fibers solidify as the solvent evaporates. The fibers are stretched to orient the molecules and to increase fiber strength. Finally they are given a slight twist and wound on bobbins. The acetone is recovered to be used again.

Acetate filaments, as spun, are a finished product —unlike rayon, which requires washing, bleaching, and so on. The staple fiber is crimped and heat-set. Figure 5–12 is a diagram of the acetate spinning process.

Delustering. This process is done by adding titanium dioxide directly to the triacetate or diacetate spinning solution. Delustered acetate is easily damaged by sunlight; bright acetate has very good resistance to sunlight damage.

When titanium dioxide is present in an oxygen containing atmosphere, ultraviolet radiation produces titanium peroxide which in the presence of moisture forms hydrogen peroxide. The hydrogen peroxide will then

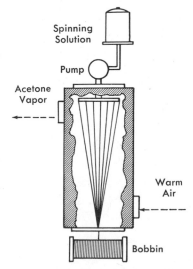

Fig. 5–12. Acetate spinning chamber. (Courtesy of the Tennessee Eastman Company.)

attack the cellulose acetate ether linkages to accelerate the molecular chain degradation.[3]

The acetate fiber Estron SLR was developed to furnish a *dull* acetate fiber for draperies and upholstery that would be more highly resistant to sunlight.

Solution-Dye. When the first acetate fiber was made, it could not be colored with the traditional dyes, and a new class of dyes—disperse dyes—was developed. It soon became evident, however, that some of these dyes, especially those containing blue, exhibited a kind of fading not caused by sunlight because fading occurred while garments were hanging in the closet. Blues and greys turned pink and greens turned brown. Tests showed that the fading was caused by gas—nitrogen oxide—coming from furnaces, gas heaters, and engines. Three possible ways to solve the problem were studied. New fade-resistant dyes worked well but were costly. Inhibitors made of various basic compounds that were applied to the fabric provided protection but were not stable to washing and dry cleaning. The most satisfactory remedy at that time was the addition of colored pigments or selected dyes to the spinning solution. The first of these *solution-dyed* (dope-dyed or producer-colored) fibers was made by the Tennessee Eastman Company and was called Chromspun.

Because the solution-dyed fibers exhibited exceptional fastness to chlorine and salt water and to sunlight, they were widely used in swim suits and in glass curtains. Limitations on the use of solution-dyed fibers are the large size of the inventory required to fill orders and the type of designs that can be made. When Arnel triacetate entered the market and found acceptance in printed jersey, the need for inexpensive fast colors became more urgent. In 1965, a new inhibitor was developed that gave greatly improved protection to the dyes under all conditions that cause fading.[4]

Fiber Identification

Acetone Test. Both diacetate and triacetate will dissolve in *acetone*. None of the other textile fibers

[3] R. C. Harrington, Jr. and C. A. Jarrett, "A New Dull Acetate for Decorative Fabrics," *Modern Textiles Magazine* **44**:67 (April, 1963).
[4] F. S. Moussalle and W. I. Myles, "Gas Fading of Acetate and Triacetate Prints," *American Dyestuffs Reporter,* **54**:1136–40 (December 20, 1965).

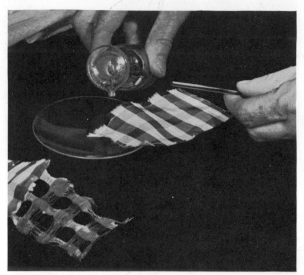

Fig. 5–13. The acetone test for identification of acetate fiber. See the text below for full instructions.

will dissolve in acetone; therefore, this is a specific identification test. Figure 5–13 shows a procedure for testing for acetate content of a fabric. Use acetone, a dropping bottle, a glass rod, watch glass, and a cleansing tissue. Test individual yarns first.

Burning Test. Diacetate and triacetate burn in a similar manner so the burning test does not distinguish one from the other, but it does differentiate them from the other textile fibers. The burning characteristics of acetate are given on page 13.

Fig. 5–14. Photomicrograph of longitudinal and cross-sectional views of acetate fiber. (Courtesy of E. I. du Pont de Nemours & Company.)

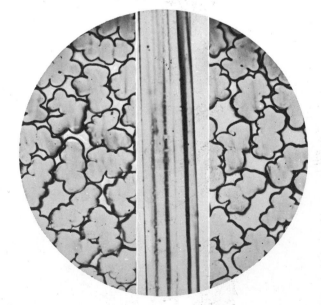

Diacetate and triacetate fibers look alike under the microscope. The cross section is lobular or flower-petal shaped. The shape results from the evaporation of the solvent as the fiber solidifies in spinning. In Figure 5–14 one of the lobes shows up as a false lumen.

Fiber Properties

Both fibers have low strength, rather high density, and have good resistance to damage from bacteria, mildew, mold, and moth.

ACETATE FIBER DIFFERENCES

	Diacetate	*Triacetate*
Safe ironing temperature	355° F	482° F
Percentage of water absorbency (70° F and 65% r.h.)	6.5	3.2
Principal end-uses	Textured knits Silk-like dresses, draperies, upholstery, bedspreads, linings	Tricot jerseys Sportswear Permanently pleated skirts
Care (general)	Dry cleanable	Wash-and-wear

The principal differences between the diacetate and triacetate fibers as shown in the table, are heat-sensitivity and low absorbency. Because of these differences, they have different end-uses that require different kinds of care.

The results of the difference in safe ironing temperature is shown in Figures 5–15. Both kinds of acetate fabric were pressed by the same iron; the diacetate fabric melted and shrank, whereas the Arnel triacetate fabric showed only a slight imprint of the iron. Compare the ironing temperatures of the acetates and the other textile fibers (page 216). Because Arnel triacetate is outstanding in its resistance to damage by heat, it is possible to heat-set fabrics at temperatures that are high enough to give a permanent "set" to pleats and flat surfaces.

Arnel has been promoted by the Celanese Corporation as the "Ease-of-Care" fiber. Its advantages are listed as washability, stability through many launderings, rapid drying, and little or no ironing. It is widely used in washable garments such as those listed in the table. The *fabric performance testing program* for Arnel is somewhat different from that of the others. The trade name is not licensed, but

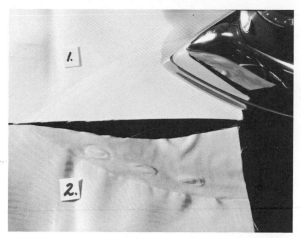

Fig. 5–15. Effect of heat on (1) Arnel and (2) acetate.

may be used by any purchaser. Instead, the official *symbol*, a black and white tent, appears on tags that are attached to Arnel products that have been tested and approved by Celanese.[5]

Diacetate was promoted as the "Beauty Fiber" because it has many silk-like qualities and is used in silk-like end-uses. The properties of high luster, crisp hand, body, and drape have made such fashion fabrics as taffeta bengaline, satin, and textured knits one of the major outlets of the diacetate fibers. For this reason, more filament fiber than staple fiber has been produced. The staple acetate fiber is crimped and used in draperies, upholsteries, and in blends with rayon. Because of diacetate's silk-like nature and its poor washability, it has usually been best to dry-clean these fabrics. In 1966, Eastman Chemical Company developed a finish for a washable acetate with the trade name Estrel. The process can be applied to many acetate fabrics but is not yet suitable for taffetas and heavy satins.

Like the other cellulose fibers, both diacetate and triacetate are low in cost per pound of fiber. They have an economic advantage in competition with silk, nylon, and the polyesters.

Special Acetate Fiber Modifications

Celacrimp and *Du Pont Type C* are self-crimping, water-crimpable continuous filament yarns for tufted bedspreads. Type F, Celacloud, and Type K, Celafil, are modified cross-section staple fibers for batting, and so on. *Loftura* is a filament yarn with 4-inch slubs. Other trade names and the acetate fiber producers are listed in Appendix C.

[5] Daniel Powderly, "Trademarks and licensing," *Modern Textiles Magazine* **45**:61 (March, 1964).

6 The Melt-Spun Fibers

The major fibers spun by the melt-spinning method are the nylons, polyesters, and olefins. Melt-spinning is the third fiber spinning method. It is a simple speedy procedure and is the only one of the three methods that can be done by hand techniques. It can be demonstrated by a simple laboratory experiment that is fun to do. A flame, a pair of tweezers, and a piece of nylon, polyester or olefin cloth are all that are needed. (An old nylon stocking serves very well.) Allow the fabric to burn until quite a little melt has formed, then quickly draw out a fiber with the tweezers as shown in Figure 6–1. Figure 6–2 shows nylon fibers emerging from the spinneret at the factory.

The extrusion for all commercial melt-spun fibers is basically the same, but some adjustments are

Fig. 6–2. Spinning nylon fiber. (Courtesy of E. I. du Pont de Nemours & Company.)

Fig. 6–1. Spinning a melt-spun fiber by hand technique.

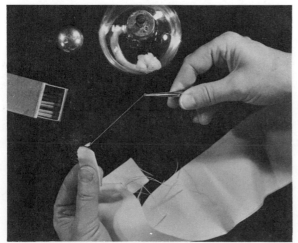

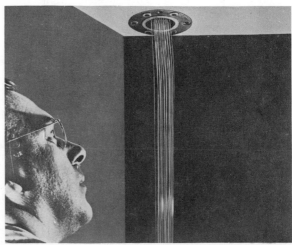

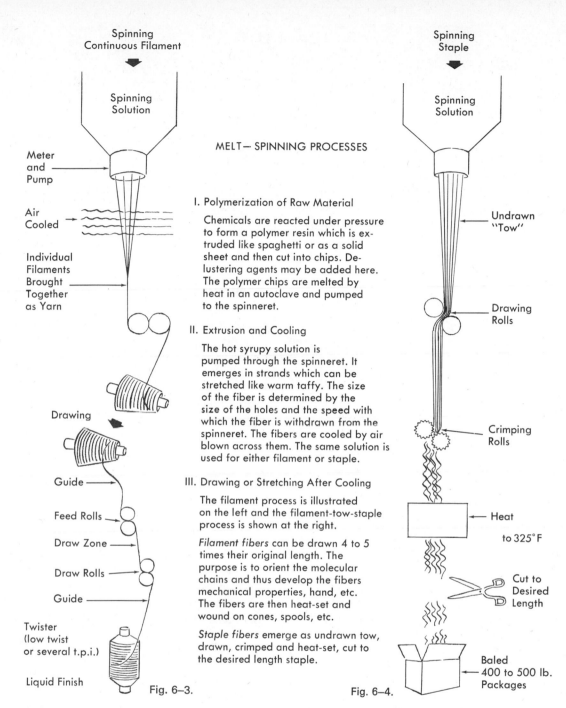

**Spinning
Continuous Filament**

**Spinning
Solution**

MELT— SPINNING PROCESSES

Meter
and
Pump

Air
Cooled

Individual
Filaments
Brought
Together
as Yarn

Drawing

Guide

Feed Rolls

Draw Zone

Draw Rolls

Guide

Twister
(low twist
or several t.p.i.)

Liquid Finish

Fig. 6–3.

**Spinning
Staple**

**Spinning
Solution**

Undrawn
"Tow"

Drawing
Rolls

Crimping
Rolls

Heat

to 325° F

Cut to
Desired
Length

Baled
400 to 500 lb.
Packages

Fig. 6–4.

I. Polymerization of Raw Material

Chemicals are reacted under pressure
to form a polymer resin which is extruded like spaghetti or as a solid
sheet and then cut into chips. Delustering agents may be added here.
The polymer chips are melted by
heat in an autoclave and pumped
to the spinneret.

II. Extrusion and Cooling

The hot syrupy solution is
pumped through the spinneret. It
emerges in strands which can be
stretched like warm taffy. The size
of the fiber is determined by the
size of the holes and the speed with
which the fiber is withdrawn from the
spinneret. The fibers are cooled by air
blown across them. The same solution is
used for either filament or staple.

III. Drawing or Stretching After Cooling

The filament process is illustrated
on the left and the filament-tow-staple
process is shown at the right.

Filament fibers can be drawn 4 to 5
times their original length. The
purpose is to orient the molecular
chains and thus develop the fibers
mechanical properties, hand, etc.
The fibers are then heat-set and
wound on cones, spools, etc.

Staple fibers emerge as undrawn tow,
drawn, crimped and heat-set, cut to
the desired length staple.

made for the physical performance of the individual
fibers.[1] Also the extrusion of filament and staple
fibers is essentially the same. As extruded the filament fibers are of little textile value due to their
amorphous state.[2] Drawing, the second part of the
melt-spinning process, develops a high level of
strength and elasticity in the fibers.

[1] Jack Press, "A New Dyeable Polypropylene Fiber,"
Modern Textiles Magazine **46**:68 (September, 1965).
[2] E. R. Higgs, "Continuous Filaments; They Create New
Horizons for Machinery," *Modern Textiles Magazine*
47:35 (April, 1966).

Melt-Spinning Process

The basic steps of the melt-spinning process are
given in the chart above and processing differences
are discussed with the individual fibers.

Properties Common to Melt-Spun Fibers

In the *drawing* part of the spinning process, an
interesting change takes place. The chain-like
molecules of the undrawn fiber are in helter-skelter

arrangement like straws in a haystack. Drawing aligns the molecules into an orderly array, placing them parallel to one another and bringing them closer together. Fiber diameter is also reduced in size. Figure 6–5 illustrates this; the molecules are represented by the short black lines. Drawing develops good mechanical properties, hand, and so on. As the molecule chains come closer together, the forces (hydrogen bonds, etc.) that attract them to one another—like the forces that attract a nail to a magnet—become stronger and the fiber develops

Unstretched   Stretched

Fig. 6–5. Diagram of orientation of molecules during stretching or cold drawing.

a great deal of strength, pliability, toughness, and elasticity. The melt-spun fibers are some of the strongest fibers made. See the table below.

COMPARISON OF THE TENACITY OF MELT-SPUN FIBERS

		(gram/denier)	
		Dry	*Wet* (% of dry)
Nylon 6,6	Regular	3.0 to 6.0	87+
Nylon 6,6	High-tenacity	5.9 to 9.5	86+
Nylon 6	Regular	4.0 to 6.8	91+
Nylon 6	High-tenacity	6.5 to 8.2	79+
Polyester (Dacron)	Regular	4.4 to 5.0	100
Polyester (Dacron)	High-tenacity	6.3 to 7.8	100
Olefin		3.5 to 13.0	100

Fiber Shape. The melt-spun fibers are unique in that they will keep the shape of the spinneret hole through which they were spun. The fiber is normally smooth and round as spun. Trilobal fibers are spun through triangular holes, flat fibers through rectangular holes, and so on. These fibers are made for special end-uses.

Moisture Absorption. The moisture absorption of the melt-spun fibers is low. Nylon has a moisture regain of 4 per cent; polyester, 0.4 per cent; and olefin, 0 per cent. This is both an advantage and a disadvantage. Fibers lose very little strength when they are wet, they dry rapidly, waterborne stains are not absorbed, and there is no fabric shrinkage because of the effect of moisture. On the other hand, fabrics made of these fibers will be uncomfortable in humid weather unless the fabrics are especially engineered to permit the moisture to pass through and evaporate. Another disadvantage is the build-up of static.

Static Electricity. Static electricity is generated by the friction of a fabric rubbed against itself or other objects. If the electrical charge is not conducted away, it tends to build up on the surface. When the fabric comes in contact with a good conductor, a shock or transfer occurs. This transfer may produce sparks that, in a gaseous atmosphere, can cause explosions. It is always a hazard in places such as dry cleaning plants and operating rooms. Nurses are forbidden to wear nylon or polyester uniforms in operating rooms because of the danger. Static tends to build up more rapidly in dry, cold regions. Other problems with static are:

1. Soil and lint cling to the surface of the fabric and dark colors become very unsightly. Brushing simply increases the problem.

2. Dust and dirt are attracted to curtains.

3. Fabrics cling to the machinery at the factory and make cutting and handling very difficult. Static is responsible for increased defects and makes a higher percentage of seconds.

4. Clothes cling to the wearer and cause discomfort and an unsightly appearance. Temporary relief can be obtained by the wearer if a damp sponge or paper towel is wiped across the surface to drain away the static. More permanent relief can be obtained by the use of *fabric softeners* available at the grocery store. These are quite effective if used in the last rinse of the laundry.

Antistatic finishes are applied to many of the fabrics at the factory but they frequently wash out or come out in drycleaning.

Oily Stains. The synthetic fibers seem to have an affinity for oily stains such as skin oil and cooking oils. They may be absorbed into the fiber if not removed immediately, and for that reason frequent washing of clothing is desirable. However, laundry research has shown that many oils, including body oils, are not removed at low temperatures; at high temperatures the oil penetrates the fibers. The following "cold-spotting" treatment is suggested by the Du Pont Company for heavily soiled areas such as collars and cuffs:

Work a *strong* solution of detergent into the spot with a sponge or brush. This emulsifies the oil. Rinse in cold water. Be sure to manipulate the spotted areas thoroughly or until the water is clear. Then wash in the regular manner.

Pilling. Pilling is a fabric problem caused by the balling up of fiber ends on the surface of the fabric. Pilling occurs on napped fabrics of wool and cotton, but the pills often break off before the garment becomes unsightly. With nylon and the polyesters, the fibers are so strong that none of the pills breaks off and they all accumulate on the surface of the garment. Pills are of two kinds: lint and fabric. Lint

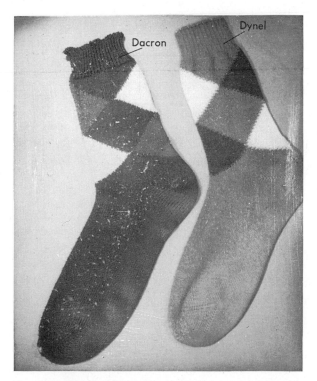

Fig. 6–6. Pilling. Sock made of Dacron on the left, sock made of Dynel on the right. Both were worn one day a week for 14 months and washed after each wearing.

pills are more unsightly, because they contain not only fibers from the garment but fibers picked up in the wash water or through contact with other garments and even through static attraction. Figure 6–6 shows two socks, one having lint pills and the other fabric pills. Observe the difference in appearance.

The best single treatment to prevent pilling is *singeing.* The construction of the fabric is a more important factor in the prevention of pilling than is the fiber content. Close weave, high twist, or plied yarns, and longer-staple fibers are recommended. Resin finishes of cottons and fulling of wool are finishes that help prevent pilling.

Nylon Fibers

Nylon is a manufactured fiber in which the fiber forming substance is any long chain, synthetic polyamide having recurring amide groups ($-\overset{\text{O}}{\underset{\|}{C}}-NH-$) *as an integral part of the molecule chain.*

Federal Trade Commission

Nylon was the first truly synthetic fiber and was announced by the Du Pont Company at the 1939 New York World's Fair. The chemicals used to produce nylon polymers were known in the 1800's, but the first research dates back to the work done by Dr. Wallace Carothers while he was at Harvard in the 1920's. Dr. Carothers joined the Du Pont Company in 1928 to work on a program of fundamental research designed to extend basic knowledge of the way in which small molecules are united to form giant molecules. In 1931, Dr. Carothers described to the American Chemical Society filaments which, when compressed, showed a springiness similar to that of wool. These first fibers were made by forcing a molten nylon solution through a hypodermic needle. In 1937, the first item of apparel —hosiery of 30, 40, and 70 denier—was knit experimentally, and the first hosiery went on sale in 1939. The first all-nylon costume was modeled at the 1940 New York Fair.

From 1941 to 1946, all nylon production was diverted to military uses such as cordage, parachutes, and so on. Some nylon hosiery was still on the market at the beginning of this period, and the desire for hosiery was so great that women would stand in lines for hours to obtain a pair. Women would rather wear mended nylons than new rayon stockings.

The Du Pont Company maintains a research and developmental laboratory that provides a continuing flow of new products. At the time of the twenty-fifth anniversary of nylon in 1964, there were 44 special *types* of nylon and 1,200 varieties that differed in twist, denier size, number of filaments, fiber shape, brightness, and color. Each was designed for a specific end-use. It was said that as a new need arose, a new type of nylon was produced to fill it. The original Du Pont patent expired in 1955, but before that time other companies had been licensed to produce nylon by the Du Pont process. About three fourths of the nylon made in the United States is made from the nylon polymer— nylon 6,6. Nylon 6, a polymer produced in Europe, is also made in the United States. The American Enka Corporation produced the first nylon 6 staple fiber in 1954. Nylon fiber producers and their trade names are listed in Appendix C.

The word "nylon" was always a *generic* name, never a trademark. Experience with a court decision that changed the company's trade name Cellophane to a generic name may have influenced the decision to use nylon as a generic name. The name "nylon" does not refer to a single material but denotes a whole family of related polyamide polymers that are designated by numbers. In the polymer nylon 6,6 each 6 indicates the number of carbon atoms in each of the two chemical compounds from which this polymer is made. Nylon 6 is made from a single compound containing 6 carbon atoms. They are compared in the table below.

Properties

Nylon has a protein-like molecule, and is related chemically to the protein fibers silk and wool. Both have amino dye sites that are important in the reaction of acid dyes. Nylon possesses only one such dye site for every 30 dye sites present in wool. Nylon is also dyed with disperse dyes, which have small molecules that penetrate the fiber and are held by the solid solution mechanism within the fiber. Nylon fabrics pick up colors very readily if washed with colored items. They are sometimes referred to as "color scavengers." It is important to wash white nylons separately.

Nylon has a long straight molecule chain with no side groups or cross-links so the molecules can be arranged in close orderly manner by stretching during spinning. Nylon's *strength* and *elasticity* are based on the strong hydrogen bonds that form between the molecular chains. Because of its high strength, nylon is used in strong sheer fabrics, long-wearing lingerie, industrial tow lines, and as a reinforcing fiber in blends with low-strength fibers. Pilling of fabrics is related to its high strength, because the fibers are strong and the pills do not break off but accumulate on the surface. Nylon's outstanding *abrasion resistance* is also based on its molecule structure. Scissors have to be sharpened frequently when used on nylon.

Nylon has higher *heat-settability* than the other synthetics. Its molecule arrangement can be changed very easily by heat-treatment to give permanent "set" to creases in trousers, pleats in skirts, shape to stockings, or wrinkles if the wash water is too hot. Heat causes the hydrogen bonds to weaken; and if the fibers are bent while hot, the

Nylon 6,6
Made of hexamethylene diamine and dibasic acid

Nylon 6
Made of caprolactum

Advantages
  Pleats, creases, etc., can be heat-set at higher temperatures
  Softening point 482° F

Advantages
  Better dye affinity
  Better weathering properties
  Softening point 428° F

bonds will break. If the fibers remain bent while they cool, new bonds will form and the bent shape will be permanent unless the fibers are again exposed to high temperature. The softening point is the point at which hydrogen bonds weaken and break. (To compare the heat-settability of nylon with that of the acrylics, turn to page 74.)

The heat-settability of nylon is high enough to make it possible to heat-stabilize fabrics permanently against shrinkage. It is a drawback in that home ironing and pressing temperatures are not high enough to press creases and pleats in home sewing or press out wrinkles acquired in washing.

The *burning test* is a very good way to identify nylon. The fibers melt and drip and some of the flame is carried down with the drip. The odor is celery-like and white smoke is given off. If no oils, pigments, or dyes are present, the melt will harden as a tan-colored bead and flammability will be low. A black bead will form when certain dyes are present.

The *transparency* of nylon fiber is evident in the photomicrograph in Figure 6–7 where the one fiber in the crosswise direction can be seen clearly through the others. Nylon's success in stockings was due to its transparency and the development of fine-denier fibers as well as to its strength, elasticity, and abrasion resistance. Transparency was a drawback in lingerie, shirts, and blouses until delustering agents were added to increase the opacity. The Schreiner finish for tricot flattens the yarns to reduce the open spaces and give better cover. Tricot finished in this way is called "satinette."

Nylon's *low water absorbency* contributes to good dimensional stability in laundering and rapid drying with little wrinkling if properly cared for. Nylon introduced the concept of "easy-care" garments. One disadvantage of low absorbency was the discomfort of the early fabrics during wear. The fibers are smooth and straight and packed together very compactly in yarns impeding ventilation. The first nylon shirts failed for this reason. They were said to feel like a film worn around the body. Nylon's bad image was not changed until the advent of textured yarns. On the basis of this experience, fiber producers began to set up Fabric Quality Control programs through which they could exercise control over the final product and thus protect the image of their fibers.

Another disadvantage of low absorbency is the development of static electricity by friction. Both

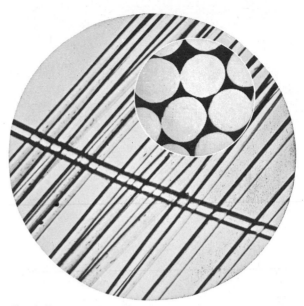

Fig. 6–7. Photomicrograph of nylon fiber. Inset is cross-sectional view. (Courtesy of E. I. du Pont de Nemours & Company.)

disadvantages can be overcome by engineered fabrics, by anistatic finishes, and by blending with low static or high-absorbency fibers. Comfort properties can be improved by use of the filament bulking process—texturing—without the necessity of resorting to blends with high-absorbency fibers.

The *chemical resistance* of nylon is generally good but it is damaged by strong acids. Soot from smoke in industrial cities contains sulfur and on damp days combines with atmospheric moisture to form an acid that has been responsible for epidemics of runs in stockings. Certain acids, when printed on the fabric, will cause shrinkage that creates a puckered "damasque" effect.

Uses

In the early years, the number of end-uses for nylon were few. Its growth has taken place in spurts, which have coincided with the development of new products. In 1959, when the hosiery, lingerie, and tire cord markets had become saturated, textured yarns for stretch and bulk started an upward swing in apparel and the trilobal heavy denier fiber, nylon 501, and Cumuloft, plus texturing made nylon one of the leading sellers in carpets. The largest amount of nylon goes into industrial and household uses and the smallest amount goes into apparel. Nylon has many more uses in filament form than in staple form. Nylon is used in larger quantities than any of the other synthetic fibers. A continuing research program produces new types of modified nylon to widen its end-use possibilities. Nylon has not been as *light-resistant*, for example, as some of the other fibers but research will probably produce a type that will make good curtains. The new developments are discussed below in the section on nylon modified fibers.

Nylon has some very interesting uses. A wheel-tire, 60 inches in diameter and covered with nylon tufted carpeting over wire mesh, is a possible means of transportation on the moon. Coated nylon is used for storage tanks for liquids, dams for rivers, and "bubble" houses. Nylon that looks like grass is used for carpets on patios and for covering football fields. The field in the Houston Astrodome is covered with this kind of carpet. Small pieces are zipped together to make one large piece that can be unzipped and stored when not in use. Ball players say the ball bounces more than it does on the regular field.

The *care* of nylon is similar to that of the other synthetic fibers. Care is discussed on page 42.

Special Modifications of Nylon Fiber

Nylon has been on the market longer than any other man-made fiber except rayon and acetate. During this time the following modifications have been made:

Low elongation nylon   Bicomponent (self-
Whiter nylons   crimping)
Nonround nylons   High-tenacity
                           Heat-resistant

Low Elongation—Nylon 420. The early nylon fibers were incompatible with cotton when used in blends. Although it had been thought that nylon with its high abrasion resistance would be a good reinforcement fiber for cotton in utility garments, in the early attempts the nylon actually wore out the cotton. Nylon fibers would elongate more under stress than cotton would and the cotton fibers would break. Nylon 420 was developed especially for use in cotton blends. It has been called the most striking example of a fiber developed to fit a need. Its elongation is more like that of cotton but its strength is still high. (See the table following.)

Because Nylon 420 is a rather expensive fiber, it is used in such a way that its use will be most effective and the cost of the blend will be competitive with

ELONGATION PROPERTIES OF NYLON AND COTTON

Fiber	Tenacity, gram/denier	Elongation at Break, per Cent
Nylon Type 200 (regular)	4.0	40
Cotton ($1\frac{1}{16}$ inch)	3.0	8
Nylon Type 420	6.5	23

SOURCE: *Du Pont Bulletin n-163* (October, 1963).

100 per cent cotton. In denims and similar twill work clothing fabrics, Nylon 420 is blended in the warp yarns only, since these are the yarns that form most of the outer surface of the cloth. Nylon 420 is referred to as the "reinforcing fiber." One of its newer uses is in blends with cotton in durable press garments. The trademark Nylon 420 appears on the label as shown in Figure 6–8.

Whiter Nylons. Whiter nylons are made by adding a fluorescent compound to the spinning solution. White fabrics made of nylon had a tendency to develop discoloration not satisfactorily removed by bleaches. This was a drawback to its use in shirts, blouses, lingerie, and particularly in girdles containing rubber, which is easily damaged by bleaches. Type 91 Nylon by Du Pont and Blanc de Blancs Nylon by American Enka are examples.

Nonround Nylons. The nonround nylons—trilobal or multilobal—are one of the most interesting of the new nylon developments. The change in

Fig. 6–8. Nylon 420 appears on the lable. Durable Press trousers are shown in the picture.

cross-sectional shape is accomplished by a change in the shape of the spinneret holes. This kind of modification is possible because the melt-spun fibers will retain the shape of the spinneret holes.

Trilobal fibers were developed in 1959 by Du Pont as a result of a five-year research study to make nylon and the polyesters more silk-like. (Silk is somewhat triangular in shape, see page 26.) The first trilobal nylon was Type 90 "Sparkling" nylon. Its shape and bright luster gave fabrics a glittery look. It is used in high-style hosiery and tricot knit fabrics. Type 860 is Du Pont's trilobal cross-section filament for general textile use. All of the apparel trilobal fibers were given the trade name *Antron*, the first trade name that the Du Pont Company had adopted for any of its nylon fibers. Later the name Antron was given also to a trilobal upholstery fiber and to a *round* cross-section filament carpet fiber.

A trilobal heavy denier fiber, Nylon 501, was developed by Du Pont at about this same time for loop-pile carpets. It was the *first continuous filament* carpet fiber to be made, and by 1966 it had become the dominant carpet fiber in the low-cost field. (Both Antron and Nylon 501 are textured for bulk, etc. Texturing is discussed on page 105.) Cadon, Cumuloft, and Enkalure are trade names of trilobal fibers made by other fiber producers.

Filament carpet yarns are inherently *resistant to pilling* and fuzzing, and there is *no shedding* of lint as there is with staple carpet yarns. However, a good latex finish on the back that seals the yarn to the carpet backing is also necessary. The trilobal shape is of great importance in nylon carpet because of its *resistance to showing soil* and its good cover. Nylon is a transparent fiber and if it has a round cross section, the fiber will show and even *magnify* any soil particles that are behind it making the carpet look dirtier than it really is. For this reason early nylon carpets were poorly accepted.

The optical behavior of the trilobal shape, on the other hand, prevents the soil from showing and *reduces the appearance of soil* in the carpet. Another advantage of the trilobal shape is that, when the sparkle is toned down by a delusterant, it has a very *desirable luster*. The *crush resistance* of the trilobal Nylon 501 fiber is exceptionally good for two reasons. First, the trilobal shape is 20 per cent stiffer than the round shape of the same denier; and second, the nature of the textured crimp—random spiral crimp—is especially good for producing bulk. With this type of yarn bulk, the carpet gives a

feeling of luxury and it also gives good cover so that if the carpet is bent (as it might be around a stair tread), the backing will not show.

Antron staple *round* cross-section carpet fiber was designed for cut-pile woven or tufted carpets that would match the overall texture and appearance of cut-pile wool woven carpets. Carpet wool is a blend of fibers having a wide range of diameters and crimp frequency. In Antron staple nylon the non-uniformity of carpet wool is simulated by a blend of fibers having varying denier per filament and crimp. The soiling characteristics of wool were matched or surpassed by use of an additive that is partially removed during dyeing and scouring. Its removal left voids in the fiber that reduced the luster and the soiling of the fiber. Bright nylon soils at a much faster rate than delustered nylon.[3]

The round cross-sectional shape was chosen for the Antron carpet fiber because this carpet was tailored for cut-pile carpet (the trilobal 501 Nylon carpet was for continuous filament loop-pile). In cut-pile carpet the cut tufts are anchored at one end only. The twist is heat-set so that it will not come out in use. Close fiber packing is a requirement for good setting and the round fiber shape is better for close packing of the fibers.

Antron nylon round continuous filament is also used in carpets, but all the fibers are of the same denier and crimp.

Both the Antron staple and filament carpet fibers have an added substance that reduces the static generation by increasing the conductivity.

Bicomponent Nylon. Bicomponent "self-crimping" nylon was introduced in 1963 as Fiber H and later given the trade name Cantrece. (This trade name had previously been used for an Orlon filament, which was discontinued.) It is a bicomponent fiber and has some similarities to the other bi-component fibers—wool (page 19) and acrylic bicomponents (page 76). The nylon bicomponent is a copolymer in which the two components each form one side of the fiber and have different shrinkage characteristics. The fibers are spun straight and are still straight when they are delivered to the knitter or weaver. Upon heating, one side of the fiber shrinks, forcing the other side to bend and the fiber assumes a spiral crimp. In hosiery, the stocking

[3] "Engineering the Fiber," *Modern Textiles Magazine* **47**:54 (May, 1966).

has clingability, a greater resistance to snags and picks, and many believe a softer, silkier feel. In tricot fabric, the advantages are better hand and bulk achieved by a method that, because the crimp is a structural part of the fiber, may be more economical than the textured process for making stretch and bulk yarn. The nylon bicomponent is the *first filament* fiber of this type, since wool and the acrylics are both staple fiber. It is used as a monofilament in hosiery.

High-Tenacity Nylons. There are several high-tenacity nylons. Most of them are made for industrial purposes. Type 704 is a deep-dyeing nylon for seat belts; 330 has improved heat and light resistance; 707 is a heavy denier used for cordage; 714 is a super-high-tenacity for tire cord.

Heat-Resistant Nylons. Nomex is the trade name of a heat-resistant fiber developed by Du Pont that does not melt or support combustion but begins to char and degrade at temperatures of 851° F and is considered to be superior to all other synthetics in its retention of tensile properties after prolonged exposure to high temperatures. It has good resistance to radiation, to caustics, and to oxidation. It is not dyeable, has a specific gravity of 1.38, tenacity of 5.8 grams/denier, and excellent electrical insulation properties at high temperatures. It uses will be in protective clothing, high-speed aircraft tires, and the like.

Multipolymer Fibers

There is no perfect fiber. Each fiber has some advantages and some disadvantages. Blending two or more fibers in a fabric has been the traditional way to capitalize on the good properties of a fiber and to minimize the poor properties. Research during the 1950's and 1960's dealt with the subject of making a blend by mixing two or more polymers before the fiber is spun in order to achieve in a single fiber the good properties of the single polymer fibers. This procedure is called *polymer blending*. Another development was a fiber with a skin-core structure in which the skin is different chemically than the interior of the fiber. Wool is a natural fiber of this sort and Avicron rayon is a man-made fiber. The bicomponent fibers were a third type of poly-

mer combination that grew out of this area of research.

The biconstituent polymer blend first introduced commercially was a 70% nylon–30% polyester fiber—AC-0001 by Allied Chemical (generic name will be applied for). It was developed for use in tire cord to reduce the "flat-spotting" that was a problem with tires made of all-nylon tire cord. "Flat-spotting" refers to the flattened area on the tire that forms when the car has been parked in one place for some time. It results in a bumpy ride.

The polymers are mixed in such a way that the extruded filament is made up of a continuous matrix of one polymer and thousands of fibrils of the other polymer are embedded in this matrix.[4] The strength and melting point of the nylon are relatively unaffected by the addition of the polyester, but the fiber modulus, important in nearly all end-uses, is doubled by the addition of 30 per cent polyester. This increases the effectiveness of the nylon in certain industrial end-uses where its strength alone was not sufficient. Sheen and better texturing properties are advantages that the fiber has in household and apparel end-uses.

Polyester Fibers

Polyester fibers are manufactured fibers in which the fiber forming substance is any long chain polymer composed of at least 85% by weight of an ester of dihydric alcohol and terephthalic acid. (p-HOOC—C$_6$H$_4$—COOH)

Federal Trade Commission

The first polyester fiber Dacron (pronounced *day-cron*) was introduced in 1953. Polyester is a polymer that is formed by reacting an acid with an alcohol. The first work was done by Du Pont's Dr. Carothers, who discontinued work on the polyesters in favor of the more promising nylon. The polyester polymer was perfected by chemists of the Calico Printers Association in England and the first fiber was made by Imperial Chemical Industries of England, who obtained the patent rights for world production. In 1946, Du Pont obtained from the original producer exclusive rights to production in the United States.

[4] R. J. Mumford and J. L. Nevin, "Multipolymer Fibers," *Modern Textiles Magazine* **48**:51 (April, 1967).

This first polyester fiber found immediate acceptance in easy-care, wash-and-wear, and durable-press garments. It had excellent wrinkle recovery, either wet or dry. Comfort properties were improved when it was used in blends with wool and cotton. In 1959, three new polyester fibers entered the market; Vycron by the Beaunit Fibers Company, Fortrel marketed by Celanese, and Kodel developed by Eastman Chemical Products, Inc. Kodel is fundamentally different from the other three polyesters. Two basic polymers were used in its production to give the fiber a higher heat resistance than the other regular polyester fibers.

The polyesters have shown the fastest rate of growth of all the synthetic fibers and by 1968 eleven companies were producing the fiber. Refer to the list in Appendix C (page 223) for other producers.

Manufacture

Polyester fibers are melt-spun from two kinds of terephthalate. The molecules are large and stiff and resist bending but recover well from bending. Molecule structure is shown below.[5]

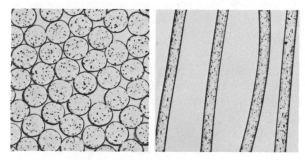

Fig. 6–9. Photomicrograph of Dacron polyester. Left, longitudinal view. Right, cross-sectional view. (Courtesy of E. I. du Pont de Nemours & Company.)

Polyethylene (glycol) terephthalate—Dacron (Fortrel and Vycron are similar)

Polycyclohexyl terephthalate—Kodel

The main difference between the two polymers is the higher heat resistance of Kodel and its lower moisture regain. There are no chemical groups on either molecule that will unite with dyestuffs. Dyeing is achieved by use of a carrier.

The original fibers (except Kodel II) are spun from a homopolymer—units joined end to end—and some of the modified types are copolymers—two somewhat unlike units polymerized together. Modified types are possible at the three different stages of manufacture. Pigments or chemicals may

[5] Rolf Quosdorf, "Dyeing of Polyester Fibres and Blends," *Canadian Textile Journal* **83**:44 (December 23, 1966).

be added to the spinning solution; the extrusion or cooling procedures may be varied, i.e., changing the shape of the spinneret hole and asymmetrical cooling; and the drawing or stretching may be nonuniform or may be done when one side of the fiber has been heated.

Properties and Related End-Uses

The polyester fibers, when seen under the microscope, are so much like nylon that identification is difficult. Both longitudinal and cross-sectional views of Dacron polyester are shown in Figure 6–9. The fibers have the smooth rod-like shape and round cross section typical of the regular or standard melt-spun fibers. The polyester fibers are not as transparent as the nylons, however.

The polyesters, like the nylons, have high strength (page 58) and abrasion resistance. They are quite different in their tensile recovery as shown by the following table.

Fiber	Tensile Form Recovery from Elongation of			
	1%	3%	5%	15%
Dacron 56 (regular)	91	76	63	40
Nylon 200 (regular)	81	88	86	77

SOURCE: Du Pont Technical Bulletin X–142 (September, 1961).

Tensile Recovery. Tensile recovery refers to the extent and manner of recovery from deformation. Notice that Dacron has high recovery when the elongation is low, an important factor in the suiting market. Only small deformations are involved in the wrinkling of a suit, and Dacron recovers better than nylon. The recovery behavior of Dacron at the elongation percentages given in the table is quite similar to that of wool at the same elongations. Nylon shows better recovery at the higher elongations, however, so it would perform better in garments that are subject to greater elongation—hosiery, for example. Dacron has lower moisture absorption than nylon. Dacron's low moisture absorption and its high recovery from low elongation make it an exceptionally good fiber for crease retention and wash-and-wear.

The other polyesters are similar to Dacron in their wet and dry wrinkle recovery. This has given them an advantage over wool in tropical suitings, since wool has poor wrinkle recovery when wet. Under conditions of high atmospheric humidity and body perspiration, polyester suits do not shrink and are very resistant to wrinkling. However, when they do acquire wear wrinkles, as often happens at the waist of a garment where body heat and moisture "set" the wrinkles, pressing is necessary to remove them.

Heat-Setting. Heat-setting is necessary for the polyesters, except Kodel II, and must be done under tension. Steam, which is often used on nylon, is less suitable for the polyesters as it may cause a loss of fiber strength so hot air or hot calender rolls are often used. Polyesters can be heat-set from 325° F to 450° F.　According to Jackle,

. . . polyesters can be re-heat-set by a second exposure to a higher temperature. If for example, a 380° F heat-set fabric were skewed (off-grain), it could be framed straight, heat-set at 410° F and the skewness permanently removed while imparting wrinkle resistance and dimensional stability.[6]

Absorbency. Absorbency is quite low for the polyesters, ranging from 0.4 to 0.8 per cent moisture regain (70° F and 65 per cent relative humidity). The advantage is that fabrics are resistant to waterborne stains and are quick drying. It is a disadvantage because fabrics are less comfortable in skin-contact apparel unless especially engineered, they are difficult to dye, and they build up static. Polyesters are more *electrostatic* than the other fibers in the heat-sensitive group. This is a distinct disadvantage because static charges attract lint to the surface of the fabric and it is difficult to keep dark-colored fabrics looking neat. Curtains soil more

rapidly. New fabrics usually have an antistatic finish but it is often removed by washing or dry cleaning. The fabric softeners available in grocery stores are good antistatic agents. Temporary relief from static can be gained by running a damp sponge over a garment.

Strength. *Wet strength* of the polyester fibers is comparable to *dry strength.* The high tensile strength of the polyesters is achieved by cold drawing or stretching to develop crystallinity and also by increasing molecular weight. The molecular weight is expressed as intrinsic viscosity (a measure of the degree of polymerization). Intrinsic viscosities of 0.9 are used in tire cords, 0.6 for regular staple and filament, and 0.4 for low-pilling staple.

Resiliency. Resiliency, quick drying, and heat-sensitivity make the polyesters good for batts in quilted fabrics (comforters, bedspreads, ski-type jackets, robes, etc.) and for furniture base and cushion constructions. The fibers can be given a permanent heat-set coil or curl during the drawing process (page 57) so they have outstanding springiness. Fibers can be spot-welded by running them under hot needles so they will not shift during use and thus pillows do not get lumpy.

Flammability. Nylon and the polyesters can be distinguished from one another by the odor and the smoke. They both melt and drip and some of the flame is carried down with the drip. Both form a tan bead when the melt hardens and both are relatively nonflammable in the unfinished state. The polyesters have an aromatic odor and a heavy black smoke containing particles of soot. Nylon's odor is celery-like and the smoke is white. It is necessary to test a large enough swatch to get enough smoke and odor to make identification positive.

Specific Gravity. The specific gravity of the polyesters varies from 1.22 to 1.38 g/d making them heavier than the nylons and acrylics.

Resistance to Chemicals and Biological Attack. The polyesters are unique because they can be treated with a caustic soda to dissolve away the surface leaving a thinner fiber, yarn, or fabric without changing the fiber basically.[7] This treatment gives the fabric a soft silky hand and is an important

[6] R. W. Jackle, "Properties of and Uses for Polyester Fibers," *American Dyestuff Reporter* **54**:112 (December 6, 1965).

[7] A. J. Hall, "Modifying Polyester Fibers To Get Sheer Silky Fabrics," *Textile World Magazine* **113**:108 (September, 1963).

part of the process, described on page 68, for making the silk-like trilobal fiber fabrics. A 5 per cent weight loss is usually enough.

Polyester fibers are generally resistant to both acids and alkalies and can be bleached with cotton-type bleaches. This is very important because the largest single use of the polyesters is in blends with cotton for durable press. They are resistant to biological attack and to sunlight damage. The polyester fibers are the most important filaments for sheer glass curtains.

Dyeing and Printing. The hydrophobic property makes the polyesters hard to dye so high pressure temperatures and modified fiber structures are used to improve dyeability. *Color crocking* has been a source of trouble with many of the printed polyesters since the color has been bound to the surface by a resin. Figure 6–10 shows a blouse in which the collar has lost its color. The collar is an area where body oils cause soiled streaks and the rubbing necessary to remove soil also removes the color. Areas subject to abrasion are affected in the same way. In 1966, a successful dye printing process, Interchem,[8] was developed.

Special Modifications of Polyester Fibers

Polyester modifications, variants, types, or "second-generation" fibers can be produced at any stage of manufacture. Type numbers are sometimes used on the labels or advertisements; Dacron T–62, for example. Special polyester modifications discussed in this section are:

> Nonround
> High-tenacity
> Crimped (helical, etc.)
> Thick-and-thin slub effect
> Optically white
> Low-pilling
> Binder fibers for nonwoven
> Low elongation

Nonround Polyesters

As the polyester fibers, like the nylons, have the ability to retain the shape of the spinneret hole, cross-sectional shape modifications are possible.

[8] Trade name for Interchemical Corporation.

Fig. 6–10. Crocking of color on the collar of a polyester blouse. Many printed polyesters may become unusable before being worn out because of color crocking.

The trilobal fiber Dacron T–62 was the first produced. Figure 6–11 shows the cross-sectional shape.

All man-made filament fibers have, in the past, lacked the unique combination of aesthetic properties possessed by silk. The development of a man-made fiber with these properties has been a long-time goal of the man-made fiber industry. The

Fig. 6–11. Photomicrograph of cross-sectional view of Dacron T-62 lobal polyester. (Courtesy of *Textile Industries*.)

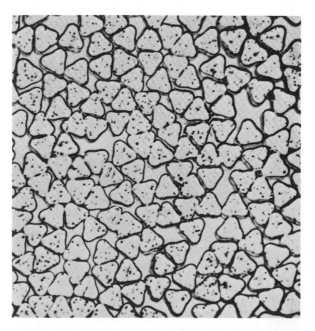

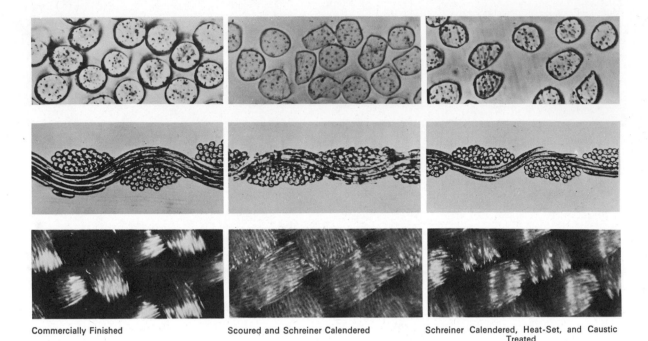

Commercially Finished   Scoured and Schreiner Calendered   Schreiner Calendered, Heat-Set, and Caustic
                                                                                                             Treated

Fig. 6–12. Photomicrographs showing effect of heat-caustic treatment. Top, Dacron polyester
fiber, cross section 1000 ×. Middle, fabric cross section, 200 ×. Bottom, fabric surface, 50 ×.
(Courtesy of E. I. du Pont de Nemours & Company.)

trilobal fiber modification Dacron T–62 (and
Antron nylon, page 63) was the result of a study
by the Du Pont Company in cooperation with a
silk-finishing company to investigate the effect of
the different stages of the silk-finishing processes
on the esthetic properties of silk fabrics, since silk
seemed to acquire added richness in the fabric
form. The results of their research showed that the
unique properties of silk—liveliness, suppleness,
and drape of the fabric, dry "tactile" hand, and
good covering power of the yarns—are due to (1)
the triangular-like shape of the silk fiber; (2) the
fine denier per filament; (3) the loose, bulky yarn
and fabric structure; and (4) a highly crimped
fabric structure.

In silk fabric, sericin (gum) makes up about 30
per cent of the weight. The boil-off finishing process removes the sericin and creates a looser, more
mobile fabric structure. If the fabric is in a relaxed
state while the sericin is being removed, the warp
yarns take on a *high degree of weave crimp*. This
crimp and the *looser fabric structure* together create
the liveliness and suppleness of the silk fiber. This
suppleness has been compared to the action of the
coil spring "Slinky" toy. The properties are quite
different when the boil-off is done under tension.

The weave crimp is much less and the response of
the fabric is more like that of a flat spring, thus the
supple nature is lost. This helps explain the difference between qualities of silk fabric.

Man-made fibers are normally processed under
tension by a continuous method rather than a
batch method. Because of the results of the Du Pont
research study of silk, the trilobal fibers are processed in a *completely relaxed* condition. Finishing
starts with a heat-setting treatment to stabilize the
fabric to controlled width, remove any wrinkles, and
impart resistance to wrinkling. The next step is a
very important caustic soda (alkali) treatment,
which dissolves away a controlled amount of the
fiber. This step is similar to the degumming of silk
and it gives the fabric structure greater mobility.
All remaining finishes are done with the fabric
completely relaxed to get maximum weave-crimp.
(Antron nylon is finished in the same way except
that there is no caustic treatment.) Because Dacron
T–62 is a copolymer, it is more susceptible to acids
and alkalies than regular Dacron and can be dyed
with silk-type dyes. Dacron T–26 is a trilobal
homopolymer and it takes different dyes from T–62.

Nonround cross-sectional shape can be obtained
in other ways. The technique shown in Figure 6–12

is a fabric finish that flattens and deforms some of the filaments by passing the fabric through a Schreiner calender (page 183). The fabrics are then treated with a caustic soda solution which gives them better hand, softness, and drape.

High-Tenacity Polyesters

High-tenacity polyesters are usually heavy denier filaments made by stretching or drawing as the last stage of the manufacturing process. Their tenacity ranges from 5.0 to 9.2 grams/denier and they are used in seat belts, tires, ropes, cordage, and fire hose. Some are designed to compete with Nylon 420.

Crimped Polyester Fibers

Crimped polyester fibers are used for fiberfill batting for pillows, furniture, carpets, and quilted apparel. Helically (spiral) crimped fibers are produced by cooling one side of the fiber faster than the other side as the melt-spun fiber is extruded. This uneven cooling causes a curl to form in the fiber. The same effect can be achieved by heating one side of the fiber during the stretching or drawing process. This helical crimp has more springiness than the conventional mechanical saw-tooth crimp, and these fibers are used where high levels of compression resistance and recovery are needed. Dacron Type 88 is used for sleeping bags and quilted fabrics. Dacron Type 76 is used in furniture base and cushion constructions which need maximum resistance. Fibers are made into bats that are needle-punched (page 119) to prevent lumping. Dacron Type 93 has a conventional mechanical heat-set crimp. Vycron Type 35 is a heat-set carpet staple. Fortrel 7 is a continuous filament fiberfill for use in pillows. *Three-dimensional* polyesters were developed by Eastman in 1966.

Thick-and-Thin Slub Effects

Thick-and-thin slub effects are produced in novelty-type filaments that have a random distribution of thick and thin places as a result of uneven drawing after spinning. When woven into cloth it gives the effect of duppioni silk. The undrawn portion of the yarn takes a deeper dye. This was thought to be a defect of the cloth until the producers learned how to use it to advantage. The uses are silk-like shantung fabrics for men's and women's suits and women's dresses. Fortrel 430 and Dacron Type 69 are fibers of this type.

Optically White Fibers

Optically white, delustered, and solution-dyed fibers are produced by adding substances to the spinning solution. Optically white fibers are designated by the following type numbers: Kodel IV, Fortrel 410 staple, Fortrel 720 filament, Vycron II, and Vycron 12. Optical whiteners are added to the solution to obtain good whites. These are usually fluorescent compounds. These whites are permanent but will not keep the fabric from picking up soil if poor laundering techniques are used.

Pill-Resistant Polyester

Pilling has always been a problem with the regular polyester staple fibers. The flex abrasion of the regular fibers is so high that, when pills form on a fabric, they do not break off as they do with weaker fibers. Instead, they accumulate and give a very unsightly appearance. Flex abrasion resistance can be reduced with little or no loss of yarn strength by modifying the polyester polymer to reduce the molecular weight (degree of polymerization or chain length). Fortrel Type 420 and Dacron Types 35, 64, 65 are examples.

Binder Staple

Binder staple is a semidull, crimped fiber with a very low melting point, which was designed to develop a thermoplastic bond with other fibers when under heat and pressure. It sticks at 165° F and will shrink 55 to 75 per cent at 200° F. Type 450 Fortrel is a fiber of this type.

Low-Elongation Fibers

Low-elongation fibers were designed for use with cotton in blends for durable press. They are reinforcing fibers similar to the Nylon 420 described previously. Vycron "Tough Stuff" and Kodel HT are examples of polyester low-elongation fibers. They are made by changing the balance of tenacity and extension. Low elongation goes with high tenacity.

Others

Various other special types are produced for use in textured yarns and in high-shrinkage yarns.

Olefin Fibers

Olefin fibers are manufactured fibers in which the fiber forming substance is any long chain synthetic polymer composed of at least 85% by weight of ethylene, propylene or other olefin units except amorphous (non-crystalline) polyolefins qualifying as rubber.

$CH_2 CH_2$; $CH_3 CH_2 CH_2 CH_3$

Federal Trade Commission

Olefin fibers are among the newest man-made fibers, and they have a combination of properties that should make them important fibers in a variety of end-uses.

Karl Ziegler spent many years in systematic study of catalysts that would polymerize *ethylene* into high molecular weight polymers. Guilio Natta discovered that crystalline polymers of very high molecular weight could be obtained from *propylene* with Ziegler's catalysts. These men were awarded the Nobel Prize in chemistry in 1963. Their work was basic to the development of the olefin textile fibers.

The discovery of steriospecific polymerization made it possible to obtain high molecular weight crystalline polymers. Steriospecific polymerization means that the molecules are specifically arranged in space so that all the methyl groups have the same location and there are no polar groups. Natta called this phenomenon *isotactic*. In the atactic form, the methyl groups are randomly oriented, resulting in an amorphous polymer that would qualify as rubber.

Methyl groups

Polypropylene fibers, discovered in 1954, were developed in Italy after six years of basic research and are produced there under the trade name of Meraklon; the name was taken from the name of one of the stars of the big bear, Merak. Marvess and Herculon are trade names of fibers produced in the United States. Refer to Appendix C (page 223) for a listing of the producers and their trade-

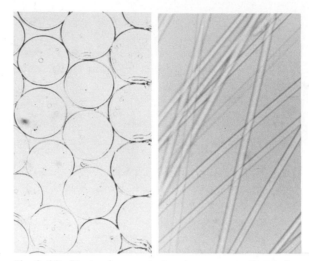

Fig. 6–13. Photomicrograph showing cross-sectional view (left) and longitudinal view (right) of Herculon (Hercules registered trademark). (Courtesy of Hercules, Incorporated.)

marks. The base polymer is used in large volume in plastics as well as in fibers. Polyethylene bags and bottles are examples.

Manufacture

The term "olefin" is derived from the Latin *oleum* meaning oil. Petroleum gas, a by-product of the petroleum industry, is converted chemically into tiny pellets, which are then melt-spun. After extrusion, the olefin filaments crystallize immediately on cooling, making them react differently in the spinning from nylon and the polyesters, which are amorphous after spinning and develop crystallinity only when stretched.

Properties

The olefins are spun as round, smooth fibers that look very much like the other melt-spun fibers. (See Figure 6–13.)

Polypropylene is the lightest fiber made. The following table shows how it compares with the other fibers.

Fiber	Specific Gravity (grams/denier)
Polypropylene	0.91
Nylon	1.14
Acrylics	1.17
Wool	1.34
Polyester	1.22–1.38
Rayon	1.5
Cotton	1.5

Because of its light weight, a pound of olefin will make more fabric than a pound of the other fibers. The low cost and low specific gravity are definite advantages in most end-uses. Because the amount of fiber per pound is greater, the *relative cost* is the lowest of all fibers. Even rayon, with its low fiber cost, has a high specific gravity so that its cover cost is approximately that of the olefins. The following table lists some of the advantages and disadvantages of the olefin fibers.

Advantages of Olefins	Disadvantages of Olefins
High strength	Very heat-sensitive
Lowest specific gravity	Difficult to dye
Good abrasion resistance	
Hydrophobic	
Excellent resistance to abrasion	
Low-cost raw material	

The greatest impact of the polypropylene fibers has been in carpeting, an end-use where no ironing is needed and where solution-dyed fibers are widely used. *Heat sensitivity*, particularly the sticking point, limits the use of olefins in apparel. If it were not so heat-sensitive, it could be used effectively in durable press garments.

END-USES OF OLEFIN FIBERS

Apparel	Home Furnishing	Industrial
Sweaters	Carpets, indoor-outdoor	Filters
Hose, socks		Cordage
Sports shirts	Carpet backing	Ropes
Work clothing	Upholstery	Tarpaulins
Underwear		Laundry bags
Neckties		
Imitation furs		
Boot liners		

At present the olefins can be used satisfactorily in 20/80 blends with cotton, but if more than 20 per cent is used, there can be pressing problems. Lightweight military items also would be important end-uses except that polypropylene cannot be used at elevated temperatures. Much research has been done to raise the melting point, but the satisfactory processes are too expensive to make the fiber competitive with nylon and the polyesters.

Olefins make *strong*, durable fabrics that have good resistance to abrasion. Tenacities as high as 13 g/d have been achieved. Seat belts, cordage, and so on are end-uses where high strength and light weight are important. Their resistance to moisture and biological attack make them good for sand bags. They are replacing jute as wool bagging, not because of strength, but because they are competitive in cost and the filaments do not shed and mix with the wool fibers.

Low absorbency of the fibers is important in stain and spot resistance and in their easy removal, but it also makes the fiber difficult to dye. The lack of polar groups means that there are no sites for dyes to lodge. Olefins can be solution-dyed but for any fiber to be commercially acceptable, it must be possible to piece-dye and print fabrics. (See Color, page 207). Dyeable olefins have compounds added to the spinning solution, which are more or less satisfactory. The fact that 300 or more patents have been issued relating to the dyeability of polypropylene indicates the extent to which companies are working in this field. The U.S. Rubber Company describes their process as developing channels in the fiber to permit the entry of the dye. A basic dye receptor is incorporated into the resin and after spinning, the fibers are chemically treated to make the channels. A new dyeable PPX is a modified fiber that requires no chemical treatment after spinning.

Low static build-up is an interesting property related to low absorbency. Other nonabsorbent fibers are notorious for static charges. It is thought that with the olefins, the charging rate is low in relation to the discharging rate.

Modifications of Olefin Fibers

Fiber types or modifications are dyeable, nondyeable, nondyeable with light stabilizers, nondyeable with heat stabilizers. The nondyeable fibers can be natural or have pigment colors. Fibers and filaments are prepared for specific end-uses:

Staple
    Silver knits and nonwovens
    Fiberfill
    Carpets
    7-inch cut for doll's hair
Tow
    Pacific Converter
Filament
    Texturing
    Sewing thread
    Textured for carpets
    With modified cross section

Bicomponent fibers with three-dimensional crimp were developed in 1966.

Split-Fiber Method

All man-made fibers have been made by the *extrusion* method—forcing a liquid through fine holes to form fine strands. In 1965, a new, limited method was developed at the Shirley Institute in England. It was noticed that under certain conditions some materials, such as polyethylene and polypropylene, in sheet form, would split directly into fibers when stretched. These fibers had strength equal to the best found in other fibers but the first fibers made were too rough to be suitable for clothing. They were used in twine, rope, and the like.

This method of making fibers costs much less than the traditional extrusion process. Use may continue to be restricted to certain fiber polymers.

7 *Acrylic, Modacrylic, and Vinyl Fibers*

The acrylic and modacrylic fibers both contain acrylonitrile but in differing amounts. The modacrylics contain less than the acrylics and they are much more sensitive to heat—a factor that has limited their use in clothing. Acrylic fibers burn freely, but the modacrylics do not support combustion. Of all of the synthetic fibers, the acrylics and modacrylics come closest to wool and silk with respect to warmth and quality of handle.

Acrylic Fibers

Acrylic fibers are manufactured fibers in which the fiber-forming substance is a synthetic polymer composed of at least 85% by weight of acrylonitrile units.

$$-CH_2-\overset{\displaystyle H}{\underset{\displaystyle CN}{C}}-$$

Federal Trade Commission

The preparation of acrylonitrile in monomeric form was first reported in 1893 and a patent for polyacrylonitrile was obtained in 1929. The extreme insolubility and the resistance to swelling in common solvents were stumbling blocks to early production. Research on acrylic fibers started in the United States in 1938 and commercial production of Orlon, the first acrylic fiber, was begun in 1950 by Du Pont. The Chemstrand Corporation[1] introduced Acrilan in 1952, Dow Chemical started commercial production of Zefran in 1958, and American Cyanamid introduced Creslan in 1959.

Manufacture

All acrylic fibers are made of at least 85 per cent acrylonitrile, but the raw material for each has been made by polymerizing it with additives that will improve the dyeability, and so on. Acrilan, Orlon, and Creslan are copolymers. Zefran is a graft polymer. In graft polymerization, the additive does not become part of the main molecular chain as it does in the copolymers but it is fastened as a side

[1] Now Monsanto Corporation.

chain. The difference between polymers, copolymers, and graft polymers is illustrated below.

```
OOOOOOOOOOOOO   Monomer
XXXXXXXXXXXXX   Monomer
OXOXOXOXOXOX    Copolymer
OXOXOXOXOXOX    Graft polymer
      |  |
      C  C
      |  |
      C  C
```

Orlon acrylic fibers are solvent-spun and the other three are wet-spun. The melt-spinning process cannot be used because acrylonitrile decomposes before it melts. In *solvent spinning*, the fibers are dissolved in a suitable solvent such as dimethyl formamide, extruded into warm air, and the fibers solidify as the solvent evaporates. After spinning the fibers are stretched 300 to 1,000 per cent of their own length, crimped, heat-set, and marketed as cut staple or tow. In *wet spinning* the polymer is dissolved in chemicals, extruded into a coagulating bath, dried, crimped, and collected as tow for use in the high-bulking process or cut into staple and baled.

Because of the excellent resistance to chemicals and to weathering, properties that are not common to some of the other man-made fibers, it was thought that *continuous filament* acrylic fibers would be widely used in industrial and out-of-doors applications. However, because production costs for the filament form were high and methods of dyeing were not successful, the volume of production was not sufficient to pursue this end-use. From time to time acrylic filaments have been introduced on the market but with little success. Orlon Cantrece was introduced in 1959 and discontinued in 1962. Creslan 63 was introduced in 1965 and discontinued in 1967.

The success of the acrylics has been in *staple* fiber end-uses in areas previously dominated by wool. In apparel end-uses they are softer, less scratchy, and lighter in weight than wool. The nonfelting and good washability of the acrylic fibers have made them important competitors of wool in sweaters and blankets because they do not shrink and it is unnecessary to block sweaters to make them keep their shape. A substantial portion of the growth of the acrylic fibers can be traced to two early developments: the high-bulk process for sweater yarns that was developed on the Turbo Stapler (page 104) and

the development of heavy denier carpet fibers. These two developments accounted for about 50 per cent of the total market by 1963.[2] Other end-uses are shown in the following table.

MAJOR END-USES OF ACRYLIC FIBERS

Apparel	Household	Industrial
Sweaters	Blankets	Uniforms
Knitted outerwear	Carpeting	Chemical
Woven flannels,	Draperies	filters
suitings	Upholstery	Weather
Blends for wool-like	Batting for	stripping
fabrics	pillows, etc.	Paint
Bathing suits		rollers
Imitation furs		
Textured hose		
Men's athletic socks		

Properties

All of the acrylic fibers have some common properties because of their acrylonitrile and they also have individual differences as shown in the table on page 75.

The most important properties that the acrylic fibers have in common are low density and high bulking power. (See Appendix A (page 223) to see how the acrylics compare with the other textile fibers.) Low density and high bulk have given the acrylics the slogan of the "Warmth Without Weight" fibers.

The high-bulking power is the result of a metastable heat-sensitive property. Acrylics cannot be given a "permanent set" like that of the nylons and polyesters.[3] This is both an advantage and a disadvantage. To the consumer it means that pleats and creases can be pressed into a garment and they will remain during wear, laundry, and/or dry cleaning but can be pressed out again if the consumer so desires. This makes it easy to lengthen hems, etc. Flat surfaces will stay flat so that the "set" gives the fabric wash-and-wear characteristics. The metastable heat-sensitivity is a disadvantage in that any hot, wet processing during manufacturing will introduce inherent shrinkage and give the fabric poor dimensional stability.

[2] David W. Chaney, "New Developments in Acrylic Fibers," *American Dyestuff Reporter* **54**:30 (March 1, 1965).

[3] H. F. Mahoney, "Some Properties of Acrilan that Affect Dyeing and Finishing," *American Dyestuff Reporter* **54**:99 (December 6, 1965).

COMPARISON OF ACRYLIC FIBERS

	Acrilan	Creslan	Orlon	Zefran	Characteristics
Cross section	Lima bean	Round	Dog-bone	Round	
Sticking temperature	——— 410° F to 455° F ———				Watch heat of iron.
	(decomposes before melting)				
Specific gravity	——— 1.16 to 1.18 g/d ———				Lightweight fabrics, good cover, warmth
Sunlight and weathering	——— Excellent resistance ———				Good for curtains and draperies
Tenacity, g/d dry	——— 2.0 to 2.6 ———			3.5–4.2	Low to medium strength; Wear is satisfactory
Tenacity, g/d wet	——— 1.6 to 2.1 ———			2.9–3.6	Wet strength is satisfactory
Moisture regain	——— 1.0 to 1.5 ———			1.5–2.5	Dries quickly; Easy spot removal; Wash-and-wear
Acids	——— Good to excellent resistance ———				
Alkali	——— Fair to good resistance to weak alkali ———				Washes satisfactorily
Flammability	——— Burns freely ———				Flameproofing desirable for napped fabrics, etc.
Drycleaning solvents	——— Good resistance ———				Dry-cleans easily

The term "metastable" refers to a middle stage in which the fiber or fabric, after a heat treatment, is stable until heat is again applied. Fibers that are hot-stretched and cooled are in a metastable state but because of the strains from stretching, have high potential shrinkage. If heat is applied without tension, the fibers will shrink back to their original length. This is the basis for the procedure used to make "Hi-bulk" yarns for sweaters and other bulky garments. Hot-stretched, high-shrinkage fibers are blended in a yarn with unstretched, low-shrinkage fibers and the yarn is exposed to heat usually in the form of steam. The high-shrinkage fibers shrink and cause the other fibers to "buckle" thus creating bulk in the yarn. The hi-bulk process is discussed on page 104. Deep pile fabrics for *fur-like coats* are made by application of this same heat-sensitive property of the acrylics. In this case, the surface fibers are a blend of high- and low-shrinkage fibers. Heat treatment causes the high-shrinkage fibers to shrink and form the downy undercoat fibers leaving the low-shrinkage fibers as the guard hairs. Figure 7–1 shows this kind of fur-like fabric. Figure 7–2 shows a label that gives directions for care.

Fig. 7–1. Furlike fabric. Notice long sleek guard hairs and soft fine undercoat.

Fig. 7–2. Label giving directions for cleaning.

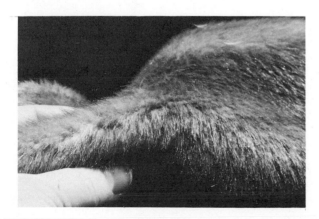

Differences between the acrylic fibers made by different companies are great enough that they cannot be used interchangeably by yarn spinners and dyers. For example, the processing of Hi-Bulk Orlon differs from the processing of Hi-Bulk Acrilan. (The nylons and polyesters can be used interchangeably.) One of these fiber differences is that of cross-sectional shape. Wet-spinning produces the round Creslan and Zefran fibers and the lima-bean-shaped Acrilan fiber, while dry-spinning gives Orlon its dog-bone shape. These differences in cross-sectional shape affect the physical and esthetic properties and thus are a factor in determining the end-use. The round and lima-bean shape are better for carpets than the flatter shape because of high bending stiffness, which contributes to resiliency. The dog-bone shape fibers are softer and because they are flatter, they are somewhat more lustrous. Figure 7–3 shows the longitudinal and cross-sectional shape of the acrylic fibers.

Another difference in the fibers is that of *strength*. Zefran, the graft polymer, is stronger than the other three.

The *burning* characteristics are similar in some ways to those of the acetates. The fibers melt, burst into flame and burn freely, then decompose to black crumbly residue. An acrylic carpet or garment would burn freely but a modacrylic carpet would be self-extinguishing.

Modifications of Acrylic Fibers

Like all man-made fibers, the acrylics are produced in various forms—filament, filament tow, and staple; various deniers—apparel fibers and carpet fibers; various lusters—bright and dull; and various staple fiber lengths—1.5 to 5 inches. Some fibers are producer-colored (solution-dyed); some have optical whiteners added for use in white fabrics.

Special modifications of acrylic fibers are discussed in the following section:

Bicomponent fiber
Controlled shrinkage
Modified surface
Modified heavy denier carpet fiber
Cross-dyeable

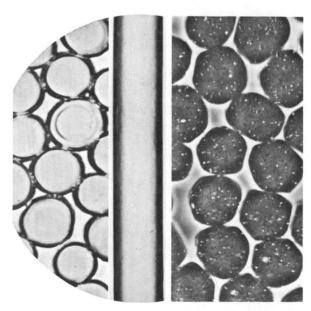

Fig. 7–3. Photomicrographs of the acrylic fibers showing cross-sectional and longitudinal views. Top: left, Acrilan; right, Orlon. Bottom: left, Creslan; bottom, Zefran. (Photomicrograph of Acrilan courtesy of Chemstrand Corporation; photomicrograph of Orlon courtesy of E. I. du Pont de Nemours & Company; photomicrograph of Creslan courtesy of American Cyanamid; photomicrograph of Zefran courtesy of the Dow-Badische Company.)

Bicomponent Acrylics

Bicomponent or self-crimping acrylics have a three-dimensional crimp similar to that of wool. This kind of crimp (also called helical) gives more bulkiness and resilience than the saw-tooth type of

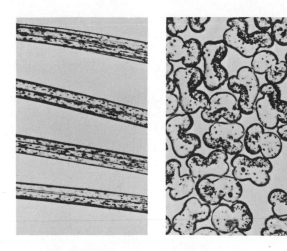

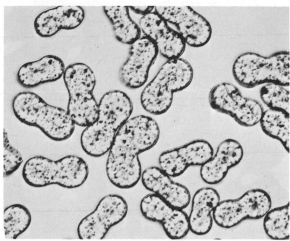

Fig. 7–4. Top, photomicrographs of 3.0 denier semidull Orlon Sayelle. Left, longitudinal view; right, cross-sectional view. (Courtesy of E. I. du Pont de Nemours & Company.) Bottom, photomicrograph of Verel, cross-sectional view. (Courtesy of Eastman Chemical Company.)

crimp. This crimp is induced by a method somewhat like that used for the self-crimping rayons. The fiber is a bilateral structure with two components side by side along the length of the individual fiber. It is produced by a special spinning process in which two different polymers are fused lengthwise.[4] Crimping occurs because the two components differ in shrinkage. Heat treatments cause one side of the fiber to shrink and forces the fiber to curl.

The fiber is straight as it is spun and as the garment is constructed. Heat is then applied and the fibers in the garment curl. When the garment is washed, one side of the fibers swells with the moisture and the curl comes out, making the garment

[4] *Textile Fibers and Their Properties*, Burlington Industries, 1966, p. 62.

much larger. If the garment is dried properly, it will resume its original size because drying removes the moisture and the curl comes back. This is called *reversible crimp*. Reversal of crimp will not occur if the curl's freedom to reverse is interfered with. The garment must be dried in a drier or laid out on a smooth surface, not on a towel. It must be "bunched" up to its original size so that there is no tension on the fibers. Some consumers are unhappy with their garments because they do not understand this principle of reversible crimp.

Figure 7–4 shows a cross section of the bicomponent fiber, Orlon Type 21 (Sayelle). The two halves show distinctly in most of the fibers. Other bicomponent acrylic fibers are Type 24 Orlon (Sayelle)—better pill resistance—and Creslan Type 68. All three are staple fibers.

Controlled Shrinkage Acrylics

Shrinkable acrylic fibers have the capacity to develop, and retain indefinitely at room temperature, a *latent* shrinkage. This shrinkage is developed by hot stretching and cooling while stretched. Upon subsequent heating the fibers will shrink back to their original length. The amount of stretching and shrinkage may be as much as 20 to 45 per cent. These fibers are used to produce high-bulk yarns and guard-hair-type fur-like fabrics, as previously discussed. They are also used in heavy denier in carpets. Orlon Type 38 and Hi-Shrunk Acrilan are apparel fibers of this type.

Modified Surface Acrylics

Modified surface (or skin-contact) acrylic fibers are produced by chemical modifications in the fiber or by treatment of the fiber surface. Orlon Type 28 is one with low surface friction; Acrilan 60 and 80 are durable antistatic, acid-dyeable fibers for blankets; and Orlon 29 is similar to Orlon 28 but is a heavy denier fiber.

Heavy Denier Acrylics

Heavy denier Acrilan 41 carpet fiber is a new polymer and an improvement over the original Acrilan 16 carpet fiber. It is cross-dyeable and is said to give more than twice the wear of wool. It has outstanding resilience and a lima-bean cross section. This illustrates the fact that products such as carpets are not the same from year to year but reflect new fiber modifications.

Another heavy denier carpet fiber, Type 33 Orlon,

is a blend of 17-denier regular Orlon and 12-denier bicomponent Orlon. Both are semidull and cut to 3.75 into staple. Type 33 has flame retardancy and low tenacity, which gives it good pill resistance. The blend of fibers of different denier makes it more like carpet wools, which are a blend of different-sized fibers. One of the *advantages* of the Type 33 fiber is the reversible crimp associated with its bicomponent nature. For example, surface depressions made by table legs can be brought back up by the drying and recrimping action that occurs after the fibers have been wetted.

Cross-Dyeable Acrylics

The standard Orlon fiber, Type 42, is dyeable with both basic dyes and disperse dyes but it has no affinity for acid dyes. Type 44 Orlon is dyeable with acid dyes but not with basic dyes. It is referred to as a cross-dyeable Orlon because it can be blended with the basic dyeable fibers. When the fabric is colored with a basic dye, Type 44 remains white. A two-color effect can be obtained if the blend is dyed in a single dye solution containing an acid dye of one color and a basic dye of another color. The other acrylic fibers have cross-dyeable types also.

Modacrylic Fibers

Modacrylic fibers are manufactured fibers in which the fiber forming substance is any long chain synthetic polymer composed of less than 85% but more than 35% acrylonitrile units.

$$-CH_2-CH-$$
$$|$$
$$CN$$

Federal Trade Commission

These fibers are modified acrylics. Dynel, produced by the Union Carbide Corporation, is a copolymer of 60 per cent vinyl chloride, $CH_2=CHCl$, and 40 per cent acrylonitrile. The composition of Verel is vinylidene chloride, $CH_2=CCl_2$, and other substances in addition to acrylonitrile. Verel is produced by Eastman Chemical Products, Inc.

Manufacture

Dynel and Verel are made by the dry- or solvent-spinning method. The raw material, in the form of a copolymer resin, is dissolved by acetone, dry-spun as filament tow, stretched, crimped, cut, and stabilized by heat-setting. Stretching is done during the manufacturing process to orient the molecules in the fiber and thus increase fiber strength. Fibers may be sold as filament tow or as staple of 1.5 to 5 inches in length. They may be heat-set, unheat-set, high-shrinkage, or low-shrinkage types of fibers. Verel III, for example, is a high-shrinkage fiber that has a potential shrinkage of 30 per cent. Different types of fibers are produced with high, low, or medium crimp. The properties of Dynel and Verel are contrasted in the following table:

COMPARISON OF MODACRYLIC FIBERS

Property	Dynel	Verel
Cross section	Irregular	Dog-bone
Specific gravity	1.35	1.37
Heat sensitivity	Softens at 300° F	Sticks at 300° F
Tenacity	3.5–4.2 g/d	2.5–2.8 g/d
Moisture regain	0.4	3.0
Acid and alkali	Excellent resistance	
Moth, mildew, etc.	Excellent resistance	
Flammability	Will not support combustion	

Structure and Properties

The shape of the modacrylic fibers shown in Figure 7–5, resembles that of the Orlon acrylic fibers, which are also dry-spun. This flattened shape is good for apparel fabrics for warmth, since they do not pack together tightly and there is considerable dead air space in the yarns. The fibers are not as lightweight as the acrylics, however. Both modacrylic fibers are used in carpets but their use in apparel is somewhat limited by their poor resistance to heat.

The modacrylics are very heat-sensitive. Dynel has high shrinkage in boiling water or in dry heat at 260° F if not under tension. They are frequently used in fabrics that do not require ironing. If they must be ironed or pressed, the lowest ironing temperature should be used and a press cloth should be placed over the fabric. Blending with natural fibers or rayon will improve their heat resistance. Dynel has been blended with wool to make felt fabrics that can be molded into hats. Bondyne is a suiting fabric, made of a blend of Dynel and wool, that can be given creases that are permanent to washing. Hair pieces, wigs, and doll's hair made of

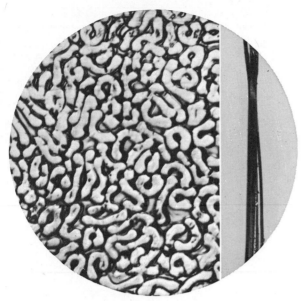

Fig. 7–5. Photomicrographs of Dynel modacrylic staple fiber; cross-sectional and longitudinal views. (Courtesy of the Carbide and Carbon Chemical Company.)

Dynel look very much like real hair and can be washed, set, brushed, and combed. Figure 7–6 shows a 100 per cent Dynel fabric that has been shrunk by the heat of an iron at low setting.

The heat-sensitivity of the modacrylics is also used to advantage in the construction of fur-like fabrics. The base fabric may be Dynel and the pile of Orlon acrylic. Heat treatment will shrink the Dynel base making the pile more dense and holding it firmly in place. Dynel may be used as the pile

Fig. 7–6. Dynel text fabric pressed with steam iron at low setting. Note shrinkage.

fibers and an embossed design will give it the look of Persian lamb or other furs.

The "guard hairs" of true furs may be simulated by making the pile of a blend of high-shrinkage and low-shrinkage fibers, then treating with heat to cause the high-shrinkage fibers to shorten thus forming the downy undercoat and leaving the low-shrinkage fibers as the long guard hairs. Proper heat finishing will give the fibers a high polish that makes them look like real fur.

The excellent chemical resistance of the modacrylics makes them useful in industrial fabrics and in laboratory coats for chemistry laboratories.

Saran

Saran is a manufactured fiber in which the fiber forming substance is any long chain synthetic polymer composed of at least 80% by weight of vinylidene chloride units. (CH_2CCl_2).

Federal Trade Commission

Saran is a vinylidene chloride and vinyl chloride copolymer developed in 1940 by the Dow Chemical Company. The raw material is melt-spun and stretched to orient the molecules. Both filament and staple forms are produced. Much of the filament fiber is produced as a monofilament for seat covers, furniture webbing, screenings, luggage, shoes, and handbags. Monofilaments are also used in doll's hair and wigs. The staple form is made either straight, curled, or crimped. The curled form is unique in that the curl is inherent and closely resembles the curl of natural wool. The staple is used in rugs, draperies, and upholstery. In addition to its use as a fiber, saran has wide use in the plastics field.

Saran has good *weathering properties, chemical resistance,* and *resistance to stretch.* It is an unusually tough, durable fiber. The fiber as seen under the microscope is perfectly round and smooth. It does not catch and hold gritty dirt particles that, when embedded in a rug, set up an abrasive shearing action. Saran *absorbs little or no moisture* so it dries rapidly. It is *difficult to dye* and for this reason, solution dyeing is used. Saran does *not support combustion.* When exposed to flame, it will soften, char, and decompose.

Vinyon

Vinyon is a manufactured fiber in which the fiber forming substance is any long chain synthetic polymer composed of at least 85% by weight of vinyl chloride units. (CH_2CHCl)

Federal Trade Commission

A patent for making fibers from a copolymer of vinyl chloride (86 per cent) and vinyl acetate (14 per cent) was obtained by the Union Carbide Corporation in 1937. The raw material is dissolved in acetone and dry-spun. The name "vinyon" was adopted as a trade name and later released for generic usage. The fiber is now produced in staple form only as Vinyon HH by the American Viscose Company with permission from Union Carbide.

Vinyon is very heat-sensitive. The fibers soften at 150–170° F, shrink at 175° F, and do not withstand boiling water or normal pressing and ironing temperatures. They are *unaffected by moisture, chemically stable, resistant to moths* and *biological attack, poor conductors of electricity,* and *do not burn*. These properties make vinyon especially good for bonding agents for rugs, papers, and nonwoven fabrics. The fibers have a tenacity of 0.7–1.0 g/d, which indicates that they are not stretched after spinning. These fibers, which are amorphous, have a warm, pleasant hand.

8 The Mineral Fibers

The mineral fibers are inorganic materials used mainly for fireproof fabrics and for insulation. The mineral fibers have more industrial uses than clothing and household uses. Glass fiber, asbestos, and stainless steel are the fibers in this group. Glass fiber has wide use in curtains and draperies, and stainless steel has been used experimentally in clothing fabrics, rugs, and carpeting.

Glass

The process of drawing out glass into hair-like strands dates back to ancient history. It is thought that Phoenician fishermen noticed small pools of molten material among the coals of the fires they built on the sands of the Aegean beaches and while poking at the strange substances, they drew out a long strand—the first glass fiber.

In 1893, at the Columbian Exposition in Chicago, the Libby Glass Company exhibited lamp shades woven of glass fibers and silk. A celebrated actress saw them and ordered a dress made from the fabric. The dress was valued at $30,000. These fabrics were not practical because they could not be folded without splitting. In 1938, commercially useful glass fiber was first produced by the Owens-Corning Fiberglas Corporation.

The raw material for glass is sand, silica, and limestone, combined with additives of feldspar and boric acid. These materials are melted in large electric furnaces (2400° F). For *filament* yarns, each furnace has holes in the base of the melting chamber. Fine streams of glass flow through the holes and are carried through a hole in the floor to a winder in the room below. The winder revolves faster than the glass comes from the furnace, thus stretching the fibers and reducing them in size before they harden. When *staple* yarn is spun, the glass flows out in thin streams from holes in the base of the furnace, and jets of high pressure air or steam yank the glass into fibers 8 to 10 inches long. These fibers are collected on a revolving drum and made into a thin web, which is then formed into a sliver, or soft, untwisted yarn. Figure 8–1 shows the round rod-like glass filaments.

Beta Fiberglas was introduced by Owens-Corning Fiberglas Corporation in 1964. This fiber has all the excellent properties of regular glass fiber but it is extremely fine in cross section. It has one sixth the denier of common fibers. The extremely fine filaments are resistant to breaking and thus more

81

Fig. 8–1. Photomicrograph of Fiberglas. (Courtesy of the Owens-Corning Fiberglas Corporation.)

resistant to abrasion. Beta Fiberglas has about half the strength of regular glass fiber, but its tenacity of 8.2 is still greater than that of most fibers. This new fiber is being used in bedspreads, mattress covers, mattress pads, and tablecloths. Intimate blends with other fibers are possible. Blankets of 30/70 Beta/acrylic are said to be softer, more stable to washing, and to have better insulating properties than 100 per cent acrylic blankets. The potential for this type of glass fiber is for all purposes rather than specific uses.

Glass fiber is extensively used in the decorator field for curtains and draperies. Here the fiber performs best if bending and abrasion can be kept at a minimum. Curtains or draperies should not be used at windows that will be kept open, allowing the wind to whip the curtains. The bottom of the curtains or draperies should not be allowed to touch the floor or window sills. The properties listed in the following table are those important in home furnishings.

GLASS FIBER PROPERTIES

Breaking tenacity, g/d	15.3–19.9
Specific gravity	2.49–2.55
Absorbency, per cent of moisture regain	None
Effect of sunlight	Resistant
Effect of acid and alkali	Resistant
Effect of heat	Flameproof

Glass fiber fabrics are preferably washed by hand. If washed by machine, a residue may be left that will get into the next wash load making skin-contact clothing very uncomfortable. If a machine is used, glass fiber articles should be washed separately and the machine should be thoroughly rinsed. Figure 8–2 shows a glass fiber laundry bag that was put in with the regular wash load. Frequent washing should not be necessary since glass fibers *resist soil*, and *spots and stains can be wiped off* with a damp cloth. No ironing is necessary. Curtains can be smoothed and put on the rod to dry. Oils used in finishing have caused graying in white curtains. Oil holds the dirt persistently and also oxidizes with age. Washing has not proved to be a very satisfactory way to whiten the material, and dry cleaning is not recommended unless Stoddard solvent is used. Of all the fibers used in curtains, glass fiber is the only one that is *flameproof* and it has the *best resistance to degradation by sunlight*. Glass fibers have a *density* higher than any other fiber. In curtains and draperies, the weight of fabrics may mean that special rods are necessary, especially if large areas are draped.

Glass fiber has wide industrial use where noise abatement, fire protection, temperature control (insulation), and air purification are needed. The excellent insulating properties of glass fiber are also

Fig. 8–2. Glass fiber laundry bag after being washed with regular family wash.

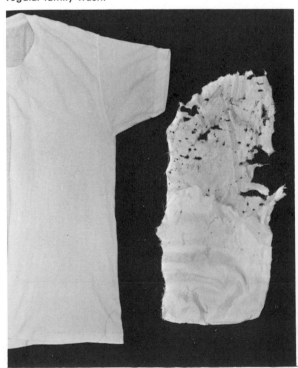

used to advantage in the clothing and household field. The fiber used for insulating clothing is much finer than that used in industrial insulation.

Coronizing

Coronizing is a process for heat-setting, dyeing, and finishing glass fiber in one continuous operation. Heat-setting is done on the fabric to set the crimp in the woven yarn. Since glass is *low in flexibility*, the yarns resist bending around one another in the woven fabric. Heat-setting softens the yarn so that it assumes a permanent bend suitable to the fabric construction. Heat-setting is done at a temperature of 1,100° F, which is high enough to soften the yarns but not melt them. Coronized fabrics have greater wrinkle resistance and softer draping qualities.

After the heat-setting treatment, the glass fabric is treated with a lubricating oil; then color and a water-repellent finish are added. For this treatment the Hycar–Quilon process is used. Hycar is an acrylic latex resin which, with the colored pigment, is padded on the fabric and then cured at a temperature of 320° F. This is followed by a treatment with Quilon, a water-repellent substance, and the fabric is again cured. Glass fiber is *nonabsorbent*, but glass will get wet, as anyone who has washed and dried windows knows. The water-repellent treatment makes the fabric resistant to wetting and increases the color-fastness. The resin used in the color treatment increases the flexibility of the fiber. However, the resin is damaged by chlorinated dry cleaning solutions, so dry cleaning should be done with Stoddard solvent.

Screen printing as well as roller printing can be done by the Hycar–Quilon process, since the color paste dries fast enough to allow one screen to follow another rapidly. The Hycar–Quilon process gives good resistance to rubbing off (crocking), which is one of the disadvantages of the other coloring methods.

Producers of glass fibers are listed in Appendix B.

Asbestos

Asbestos is a natural fiber that occurs as veins or strips in rocks. While there are three minerals classified as asbestos, the most important commercial variety is the Canadian serpentine. Other deposits are found in Russia, Arizona, and Africa. The fiber is obtained by mining or quarrying. The fiber is carefully separated from the crushed rock and sorted according to fiber length.

Properties

Asbestos fibers are $\frac{3}{8}$ inch to $\frac{3}{4}$ inch in length and are quite small in diameter. The diameter has never been definitely determined because the fibers can be split to infinite fineness. The finest ever measured was made of several fine fibers. Under the microscope the fibers look like tiny polished rods, very straight, with no rough surfaces. The physical structure of the fiber makes it very difficult to spin into yarns because it is lacking in length and cohesiveness. For textile uses, 5 to 20 per cent cotton is blended with asbestos.

Asbestos is white or grayish-white in color. Asbestos fibers do not take dye readily but since most textile uses are utilitarian, color is not important. Some fire screens and draperies have been printed.

Asbestos is used for padding, for laundry presses and mangles, brake linings, gloves, aprons, belting for conveying hot materials, etc.

Stainless Steel

For ages man has made yarns from gold and silver and, more recently, from aluminum for decorative clothing. In 1965, the Brunswick Corporation developed a superfine stainless steel filament, 6 to 12 microns, that could be woven or knitted. It has been described as the newest development since the nylons in the 1930's. Stainless steel was first known in the early 1960's and was used in space travel for uses where glass and ceramic fibers would be completely destroyed by the high temperatures.

In manufacture, a bundle of fine wires (0.002 inch) is sheathed in dissimilar alloys and drawn to its final diameter, pickled in nitric acid to remove the sheath, and the yarn of several filaments is ready for sizing, warping, and weaving. The early fibers were costly, $25 per pound, and there were a number of problems to be solved. One was with twist. Each filament tended to act as a tiny coil spring. The fibers cannot be dyed; and if blended with white fibers, a good white cannot be obtained in the fabric.

Stainless steel fibers are expected to be useful in eliminating static, in preventing pilling, and because of antistatic properties repelling soil that is attracted by static. Since only 1 per cent is needed, it was thought that in spite of the high cost, it would be cheaper than an antistatic compound and the cost of application.

An interesting possibility for fabric blends is that, when hooked up to the proper power source, they can be used for heated clothing and for wall and floor coverings that supply radiant heat. The fiber is still experimental.

9 *Fiber Blends*

A *blend* is an intimate mixture of staple fibers of different composition, length, diameter, or color spun together into a yarn. A *mixture* is a fabric that has yarn of one fiber content in the warp and yarn of a different fiber content in the filling. A *combination* yarn has two unlike fiber strands twisted together as a ply. Blends, mixtures, and combinations give properties to fabrics that are different from those obtained with one fiber only. The following discussion relates to blends, although most of the facts are true for mixtures and combinations as well.

Blends are not new, but in the past ten years, they have become very important. *Viyella*[1] *flannel* is one of the oldest blends. It is a 55 per cent cotton and 45 per cent wool fabric that has been woven in England for many years. It feels like a lightweight wool but does not felt and is washable. Long Johns are made from a combination of wool and cotton. Covert, a fabric specially designed for hunting, is also a blend of cotton and wool. Today it is possible to obtain all basic fabrics in fiber blends.

There is no perfect fiber. All fibers have good, fair, and poor characteristics. Blending enables the technician to combine fibers so that the good qualities are emphasized and the poor qualities minimized. Blending requires knowledge of both science and art.

Reasons for Blending

Blending is done for several reasons:

1. To obtain cross-dyed effects or create new color effects such as heather, when fibers with unlike dye affinity are blended together and then piece-dyed.
2. To improve spinning, weaving, and finishing efficiency for uniformity of product, as with self-blends of natural fibers to improve uniformity.
3. To obtain better texture, hand, or fabric appearance. A small amount of a specialty wool may be used to give a buttery or slick hand to wool fabrics, or a small amount of rayon may give luster and softness to a cotton fabric. Fibers with different shrinkage properties are blended to produce bulky and lofty fabrics or fur-like fabrics with guard hairs.

[1] Copyrighted trade mark.

FIBER PROPERTIES

Properties	Cotton	Rayon	Wool	Acetate	Nylon	Polyester	Acrylic	Modacrylic	Olefin
Bulk and loft	−	−	+++		−	−	+++	+++	
Wrinkle recovery	−	−	+++	++	++	+++	++	++	++
Press (wet) retention	−	−	−	+	++	+++			
Absorbency	+++	+++	+++	+	−	−	−	−	−
Static resistance	+++	+++	++	+	+	−	+	+	++
Resistance to pilling	+++	+++	+	+++	+				++
Strength	++	+	+	+	+++	+++	+	+	+++
Abrasion resistance	+	−	++	−	+++	+++	+	+	+++
Stability	++	−	−	+++	+++	+++	+++	+++	+++
Resistance to heat	+++	+++	++	++	+	+	++	−	−

+++ Excellent   ++ Good   + Fair   − Deficient

4. For economic reasons. Expensive fibers can be extended by blending them with more plentiful fibers. This use is sometimes unfair to the consumer, especially when the expensive fiber is used in small amounts but advertised in large print; for example, CASHMERE and wool.

5. To produce fabrics with better performance. This is perhaps the most important reason for blending. In end-uses where durability is very important, nylon or polyester blended with cotton or wool provide strength and resistance to abrasion, while the wool or cotton look is maintained. A classic example is in durable-press garments where 100 per cent cotton fabrics are not as durable as polyester/cotton blends.

In the above chart some fiber properties are rated. Notice that each fiber is deficient in one or more important property. Try different fiber combinations to see how a blend of two fibers might give different performance than either fiber used alone.

Blend Levels

For a specific end-use, a blend of fibers that complement each other will give more satisfactory all-round performance than a 100 per cent fiber fabric.

M. J. Caplan,[2] in his article "Fiber Translation

[2] M. J. Caplan, "Fiber Translation in Blends," *Modern Textiles Magazine* **40**:39 (July, 1959).

in Blends," used the following example to show that a blend will yield a fabric with intermediate values. He took two fibers, *A* and *B*, each of which could be used to make a similar fabric, measured five performance properties of each of these 100 per cent fabrics, and then predicted the performance of a blended fabric 50/50 *A* and *B* by averaging the values of each fabric in the blend.

	Known Values		Predicted Values
Property	A	B	50/50 *A and B*
1	12	4	8
2	9	12	10.5
3	15	2	8.5
4	7	9	8
5	12	8	10

Notice that the predicted value for the blend is lower than the high value of one fabric, and is greater than the low value of the 100 per cent fabric. By blending them, a fabric with intermediate values is obtained. Unfortunately, the real values do not come out in the same proportion as the respective percentage in a blend.

Much research has been done by the fiber manufacturers to determine just how much of each fiber is necessary in the various fiber constructions. It is very difficult to generalize about percentages, because the percentage varies with the kind of fiber, the fiber construction, and the expected performance. For example, a very small amount of nylon (15 per cent) improves the strength of wool, but 60 per cent nylon is needed to improve the strength of rayon. For stability, 50 per cent Orlon blended with wool in a woven fabric is satisfactory, but 75 per cent Orlon is necessary in knitted fabrics.[3]

Fiber producers have controlled blend levels fairly well by setting standards for apparel or fabrics identified with their trade mark. For example, the Du Pont Company recommends a blend level of 65 per cent Dacron polyester/35 per cent cotton in light or mediumweight fabrics, while 50/50 Dacron/cotton is satisfactory for suiting weight fabrics. This assures satisfactory performance of the fabric and maintains a good fiber "image" for Dacron. The fabric manufacturer profits from large-scale promotion carried on by the fiber producer.

If fiber trade names become less important and fabric or apparel producers are willing to use generic names only, they can set their own blend levels. These should be satisfactory to most consumers, however, because fabrics will have to meet minimum standards to compete in the retail market.

Blending Methods

Blending can be done at any stage prior to the spinning operation. Blending can be done during opening-picking, drawing, and roving. One of the disadvantages of direct spinning is that blending cannot be done before the sliver is formed.

The earlier the fibers are blended in processing, the better the blend. The drawing in Figure 9–1

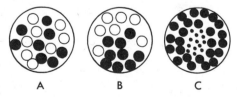

Fig. 9–1. Cross section of yarn showing the location of the fibers in the blend.

shows a cross section of a yarn *A*, in which the fibers were blended in opening, and yarn *B*, a yarn in which the fibers were blended at the roving stage.

Variations occur from spot to spot in the yarn and also from inside to outside. Long, fine fibers tend

[3] E. I. du Pont de Nemours & Company, "Properties of Blended Fabrics," Bulletin X–21, Wilmington, Del., no date.

to move to the center of a yarn, while coarse, shorter fibers migrate to the periphery of the yarn *C*. The older methods of blending involve much hand labor.

Fig. 9–2. Sandwich blending of wool fibers.

Opening Picking

In one method, several bales of fiber are laid around the picker and an armful from each bale is fed alternately into the machine. Another method is called *sandwich blending*. The desired amounts of each fiber are weighed out and a layer of each is spread over the preceding layer to build up a sandwich composed of many layers. Vertical sections are then taken through the sandwich and fed into the picker. (See Figure 9–2.) *Feeder blending* is an automatic process in which each type of fiber is fed to a mixing apron from individual hoppers. (See Figure 9–3.)

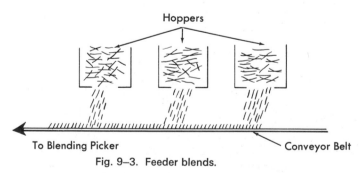

Fig. 9–3. Feeder blends.

Blending on the Drawing Frame

When the physical properties of two fibers differ, it is not always practical to blend them before carding, so they are picked and carded separately and then blended in the drawing frame. The problem of mixed wastes is eliminated with this process. (See page 95.)

Blending on the Roving and Spinning Frame

Both these operations combine fiber strands to reduce size and increase amount of twist until the final size and twist are achieved. Blending colors is the primary purpose at this stage. (See page 94.)

Blending is a complicated and expensive process, but it makes it possible to build in a combination of properties that are permanent. Not only are blends used for better functionability of fabrics, but they are also used for beauty of appearance and hand.

Polymer blends are a new approach to the problem of blending. Polymer blending creates the possibility of a whole new field of fibers. (See "Multipolymer Fibers," page 64.)

10 *Conventional Yarn Spinning*

Yarn is the generic name for an assemblage of fibers that are laid or twisted together. Yarns are classified as: (1) spun yarns, made of staple fiber, and (2) continuous filament yarns, made of filament fiber. A spun yarn is turned into a thread if it is given considerable twist by doubling, twisting, winding, and in some cases, gas singeing.

The yarn may be as important in determining fabric characteristics as the fiber, the weave, or the finish. The two fabrics in Figure 10–1 are 100 per cent cotton but have very different performance characteristics because of the yarn structure (and the weave). The yarn can enhance good fiber performance or compensate for poor fiber performance. The structure of the yarn is a basic factor in a finish such as napping, or it may determine the effectiveness of finishes such as the Schreiner finish for luster of sateen fabrics. Some fabric characteristics that are related to the nature of the yarn are:

1. Texture—smoothness, softness, crepiness, etc.
2. Beauty—luster, dullness, slubbiness, etc.
3. Weight—sheer, medium, suiting, etc.
4. Comfort—warmth, coolness, absorbency, etc.
5. Performance—resiliency, pilling, soiling, etc.

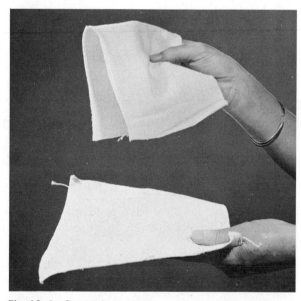

Fig. 10–1. Comparison of yarn properties as shown by the limpness of the elastic fabric above and the stiffness of duck below.

Spinning is the term applied to the processes of making yarn. Spun yarns are made by the *mechanical spinning* of natural or man-made staple fiber. Continuous filament tow and yarn are produced by

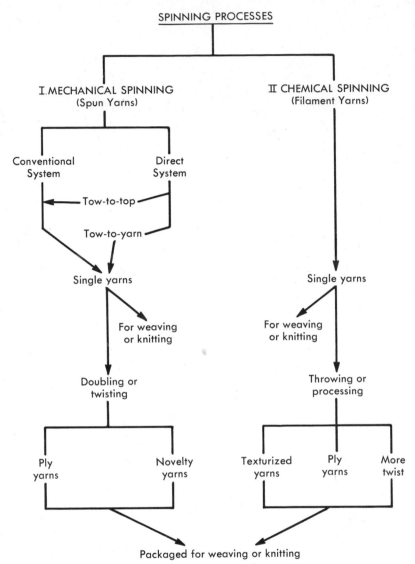

Fig. 10–2. Diagram of yarn spinning processes.

chemical spinning—the extrusion of a solution through a spinneret. The chart in Figure 10–2 outlines these two major spinning processes.

Mechanical Spinning

Mechanical spinning consists of a series of operations designed to clean and parallel staple fibers, draw them out into a fine strand, and twist them to make a *spun yarn*. Mechanical spinning is one of the oldest manufacturing arts, and has been described as an invention as significant as that of the wheel.

The earliest primitive spinning consisted of simply twisting the fibers between the fingers. Later primitive man bound the fibers to a stick called a distaff, which was held under the arm leaving the fingers free to draw out the fibers. When the strand was about a yard long, the free end was fastened to a rock or spindle, which had enough weight to help draw out the fibers and could be spun like a top to twist the yarn, as shown in Figure 10–3.

This method was satisfactory for the spinning of wool and flax, but primitive man found that the weight of the spindle was too great for the shorter,

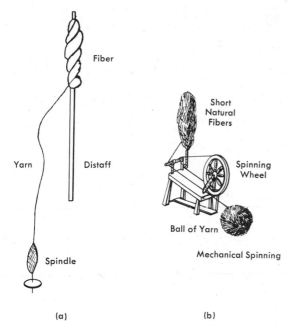

Fig. 10–3. (a) Distaff and spindle used in primitive spinning of yarn. (b) A spinning wheel.

less cohesive cotton. A small spindle set in a bowl with a little water made the cotton fibers moist and cohesive and relieved them of some of the weight of the spindle. Thus primitive spinners varied the spinning process according to the characteristics of the fiber to be spun and also developed two spinning processes—the intermittent twisting and winding of the wool fiber, which is comparable to the mule-spinning of wool as used today, and the continuous twisting and winding of cotton yarn, which is comparable to the continuous ring-spinning of the modern cotton spinning mill.

The spinning wheel was developed by the spinners of India who turned the spindle in a horizontal position and attached it to a wheel, which was turned by a foot pedal. The spinning wheel was introduced into Europe in the fourteenth century. The factory system began in the eighteenth century when spinning was done by a class distinct from the weavers. In 1764, an Englishman named James Hargreaves invented the first spinning jenny —a machine to turn more than one spinning wheel at a time. Other inventions for improving the spinning process followed, and the Industrial Revolution made mass production possible as power-operated machines took over the hand process.

The basic principles of spinning are the same now as they were when man first made yarn. Also, modern spinning systems[1] are specialized to adapt them to the characteristics of the fibers used— length, cohesiveness, diameter, elasticity, and surface contour. These spinning systems are spoken of as conventional spinning systems because they are an outgrowth of the traditional methods. The cotton system of spinning is discussed in the section that follows.

The Cotton System

Because the cotton system of spinning yarn is representative of the others, it is discussed here in detail. References are made to the woolen system.

The steps in spinning staple fiber into yarn are designed to clean and parallel the fibers, to draw them out into a fine strand, and twist them to give strength to the finished yarn.

THE COTTON SYSTEM

Operations	Purpose
Opening	Loosens, blends, cleans, forms lap
Carding	Cleans, straightens, forms sliver
Combing	Straightens, removes short fibers, forms sliver
Drawing	Parallels, blends, reduces size, forms sliver
Roving	Reduces size, forms roving with slight twist
Spinning	Twists, winds finished yarn on a bobbin
Winding	Rewinds yarn from bobbin to spool or cone

Conventional spinning traditionally has been a series of operations done by individual machines and a great deal of hand labor was involved. In the early 1950's, an *automated continuous spinning system* began to develop in which the operation of each machine and the movement of the fibers from machine to machine is controlled automatically.

Opening. Cotton fibers have been compressed very tightly in the bale and may have been stored in this state for a year or more. The initial step of opening (loosening) is necessary to make the fibers ready for carding. Also, machine-picked cotton contains a much higher percentage of dirt and trash than does hand-picked cotton; consequently, the work of cleaning it has become more complicated.

[1] The five spinning systems are the cotton, woolen, American, Bradford, and French systems.

Fig. 10–4. A Karousel opener picker machine. (Courtesy of American Reiter.)

(Part of this is done at the gin.) Cotton varies from bale to bale; during the various spinning operations, the fibers from several bales are blended to give yarns of uniform quality.

Opening is the first operation and it loosens, cleans, and blends the fibers. Two types of units are used. One, shown in Figure 10–4, is a merry-go-round-like unit[2] with a circular stage containing compartments for several bales. The stage rotates over a stationary platform containing a number of beaters (pluckers). The beater is a device that plucks small tufts of fiber from the underside of a bale as the stage revolves and drops the tufts on a screen or lattice. At the same time, dirt and trash are removed by high-velocity air.

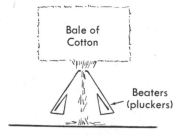

Fig. 10–5. How the beaters (pluckers) work.

[2] Carousel or Karousel, trade name of the American Reiter Company.

The other type of opening unit is the chute-feed system in which the bales travel in a straight line across the beaters. The diagram in Figure 10–5 shows how the beaters work. The loosened and cleaned fibers are fed to a line of carding machines.

Carding. Carding is done by a machine consisting of two cylinders covered with heavy card clothing—a heavy fabric embedded with especially bent wires. The fibers are fed between the two cylinders, which straighten them and form them into a thin web that is brought together as a soft rope called a *card sliver.* In automatic spinning, the carded web is formed into a sliver ribbon, which is combined with the ribbon slivers from the other machines in the line and is then fed into a sliver can which is automatically filled and delivered to the drawing frames. (See Figure 10–6.)

Short cotton fibers are processed on the carding machine and yarns made from them are called *carded yarns.*

In the woolen spinning system, short wool fibers that are carded but not combed are made into *woolen yarns.* Although carding straightens the fibers somewhat, the carded web is divided into ribbons, which are given a sideward roll to form the roving. Thus the fibers in the finished woolen

Fig. 10–6. Carding. (Courtesy of Coats & Clark Inc., New York, N.Y.)

yarn lie in every direction. (See Figure 10–7.) Remember that the term "woolen" has a specific meaning and is not a synonym for the word "wool."

Worsted Yarns

Woolen Yarns

Fig. 10–7. Top, combed yarn made from long staple wool fiber—worsted yarn. Bottom, carded yarn made from short staple wool fiber—woolen yarn.

Combing. Combing is the operation that follows carding when long-staple fibers are to be spun. The fundamental purpose of combing is to separate any short fibers from the long staple so that the combed fibers will be of a much more uniform length and of longer average staple. Combing is quite expensive and adds considerably to the cost of the yarn. Long-staple fibers cost more per pound than short staple and as much as one fourth of the fiber is combed out as waste.

Fibers emerge from the combing machine as *combed sliver* (see Figure 10–8), and yarns made

Fig. 10–8. Combing. (Courtesy of Coats & Clark, Inc., New York, N.Y.)

from combed cotton fibers are called *combed yarns*. Wool fibers that are suitable for combing range from the long, coarse, lustrous fiber processed on the Bradford system to the fine, short, crimpy wool fiber processed on the French system. Combed wool sliver is referred to as *top* and the yarns made from them are *worsted yarns*. The short fibers that are combed out are called *noils*. The noils are used to make woolen yarns.

Combing produces yarn of high quality, great uniformity, more strength, and finer count.[3] The diagram in Figure 10–7 shows the parallelism of fibers in a worsted yarn. The chart at the right gives a comparison of woolen and worsted yarns.

Drawing. Drawing blends several slivers together and parallels the fibers. This further blends the fibers and contributes to a more uniform yarn. It is done by four *sets* of rolls, each running successively faster than the preceding set. The speed is adjusted so that it produces one drawn sliver comparable in size to the individual slivers that were fed into the drawing machine. The drawn sliver comes out much faster than the carded (or combed sliver) is fed in. (See Figures 10–9 and 10–10.)

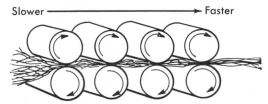

Slower ⟶ Faster

Fig. 10–9. Diagram of drawing rolls.

Fig. 10–10. Drawing operation. (Courtesy of Coats & Clark, Inc., New York, N.Y.)

[3] Count refers to the size of a *spun* yarn.

EFFECT OF WOOLEN AND WORSTED YARNS IN FABRICS

Woolens	Worsted
Yarns have medium to low twist	Yarns have medium to high twist
Less strength, bulkier	Lighter weight
Softer, rougher texture	Smoother surface
Fuzzier surface	
Do not hold shape as well as worsteds	Do not sag
Becomes baggy at areas of stress	Takes and holds a press better
Breaking load relatively low	Longer wearing, stronger
Widely used for blankets, soft fabrics, washable woolens	Widely used for suiting for men and women because it tailors well

Roving. Roving is a term applied to both a process and its product. The purpose of the process is to draw out (draft) the drawn sliver to a size suitable for spinning. This drafting is done by a set of rollers similar to those of the drawing machine. Also, it increases the parallelism of the fibers, and when two or more slivers are drawn out together (doubling), the uniformity of the yarn will be improved. Roving, the product, is not coiled in a can, as was carded or combed sliver, which has very little strength, but it is given a slight twist and wound on a bobbin. The twist is inserted by a flyer, as shown in Figures 10–11 and 10–12. A roving is a continuous, soft, slightly twisted strand of fibers produced from a sliver. A roving is comparable in size to a thin pencil.

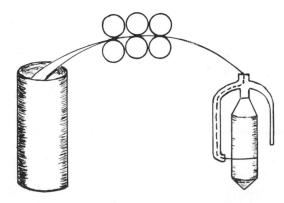

Fig. 10–11. Diagram of roving machine.

Fig. 10–12. Roving machine. (Courtesy of Coats & Clark Inc., New York, N.Y.)

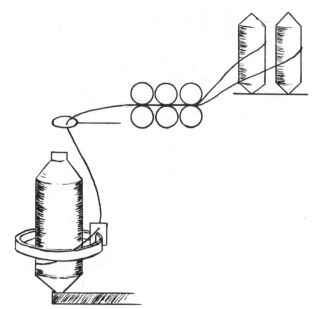

Fig. 10–13. Diagram of spinning machine.

Spinning. Spinning is the final operation in the making of a single yarn. Spinning inserts the twist that gives strength to the yarn and winds the finished yarn on a bobbin. The *ring* spinning machine, a down-twisting machine, draws, twists, and winds in one continuous motion. Drafting rolls draw out the roving to its final size. A traveler, which glides freely around a ring, inserts the twist as the spindle rotates a bobbin on which the yarn is wound. (See Figures 10–13 and 10–14.) *Mule* spinning is done on a spinning frame with an intermittent action and it is used in the woolen spinning system. The yarn is drawn out and twisted, then the twisting stops while the twisted portion of yarn is wound on the bobbin.

A spinning *frame* is a multiple machine with a large number of individual units.

Winding. The spun yarn is wound from the bobbin to spools or cones. The spools are placed on a large creel and the yarns are wound from the spools onto a warp beam, ready for weaving as shown in Figure 10–15. This operation is called *creeling* and may be performed at the weaving mill.

Characteristics of Spun Yarns

The first spun yarns were made from wool, linen, and cotton, all of which are staple fibers. Yarns made from man-made fibers give fabrics a cotton-like, wool-like, or linen-like appearance. Spun yarns are suited to fabrics for clothing in which absorbency, bulk, and warmth are desired. The

Fig. 10–14. A spinning frame. (Courtesy of the Roberts Company.)

fiber ends hold the yarn away from close contact with the skin; thus a spun yarn is more comfortable on a hot humid day than a fabric of smooth filament yarns.

Spun yarns are characterized by *protruding fiber ends.* Carded yarns, made of short fibers, have more protruding fiber ends than combed yarns, which are made of long-staple fibers. Protruding ends contribute to a dull fuzzy appearance, to the

Fig. 10–15. Creeling yarns onto a wrap beam. (Courtesy of Barber Coleman.)

shedding of lint, and to the formation of pills on the surface of the fabric. Fuzzy ends can be removed from the yarn or from the fabric by singeing (page 182).

The *strength* of the individual staple fiber is less important as a factor in yarn strength than it is in filament yarns. Instead, spun yarn strength is dependent on the cohesive or clinging power of the fibers and on the points of contact resulting from pressure of twist. The greater the number of points of contact, the greater the resistance to fiber slippage within the yarn. Fibers with crimp or convolutions make a greater number of points of contact. The friction of one fiber against another gives resistance to lengthwise fiber slippage. A fiber with a rough surface—wool scales, for example—creates more friction than a smooth fiber. (See page 98 for a chart giving a comparison of spun yarn and filament yarn characteristics.)

Chemical Spinning

Chemical spinning produces filament fiber, filament yarn, and filament tow. (Filament tow is made into staple and processed by mechanical spinning.) It is a process in which a polymer solution is extruded through a spinneret, solidified in fiber form, and the individual filaments are *immediately brought together* with or without a slight twist to make the yarn, which is then wound on a bobbin. Thus, filament fiber spinning and filament yarn spinning are parts of the same process. (See Figure 10–16.)

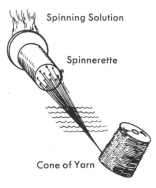

Fig. 10–16. Chemical spinning of filament yarn. (Courtesy of the FMC Corporation, American Viscose Division.)

Before the twentieth century, the only continuous filament yarn was silk, an item of luxury. All utility fabrics were made with yarns containing staple fibers. Man-made continuous filament yarns made silk-like fabrics available for the mass market. Continuous filament yarns are classified into two groups: *regular filament yarns*, discussed in the section that follows, *and textured filament yarns*, discussed on page 105. (See Figure 10–17.)

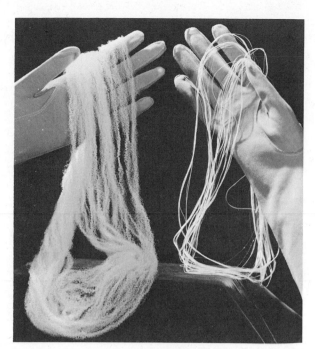

Fig. 10–17. Regular filament and textured yarn.

Regular Filament Yarns

When a new fiber is being developed, filament yarn production usually precedes production of tow for staple. Filament yarns are more expensive in price per pound; however, the cost of making tow into staple and then spinning it into yarn by the mechanical spinning process usually makes the final cost about the same. The number of holes in the spinneret determines the number of filaments in the yarn.

The filament yarn is a finished product unless additional twisting or finishing is required in which case the yarn is sent to a throwing mill.

Throwing is a term that originally meant twisting and/or plying (doubling) of filament yarns. It now includes finishing and texturizing. Throwing provides the weaver or knitter with the type of yarn needed for the particular fabric to be made—crepe or voile, for example. Throwsters work in two ways: They buy raw yarn, process it, and sell the processed yarn; or they work on a commission basis in which the customer buys the raw yarn, sends it to the throwster who processes to order, and returns it to the customer, charging for his services. The latter plan benefits the customer because he can meet seasonal demand and fashion changes without investing in specialized equipment.

Characteristics of Filament Yarn. Regular filament yarns are smooth and silk-like as they come from the spinneret. Their smooth nature gives them more *luster* than spun yarns, but the luster varies with the amount of delustering agent used in the fiber spinning solution and the amount of twist in the yarn. Maximum luster is obtained by use of bright filaments, which are laid together with little or no twist. Crepe yarns, of very high twist, were developed as a means of reducing the luster of the filaments. Filament yarns are generally used with either high twist or low twist.

Filament yarns have no protruding ends so they do not shed lint; they resist pilling, and fabrics made from them shed soil. Filaments of round cross section pack well into compact yarns, which give little bulk, loft, or cover to a fabric. Compactness is a disadvantage in some end-uses where bulk and absorbency are necessary for comfort.

The strength of a filament yarn depends on the strength of the individual fibers and on the number of filaments in the yarn. Filament fiber strength is usually greater than that of staple fibers. For example:

1. Polyester filaments—5 to 8 grams/denier tensile strength.
2. Polyester staple—3 to 5.5 grams/denier tensile strength.

The strength of each filament is fully utilized. In order to break the yarn, the filaments must be broken. Therefore, it is possible to make very sheer fabrics of fine filaments that have good strength. Filament yarns reach their maximum strength at about 3 turns per inch; then strength remains constant or decreases.

Fine filament yarns are soft and supple. However, they are not as resistant to abrasion as coarse filaments; so for durability, it may be desirable to have fewer, but coarser filaments in the yarn. Filament yarns are made with a denier (size) designed for a particular end-use.

1. 15 denier for sheer hosiery
2. 40 to 70 denier for tricot lingerie and blouses and shirts
3. 140 to 520 denier for different types of apparel
4. 520 to 840 denier for upholstery
5. 1040 denier for yarn for carpets.

A comparison of spun yarns and filament yarns is given in the following chart.

COMPARISON OF SPUN YARNS
AND FILAMENT YARNS

Spun Yarns	Filament Yarns
Strength of fibers is not completely utilized.	Strength of fiber is completely utilized.
	Long continuous, closely packed strand
Have protruding ends.	1. Smooth, lustrous
1. Dull, fuzzy look	2. Do not lint
2. Lints	3. Do not pill readily
3. Subject to pilling	4. Shed soil
4. Soil readily	5. Cool
5. Warm	6. Give little loft or bulk to fabrics.
6. Loft and bulk depend on the size and twist of yarn.	
Are absorbent.	Absorbency depends on fiber content.
1. Good for skin-contact fabric	1. Silk, rayon, acetate are absorbent. Thermoplastics are low in absorbency
2. Resistant to static build-up	2. Static build-up is high in thermoplastics

Yarn Classification

Yarns are classified by size, twist, number of parts, and appearance.

Classification by Size. The size, number, or count of spun yarns and of filament yarns is determined by different systems.

Spun yarn size is expressed in terms of length per unit of weight. It differs according to the kind of fiber. The cotton system is given here. In the cotton system, the count is based on the number of hanks (one hank is 840 yards) in one pound of yarn. Weaving yarns and sewing thread are numbered by this system. The cotton system is an indirect system since the finer the yarn the larger the number. See the following chart.

Number or Count of Spun Yarn	Hanks	Weight
No. 1	1 (840 yds.)	1 lb.
No. 2	2 (1,680 yds.)	1 lb.
No. 3 etc.	3 (2,520 yds.)	1 lb.

Some examples that show how the size of the weaving yarn affect the weight of the fabric are given in the following chart.

Fabric Weight	Yarn Size	
	Warp	Filling
Sheer lawn	70s*	100s
Dress weight percale	30s	40s
Suiting weight Indian Head	13s	20s

* The "s" after the number means that the yarn is single

Filament yarn size is dependent partly on the size of the holes in the spinneret and partly on the rate at which the solution is pumped through the spinneret and the rate at which it is withdrawn. The size of filament yarns (and filament fibers) is expressed in terms of weight per unit of length—denier (pronounced "den-yer"). In this system the unit of length remains constant. The numbering system is direct because the finer the yarn the smaller the number.

1 denier	9,000 meters weigh 1 gram
2 denier	9,000 meters weigh 2 grams
3 denier	9,000 meters weigh 3 grams

Classification by Twist. Twist is defined as the spiral arrangement of the fibers around the axis of the yarn. Twist is produced by revolving one end of a fiber strand while the other end is held stationary. Twist binds the fibers together and gives the yarn strength.

DIRECTION. The direction of twist is described as S-twist and Z-twist. These terms have largely replaced the terms "regular," "reverse," "right," and "left," which are used with opposite meaning by various segments of the textile industry. A yarn has S-twist if, when held in vertical position, the spirals conform to the direction of slope of the central portion of the letter "S". It is called Z-twist if the direction of spirals conforms to the slope of the central portion of the letter "Z". Z-twist is the standard twist used for weaving yarns. (See Figure 10–18.)

AMOUNT. The amount of twist varies with the length of the fibers, the size of the yarn, and the intended use. Increasing the amount of twist up to a certain point will increase the strength of the yarns. Too much twist places the fibers at right angles to

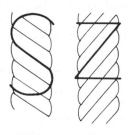

S-Twist   Z-Twist
Fig. 10–18. S and Z twist.

the axis of the yarn and causes a shearing action between fibers and the yarn will lose strength. (See Figure 10–19.)

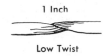

1 Inch

Low Twist

High Twist

Fig. 10–19. Diagram showing high and low twist.

Yarns with long fibers do not require as much twist as yarns with short fibers, since they establish more points of contact per fiber and give stronger yarn for the same amount of twist. Fine yarns require more twist than coarse yarns. Knitting yarns have less twist than the filling yarns used in weaving. It is important for knitting yarns to be very uniform to prevent the formation of thick and thin places in the fabric. The chart and the discussion that follow give some examples of different amounts of twist.

AMOUNT OF TWIST

Amount	Example
Low twist	Filament yarns; 2 to 3 t.p.i.*
Napping twist	Blanket warps; 12 t.p.i.
	Filling; 6 to 8 t.p.i.
Average twist	Percale warps; 25 t.p.i.
(Usually spun	Filling; 20 t.p.i.
yarn)	Nylon Hosiery; 25 to 30 t.p.i.
Voile twist	Hard twist singles; 35 to 40 t.p.i.
	are plied with 16 to 18 t.p.i.
Crepe twist	Singles; 40 to 80 or more t.p.i.
	are plied with 2 to 5 t.p.i.

* Turns per inch.

Low twist is used in filling yarns of fabrics that are to be napped. The low twist permits the napping machine to tease out the ends of the staple fibers and create the soft fuzzy surface. (See "Napping," page 170.)

Average twist is that most frequently used for yarns made of staple fibers and is very seldom used with filament yarns. The amount of twist that gives warp yarns maximum strength is referred to as standard warp twist. Warp yarns need more twist than filling yarns because warp yarns are under high tension on the loom and they must resist wear caused by the abrasion of the shuttle moving back and forth. The lower twist of the filling yarns makes them softer and less apt to kink.

High, hard twist (voile twist) yarns have 30 to 40 turns per inch. The hardness of the yarn results when twist brings the fibers closer together and makes the yarn more compact. This effect is more pronounced when a twist-on-twist ply yarn is used. Twist-on-twist means that the direction of twist in the singles is the same as the direction of plying twist. (See Figure 10–20.) This results in a build-up of the total amount of twist in the yarn. (See "Voile," page 140.)

Fig. 10–20. Twist on twist yarn.

Crepe yarns are made of either staple or filament fiber. They are made with a high number of turns per inch (40 to 80) inserted in the yarn. This makes the yarn so lively and kinky that it must be twist-set before it can be woven or knitted. Twist-setting is a finishing process in which the yarns are moistened and then dried in a straightened condition. After weaving, the cloth is moistened and the yarns become lively and kinky once more and thus produce the crinkle characteristic of true crepe fabrics. All of the common natural fibers and rayon can be used in crepe twist yarns because they can be twist-set in water. The thermoplastic fibers are not used in high-twist crepe yarns because they are not affected by water; and if the twist is set by heat, the liveliness of the twist is deadened. Increasing the amount of crepe yarn twist and alternating the direction of twist will increase the amount of crinkle in a crepe fabric. For example, 6S and 6Z will give a more prominent crinkle than 2S and 2Z.

To identify crepe yarns, ravel adjacent sides to obtain a fringe on each of the two edges. Test the yarns that are removed by pulling on the yarn and then letting one end go. The yarn will "kink up" as shown in Figure 10–21. Do not confuse kink with yarn crimp. Examine the fringe of the fabric. If yarns other than crepe yarns are used in the fabric, they will probably be of very low twist. The majority of crepe fabrics have crepe yarns in the crosswise direction, although some are in the lengthwise direction and some have crepe yarns in both directions.

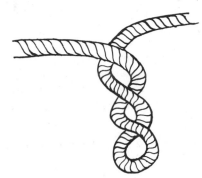

Fig. 10–21. Kink in crepe yarn.

Classification by Number of Parts and by Appearance.

A simple yarn is alike in all its parts. A novelty yarn has unlike parts; it is irregular at regular intervals.

SIMPLE YARNS. Simple yarns are classified as single, ply, and cord.

A *single yarn* is the product of the first twisting operation that is performed by the spinning machine. (See Figure 10–22.)

Fig. 10–22. A single yarn.

A *ply yarn* is made by a second twisting operation that combines two or more singles. (See Figure 10–23.) Each part of the yarn is called a ply. The twist is inserted by a machine called a twister. Most ply yarns are twisted in the opposite direction to the

Fig. 10–23. Two-ply yarn.

twist of the singles from which they are made; thus the first few revolutions tend to untwist the singles and straighten the fibers somewhat from their spiral position and the yarn becomes softer. Plying tends

to increase the diameter, strength, and quality of the yarn.

A *cord* is made by a third twisting operation that twists ply yarns together. (See Figure 10–24.) Some types of sewing thread and some rope belong in this group.

Fig. 10–24. A cord yarn.

NOVELTY YARNS. Novelty yarns have regular cycles of uneven arrangement and may be unlike in all parts. They are made on twisters with special attachments for giving different tensions and rates of delivery to the different plies and thus allow loose, curled, twisted, or looped areas in the yarn. Slubs and flakes of color are introduced also into the yarn by special attachments. The durability of novelty yarn fabrics is dependent on the size of the novelty effect, how well the novelty effect is held in the yarn, and on the firmness of the weave of the fabric. Generally speaking, the smaller the novelty effect the more durable the fabric, since the yarns are less affected by abrasion and do not tend to catch and pull out so readily.

A typical novelty yarn has three basic parts: the ground or foundation, the fancy or effect, and the binder. (See Figure 10–25.)

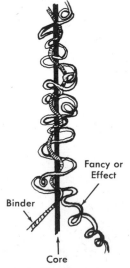

Fig. 10–25. A novelty yarn.

Ratiné is a typical novelty yarn. The effect ply is twisted in a somewhat spiral arrangement around the ground ply; but at intervals a longer loop is

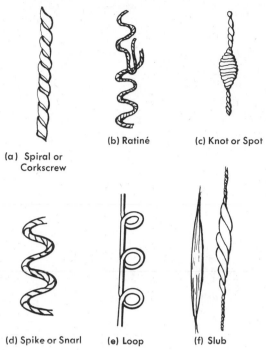

(a) Spiral or Corkscrew   (b) Ratiné   (c) Knot or Spot

(d) Spike or Snarl   (e) Loop   (f) Slub

Fig. 10–26. The fancy or effect ply in several kinds of novelty yarns.

thrown out, kinks back on itself, and is held in place by the binder.

The *spiral or corkscrew* yarn is made by twisting together two plies that differ in size or in twist. These two parts may be delivered to the twister at different rates of speed. (See Figure 10–26(a).)

The knot, spot, nub, knop yarn is made by twisting the effect ply many times in the same place. (See Figure 10–26(c).) Two effect plies of different colors may be used and the knots arranged so the colored spots are alternated along the length of the yarn. A binder is added during the twisting operation.

In the *spike or snarl*, the effect ply form alternating unclosed loops along both sides of the yarn. (See Figure 10–26(d).)

The *loop, curl, or bouclé yarn* has closed loops at regular intervals along the yarn. (See Figure 10–26(e).) These yarns are used in woven or knit fabrics to create a looped-pile that resembles caracul lambskin and is called *astrakhan cloth*. They are used to give textured effects to other coatings and dress fabrics

Slub effects are achieved in two ways. (See Figure 10–26(f).) True slubs are made by varying the

tightness of the twist at regular intervals. Intermittently spun flake or slub effects are made by incorporating soft, thick, elongated tufts of fiber into the yarn at regular intervals. A core or binder is needed in the latter.

Metallic yarns have been used for thousands of years. The older yarns were made of pure metal (lamé) and were heavy, brittle, expensive, and had the disadvantage of tarnishing.

The new metallic yarns are made by laminating a layer of aluminum foil between two layers of plastic film. This laminate is then cut into strips that range from $\frac{1}{120}$ of an inch to $\frac{1}{8}$ of an inch. The sheets of film may be colorless, giving the yarn the natural aluminum color, or the film or adhesive may be colored before the laminating process. The colors are gold, silver, copper, and pastel or "porcelain" colors. (See Figure 10–27.)

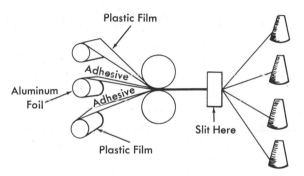

Fig. 10–27. Laminating metal yarn.

The first plastic film was acetate. Polyester film was produced in 1954 and was stronger, more flexible, and washable. In 1957, a metalizing process was developed. Aluminum, vaporized under high pressure was deposited on the polyester film. A very small amount of metal was required and the metalized film could be laminated between two layers of clear film or it could be used with only one other layer of film. Fabric containing a large amount of metal can be embossed. Ironing is a problem when the metallic film yarns are used with cotton, since a temperature high enough to take wrinkles out of the cotton will melt the plastic. The best way to remove wrinkles is to tip the iron on its side and draw the edge of the sole of the iron across the fabric.

11 Special Yarn-Spinning Processes

The long straight continuous nature of filament yarns has limited their use in utility garments and in garments for comfort and warmth. Early efforts to overcome these limitations in the man-made fibers consisted of collecting continuous filaments in large ropes called tow, as they come from the spinneret, then cutting them into staple lengths, baling them, and spinning them into yarn on one of the mechanical spinning systems.

More recent methods have been concerned with:

1. Retaining the continuity of the filament tow strand while the fibers are "stapled" and made into yarn—the direct spun system.
2. Retaining the continuous nature of the fibers while imparting spun-like characteristics—texturizing yarns.

Direct Spun Yarns

The direct spinning systems were developed as a way of by-passing some or all of the conventional system without disrupting the continuity of the strand of filament tow. The tow-to-yarn process and the tow-to-sliver process are examples.

Tow-to-Yarn System

The *Direct Spinner* performs all the operations of stapling (making tow into staple) and spinning. It is a Perlock machine that processes 4,400 denier high-tenacity viscose rayon.

The tow is fed into the machine through leveling

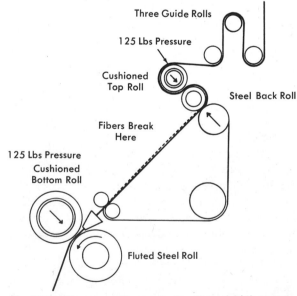

Fig. 11–1. Diagram of direct spinning. Perlock high tow-to-yarn system.

rolls, passes between two nip rolls, across a conveyor belt to a second pair of nip rolls, which travel at a faster rate of speed and create tension that causes the fibers to break at their weakest points. The strand is then drawn out to yarn size, twisted, and wound on a bobbin. (See Figure 11–1.)

Direct spun yarns have a higher degree of strength and uniformity than conventionally spun yarns. They can be distinguished from conventionally spun yarns by "backing" the twist out of a single yarn. The fibers will have a staple length in excess of six inches, whereas conventionally spun yarns have fibers which are usually less than two inches in length.

There is no control over the average staple length and there is not sufficient time after stretching and before winding for the fibers to relax, so that the yarns have high potential shrinkage, 14 per cent in wet-finishing operations. This shrinkage makes it possible to produce fabrics such as those in Figure 11–2. High-shrinkage yarns in the filling are alternated with low-shrinkage yarns. In wet finishing, the low shrinkage yarns are puckered by the contraction of the high-shrinkage, direct spun yarns.

Dense, compact rainwear fabrics can be made by using the direct spun yarns in the filling direction.

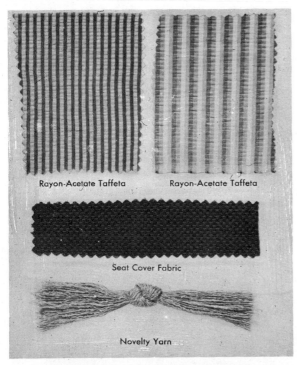

Fig. 11–2. Direct spun yarns and fabrics.

When these shrink, they bring the warp yarns closer together.

Novelty yarns are produced by combining a high-shrinkage ply with a low-shrinkage ply to produce a bouclé effect. (See Figure 11–2.)

The strength of direct spun yarns is best utilized in upholstery fabrics. The disadvantages are expense, lack of crimp, and no way of producing blends.

Tow-to-Top System

The tow-to-top process reduces the tow to staple and forms it into *sliver* on either the Pacific Converter or the Perlock heavy tow machine.

Fig. 11–3. The Pacific Converter. (Courtesy of the Warner & Swasey Company.)

The Pacific Converter,[1] shown in Figures 11–3 and 11–4, was invented in 1939. It is a diagonal-cut stapling machine that changes tow into staple of equal or variable lengths, and forms it into a crimped sliver ready for further drawing, blending, and spinning operations.

The tow enters the machine through a series of leveling rolls which spread the fibers out in a sheet about 14 inches wide.

The Pacific Converter operates like a lawn mower. A helical cutting blade cuts the fiber band in diagonal strips while it is carried along on a

[1] The Greenfield Top and N. Stuart Campbell machines are similar.

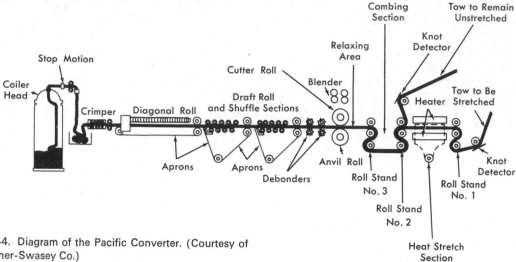

Fig. 11–4. Diagram of the Pacific Converter. (Courtesy of the Warner-Swasey Co.)

conveyer belt, thus preventing disruption of the parallelism of the fibers. The cut fibers are flexed to break open any sections that might have fused together and are drawn lengthwise to make them into a thinner sheet. They are moved by serpentine action between fluted rolls which cause further separation. The thin sheet is then rolled into a continuous sliver and a slight crimp is imparted to the fibers by the crimping unit. The sliver is collected and coiled in a can ready to be taken to a conventional drawing or roving machine.

The spinning of the yarn is done on conventional spinning machinery. Natural fibers are not processed on the Pacific Converter except when wool top is to be added for a blend. Then a blending attachment is used with the converter.

The *Perlock machine* operates on the principle that, when tow is stretched, the fibers will break at their weakest points (random breakage) without disrupting the continuity of the strand. A sheet of tow nine inches wide (180,000 denier or more) enters the machine through leveling rolls and then passes between two sets of nip rolls that apply the breaking tension. Breaker bars between the sets of rolls control the length of the staple. As the tow travels through the breaking zone, tension is applied suddenly and the fibers break in the breaker bar area. This process is then repeated as more tow enters the breaking zone. The fiber strand moves on through another set of rolls into a crimping box and emerges as crimped *sliver*. The rest of the yarn-making process is completed on conventional spinning machinery.

Hi-Bulk Yarns

Bulk is desirable for warmth, texture, and cover. Bulking characteristics result when the curl or crimp of the fibers prevents orderly arrangement and creates air spaces within the yarn.

Thermoplastic fibers can be used to make hi-bulk yarns by processing them on either the Perlock machine or the Pacific Converter if a heat attachment is added. A Perlock heavy tow machine is called a Turbo-Stapler. (See Figure 11–5.) Thermoplastic fibers, in a flat sheet, are heat-stretched as they are passed between the heater plates and are then changed to staple in the breaking zone. This

Fig. 11–5. The Turbo-Stapler. (Courtesy of the Turbo Machine Company.)

gives the fibers high shrinkage properties. Acrylics will shrink 20 per cent or more when they are subsequently relaxed by another heat treatment. The fibers are crimped and a portion of the heat-stretched sliver is sent in louvered cans to a Fiber-Setter. Steam enters the can through the slot openings and relaxes the fiber from the strains of heat-stretching. This shrinks it so that it loses its high-shrinkage properties. It then rejoins the portion that was not heat-relaxed.

The Pacific Converter processes hi-bulk in two different ways. If a heat-stretching attachment is added, part of the tow is passed through the heat-stretching attachment while the remainder is passed above it. The two parts of the tow are combined before entering the cutting zone where it is cut into staple. The yarn at this stage is similar to other yarn, since the bulk has not been developed. Subjecting the stapled tow to high temperature, usually in the dyeing process, causes the heat-stretched fibers to shrink; and as they shorten, they force the rest of the fibers to "buckle" and thus create the bulk. The yarn usually consists of 40 per cent nonrelaxed and 60 per cent heat-relaxed fibers, but other percentages may be used.

In the second method of producing hi-bulk yarns on the Pacific Converter, the tow is purchased as high-shrinkage and low-shrinkage types and blended before it enters the converter. The spun yarn is heat-treated to create the bulk.

Much hi-bulk yarn has gone into the knit apparel trade, especially sweaters. These are labeled as "Hi-Bulk Orlon" or as "Turbo Orlon." Hi-bulk

Fig. 11–6. High-bulk yarn. Left, before steaming. Right, after steaming.

yarns are used also in woven apparel. Figure 11–6 shows a diagram and a photograph of hi-bulk yarns before and after steaming.

Textured Filament Yarns

Textured yarns are those in which the individual filaments are displaced from their natural and relatively closely packed position into various configurations. Man-made filaments have always been made to resemble silk, but they neither feel nor behave like silk. The thermoplastic filaments are superior to silk in resiliency, ability to be heat-set, easy care, and uniformity, but they have certain disadvantages; namely, static build up, poor hand (dead feeling rather than live), poor cover (opacity), and low absorbency. Textured filament yarns are superior to regular filament yarns in that the individual filaments

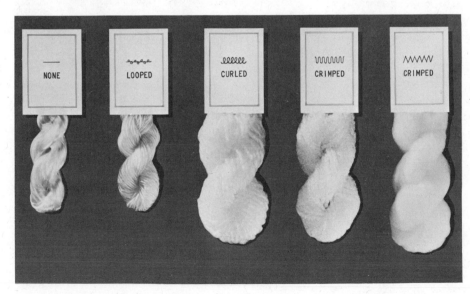

Fig. 11–7. Appearance and bulk of continuous filament textured yarns. (Courtesy of Allied Chemical.)

are no longer in a closely packed parallel arrangement but have loops, curls, coils, or crimps to give bulk, stretch, and surface texture. The textured yarns are more absorbent, since they have more air spaces and do not cling to the skin surface as closely. They should not build up as much static, since there is a direct relationship between absorbency and static build-up. Filaments pill less than spun yarns and in carpets, they do not shed as the spun yarns do.

Textured filament yarns are classified as bulk-type, stretch-type, and textured surface "set" yarns. Figure 11–7 shows yarns with different textured configurations.

Bulk-Type Yarns (No-torque)

Bulk yarns are those in which the filaments have been modified to give greater mass per unit length and are of two types; loop and crimp. (A yarn has torque if when held by one end, the free end tends to rotate.)

Loop-type bulk yarns are made by feeding regular filament yarn over an air jet at a faster rate than it is drawn off by the take-up rolls. The blast of air forces some of the filaments into tiny loops. The rate at which the yarn is fed into the nozzle determines the amount of yarn thrown into loops; the velocity of the air affects the size of the loops.

Volume increase is between 50 and 150 per cent. The yarn maintains its size and bulkiness under tension, since the straight sections of the fiber bear the strain and allow the loops to remain relatively unaffected. The yarns have little or no stretch. This process can be used on any kind of filament, since heat-setting is not necessary. The looped yarn does not look like a novelty yarn when viewed without magnification. Taslan, Skyloft, and Lofted Acetate are some trade names for loop-type yarns. (See Figure 11–8.)

Crimp-type yarns are bulk yarns made by compressing regular filament yarns in a stuffing box, causing the individual filaments to take on a sawtooth crimp. The yarn is then heat-set. The bulked single yarns are usually plied to hold the filaments together and minimize snagging.

The apparent volume increase is approximately 200 to 300 per cent. The yarns have some elasticity, but not enough to be classified as stretch yarns. Registered trade marks are Textralized and Spunized. (See Figure 11–9.)

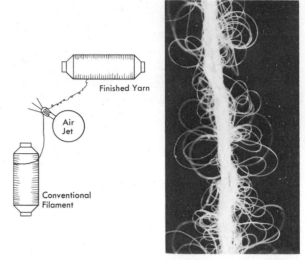

Fig. 11–8. Left, diagram showing the jet air process. Right, a Taslan textured yarn. "Taslan" is Du Pont's registered trademark used to designate textured yarns made in accordance with quality standards set by Du Pont. (Courtesy of the Chemstrand Corporation.)

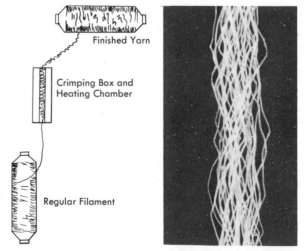

Fig. 11–9. Left, diagram of the "stuffing-box" process. Right, a Textralized yarn used in Ban-lon garments. "Textralized" and "Ban-lon" are trademarks for end-products and continuous filament yarns modified by a process licensed by Joseph Bancroft and Sons. (Courtesy of the Chemstrand Corporation.)

Stretch-Type Yarns (Torque and No-torque)

Stretch yarns have both bulk and stretch. They are used in hosiery, underwear, sweaters, gloves, and swim suits, and they make possible the manufacture of a one-size item that fits several wearers. The retailer needs to stock fewer sizes and can stock

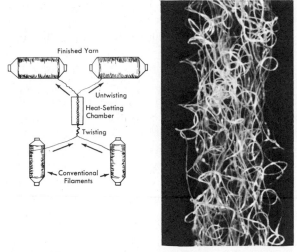

Fig. 11–10. Left, diagram of the conventional stretch process. Right, a Helanca (conventional) yarn. "Helanca" is the registered trademark of Heberlein Patent Corporation. (Courtesy of the Chemstrand Corporation.)

more depth in each size. Stretch yarns are of two types: coil and curl.

Coil-type stretch yarns are made in two ways. (1) The conventional process developed by the Heberlein Co. of Switzerland is based on twisting, heat-setting, and untwisting in separate steps. (2) In the false-twist process, a single yarn is twisted, heat-set, and untwisted very quickly.

The *conventional* or *step-by-step process* inserts twist comparable to crepe twist (75 t.p.i.).[2] Bobbins of twisted yarn are heat-set to give the maximum "memory" of the twisted condition. Yarn is cooled and then twisted again but in the opposite direction so that the finished untwisted yarn will have zero twist. (See Figure 11–10.)

The yarn may be used as singles with alternating S-twist and Z-twist yarns in the fabric or they may be plied by twisting singles of opposite twist together. When the yarn is in the relaxed state, the effect is that of soft staple or spun yarn. The yarns have a bulk increase of 300 per cent. They stretch 300 per cent in heavy denier and 400 to 500 per cent in finer yarn. Helanca is the trade name of the process. Helanca Hi-Test is the yarn with maximum stretch.

The *false-twist coil-type* yarns are made by a continuous process in which the twisting and untwisting is done in a four-to-ten-inch space and takes less than a second. The yarn is led from the supply

[2] Dacron crepes such as "whipped cream" by Klopman Mills.

package to a heating chamber, then to the false-twist spindle, which consists of a rapidly revolving tube with an electrically located guide or hook. The yarn is twisted, heat-set, and untwisted as it travels through the tube. (See Figure 11–12.) The false-twist process can be demonstrated by tying the ends of a string together into a loop, holding the loop over the thumb and forefinger, inserting a pencil between the two strands, and twisting. As the pencil turns, there will be an S-twist on one side of the pencil, and a Z-twist on the other. (See Figure 11–11.) As the pencil is moved up between the fingers, the twist is removed; as the pencil turns, twist is put in.

Variation in the yarn can be obtained by differences in the amount of false twist, differences in the heat-setting temperatures, and differences in the degree of tension on the feed roll. The yarns can be given right or left twist or they can be given alternate right and left twist by reversing the false-twist spindle at controlled time intervals. The yarn can be used as a single, or yarns can be plied by combining singles of right and left twist.

Superloft, Fluflon, Saaba, Helanca SS, and Helanca SW are trade marks for false-twist coil-type

Fig. 11–11. Diagram of the technique for demonstrating false-twist principle.

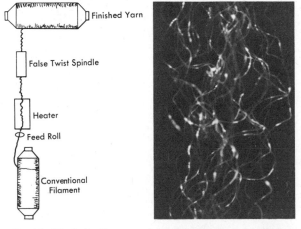

Fig. 11–12. Left, diagram of the false-twist coil-type texturizing process. Right, Fluflon yarn. "Fluflon" is a registered trademark of Marionette Mills Inc. (Courtesy of the Chemstrand Corporation.)

yarns. The Helanca trade mark can be used for both conventional and false-twist yarns if the producer maintains the quality set by the Heberlein Co. One requirement for Helanca yarns is that the yarn must be capable of being extended at least 200 per cent. (See Figure 11–12.)

Knit-de-knit is a no-torque stretch yarn. This was one of the older methods that was not used much until 1965 when it became very popular. A tube of nylon is knit at a rapid speed, heat-set for 20 minutes at 215° F or 30 minutes at 240° F depending on the product, dyed and unraveled, and wound on cones. Crimp size and frequency can be varied by difference in stitch size and tension. Figure 11–13 shows the knit-de-knit crimp.

Fig. 11–13. Diagram showing knit-de-knit crimp.

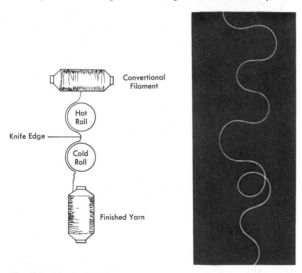

Fig. 11–14. Left, diagram showing curl-type yarn. Right an Agilon yarn. (Courtesy of Deering-Milliken Research Corporation.)

The knitting stitch for the garment must be of a different gauge than that of the knit-de-knit crimp or pin holes will form where the crimp gauge and knit gauge match.

Curl-type stretch yarns are made by drawing heated filaments over a knife-like edge, which flattens the filaments on one side and causes the yarn to curl with an effect similar to that obtained by pulling Christmas ribbon over scissors to curl it. The yarn is then cooled. This process can be used on monofilaments as well as multifilament yarns. The yarn is used primarily for hosiery. Agilon is the trade name of the Deering-Milliken Research Corporation. (See Figure 11–14.)

Textured "Set" Yarns

In 1963, interest swung to texturing yarns for esthetic fabric properties such as hand, appearance, and drapability. These textured yarns are "set" yarns. To "set" the yarn, it is first false-twisted, heat-set, and wound *loosely* on the package just as for regular textured yarn. Then the loosely wound package is heat-set again by steaming. This takes the stretch out of the yarn and stabilizes it with bulk and texture. The yarn has only the stretch that exists in the crimp. The yarn loses most of its torque.

Textured acetate is the largest seller in the market. These fabrics, however, cannot be dyed in the piece without removing most of the crimp and garments must be dry-cleaned to retain their crimp during use. The knits look like Italian silks. They are wrinkle-free and retain their shape and appearance during wear.

Textured polyesters are higher-cost fibers than the acetates but they have the advantage of retaining crimp during use and can be washed as well as dry-cleaned.

12 The Stretch Concept:

Fibers, Yarns, Fabrics

Elastic and stretch materials extend beyond and return to their normal dimensions. The general definition for "stretch" is to extend or draw out and does not imply snap-back. In textiles, when "stretch" is used with "yarn" or "fabric," the meaning is specific as stated in the first sentence.

Apparel made from woven fabric of nonelastic fibers and nonelastic yarns must have sufficient ease (extra fabric) to allow for knees, arms, and the torso to bend and for the arms to move forward and upward. Stretch fabrics make it possible to have close-fitting garments. Apparel made from stretch fabric is more comfortable, since it extends and contracts as needed during body movements.

Elastic materials support and shape the figure. This property is called "holding power." It means that the fabric stretches over the body, drawing in or firming body flesh as the fabric contracts.

Stretch in fabric is obtained in several ways:

1. By using elastic fibers or eleastic yarns
2. By using stretch yarns
3. By using knit constructions
4. By slack mercerization
5. By combining three with one or two

Elastic Fibers: Rubber, Lastrile, Spandex

An elastic fiber or yarn has a high break elongation (more than 200 per cent) and both a high degree and a rapid rate of recovery. Fibers contain hard and soft segments in the polymer chain, the soft segments providing the stretch and the hard segments holding the chain together.

An elastic yarn is essentially the same as an elastic fiber. Filaments from the spinnerets may be used as yarns without further processing, covered with yarns of rigid fibers, or used as a core with staple fibers spun around them.

End-uses where *holding power* and *elasticity* are important are foundation garments, surgical support garments, swim suits, garters, belts, and suspenders. Elastic fibers and yarns are used in other fabrics and apparel where *elasticity* only is desired.

Rubber was the first elastic fiber or yarn to be used. Spandex, the first man-made elastic fiber, was introduced in the late 1950's. Lastrile was developed in the 1960's. In 1967, a new yarn, as yet unnamed, was introduced.

Rubber

Rubber is a manufactured fiber in which the fiber-forming substance is comprised of natural or synthetic rubber.

Federal Trade Commission

Natural rubber is concentrated from the sap of certain trees while synthetic rubber is polymerized from petroleum products. Before 1930, rubber yarn was quite coarse and fabrics made from it were relatively heavy. Yarns were made by cutting sheets of rubber into the desired size. In 1930, a technique for making rubber from liquid latex was developed. In this process, liquid latex is extruded through spinnerets into a coagulating bath, washed, treated, and vulcanized, resulting in single round yarns.

Rubber *must be covered* (see page 112) by other yarns to prevent rupture of the core. It is harmed by high temperature, bleaches, and dry-cleaning solvents. It is nonabsorbent and will not take dyes. It is less expensive than any of the man-made elastic fibers.

Lastrile

Lastrile is a manufactured fiber in which the fiber-forming substance is a co-polymer of acrylonitrile and a diene (such as butadiene) composed of not more than 50%, but at least 10% by weight of acrylonitrile units.

Federal Trade Commission

Lastrile fibers are said to be approximately 50 per cent more expensive than rubber but half as expensive as spandex. Butadiene is a synthetic rubber. Orofil is the trade mark for Rohm and Hass' lastrile. This fiber is white, readily dyeable, has a rectangular cross section, a specific gravity of 1.30, and an elongation of 600 to 670 per cent. Its resistance to bleaches is better than most spandex. One disadvantage is that the fiber takes a "cold-set" if held in an elongated state for 24 hours or more and will not return to its original length.[1]

Spandex

Spandex is a manufactured elastomeric fiber in which the fiber-forming substance is a long chain polymer consisting of at least 85% segmented polyurethane.

Federal Trade Commission

[1] "Textile Fibers and their Properties," Burlington Industries Inc., 1965.

After about ten years of research, Du Pont introduced the first man-made elastic fiber in 1958, calling it Lycra. Two years later U.S. Rubber brought out Vyrene. In the early 1960's, the promotion of nylon stretch yarns (see page 107) in casual and sports wear had aroused much interest and excitement in the "Stretch Concept." Woven stretch fabrics were the "new" development and it was predicted that by 1970 all apparel would be stretch. As is natural with any new development, everyone wanted a "piece of the business." By 1965, eight companies were producing spandex. See the historical chart and list of producers in Appendix B. Four of these companies discontinued production in 1967. The reasons given by the companies were that predicted end-uses did not materialize and that the durable-press concept for apparel affected spandex from the marketing viewpoint. In handling any new development that requires special or different sewing and pressing techniques in apparel production, there is always the time-consuming and costly problem of training workers and changing production patterns. Both stretch and durable-press required new learnings. It seems that the ready-to-wear industry can only cope with one completely new development at a time; and in the late 1960's, durable-press seemed more important than stretch. Stretch fabrics are and always will be important.

Manufacture. Spandex is made by either dry or solvent spinning. Like all man-made fibers, the spinning solution may contain delustering agents, dye receptors, whiteners, and lubricants. Varying proportions of hard and soft segments are used depending on the amount of stretch desired. Fibers are produced as monofilaments or multifilaments and in sizes from fine to coarse. The multifilament yarns differ from other multifilament yarns in that they are held together by positive bridging. (See Fig. 12–1.) A pin inserted in the yarn cannot be pulled through the entire length but will be stopped by these joinings. Companies making multifilaments say the advantage of these yarns is that in sewing fabrics, the machine needle will go between the fine filaments and thus there is no danger of breaking them. Companies making monofilaments say that blunt needles are used to sew elastic fabrics and they push the monofilament to one side so there is no danger of rupturing it.

Fig. 12–1. Photomicrograph of spandex. Left, cross-sectional and longitudinal views of Lycra. Right, cross-sectional and longitudinal views of Vyrene. (Courtesy of E. I. du Pont de Nemours & Company.)

Properties. Spandex has the following properties:

Property	Importance to Consumer
1. Very elastic	1. Foundation garments and support garments can be lighter in weight.
2. Good holding power No. 1 spandex yarn has the same power as No. 1.8 rubber yarn.	
3. Twice as strong as rubber	2. Can be used bare. This reduces the cost by eliminating cost of cover yarns and further reduces fabric weight.
4. Specific gravity is 1.0. (Rubber 1.4.) Spandex is ⅓ lighter in weight.	
5. Can be dyed	

Elasticity and recovery from stretch are the most important properties of spandex. The elasticity is due to the long, flexible molecules that are in a coiled and tangled position when relaxed and straighten when force is applied. They return to the coiled position when stress is removed because of the intermolecular bonds or cross-links that hold the molecular chains in a sort of network.

Spandex has good flex life and can be stretched repeatedly. Numa[2] can be flexed 200,000 times without breaking. Spandex can be made in deniers ranging from 40 to 2,240.

Spandex has better resistance to cosmetic lotions, body oils, and powders than rubber. Chart I compares rubber, spandex, and nylon. Nylon is included to show a comparison of an elastic hard fiber with elastic soft fibers. Chart II is a comparison of spandex from different companies.

CHART I*

Property	Rubber	Spandex	Nylon
Tenacity, g/d	.34	1.2	4.2
Elongation	540%	625%	25%
Dyeability	Poor	Good	Good
Durability	Fair	Excellent	Excellent
Minimum denier	100	20	10

* Albert F. Smith, "Spandex Elastic Fibers," *American Dyestuff Reporter*, **56**:6 (March 15, 1965).

[2] Tad Henke, "Numa—Cyanimid's New Spandex Fiber," *Modern Textile World* **47**:31 (May, 1965).

CHART II*

Property	Glospan	Lycra	Numa	Vyrene
Tenacity	0.7	0.6–0.8	0.6–0.9	
Elongation	600–700%	520–610%	500–600%	700%
Specific gravity	1.2	1.2	1.21	1.2
Absorbency less than	1.0	1.3	1.0	0.3
Effect of heat	Good stability	Yellows degrades at over 300° F. Sticks at over 347° F.	Sticks at 434° F.	Some thermoplasticity above 300° F.
Resistance to bleaches	Discolors slightly	Discolored by hypochlorite bleach	Good	Slightly discolored by chlorine bleach

* "Man-Made Fiber Chart," *Textile World*, 1966.

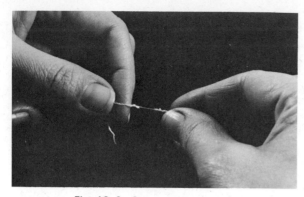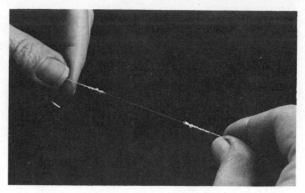

Fig. 12–2. Core-spun spandex. Left, relaxed yarn—cotton fiber removed to show core. Right, extended yarn.

Elastic Yarns

Elastic yarns are the forms in which elastic fibers are knitted, woven, or otherwise fabricated into cloth. (Stretch yarns are made from nonelastic or rigid filaments, which are coiled or curled and heat-set in that configuration.) (See page 107.) Elastic yarns vary in size from very fine to very heavy. Bare,

covered, and core spun elastic yarns are contrasted in the chart below. One new elastic yarn developed by the Deering-Milliken Research Corporation is "a composite yarn comprised of non-elastic staple fibrous material spun helically around a core of a continuous strand of flexible cellular plastic foam with about 60–95 cells per linear inch."[3]

[3] *Textile Industries* **131**:2 (February, 1967).

KINDS OF ELASTIC YARNS

	Bare (*lastrile, spandex*)	*Covered* (*rubber, spandex, lastrile*)	*Core-Spun* (*spandex*) (*See Figure 12–2.*)
Description	No cover (eliminates high cost of adding ply cover)	Covered with spiral (helical) wrap of filament or spun yarn Single wrap or double wrap	Spandex core surrounded by staple sheath. Sheath is a roving or drafted staple
How spun	Fiber chemical spinning	Stretched Spandex or rubber fiber (yarn) plied with cotton, nylon, etc., yarn for single wrap Second spindle on same *twister* twists second cotton, nylon, etc., ply in opposite direction	Plied on twister Spandex core stretched 3.5 to 4.5 times its original length and roving (yarn) wrapped helically around it Roving (yarn) 12 to 26 t.p.i.
Comments	Sheer Very thin garments are possible Supple, comfort, no grin-through	More absorbent than bare yarns. Makes color possible with rubber. Controls extensibility	Fabrics have same appearance as those made without stretch Caused change in labeling law Lack of progress due to industry and consumer emphasis on durable-press Has potential for comfort clothing
Uses	Foundation garments Sock tops	Foundation garments Swim suits	Woven and knitted outerwear of all weights from lawn to duck

Stretch Fabrics

Stretch fabrics extend when needed and contract when stress is removed. Stretch in fabric is desirable for the following reasons:

1. Garments are more comfortable.
2. Garments can be form-fitting or close-fitting and still permit the body to move naturally.
3. Garments can have less precise or less accurate fit. This means that fewer sizes need to be stocked by the retailer and that fewer alterations are needed.
4. Elastic stretch garments provide support to the body.

Why Fabrics Stretch

In order for fabrics to stretch, one or more of the fabric components must stretch. Fabrics stretch, therefore, if they contain elastic fibers or yarns (see page 109: stretch yarns, page 107), if they are knit constructions, or if they are finished to induce yarn crimp in the fabric.

In the chart below, a comparison is made of elastic fibers, stretch yarns, and stretch by fabric finish. Knitting is not included.

Kinds of Stretch

Two kinds of stretch are *power* stretch and *comfort* stretch. The terms are self-explanatory and are compared in the table on page 114.

Stretch garments may have *warp* stretch, *filling* stretch, or *two-way* stretch. Warp stretch is used primarily in tensioned pants or as insets in foundation garments. Two-way stretch is present in knit-fabrics and filling stretch is in most other apparel.

Comfort Stretch Apparel

Comfort stretch garments look no different than garments made from rigid fabrics. However, the problems involved in producing satisfactory stretch fabrics and garments were many. Answers to the following questions had to be found.

1. How much stretch is necessary for comfort?
2. How much growth is acceptable in stretch garments?
3. How much smaller should garments be cut?

	Stretch Fiber	*Stretch Yarn*	*Fabric Stretch*
Stretch component	Rubber, spandex, lastrile	Textured yarns (a) crimp type (b) coil type (c) crinkle type	Slack mercerization
Reasons for stretch	Molecular chains lie in coiled configuration. When force is applied, they straighten out.	Thermoplastic filaments are (1) coiled (2) curled or (3) knitted, heat-set. When force is applied, they straighten out.	Fabrics in a relaxed condition are treated with sodium hydroxide. Process causes yarns to crimp. When force is applied, the yarns straighten out.
Appearance in fabric or raveled from fabric	Relaxed Extended	Relaxed Extended	Relaxed Extended
Identification	TEPIA requires fiber content labeling. Look for spandex, lastrile, rubber.	Look for trade name, thermoplastic, filaments: nylon, polyester, olefin.	100% cellulosic fiber, usually cotton.
Per cent stretch*	500–700%, depends on molecular weight of soft segments.	300–500%; *a* and *b* depend on amount of disfiguration of yarn; *c* depends on gauge of knit stitch.	Depends on amount of yarn crimp developed.

* In fabrics, especially woven stretch fabrics, the potential stretch of fiber or yarn is not attainable because of the nature of fabric construction.

	Power Stretch	*Comfort Stretch*
Definition	Garments have "holding power."	Garments give with the body.
Advantages	Support muscles and body organs. Reduce apparent body size. Firm and shape body flesh	
End-uses	Special-purpose garments	Not special-purpose
Stretch level	10%–200% extensibility	15%–50% extensibility
Fibers and yarns	Spandex, lastrile, rubber	Textured nylon or polyester Core-spun spandex Regular cellulosic yarns
Yarn size	Fairly heavy	Fine to medium

4. Are different cutting and sewing techniques necessary?
5. How should stretch be marketed and promoted?

To answer the first question, comprehensive studies of the body were made. Average increases, when the knees and elbows were bent, when the arms were extended, and when the body was seated are shown on page 115. The amount of stretch in stretch fabric should be comparable to the percentage of elongation of the body. The amount of stretch in fabric is called the *stretch level*.

In making stretch fabrics, the manufacturer must consider recovery of the fabric as well as the stretch level. Stretch fabrics do not return completely or immediately to their original size after being stretched. This failure to recover is called *growth*. In determining the amount of acceptable growth, most researchers agree that some distortion can be tolerated and the amount depends on the end-use. This probably means that growth is a necessary evil at present and until someone discovers a means of preventing it, both manufacturers and consumers need to recognize growth limits.

In producing apparel from stretch fabrics, garment producers had to develop new basic patterns with less ease and straighter curves. They had to modify their cutting procedure, since stretch fabric must be completely relaxed (laid out flat for 12 to 24 hours) and it was discovered that fewer plies had to be cut at once. New sewing techniques were necessary to ensure that seams and hems would stretch.

In promoting and marketing stretch apparel, attempts are made to inform the consumer about the product. In some of the early comfort stretch garments, the fabrics used had too little stretch, too much growth, and were too light in weight to be satisfactory to the consumer. Fiber, yarn, and fabric producers are working on standards for stretch fabrics.

The standards thus far are not uniform but some fiber producers restrict the use of their trade names to those fabric or garment producers that meet the standards for stretch set by the fiber producer. For example, Du Pont uses a symbol resembling a tic-tac-toe for garments made from Lycra, core-spun Lycra, and their producer-textured yarns. Chemstrand has an Action Wear Label for approved apparel made from their stretch yarn. (See Figure 12–3.)

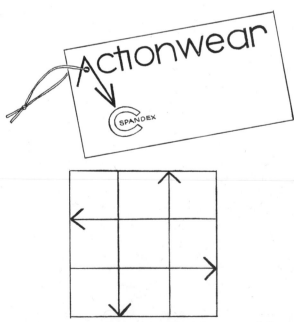

Fig. 12–3. Labels for stretch garments that meet minimum standards set by fiber procedures.

AMOUNT OF INCREASE FROM STRAIGHT TO BENT POSITION

	Back–Across Shoulders	Elbow– Horizontal	Elbow– Vertical	Knee– Horizontal	Knee– Vertical	Seat– Horizontal
Elongation, in per cent	13–16	15–22	35–40	12–14	35–45	4–6

The Good Housekeeping Institute tests products to see if they perform as advertised. For stretch apparel to be shown in their magazine, the standards shown in the table below must be met.

In addition to the stretch requirements, fabrics and garments must meet acceptable standards for color fastness, shrinkage, and construction.

Several years ago a Commercial Standard CS234–61, Stretch Socks, and Anklets was established to provide for definite stretch allowances for stretch socks for infants, children, misses, boys, and women. The socks should be smaller than the smallest size on the label and when stretched, should be larger than the largest size indicated. For example, in men's socks, size 10–11½, the foot should stretch to 14½ inches and unstretched should be 9½ inches or shorter.

In comfort stretch apparel, it is important to select garments that fit properly. Fabrics should not be extended except when the body moves.

There is a tendency to use infant's and children's stretch garments too long. Outgrown clothing, particularly socks and sleepers, may be harmful to the child.

Good Housekeeping STANDARDS FOR STRETCH

	Stretch Level	Maximum Growth Allowed After 1 Hr.	Maximum Permanent Set After 5 Laundry or Dry Cleanings
		(in per cent)	
Tailored wear	20	2.5	1.5
Casual wear	25	5.0	2.0
Active sportswear	30–35	6.0 weaves 7.5 knits	2.0

13 Fabric Construction

A fabric is a structure made from fibers, from yarns, or from nonfibrous substances (plastics, rubber, metal). Of these, the fabrics made from yarns are more complex and usually more expensive than those made directly from fibers or nonfibrous materials. Fabrics are usually pliable, and they can be made into garments, fitted over furniture frames, or used in the home and industry for specific purposes.

The fabric construction chart on pages 118–119 gives an overview of the many methods used to make fabrics. There are many variations on each method.

Felt and Nonwoven or Web Textiles

Felt refers to fabrics made from wool, whereas nonwoven applies to fabrics made from other fibers. In both the felting and the nonwoven processes, the fabric is made *directly* from the fiber.

Felt

True felt is a mat or web of wool or part wool fibers held together by the interlocking of the scales of the wool fibers. Felting is one of the oldest methods of making fabrics. Primitive peoples made felt by washing wool fleece, spreading it out while still wet, and beating it until it had matted and shrunk together in fabric-like form. In the modern factory, layers of fiber webs are built up until the desired thickness is attained and then heat, soap, and vibration are used to mat the fibers together and to shrink or full the cloth. Finishing processes for felt resemble those for woven fabrics.

Felt has many industrial and some clothing uses. It is used industrially for padding, soundproofing, insulation, filtering, polishing, and wicking. Felt is not used for fitted clothing because it lacks the flexibility and elasticity of fabrics made from yarns. Felt has wide use in such things as hats, house slippers, and clothing decorations and pennants. Because felt does not fray, it needs no seam finish. Colored felt letters or decorations on white sport sweaters or other garments often fade in washing, and should be removed or the garments should be sent to a dry cleaner who knows how to treat them.

Nonwoven Fabrics

Nonwoven fabrics are fibrous sheets made by bonding and/or interlocking textile fibers by mechanical, chemical, thermal, or solvent means or by a combination of these processes. The term "nonwoven" applies to needled fabrics (needle-punched felts, etc.), to bonded web or paper-like fabrics (see Figure 13–1), to battings, and to waddings.

Needled Fabrics. Needle punching consists of passing a properly prepared web over a needle loom as many times as is necessary to produce the desired strength and texture. A needle loom consists of a board with barbed needles protruding two or three inches from the base. As the needle pushes through the web, the barbs catch a few fibers causing them to interlock mechanically. (See Figure 13–2.) Needled fabrics are finished by pressing, steaming, calendering, dyeing, and embossing as woven fabrics are finished.

Fig. 13–1. Paper dresses.

FIBERWOVEN PROCESS

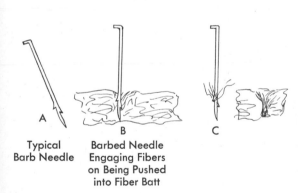

A — Typical Barb Needle

B — Barbed Needle Engaging Fibers on Being Pushed into Fiber Batt

C

FIBERWOVEN PROCESS
Action of Cooperating Pair of Barbed Needles

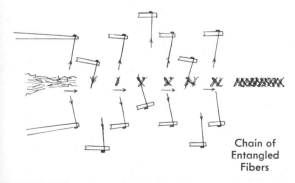

Chain of Entangled Fibers

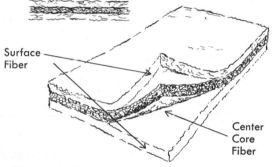

Surface Fiber

Center Core Fiber

Fig. 13–2. Fiberwoven Process.

Top, left, diagram shows pointed needle with two barbs. If such a needle is pushed into an assemblage of fibers, a number of them, 10 to 30 fibers, will be caught by the barbs.

Bottom, left, the motion of a needle pair and the synchronized sequence of the Fiberwoven Process are represented in the drawing. Action is as follows:

1. The top needle picks up and carries fiber downward and withdraws.
2. The fiber batt advances a small increment.
3. The lower needle picks up the fiber, passes it through the fiber loops, previously positioned by the partner needle, and withdraws.
4. The fiber batt again advances a small increment.

The sequence repeats itself, and continuous chain of interlooped, entangled fibers results from the action of two needles.

Top, right, because of simplicity of the process, the Fiberwoven technique lends itself to the fabrication of layered structures; fiber denier, fiber type, and fiber quality can differ in the layers. Fiber to give a desirable hand—for example, wool or acrylic—can be placed on the outer surface of a center section of fiber chosen for durability and shrink properties. The figure illustrates such a blanket construction. (Courtesy of The Chatham Mfg. Co.)

FABRIC CONSTRUCTION

Method	Simple Description	Diagram or Photograph of Typical Fabric	Major Characteristics	Reference
Felting	Wool fibers are carded (and combed), laid down in a thick batt, sprayed with water, and run through hot agitating plates, which cause the fibers to become entangled and matted together.	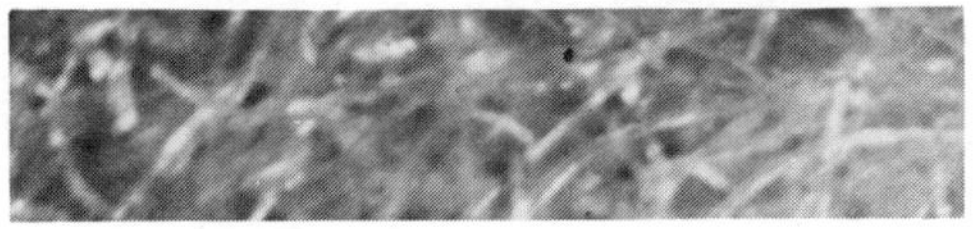 Fig. 13–3. Felt.	No grain. Does not fray or ravel. Absorbs sound.	Page 116
Nonwoven (Fiber web)	Fibrous sheets are produced by bonding and/ or interlocking textile fibers by mechanical, chemical, thermal, or solvent means or combinations of these processes.	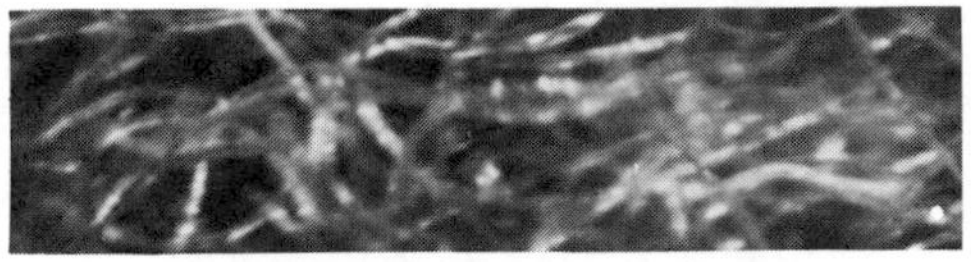 Fig. 13–4. Nonwoven fabric.	Cheaper than woven or knitted fabrics. Widely used for disposable items. May have grain but usually do not.	Page 117
Films	Solution is extruded through narrow slits into warm air or cast onto a revolving drum. Moulding powders may be pressed between hot rolls.	 Fig. 13–5. Films.	Waterproof. Low cost. Resistant to soil. Finished to look like leather, lace, woven fabrics, etc.	Page 123
Lace	Yarns are knotted, interlaced, interlooped, or twisted to form open-work fabrics, usually with some figures.	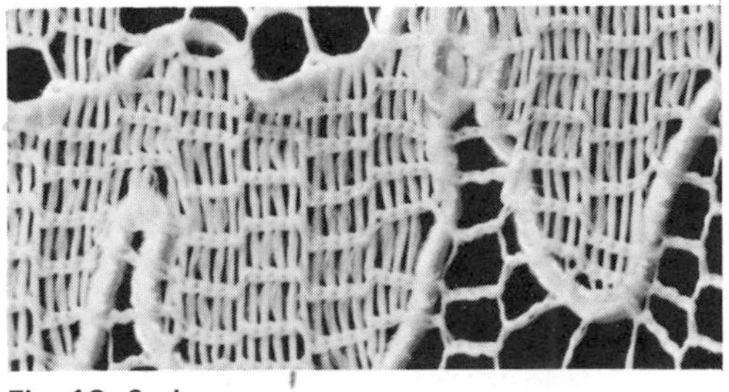 Fig. 13–6. Lace.	Decorative edgings, insertion, or entire fabric.	(Not included in text)
Braid	Yarns are interlaced lengthwise and diagonally.	 Fig. 13–7. Braid.	Narrow fabrics used for trimming. Circular braids good for shoe laces.	(Not included in text)

Technique	Description	Figure	Notes	Reference
Weaving	Two or more sets of yarns are interlaced *at right angles* to each other.	 Fig. 13–8. Plain-weave woven fabric.	Fabrics have grain. Sides can be raveled. Fabrics may ravel. Many different interlacing patterns give interest to fabrics. Most widely used fabric construction technique.	Chapters 15, 16, 17
Knitting	One or more yarns are formed into a series of interlocking loops.	 Fig. 13–9. Knitted.	Faster technique than weaving. Very pliable and stretchy. Wrinkle-resistant.	Chapter 14
Knit-sew (Malimo)	A layer of warp yarns is placed over a layer of filling yarns (not interlaced) and the two layers are locked together with a chain stitch.	 Fig. 13–10. Malimo, knit-sew.	Inexpensive construction technique because of speed of process.	Chapter 21
Multi-component	Components (fabrics, foams, films) are held together by quilting (machine stitched), adhesive or foam-flame bonding, embossing, or other techniques.	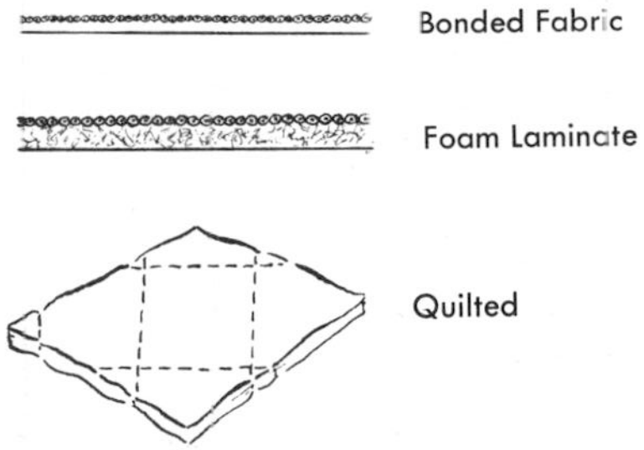 Bonded Fabric / Foam Laminate / Quilted — Fig. 13–11. Multicomponent.	Lightweight fabrics can be used for outer wear. Lower cost than double-woven or knitted cloth. Lining and face as one shortens garment production time and therefore the cost. Warmth without weight.	Page 176
Tufting	Yarns carried by needles are forced through an already made fabric and formed into cut or uncut loops.	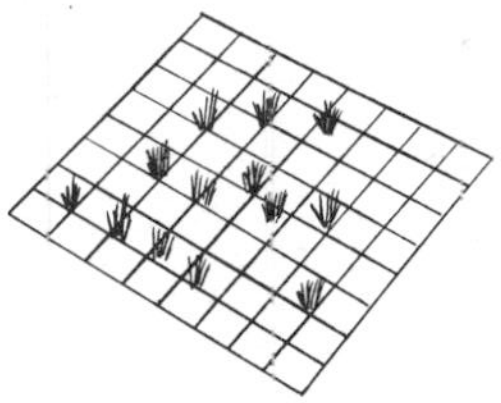 Fig. 13–12. Tufted.	Cheaper than woven pile fabrics because of speed of production.	Page 165

This process has been used for over a century to make thick felts of coarse fiber and hair for carpet underlays, saddle pads, and the like. In the past few years, attractive blankets and carpeting have been made by needle punching. In the Fiberwoven[1] blanket, 100 per cent Acrilan acrylic fiber or blends of acrylic and other fibers have been used. Fiber denier, fiber type, and fiber quality may differ. Blankets may be lofty or compact.

Indoor-outdoor carpeting using olefin fibers is being used rather extensively for putting greens, poolsides, or patios and porches. The construction process makes this carpeting inexpensive, and the fiber content makes it impervious to moisture.

Corfam, a Du Pont product similar to leather in appearance, has a needle-punched base covered by a woven fabric and an outer surface of vinyl.[2]

The Arachne and Maliwatt systems can be used without stitching threads to make webs. In these processes, a closed needle penetrates the web. The hook opens, grabs some fibers, and as it is lifted, it draws these fibers back as a yarn-like structure, which is chain-stitched through the web.[3]

Locktuft,[4] a primary carpet backing designed especially for carpet tufting, is a needled nonwoven of Marvess olefin fibers.

Bonded-Web or Paper-like Fabrics. In these fabrics, one or more layers of fibers are sealed together by use of solvents, heat, or bonding substances. They compete with both paper and fabrics made from yarns. They have a more cloth-like appearance, higher wet strength, better drape, and less tendency to lint than paper. They are widely used in disposable items: disposable diapers and rainwear are a convenience in travel; disposable sanitary and medical goods often cost less than laundering the original article; disposable wash cloths and damp napkins eliminate lint, which might float around inside a space capsule and be inhaled by astronauts.

Bond-web fabrics are available in many weights and textures for use as interfacings where they are

[1] Registered trade name of Fiberwoven Corp., Elkin, North Carolina.

[2] "New Methods of Fabric Forming On the Move," *Modern Textiles Magazine* **47**:7 (July, 1966).

[3] W. J. Kennedy, "Needle Punching, State of the Art," *Modern Textiles Magazine* **47**:7 (July, 1966).

[4] Heywood V. Simpson, "Locktuft, A New Concept in Backing Materials," *Modern Textiles Magazine* **46**:12 (December, 1965).

Fig. 13–13. Wonder-under (Pellon) spun-bonded nonwoven used in the hem of a skirt.

more economical to cut since they have no grain. Some may be used as bonding agents between fabric layers to give body and smoothness in the bands of collars and cuffs of men's dress shirts and to eliminate hand or machine hemming in dresses and skirts. (See Figure 13–13.) Some of the bonded-web fabrics that will withstand several washings are used as place mats, towels, and draperies.

Any kind of fiber can be used in nonwovens. The choice depends on the end-use, cost, processing characteristics, and properties of the fiber. Reused and reprocessed fibers as well as new fibers of various lengths are used. Cotton, rayon, and acetate require the use of a binder to hold them together. They tend to make heavier, denser fabrics than other fibers. Nylon and polyester are more expensive, but they are heat-sensitive and can be self-bonding. Continuous filaments have recently been introduced in nonwovens. A fiber web called Reemay[5] is a spun-bonded polyester. (See Figure 13–14.) This product is made by depositing the filaments from the spinnerets in random fashion on a moving belt and then heat-setting in this position.

Bonded-web fiber fabrics also vary in the web formation, the bonding technique used, and the curing or drying process.

Fiber webs are made in two ways—oriented webs and random webs. Oriented webs are made on conventional carding equipment. The web comes from the card onto the conveyor apron. Several webs may be superimposed to obtain the desired thickness. The fibers can all go in the same direction (lengthwise) or some webs may be laid with the fibers at

[5] Trade name.

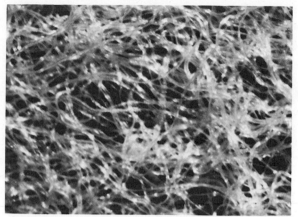

Fig. 13–14. A spun-bonded polyester fiber web called *Reemay*.

right angles to the fibers in other webs. In the latter case, the fabric will have strength both lengthwise and crosswise, while in the former case, the strength will be lengthwise. Random webs are made on special machines, which operate by suspending the fibers in a rapidly moving airstream and carefully depositing them on a collecting screen. These webs have equal strength and elasticity in all directions.

Solvent bonding is done by applying suitable solvent to gelatinize the fibers which are then bonded together by pressure. This makes a stiff fabric. Heat setting of thermoplastic fibers is done by passing the web through heated rollers. Du Pont has developed synthetic fibrous particles that they call "fibrids." These fibrids are $\frac{1}{16}$ to $\frac{1}{32}$ of an inch long and have twig-like projections, which hold the fibers in the web in place until they are fused together by heat. The name Textryl has been given to interfacing fabric made in this way. The fabric is usually tough and durable.

Printing a bonding substance on the web in the form of crosswise stripes, bars, or diamonds forms a discontinuous bonded web. These nonwovens have good drape and a fabric-like hand, but often have poor strength properties.

Padding is done by running the web through an impregnating bath and then through a padder to remove excess bonding emulsion to form a continuous bonded web. This technique is used primarily on thin or moderately thick webs. Flexibility of the fabric depends on the bonding agent used. An alternative method is one in which the

COMPARISON OF PROPERTIES OF DIFFERENT BATTINGS

Fiber	Density	Resiliency	Resistance to Shifting	Care	Cost
Cotton	1.48	Poor	Poor	Washable but slow drying	Inexpensive fibers not long enough for spinning can be used
Cotton sprayed with resins Cotton Flote (trade name)	1.48	Much better than regular cotton	Improved		More expensive than regular but less cotton can be used
Wool	1.30	Good	Poor	Dry cleaning is best	Expensive. Reused wool can be used but is not as lofty
Down	Lightweight	Excellent	Poor	Dry-cleanable	Most expensive
Acetate	1.30	Fair	Poor	Washable Dries quicker than cotton	Low cost
Polyester	1.30–1.38	Good	Good—can be spot-welded	Quick drying Washable	Expensive, but less than wool
Acrylics	1.18	Good	Good—can be spot-welded	Quick drying	Fairly expensive
Nylon	1.14	Fair	Good—can be spot-welded	Quick-drying	Expensive
Beta Fiberglas	2.56	Good		Quick drying	

web does not enter the bath but passes between rollers with the lower roller dipping into the bath and depositing the binder to give a loftier fabric.

Over 200 products are used as bonding agents, ranging from starch, glue, and casein to thermoplastic and thermosetting resins.

Batting, Wadding, and Fiberfill. These are not fabrics, but they are important components in apparel for snow suits, ski jackets, quilted garments of all sorts, and in household textiles for quilts, comforts, paddings for furniture, and in mattresses and mattress pads.

Batting is made from new fiber, wadding is made from waste fiber, and fiberfill is the name given to a man-made staple made especially for these end-uses. Carded fibers are laid down to form the desired thickness and are often covered with a sheet of nonwoven fabric. The table on page 121 presents a comparison of batts made of different fibers. This comparison is helpful in the selection of comforters, quilted robes, and quilted jackets.

The importance of *density* is that, for a unit volume, the fabric will be heavy or light. Today people want lightweight fabrics, especially for outer garments. *Resiliency* is important because fabrics that maintain their loft incorporate more air space. When fibers stay crushed, the fabric becomes thinner and more compact. *Resistance to shifting* is important in maintaining uniformity of thickness in the fabric. For instance, down comforters need to be shaken often because the filling tends to shift to the outer edges. The thermoplastic fiber batts can be run through a needle-punch machine in which hot needles melt parts of the fibers that they touch, causing them to fuse together to form a more stable batt. The thicker the batt, the warmer the fabric regardless of fiber content. In apparel, there is a limit to the thickness, however, because too much bulk restricts movement and is a limiting factor in styling.

Leather—Films—Foams— Poromeric Materials

These materials may not be textiles, but they can have a fabric-like hand and drape and are used as textiles. In fact, the use of films, film-coated fabrics, and the development of new fabrics is increasing rapidly. The end-uses are many and varied. Leather, a natural product, is included because many of the man-made films are finished to resemble leather.

Leather

Leather is a product manufactured from skins and hides of animals, reptiles, fish, and birds. It is an organic substance derived from living animals and, therefore, varies greatly in uniformity. The hides and skins vary in size, thickness, uniformity, and grain, and often are marred by scratches, brands, and so on. Animals are not raised for their hides, but for meat and fiber. Leather is a relatively unimportant by-product. Since the value of the hide is only 5 per cent of the value of the animal, an increase in the demand for leather would not lead to an increase in the number of animals raised.

Hides go through many processes in becoming leather:

1. In the packing plant, the skin is removed (flayed) and dropped down a chute to a hide cellar and allowed to cool. Hides are covered with salt on the flesh side to prevent putrefaction. They are piled into packs and allowed to cure for 30 days at 50–60°. These are green, salted hides.

   In the past few years pig skin has become a fairly plentiful raw material for leather because of the popularity of packaged bacon rather than slab bacon. Some leather firms supply flaying machines to packing plants to be sure of obtaining a supply of well-flayed hides.
2. Hides are cleaned by removing hair, epidermis, and flesh and opening up the pores.
3. Hides are tanned. Tanning comes from the Latin *tannare* meaning oak bark. Tannin is extracted from the bark of various trees. In the early days, tanners maintained their own bark sheds where the bark was stacked, cured, and seasoned. Today the tanners buy a tanning liquor.

Vegetable tanning, the most expensive process, takes from several days to six months and produces leather that has excellent abrasion resistance, is tan in color, and has the characteristic leather smell. *Chrome tanning* is a one-bath process producing leather that is soft, pliable, and grayish in color. *Oil tanning* produces chamois.

Many other processes are necessary to improve the strength and appearance of the leather: bleaching, stuffing (adding hot oils to make it pliable and

Fig. 13–15. Cross-sectional drawing of a strip of leather showing variations in density of fiber.

resistant to cracking), dyeing, staking (flexing and stretching), boarding (developing the grain), buffing and snuffing (skinning off a thin layer or passing over an emery board), and embossing if the grain surface is poor.

Notice in Figure 13–15 that the leather varies in density of fibers from the flesh side to the skin side. Leathers are often split to make them more pliable and more economical. The first layer is called Top Grain and it has the typical animal grain, takes the best finish, and wears well. Splits must be embossed to have a leather-like grain. Suedes are napped on the flesh side. (See Figure 13–16.)

Fig. 13–16. Split leather.

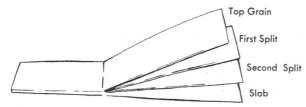

In making articles from leather, much skill is needed in cutting garments, gloves, shoe uppers, and handbags, from the relatively small skins. It is said that the French derived the reputation of making the best kid gloves not because the leather was better, but because they knew how to cut more gloves from one skin.

Films

Man-made products have the advantage of being sold by the yard in various widths and gauges (thicknesses) and they are uniform throughout. The cost varies with the "fabric" but the end product is usually cheaper when constructed from a man-made product than from leather.

Films are plain or expanded, The plain film is firm, dense, and of uniform consistency, while the expanded film is spongy, softer, and plumper due to tiny air cells made by a blowing agent incorporated into the vinyl compound. The expanded films arc less resistant to abrasion than the plain films. They are leather-like in appearance and used wherever leather is used.

Plastic "fabrics" are of two types: unsupported film and supported film. The supportcd film has a woven, bonded, or knit fabric backing. It is more expensive than the unsupported film, but it has greater sewability and is less apt to tear along seams or where it is tacked to furniture.

Most films or film coatings are made of resins of polyvinylchloride, polyurethane, or polyethylene. Mylar film, a polyester, has been used as a coating on leather shoes to give luster and greatly increased durability.

Plastic films are made by the following methods:

1. Extruding a solution through long, very narrow slits into warm air or a liquid-hardening bath. This is very similar to the methods of making fibers.
2. Casting a solution on a large revolving drum where it dries and is then stripped off.
3. Calendering or pressing a moulding powder between hot rolls which exert tons of pressure and transform it into film.

If the film is applied to fabric, the film is formed on the calender. The fabric is inserted and the hot plastic is pressed on it.

Plastic films and coated fabrics can be embossed to resemble any woven fabric or any grain leather. Overall flocking is done to give a suede look.

The advantages of plastics are ease of maintenance, resistance to soil, good wrinkle recovery, high durability, waterproofness, and low cost. They can vary in thickness from very thin, transparent film to heavy leatherette.

The disadvantages that still require research are the unpleasant odor present in some of the vinyl

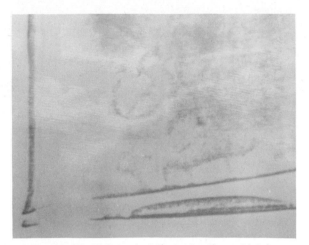

Fig. 13–17. Yellow vinyl film stained by red fabric.

plastics, stiffening at low temperatures, shrinking at high temperature, and cracking as a result of volatilization of the plasticizer.

Vinyl plastics are color scavengers. The plasticizing agents used often dissolve color from textiles in contact with the vinyl, causing stains on the vinyl that are almost impossible to remove. When this happens, there is a tendency to blame the other textile rather than the vinyl. (See Figure 13–17.)

Vinyl films tend to stiffen and shrink when dry-cleaned. Unless the label on a garment says "dry cleanable," the best method of cleaning is washing, using a washing formula suited to the fabric with which the vinyl is combined.

Almost everything one can think of is made or can be made of plastic. No other material is as good for waterproof apparel, hospital bed coverings, and baby pants. For leather-like apparel, handbags, shoes, luggage, etc., plastics make the "leather look" available to all. In home furnishing, the end-uses are many—place mats, table linens, upholstery, slipcovers, draperies, and so on.

Foams

Foams are used in fabric laminates, as carpet backings, in mattresses, cushions, pillows, and pads of various sorts. Most foams are rubber or polyurethane.

Polyurethane is a type of plastic material prepared by the reaction of di-isocyanate with a compound containing two or more hydroxyl groups in the presence of a suitable catalyst. By the selection of chemicals, polyurethane foams may be obtained with a wide range of physical properties—very stiff and brittle to soft and rubbery. The size of the cells or holes can also be controlled. Chemicals and foaming agents are mixed together thoroughly. After the foam is formed, it is cut into blocks 200 to 300 yards long and strips of the desired thickness are cut from these blocks.

Chemback[6] is a foam product especially designed as a primary backing for carpet tufting. This product consists of a nylon scrim encapsulated in a polyurethane foam, which is approximately $\frac{1}{8}$ inch thick. It is said to have better processability than jute or duck. Because it does not ravel, the carpet requires no edge finish and the performance is improved.

Poromeric Material

Poromeric material[7] is a generic term coined from the two major characteristics of the material—a porous structure and polymeric composition. Poromeric material is defined as a microporous and permeable cariaceous sheet material comprising a urethane polymer material reinforced with polyester. Corfam is a registered trade mark of the Du Pont Company.

Corfam is not considered a plastic, an imitation leather, or a leather replacement, but rather a new basic material. The first end-uses were shoe uppers and gaskets, packings, and beltings for industrial equipment. Other uses are handbags, luggage, upholstery, and home furnishings and ready-to-wear clothing. It is interesting to note that the end-uses are the same as for leather.

Corfam is like leather in its fibrous structure. In cross section, the Corfam changes from a loosely arranged fibrous structure at the base to a rather tightly built structure at the top. Corfam is easy to clean, resistant to scuffing, holds its shape, and can be finished to resemble leather or in ways leather can never be finished.

[6] Durwood B. Finn, "Chemstrand's New Carpet Tufting Medium," *Modern Textiles Magazine* **46**:12 (December, 1965).

[7] "53 Questions about 'Corfam' Poromeric Material," Product Information Service, Public Relations Department, E. I. du Pont de Nemours & Co.

14 *Knitting*

Knitting is a process by which needles are used to form one or more yarns into a series of interlocking loops. A knitting machine can make fabric two to five times faster than a loom. It is possible to "fashion" garments by knitting so that they need not be cut and sewn as are woven fabrics. Knitted fabrics are in unprecedented demand today. The increased opportunity for travel, interest in sports, informal relaxed living, and the emphasis on easy-care fabrics have been responsible for the expansion of knits in the fields of outerwear apparel, home furnishing, and automotive textiles. New technological developments in knitting machinery, new ideas in knit construction, and new finishes have contributed to the use of knits in high-fashion garments. Laminating knits to polyurethane foams has made it possible to use thin, and in some cases unevenly knit, jerseys for outerwear. In bonded fabrics, acetate filament tricot is widely used as a backing fabric.

Knits are very desirable because they do not wrinkle easily, shape to the body without binding, are elastic, porous, yet light and warm. Some of the advantages are also disadvantages. The unstable shape of the knit stitch results in loss of shape and size in many cotton, rayon and wool garments.

(See page 195.) They are warm in still air, but must be covered by a wind-repellent layer to keep the body warm on a windy day. On a warm humid day, knits may be too warm because they tend to fit snugly and keep warm air close to the body.

Knits may be made of any fiber. Spun yarns used in knitting are of rather low twist and they must be made very uniform or thick-and-thin places will occur in the fabric. Synthetic filaments are uniform and easy to knit.

Methods of Knitting

The two methods of knitting are warp knitting and filling knitting. These terms are borrowed from the weaving techniques and refer to the way the loops are formed.

Warp Knits

Warp knits are machine knit from one or more *sets* of yarns placed side by side, as warp yarns are placed for weaving. Warp knitting started about 1775 with the invention of the tricot machine (or

COMPARISON OF WARP AND FILLING (WEFT) KNITTING

	Warp Knit	*Filling Knit*

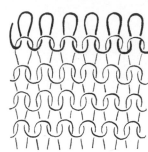

Fig. 14–1. Comparison of warp and filling knit. Left, warp knit. Right, filling knit.

	Warp Knit	*Filling Knit*
Definition	Warp yarns are wound on a warp beam and looped together by a long bar of needles	One yarn is carried back and forth or around in a circle, interlooping in the process
Machines used	Warp knitting machine: spring board needle* Rachel: latch needles Lace knitting machine: latch needles Galleon crocheting machine: latch needles (Always done on a machine)	Flat knitting machine: latch needles Circular knitting machine: latch needle Links and links: flat and circular Flat knitting machine: spring board needles* (Can be a hand process)
Identification	Tricot—lengthwise wales on right side; chevron courses crosswise on wrong side	Jersey or stockinette—lengthwise wales on the right side; wavy courses on the wrong side
Common fabrics	Laces, nets, foundation garment fabrics, carpets, tricot, glove fabric	Full-fashioned goods (hose, sweaters), wool jersey, stockinette, fur-like fabrics, double knits
Properties	Garments must be cut and sewed Not much lengthwise stretch Run-resistant	Garment parts can be knitted to shape or fabrics can be cut and sewed Stretch both crosswise and lengthwise Will run or ladder

* Makes finer fabric than the latch needle.

warp loom) by Crane of England. This machine knitted fabrics 16 inches wide and was primarily used for silk stocking cloths. The development of this machine was unique in that there is no evidence that warp knitting was practiced as a hand technique. In 1880, Kayser established a warp knitting mill in the United States. Figure 14–2 shows a modern tricot knitting machine.

Warp knitting provides the fastest means of cloth fabrication. The loops are all made simultaneously by interlooping individual warp yarn into the loops of adjacent warp yarns. The loops form vertical wales on the right side and horizontal wales or courses on the wrong side. (See Figure 14–3.)

A modern warp knitting machine can knit fabric up to 168 inches wide and can produce 1,000 courses and 4,700,000 stitches per minute. Fabrics

are usually knit flat and are made on several different types of machines. Those most commonly used are *tricot machines* employing a single needle bar with two guide bars for plain fabrics (Figure 14–3), or two to four guide bars for patterned fabrics, and *Raschel machines* having one or two needle bars and up to 30 guide bars. The guide bars lay the threads around the needles. (See Figure 14–4.)

Tricot. Tricot (pronounced *tree'-ko*) comes from the French word *tricoter* meaning "to knit" and is the name given to warp knit fabrics, which are widely used in underwear, dress and blouse fabrics, and backing fabrics. Tricot knits are stronger, less sheer, and have less stretch than filling knits. They are either run- or snag-resistant or runproof.

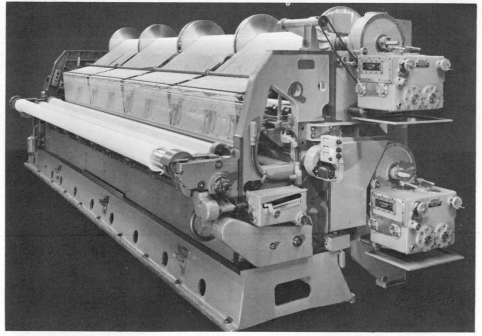

Fig. 14–2. The two-bar high-speed knitting machine for tricot fabrics. (Courtesy of Textile Machine Works.)

Fig. 14–3. Two-bar tricot fabric. Top, face side. Bottom reverse side.

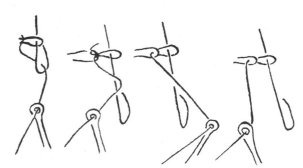

Fig. 14–4. Diagram showing motion of the guide bars in knitting.

Tricot jersey fabrics are knit 160 inches wide and cut into 40-inch widths for sale as yard goods or for use in ready-to-wear garments. Most tricot fabrics are made of filament yarns. Nylon jersey is heat-set to stabilize the fabric. If it is off grain, it *cannot* be straightened because the yarns have been set and will not assume another position when they are wet. Acetate tricot is used for the backing in most bonded fabrics and has wide use in textured knit for dresses. (See page 107.) Arnel tricot is less expensive than nylon and is employed in the same end-uses.

New developments in tricot have been made by stitch construction, by yarn construction, by finishing, or by combining these. Effects achieved by stitch construction are: (1) all-over clipped dots made by a third set of yarns put in as a lappet design as is done in woven fabric, (2) a tucked fabric, (3) a ruffled tuck, and (4) simulated pleats in which some of the fabric is sheer and some heavier.

Effects achieved by yarn construction have been mainly in improving the feel or hand of the tricot. Using trilobal nylon (Antron) has given a warmer, more silk-like hand. Textured nylon and acetate (Taslan, Ban-Lon) yarns are used to give a better hand. Crepeset nylon makes sheer tricot. This fabric looks like chiffon or georgette and has the appearance of true crepe without the high potential shrinkage due to high-twist crepe yarns. Novelty yarns can be used for special effects, but at present they are little used.

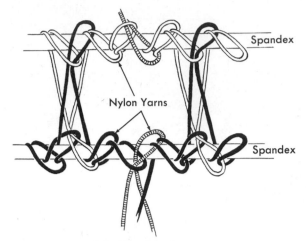

Fig. 14–5. Drawing of a power net.

Fig. 14–7. Plain jersey stitch. Left, face side. Right, reverse side.

Effects achieved by finish include cross-dyeing for striped designs or leather effects, embossing for surface design, or opaqueness and burnt-out designs. The most important embossed finish is Schreinering, a process in which round yarns are flattened to give more cover—to make fabrics look and feel flatter. Other embossed finishes give a leather-like look to fabrics. Burnt-out designs are made by

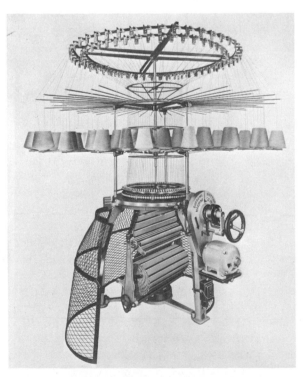

Fig. 14–6. Circular knitting frame for filling knits. (Courtesy of the Singer Company, Knitting Machinery Division.)

knitting in an extra yarn of unlike fiber content and printing an acid or caustic on the fabric to remove sections of the extra yarn.

Raschel knitting machines combine high productivity with extensive pattern designs. They knit anything from very fragile hair nets, tulles, and veilings to coarse rugs and fur cloths. Elastic fabrics for foundation garments are made on Raschel machines. Figure 14–5 shows a drawing of power net.

Filling Knits

Filling knits are made with one or more yarns carried back and forth to make a flat fabric or are knit completely around to make a circular fabric. Filling knits are made both by hand and by machine. An experienced hand knitter might produce 60 stitches per minute while a machine can produce as many as 3 million stitches per minute.[1] (Figure 14–6 shows a circular knitting machine.) Filling knit fabrics are usually plain knit or rib knit. A third stitch, or purl stitch, is used to make some imitations of hand-knit garments for children and in combination with plain or rib knit in patterned fabrics.

Plain knit is one in which the loops are drawn to one side of the fabric. These knits have a definite right and wrong side with wales on the face side and courses on the reverse side, as shown in Figure 14–7. The face of the fabric has more sheen than the back. Plain knit is also called jersey stitch, named for the turtle neck sweaters originally worn by sailors from the Isle of Jersey. This stitch is

[1] *Knitting*, Underwear Institute, p. 6.

Fig. 14–8. Plain 1 and 1 rib stitch.

Fig. 14–9. Purl stitch.

used in knitting sweaters, yard goods in dress and suiting weights, sport shirts, and hosiery.

Rib knit is made by drawing every other stitch to the face of the fabric. These fabrics look the same on the right and wrong side. Rib knits have more elasticity crosswise than plain knits and are, therefore, used as wrist and neck bands on sweaters. Rib stitch is also used in making bulky knits. It is seldom used in yard goods for outerwear garments but is used in underwear fabrics. Rib stitch fabrics do not curl at the edges as do plain knits. (See Figure 14–8.)

Purl stitch knits look the same on the face and the reverse side and look like the reverse side of jersey. This stitch is used to make sweaters, especially for infants and children, and booties. The fashion for bulky knits has increased the use of this stitch. Purl knits have excellent stretch both crosswise and lengthwise. (See Figure 14–9.)

Tuck stitches are made by collecting more than one loop on a needle and then drawing a single loop through them. Lacy or mesh fabrics are formed in this manner.

Jersey, which is made in tubular form, is seldom pressed at the factory with the wales parallel to the creases of the fabric, and the courses or crosswise ridges straight with the cut edge. Before cutting a garment from jersey, put a basting line or a line of pins along a wale to mark straight lengthwise grain, refold the cloth, and then straighten by steam pressing or wetting the fabric. A very small needle should be used in stitching.

Double knits are made with two sets of needles,

creating firm fabrics that have more body and durability than single knits. They have the good characteristics of regular knits, and in addition are less apt to "sit out," require no skirt lining, and can be hung on hangers. They are easier to handle in cutting and sewing since they do not curl on the edges.

The most commonly used stitch is the double piqué stitch, which gives a subtle diamond-effect surface. The double piqué stitch is made on specially designed circular equipment and is most attractive in finer gauges. Other double-knit constructions are ribs, single piqué, and bourrelet. Bourrelet is a ripple stitch or corded fabric made by raising loops across the surface.

Hosiery

A study of hosiery includes fiber content, yarns, knitting stitches, and styles. The table on page 130 shows the many variables to consider in buying hose.

When nylon was introduced in 1939, women were wearing silk hosiery—2 or 3 thread for dress and 6 or 8 thread for service. Silk hosiery was comfortable but not very durable. Hose were expensive and most women bought a new pair every week. Nylon was much superior to silk and it is estimated that today the American woman buys approximately 14 pairs per year.[2]

[2] Jules LaBarthe, *Textiles: Origins to Usage.* New York: The Macmillan Co., 1964, p. 300.

HOSIERY

	Women's	*Men's*
Fibers	Sheer—nylon, olefin Textured hose—nylon, acrylic, wool, cotton Support and surgical—spandex	Wool, cotton, nylon (staple and filament), polyester, acrylic, olefin, spandex, and blends of the above
Yarns	Monofilament, multifilament, stretch yarns, bulk-type yarns, covered spandex	Multifilament, stretch yarns, bulk-type yarns, covered spandex, core-spun spandex, ply yarns, mercerized cotton ply yarns (lisle)
Knitting stitches	Plain knit, mesh knit, fancies	Plain knit, rib-knit, pile knit, double knit
Styles	Seamless, full-fashioned, anklets, knee-length, panti-hose, tights, support, surgical	Seamless, short, hi-rise, support, surgical

The first nylons were 30 denier. Denier refers to the size of the yarn. It is the weight in grams of 5,000 meters of yarn. The higher the denier number, the coarser the yarn. Finer yarns are used to make gossamer sheer hose. A 70-denier stocking is extremely heavy and durable while a 7-denier one is sheer and fragile. The nylon yarns used in hose are 7, 10, 12, and 15 denier monofilaments and 15, 20, 30, 40, 50, and 70 multifilaments. (See Figure 14–10.) In 1955, double- and triple-loop hose were introduced. These are not ply yarns but rather two or more monofilaments knitted as one. For example, a 7-denier and a 10-denier yarn are knitted together on the same needle. The advantage of the multiple loop is that when snagged, only one of the yarns may break.

The *size of the knit stitch* is referred to as *gauge*. It means the number of needles in 1.5 inches of the needle bar across the machine. The size of the stitch in circular knits is given as the number of needles in the circle of the knitting machine. The range is from 260 to 474. In 1949, the Federal Trade Commission permitted the use of the word "gauge" in descriptions of circular knit hose provided that the word is accompanied by the term "circular knit," "seamless," or "no-seam." Gauges range from 42 to 90. A 474 needle circular knit is comparable to 60 gauge. The higher the gauge number, the smaller the knit stitch. High-gauge gives more elasticity to the stocking and increases its resistance to snagging. The most commonly used gauge is 51.

Hosiery is made of filling knit because it is very elastic, can be shaped, and can be made more sheer than warp knit. Two types of hose are full-fashioned and circular. Full-fashioned hose are knit flat and are shaped by dropping stitches (fashion marks) so that the hose is shaped like a leg.

Circular knit hose are also called seamless or no-seam. To give shape to these hose, the ankle area is knit with smaller needles. It is possible to decrease the size of the knit stitch 100 times from the top to the ankle without changing the number of the stitches.

To make hose cling better and to present fewer sizes, bicomponent nylon fibers (Figure 14–11) and stretch yarns (page 106) are used.

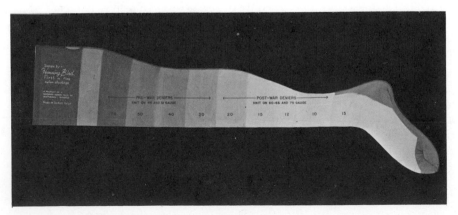

Fig. 14–10. Full-fashioned hose showing different denier sizes. Coarser to finer; 70 to 10 denier.

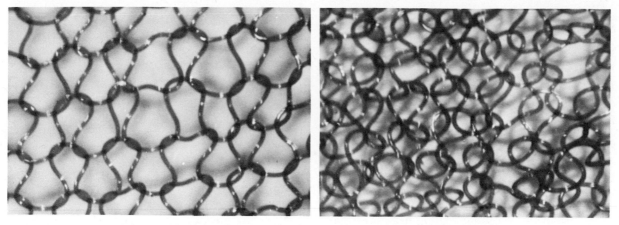

Fig. 14–11. Nylon Cantrece. Left, Stretched as when worn. Right, relaxed.

Support vs. Surgical Hose

Support hose are worn by both men and women to prevent muscle fatigue; surgical hose are prescribed by doctors for leg disorders such as varicose veins.

Support hose are worn by people who are on their feet a lot and by pregnant women. They are available in 100 per cent stretch nylon-covered spandex. They are made in a wide range of colors, full-fashioned or seamless, regular knit or mesh and in several deniers ranging from 30 to 70. Support hose for both men and women look like regular hose.

Surgical hose are much heavier than support hose. They may be purchased singly or in pairs, with or without heels and toes, in various lengths—ankle, knee, or over the knee. It is very important to choose the correct size so the support from the stocking is applied correctly. The yarns use rubber or spandex for the elastic core and cotton and nylon are used as wraps. Surgical hose are quite expensive and can be made to order.

15 Weaving and the Loom

Weaving is the process of interlacing two or more sets of yarns at right angles to each other, one set running in the lengthwise direction called the warp and the other inserted crosswise and called the filling. An *interlacing* is defined as the point at which a yarn changes its position from the surface of a fabric to the underside of a fabric or vice versa, by passing over or under one or more yarns. The number of interlacings is important in fabric properties such as firmness, flexibility, resilience, slippage, and raveling. There are fewer interlacings in a fabric when a yarn from one direction *floats*

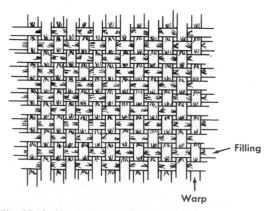

Fig. 15–1. Yarn arrangement in weaving.

over two or more yarns from the other direction. A fabric can be identified as a woven fabric if yarns can be raveled from *adjacent* sides. (See Figure 15–1.)

Loom Developments

Weaving is done on a machine called a *loom*. The primitive loom consisted of a frame that held the warp yarns in position as the filling yarn was woven over and under the warp by the fingers. A wooden bar was the first device used to separate the warp. The harness of heddles, which was developed later, is still a major part of the modern loom. A *heddle* is a wire with a hole in the center through which a warp yarn is threaded. A *harness* is a frame to hold a number of heddles. The simplest plain weave can be made on a loom with only two harnesses. (See Figure 15–2.) By the use of additional harnesses, more intricate patterns can be woven. Notice in the diagram that, as one harness is raised, the yarns form a *shed* through which the filling yarn can be inserted. A beam at one end of the loom holds the

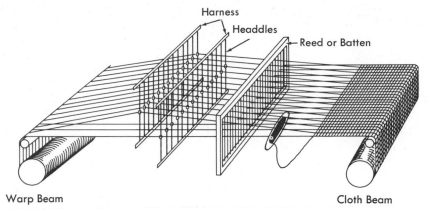

Fig. 15–2. Simplified diagram of a two-harness loom.

warp yarn and the woven cloth is wound on a beam at the other end of the loom. A shuttle carries the filling yarn through the shed and a *reed* or *batten* beats the filling yarn back into the cloth to make the weave firm.

Before the warp creel-beam is placed on the loom, the yarns are unwound from it and run through a starch bath to seal the fiber ends and strengthen the yarns so that they will withstand the stresses of weaving. This treatment is called *slashing*. (See Figure 15–3.)

All the weaves that are known today could be made by the primitive weaver. The loom has changed in many ways, but the basic principles and operations are still the same. Weaving consists of these three steps:

1. Shedding: the raising of one or more harnesses to separate the warp yarns and form a shed.
2. Picking: passing the shuttle through the shed to insert the filling.
3. Beating up: the reed pushes the filling yarn back into place in the cloth.

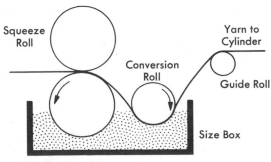

Fig. 15–3. Slashing warp yarns to prepare them for weaving.

Loom developments over the years have centered around (1) devices to separate the warp for more intricate weave patterns, (2) speedier methods of inserting the filling, and (3) the use of computers and electronic monitoring systems.

The number of harnesses that a loom can operate efficiently is limited. When the repeat of the woven pattern requires more than six harnesses, an attachment is added to the loom to control the raising and lowering of the warp yarns. For small-figure patterns requiring not more than 25 interlacing patterns, a dobby-head attachment is used. (See page 151.) The weave pattern is controlled by a chain of wooden bars with steel pegs, or punched paper patterns or, more recently, punched plastic tape. Large-figured weaves are made on a Jacquard loom, which was invented in France in 1805. It was one of the first *automated* looms, since each warp was controlled individually by punch cards. (See page 153.) Other attachments used on the loom are the swivel attachment for dotted swiss, the box loom for weaving yarns of different size, color, etc., the doup attachment for leno weave, and the lappet attachment for extra-yarn woven figures.

In the simple loom, a "flying" shuttle is "batted" across through the shed of warp yarns by a picker-stick at the sides of the loom. The speed with which it can be sent back and forth is limited—usually less than 200 picks per minute. (Pick is another name for filling yarns.) Manufacturers have long sought a way to replace the shuttle and increase the speed of weaving. Three different types of shuttleless looms have been developed. All the new shuttleless looms give higher weaving speeds and reduction in noise level in the factories—a factor of great importance to the workers.

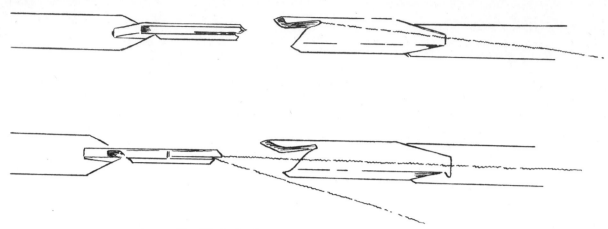

Fig. 15–4. Carrier arms of rapier-type shuttleless loom.

The *rapier-type* loom weaves (primarily) spun yarns at 200 to 250 p.p.m (picks per minute.)[1,2] It has two metal arms about the size of a small pen knife called carriers or "dummy shuttles"; one on the right side and the other on the left side of the loom. A measuring mechanism on the right side of the loom measures and cuts the correct length of filling yarn to be drawn into the shed by the carriers. The two carriers enter the warp shed at the same time and meet in the center. The left-side carrier takes the yarn from the right-side carrier and pulls it across to the left side of the loom. After each insertion, the filling threads are cut near the edge and protruding ends tucked back into the cloth to reinforce the edge. Figure 15–4 shows the carrier arms.

The *water-jet loom* was developed in Europe. The looms are compact and take up less room than the conventional loom. They can operate at speeds of 440 p.p.m.[3] Hydrophobic yarns such as nylon filament are more suitable than hydrophilic yarns such as cotton, which require a special drying device. Water-soluble sizings such as the starch usually used on cotton yarns would be washed away. The filling yarn comes from a stationary package at the side of the loom, goes to a measuring drum which controls the length of each pick, then continues through a guide to a water nozzle where a jet of water carries the filling through the shed. After the yarn is beaten back, it is cut off at both sides of the cloth. If thermoplastic fibers are used in the yarns, they are cut by electronically heated wires. Water is

removed by a slanted warp line or by a special suction device. Very little tension can be applied to the filling and for this reason, weaving of stretch fabrics is not yet possible. Also, box looms for weaving colored yarns are not practical. Figure 15–5 shows a water-jet loom.

Fig. 15–5. A water-jet loom. (Courtesy of Bowlin Associates, Inc.)

The *air-jet loom* or pneumatic method was developed in Sweden by a textile engineer who got the idea while sailing. He noticed the short regular puffs that came from the exhaust of a diesel motor.[4] His first loom used a bicycle pump to furnish the compressed air. The first loom was sold in 1955, and by 1960 there were 100 in use. The filling is premeasured and guided through a nozzle, where a blast of air sends it across. The loom can operate at 320 p.p.m.

---

[1] "Draper's New Shuttleless Loom," *Modern Textiles Magazine* **40**:22 (January, 1959). *Ibid.*, **43** (September 1962); *ibid.*, **33** (November, 1952).

[2] J. B. Goldberg, "Shuttleless Looms," *Modern Textiles Magazine* **47**:54 (June, 1966).

[3] Picks per minute.

[4] "He Invented a Shuttleless Loom," *Modern Textiles Magazine* **41**:28 (September, 1960).

Computers and electronic devices now play an important part in weaving and also other areas of textile manufacture. Computers have been used to develop design tables for setting up weaves of "maximum weavability" for properties such as tightness and compactness in wind-repellent fabrics, ticking, etc., of any fiber content. The computer plays a part in textile designing. It can be programmed to prepare a paper from which punched cards can be made to control the operation of the loom. The computer does not replace the designer but releases him from some of the more technical aspects of designing. The computer is also used to control temperature and pressure in dyeing and bleaching.

Electronic tools play an important part in quality control. Photofeelers, for example, can sense the amount of yarn on the bobbin and signal for a bobbin transfer. *Cloth straighteners* are photoelectric devices attached to the tenter frame to keep the crosswise yarns at right angles to the lengthwise yarns as the fabric is dried and thus eliminate the "off-grain" fabrics that create such a problem to the home sewer as well as to the garment manufacturer.

Similarities of Woven Fabrics

The width of the loom determines the width of the fabric. Hand-woven fabrics are usually 27 to 36 inches wide. Before the 1950's, machine-woven cottons were traditionally 36 inches wide. However, wider fabrics are more economical to weave and the garment cutter can lay out patterns to better advantage. The new looms weave cotton 45 inches wide. Wool fabrics are 54 to 60 inches wide and silk-type fabrics are 40 to 45 inches wide.

The arrangement of warp and filling yarns is always at *right angles* to one another, a yarn position that gives the cloth more firmness and rigidity than the yarn arrangement in knits, braids, and laces. Yarns can be raveled from adjacent sides of the fabric. Yarn position also indicates the grain of the fabric.

The warp and filling yarns differ because of the performance requirements of the loom and because they serve different functions in the fabric. The warp yarns (ends) usually have more twist and are made of better quality fibers because they must resist the high tensions put on them by the loom and because of the abrasion of the shuttle as it flies back and forth. It is very important to recognize the warp and filling directions of a fabric because:

1. The fabric is stronger in the warp direction and it usually stretches least in this direction.
2. Fabrics are often stiffer in the warp direction because the warp yarns have more twist. Therefore, the warp and the filling drape differently.
3. The fabric will shrink more in the warp direction. The picture of the bias slip in Figure 15–6 shows the difference between warp and filling shrinkage.

It is difficult to recognize a difference in the warp and filling directions of plain woven fabrics, but a trained eye can see the difference. Except for the first method given here, no one method fits all fabrics. Some of the methods given will be easier to understand as fabrics are studied so reference should be made to the list on page 136.

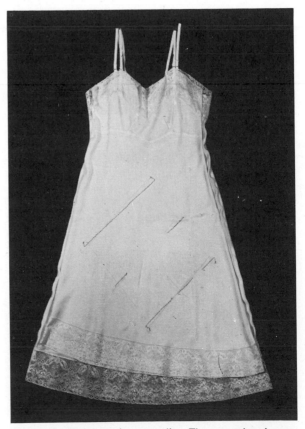

Fig. 15–6. Shrinkage in crepe slips. The warp shrank more than the filling.

1. The selvage always runs in the warp direction (lengthwise) of the fabric.
2. Most fabrics stretch less in the warp direction.
3. Warp yarns usually appear to be straighter in the fabric. This is the result of tension on the yarns during weaving.
4. Warp yarns are usually the regular yarns, while filling yarns may be decorative or functional yarns. (Regular yarns are the ordinary weaving yarns of medium size and medium twist and of uniform construction. Example: the yarns in a percale fabric.)
5. Many fabrics have certain characteristics that indicate the warp and filling direction. For example: poplin always has a filling rib, satin always has warp floats, and flat crepe has crepe yarns in the filling and low-twist yarns in the warp.

All woven fabrics have grain and selvages. *Grain* is a term used in sewing to indicate the warp and filling yarns of the fabric. *Lengthwise grain* is any position along a warp yarn and *crosswise grain* is any position along a filling yarn. *True bias* is the diagonal of a square and *garment bias* is any position on the cloth between true bias and either lengthwise or crosswise grain. Figure 15–7 shows why a garment bias edge will ravel more than any of the others.

A *selvage* (selvedge) is the self-edge of a fabric formed by the filling yarn when it turns to go back across the fabric. The conventional loom makes the same kind of selvage on both sides of the fabric but

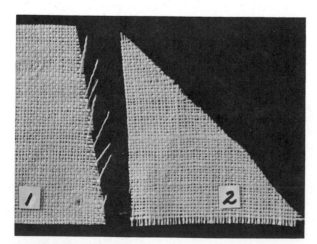

Fig. 15–7. Grain position of cut edges. (1) Garment bias. (2) True bias.

the new shuttleless looms have different selvages because the filling yarn is cut and the cut ends are tucked back in by a special leno shedding mechanism. In some fabrics stronger yarns or a basket weave arrangement are used.

Plain selvages are similar to the rest of the fabric. They do not shrink and can be used for seam edges in garment construction. *Tape selvages* are made of larger and/or ply yarns to give strength. They are wider than the plain selvage and may be of basket weave for flatness. An example is the selvage on sheets. *Split selvages* are used when narrow items such as towels are made by weaving two or more side by side and cutting them apart after weaving. The cut edges are finished by a machine chain stitch or a hem. *Fused selvages* are the heat-sealed edges of ribbon or tricot yard goods made from wide fabric and cut into narrower widths.

Differences in Woven Fabrics

Woven fabrics differ from one another in the pattern of interlacing—identified by weave names, such as plain, twill, satin—the thread count, and the balance. Specific woven fabrics within one weave group differ because of the fiber content, yarn structure, and the fabric finish.

Thread or cloth count is the number of warp and filling per square inch of gray goods (fabric as it comes from the loom). This may be changed by shrinkage during dyeing and finishing. Thread count is written with the warp number first, for example, 80 × 76; or it may be written as the total of the two, as 156. (Thread count should not be confused with yarn count or number, which is a measure of yarn size. See the discussion on page 98.)

Thread count is an indication of the quality of the fabric—the higher the count, the better the quality for any one fabric—and can be used in judging raveling, shrinkage, and durability. Higher count also means less potential shrinkage and less raveling of seam edges.

Thread count is sometimes printed on the selvage of percale and on the labels of bed sheets. Mail-order houses frequently give the thread count since the customer must judge the quality from printed information rather than from the fabric itself.

A standard method of making a thread count may

Fig. 15–8. Thread counter. (Courtesy of the Alfred Suter Company.)

be found in the American Standards for Testing Materials (A.S.T.M.). The count is made with a thread counting instrument. (See Figure 15–8.) It is possible to use a "hand" method by which the area is measured by a ruler and counted by sight or yarns raveled off and counted.

Percale fabrics have, in the past, had a standard thread count of 80 × 80 and were called 80-Square fabrics. In February, 1960, the *Women's Wear Daily* announced that, due to cost factors, a 78 × 78 fabric would now be the basic print cloth used. (Print cloth is the percale fabric as it comes from the loom before any finishing has been done.)

Balance is the *ratio* of the warp yarns to filling yarns in a fabric. A well-balanced fabric has approximately one warp yarn for every filling yarn, or a ratio of 1:1. Examples of typical unbalanced fabrics are cotton broadcloth with a thread count of 144 × 76 and a ratio of about 2:1 and nylon satin with a thread count of 210 × 80 and a ratio of about 3:1.

Balance is helpful in recognizing and naming fabrics and in distinguishing the warp direction of a fabric. Balance is *not always* related to quality. Balance plus thread count is helpful in predicting slippage. If the count is low, there seems to be more slippage in unbalanced fabrics than there is in balanced fabrics.

16 The Three Basic Weaves

The three basic weaves—plain, twill, and satin—can be made on the simple loom without the use of any attachment.

Plain Weave

Plain weave is the simplest of the three basic weaves that can be made on a simple loom. It is formed by yarns at right angles passing alternately over and under each other. Each warp yarn interlaces with each filling yarn to form the maximum number of interlacings. Plain weave requires only a two-harness loom and is the least expensive weave to produce. It is described as a 1/1 weave; one harness up and one harness down when the weaving shed is formed. Figures 16–1, 16–2, and 16–3 show the pattern of interlacing.

Fig. 16–2. Checkerboard design of plain weave.

Fig. 16–3. Plain weave fabric.

Fig. 16–1. Cross-sectional view of plain weave.

Characteristics

Plain weave fabrics have no right and wrong side unless they are printed or given a surface finish. Their plain, uninteresting surface serves as a good background for printed designs, for embossing, and for puckered and glazed finishes. Because there are many interlacings per square inch, plain weave fabrics tend to wrinkle more, ravel less, and be less absorbent than other weaves. Interesting effects can be achieved by use of different fiber contents, novelty or textured yarns, yarns of different sizes, high- or low-twist yarns, filament or staple yarns, and different finishes.

Balance in plain weave fabrics is helpful in recognizing and naming fabrics and in distinguishing the warp direction of the fabric. The plain weave fabrics in this section are organized as shown in the following chart.

PLAIN WEAVE FABRICS

Balanced Fabrics	Unbalanced Fabrics	Variations
Sheers	Sheers*	Basket
Low count		
High count		
Medium weight	Medium weight	
Converted		
Yarn-dyed		
Suiting weight	Suiting weight	
Heavy fabrics†		

* Not discussed in the text.
† Seldom made.

Plain Weave Balanced Fabrics

Plain weave balanced fabrics have a wider range of end-uses than fabrics of any other weave and are, therefore, the largest group of woven fabrics. They can be made in any weight from very sheer to very heavy.

Sheer Fabrics. Sheer fabrics are very thin, lightweight fabrics that are transparent or semitransparent because of very few yarns or very fine yarns. They are used for glass curtains, which give privacy but let in light, for summerweight shirts, blouses, and dresses, and for lingerie. Garments made of sheer fabrics may require shorter wash cycles and lower ironing temperatures to prevent scorching. Because they dry faster, they may need to be re-dampened during ironing. Small hems and en-

closed seams are used to enhance the daintiness of the fabric and to prevent pulling out during use and care.

Low-count sheers are characterized by open spaces between the yarns. They are made of carded yarns similar in size to the yarns used in the medium-weight fabrics. (See the charts that follow.) They are neither strong nor durable, are seldom printed, and differ in the way they are finished.

LOW-COUNT SHEERS

Fabric	Range in Thread Count	Yarn Size Warp	Filling
Cheesecloth (or tobacco cloth)	10 × 12 to 48 × 44	28s*	39s
Crinoline	Same as above	30s	42s

* The "s" after the number means that the yarn is a single thread. If a ply yarn is used in the fabric, it is indicated by writing the number as 38/2 or 44/2, etc.

Cheesecloth has a very soft texture and may be natural color, bleached, or dyed. It is used for interlinings, flag buntings, and sign cloths. Cheesecloth of very low count is used for covering tobacco plants that must be grown in the shade, and is called tobacco cloth.

Crinoline is a cheesecloth that has been stiffened with sizes, glue, or resins. It is usually black or white and is seldom color fast. Some have a nonwoven material pressed on the back to make them more comfortable to wear.

High-count sheers are characterized by transparency due to fineness of yarns. The cotton sheers —lawn, organdy, and batiste—are finished from the same gray goods (lawn gray goods). They differ from one another in the way they are finished. The better qualities are made of combed yarns.

MEDIUM- TO HIGH-COUNT SHEERS

Fabric	Typical Thread Count	Yarn Size Warp	Filling
Lawn	88 × 80	70s	100s
Organdy	Similar to lawn	Similar to lawn	
Batiste	Similar to lawn	Similar to lawn	

Organdy is the sheerest cotton cloth made. Its sheerness and crispness are the result of an acid finish. (See page 189.) Because of its stiffness, it wrinkles badly and is not suitable for handkerchiefs or baby clothes. Lawn has a starched or resin finish and is often printed. Batiste is the softest of the three. It is highly mercerized and is often used in whites or pastels. Batistes of polyester/cotton blends have good wrinkle recovery so are suitable for wash-and-wear end-uses. Batiste of 100 per cent polyester is not as soft and opaque as the blend fabric and is often an unbalanced fabric.

Tissue ginghams and chambray are similar to lawn but are yarn-dyed.

Filament yarn sheers are often designated by the fiber content; for example, polyester sheer or nylon sheer, or they may be called by the name of the cotton fabric they resemble; for example, silk organdy. *Ninon* is a filament sheer widely used for curtains. *Georgette* and *chiffon* are made with crepe yarns, the latter being smoother and more lustrous.

Voile is a sheer made with special high-twist or twist-on-twist yarns. (See page 99.) Voile was originally a cotton or wool fabric, but it may be found on the market in other fiber contents now.

Mediumweight Fabrics. The largest group of plain weave fabrics are of medium weight, as a mediumweight fabric has many more uses than either a lightweight or a heavyweight fabric. These fabrics have medium-sized yarns, a medium thread count, carded or combed yarns, and may be finished in different ways or woven from dyed yarns.

CONVERTED (FINISHED) FABRICS*

Fabrics	Range in Thread Count	Yarn Size Warp	Filling
Percale, carded (muslin, plissé, calico, chintz, etc.)	80 × 80 to 44 × 48	30s	42s
Combed cottons	96 × 80	40s	50s

* Other fabrics such as pigment taffeta, challis, and dress linen are given in the glossary.

The carded yarn fabrics in this group are converted from a gray goods cloth called *print cloth*. Most print cloth is made into *percale*, a smooth, slightly starched, printed or plain-colored fabric. It is called a *wash-and-wear cotton* if it has a resin finish; *calico* if it has a small quaint printed design: *chintz* if it has a large printed design and *glazed chintz* if it is

given a glazed resin finish. Glazed chintz is made in solid colors as well as prints. The name chintz comes from the Hindu word meaning "spotted." These fabrics are often made with blends of cotton and polyester or high-wet-modulus rayon. They are used for shirts, dresses, blouses, pajamas, and aprons.

Any plain woven, balanced fabric ranging in weight from lawn to heavy bed sheeting may be called *muslin*. It is also a specific name for medium-weight fabric that is unbleached or white.

YARN-DYED FABRICS

Fabrics	Range in Thread Count	Yarn Size Warp	Filling
Gingham, cotton Carded	64 × 76 to 48 × 44	Same as percale	
Combed	88 × 84 to 84 × 76		

Chambray and gingham madras are similar to gingham.

Ginghams are yarn-dyed fabrics with checks, and plaids, or they may appear to be solid color. Chambrays appear to be solid color but have white filling and colored warp yarns or they may have darker yarns in the filling—iridescent chambray—or they may have stripes. Some chambray is unbalanced with high warp count, which produces a filling rib similar to that of broadcloth and poplin.

Ginghams and chambray are made of cotton or cotton blends and are usually given a wash-and-wear or durable-press treatment. When they are made of fiber other than cotton, the fiber content is included in the name, for example, silk gingham. In filament rayon, these fabrics are given a crisp finish and called *taffetas*. In wool, similar fabrics are called wool checks, plaids, and shepherd's checks.

The construction of gingham and chambray is a more costly process than the making of converted goods because the loom must be rethreaded for each new design and threading a loom for yarn-dyed fabrics requires more skill than threading it with undyed yarns. It is necessary also for the manufacturer to carry a larger inventory, which requires more storage space.

Stripes, plaids, and checks present problems that are not present in plain-colored fabrics. Crosswise lines must be parallel to the floor in draperies, must

Fig. 16–4. Gingham. Top, balanced plaid. Bottom, unbalanced plaid.

be lined up with the edges of furniture, and must be properly balanced in apparel. Ginghams may have an up-and-down, a right-and-left, or both. These are called *unbalanced plaids*. Compare the unbalanced plaid in the picture in Figure 16–4 with the balanced plaid. More time is needed to cut out a garment in plaid than in plain material and more attention must be given to the choice of design. Plaids in inexpensive garments seldom match

except at the center front and back seams, places where failure to match is seldom noticeable.

Imitations of gingham are made with printed designs. There is, however, a right-and-wrong-side to the print, whereas true gingham is the same on both sides. Lengthwise printed stripes are usually "on-grain" but the crosswise stripes are frequently "off-grain," as shown in Figure 16–5.

Suiting Weight Fabrics. Suiting weight fabrics are heavy enough to tailor well. Filling yarns are usually larger than the warp yarns due to slightly lower twist. Uses are slacks, trousers, shorts, jackets, suits and coats, upholstery, slipcovers, and draperies. Because of their weight, they usually are more durable and more resistant to wrinkling than sheer or mediumweight fabrics but they tend to ravel more because of their low thread count.

SUITING WEIGHT FABRICS*

Fabric	Typical Thread Count	Typical Yarn Size
Cotton suiting	48 × 48 to 66 × 76	13s to 20s

* Tropical worsteds, linen suitings, cretonne, crash, Butcher rayon, flannel, tweed, sailcloth, homespun, etc., are suitings that vary in yarn construction and fiber content. (See Glossary for those not discussed here.)

Cotton suiting is converted from a gray goods called *coarse narrow sheeting*. Indian Head is a manufacturer's trade name. Cotton suiting is plain color or printed. *Cretonne* is similar to cotton suiting except that it has large floral designs.

Crash is made with yarns that have thick-and-thin

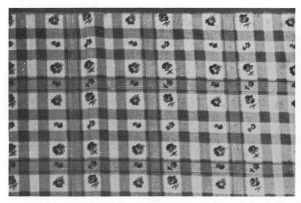

Fig. 16–5. Left, "on-grain" fabric. Right, "off-grain" fabric.

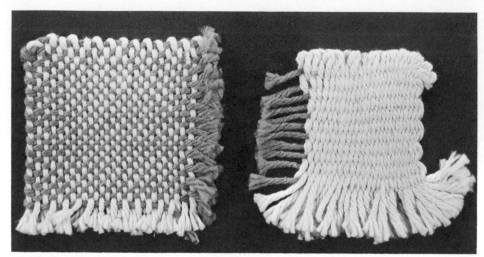

Fig. 16–6. Ribbed fabric shows high warp count and warp surface. Left, plain weave—balanced. Right, plain weave—unbalanced.

areas that give it an uneven nubby look. It shows wrinkles less than a plain surface does.

Butcher rayon is a crash-like fabric of 100 per cent rayon or rayon/acetate blends. In heavier weights it looks like linen suiting.

Tweed is made of any fiber or mixture of fibers and is always characterized by nubs of different colors. The name comes from the Tweed river in Scotland. Harris tweed is hand woven in the Outer Hebrides Islands and Donegal tweed is hand-woven in Donegal County, Ireland.

Plain Weave Unbalanced Fabrics

When the number of *warp* yarns in a plain woven fabric is increased until it is about *twice* that of the filling yarns, the fabric has a crosswise ridge called a *filling rib* and a warp surface in which the warp yarns completely cover the filling yarns. If the yarns are of different color, the only color showing on the surface will be that of the warp yarns. Small ridges are formed when the warp and filling yarns are the same size, and larger ridges are formed where the filling yarns are larger than the warp. Yarn sizes are given in the fabric chart. Figure 16–6 shows the high warp count, the warp surface, and a difference in color in a ribbed fabric.

Ribbed fabrics such as broadcloth look very much like percale. If the following technique of analysis is used, the difference between the two fabrics will become evident.

1. Use a two-inch square of broadcloth and of percale.

2. *Ravel* adjacent sides of each fabric to make a ¼-inch fringe.

3. Observe the difference in the number of yarns in each fringe. Broadcloth will have a very thick fringe of warp yarns (144 × 76); whereas in the percale fabric, the fringe of warp yarns will be about the same as the fringe of filling yarns (80 × 80).

Slippage is a problem in ribbed fabrics made with filament yarns, especially those of lower quality and lower count, as shown in Figure 16–7. This occurs at points of wear and of tension such as at seams and buttonholes. If the yarns are of different color, as they are in iridescent taffeta, slippage is particularly obvious. For example, a black/red iridescent taffeta with black warp and bright red filling would show a bright red streak along a seam

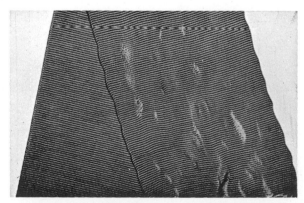

Fig. 16–7. Slippage of yarns in a ribbed fabric.

where slippage had occurred, and the main portion of the garment would remain black.

Wear always occurs on the top of the ribs. The warp yarns wear out first and splits occur in the fabric. The filling yarns, which are covered by the warp, are protected from wear.

Ribbed fabrics with fine ribs are softer and more drapable than comparable balanced fabrics. Those with large ribs have more body and less drapability and are good for garments where a bouffant look is desired.

Mediumweight Ribbed Fabrics. Sheer ribbed fabrics are seldom made except in glass curtain fabrics, while mediumweight ribbed fabrics are the largest group of the plain weave unbalanced fabrics.

Broadcloth has the finest rib of any of the staple fiber fabrics because the warp and filling yarns are the same in size. Better qualities are made of long-staple cotton, ply yarns, and are usually mercerized for luster. They have a very silky appearance. The term "Pima Broadcloth" on a label refers to the use of long-staple fiber. Combed broadcloth will cost from two to four times as much as carded broadcloth. *Slub broadcloth* is made with a yarn that contains slubs at regular intervals. *Silk broadcloth* has filament warp and staple filling.

Poplin is similar to broadcloth but has heavier ribs made by larger filling yarns.

MEDIUMWEIGHT UNBALANCED RIBBED FABRICS*

Fabric	Thread Count	Yarn Size Warp	Filling
Staple Fiber			
Combed broadcloth	144 × 76	100/2	100/2
Carded broadcloth	100 × 60	40s	40s
Combed poplin	102 × 50	50/2	28s
Carded poplin	100 × 44	30s	24s
Filament Fiber			
Rayon taffeta	60 × 15	10/2	3s
Acetate taffeta	140 × 64	75 denier	150 denier
Faille	200 × 64	75 denier	200 denier

* Ribbed fabrics and ribbed weave should not be confused. Ribbed weave is not discussed in this text.

Taffeta is a fine rib, filament yarn fabric with crispness and body. In acetate taffeta, crispness is due to the fiber and the finish, and in rayon taffeta it is due to the finish only. *Moiré taffeta* has a watermarked embossed design. This design is durable on acetate taffeta but temporary on rayon taffeta unless resin treated, as shown in Figure 16–8.

Faille (pronounced *file*) is usually made of filament warp and staple filling yarns. The filament yarns are usually acetate or rayon.

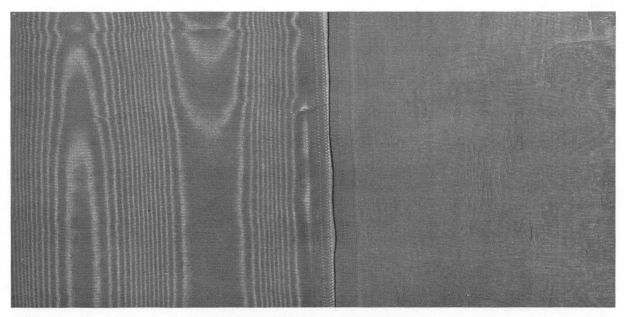

Fig. 16–8. Moiré before and after washing.

Shantung has an irregular rib surface produced by long irregular areas in the yarn. It may be made in medium or suiting weight and of various kinds of fiber.

Suiting weight unbalanced ribbed fabrics are given in the following chart.

SUITING WEIGHT UNBALANCED RIBBED FABRICS

| | | Yarn Size | |
Fabric	Thread Count	Warp	Filling
Rep	88 × 31	30/2	5s
Bengaline	92 × 40	150 denier	15s spun
Shantung	140 × 44	150 denier	30/2

Rep is a heavy coarse fabric with a pronounced rib effect. *Bengaline* is similar to faille and is often made with rayon warp and cotton filling. It is sometimes woven with two warp at a time to emphasize the rib. *Grosgrain* (pronounced *grow'-grane*) has a rounder rib than faille. Grosgrain ribbon may shrink as much as 2 to 4 inches per yard. It is often used at the button closure of sweaters and causes an unsightly appearance when it shrinks.

Plain Weave Variation: Basket Weave

Basket weaves are made with two or more warp used as one, and with two or more filling placed in the same shed. The most common basket weaves are 2 × 2 and 4 × 4 but other combinations are 2 × 1, 2 × 3, 3 × 3, etc. These fabrics have flexibility and wrinkle resistance because there are few interlacings per square inch. The fabrics have a flatter appearance than a comparable plain weave fabric would have. Long floats will snag easily. Figure 16–9 shows a 2 × 2 basket weave.

Oxford is one of the most important commercial shirtings. The oxford weave is a 2 × 1 interlacing with fine warp and a larger filling. It may have a yarn-dyed warp and white filling and be called an oxford chambray. Because of soft yarns and loose weave, yarn slippage occurs at the seams and within the fabric itself. Loose-weave fabrics will snag and pill. Filling yarns have a little higher breaking strength than the warp. Oxford fabrics are soft, porous, and lustrous.

Monk's cloth is one of the oldest homespun-type fabrics. Others are called friar's cloth, bishop's cloth, druid's cloth, or mission cloth. They are heavy, coarse fabrics in a 2 × 2 or a 4 × 4 basket weave, and are usually brownish white or oatmeal

Fig. 16–9. Basket weave.

color, but may be white or piece-dyed. The oatmeal color is obtained with ply yarns, one unbleached cotton and the other brown, or with a blend of natural and dyed cotton fibers. The yarns are carded, soft spun in sizes 7/2 to 10/2 or 3s to 5s. Monk's cloth is used for draperies, wall and bulletin-board coverings, bedspreads, and dresser scarves.

Hopsacking is an open basket weave fabric made of cotton, linen, or wool. It is primarily used for coats and suits. It gets its name from sacks used to gather hops.

Basket weave can be varied by combining it with other types of weaves.

Twill Weave

Twill weave is one in which each warp or filling yarn floats across two or more filling or warp yarns with a progression of interlacings by one to the right or left to form a distinct diagonal line or *wale*. A *float* is that portion of a yarn which crosses over two or more yarns from the opposite direction. Twill weaves vary in the number of harnesses used. The simplest twill requires three harnesses. The more complex twills may have as many as 15 to 18 harnesses and are woven on a loom with a dobby attachment. Twill weave is the second basic weave that can be made on the simple loom.

Twill weave is often designated by a fraction (for example, 2/1) in which the numerator indicates the number of harness that are raised and the denominator indicates the number of harness that are lowered when a filling yarn is inserted. The fraction

Fig. 16–11. Twill wales in lapel look unbalanced.

Fig. 16–10. Top, drawing of a twill weave 2/1. Bottom, twill weave fabric—three-harness 2/1.

2/1 would be read as "two up, one down." A 2/1 twill is shown in Figure 16–10. The floats on the surface are warp yarns, making it a warp surface or warp-faced twill.

Characteristics

All twill fabrics are characterized by diagonal wales, which vary in prominence, direction, and degree of angle.

The *prominence* of a twill wale may be increased by the use of long floats, combed yarns, ply yarns, hard-twist yarns, twist of yarns opposite to the direction of the twill line, and by use of high thread count. Fabrics with prominent wales, such as gabardine, may become shiny because of flattening due to pressure and to wear. If the ridges have been flattened by pressure, steaming will raise them to remove the shine. Pure white vinegar (5 per cent) or sandpaper may be used to remove shine caused by either pressure or wear. Dip a piece of terry cloth in the vinegar, wring it out, and rub hard and fast in both directions of the cloth in the shiny area. As the cloth dries, the odor will disappear. Do not iron or press, as either process may flatten the ridges again. Use the sandpaper with a gentle rubbing motion.

The *direction* of the twill wale usually goes from lower left to upper right in wool and wool-like fabrics—right-hand twills—and from lower right to upper left in cotton or cotton-like fabrics—left-hand twills. This fact is important only in deciding which is the right and wrong side of a twill fabric. In some fabrics that have a very prominent wale or are made with white and colored yarns, the two lapels of a coat or suit will not look the same. (See Figure 16–11.) This cannot be avoided and if it is disturbing, a garment of a different design should be chosen.

The *degree of angle* of the wale depends on the balance of the cloth. The twill line may be steep, regular, or reclining. The greater the difference between the number of warp and filling yarns, the steeper the twill line will be. Steep twill fabrics have a high warp count and, therefore, are stronger in the warp direction. The importance of the angle is that it serves as a guide in determining the strength of a fabric. Figure 16–12 is a diagram that shows how the twill line changes in steepness when the number of warp yarns changes and the filling yarns remain the same in number.

Twill fabrics have a number of common characteristics. They have a right and wrong side. If there are warp floats on the right side, there will be filling floats on the wrong side. If the twill wale goes up to the right on one side, it will go up to the left on the other side. Twill fabrics have no up-and-down. Check this fact by turning the fabric upside-down and then examining the direction of the twill wale.

Sheer fabrics are seldom made with a twill weave. Printed designs are seldom used, except in silk and lightweight twills, because a twill surface has interesting texture and design. Soil shows less on the

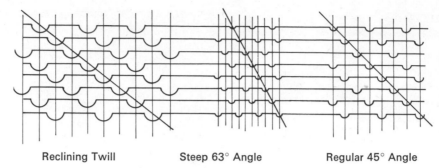

Reclining Twill   Steep 63° Angle   Regular 45° Angle

Fig. 16–12. Twill angle depends on ratio of warp to filling.

uneven surface of twills than it does on smooth surfaces.

Fewer interlacings give the fabric more softness, pliability, and wrinkle recovery than a comparable plain weave fabric would have because the yarns can move more freely. When there are fewer interlacings, yarns can be packed closer together to produce a higher count fabric with more weight and durability. If a plain weave fabric and a twill weave fabric had the same kind and number of yarns, the plain weave fabric would be stronger because of more interlacings.

Classification of Twill Fabrics

Twill weave fabrics are classified, according to the kind of yarn exposed on the surface, as even-sided twills, warp-faced twills, and filling-faced twills.[1]

Even-Sided Twills. Even-sided twills have the same amount of warp and filling yarn exposed on both sides of the fabric. They are sometimes called reversible twills because they look alike on both sides although the direction of the twill line differs. Better quality filling yarns must be used in these fabrics than in the warp-faced twills since both sets of yarn are exposed to wear. They are 2/2 twills and have the best balance of all the twill weaves. (See Figure 16–13.)

Filling

Warp

Fig. 16–13. Reversible twill 2/2—even-sided. Notice change of warp and filling. Warp yarns are dark to correspond the checkerboard design.

[1] Filling-faced twills are not discussed in this text because they are seldom used. They are usually reclining twills.

EXAMPLES OF EVEN-SIDED TWILLS*

Fabric	Thread Count	Range in Yarn Size	
		Warp	Filling
Serge	48 × 34 to 62 × 58	Vary with fiber content	
Flannel	56 × 30 to 86 × 52	Vary with fiber content	
Surah			

* See Glossary for other twill fabrics.

Serge is a 2/2 twill with a rather subdued wale, which is still quite apparent. Cotton serge of fine yarn, high count is often given a water-repellent finish and used for jackets, snow suits, and raincoats. Heavy yarn cotton serge is used for work pants. Wool serge gets shiny from abrasion and repeated pressing but is not subject to flattening of the wale as is gabardine. Luster comes from the smoothness of the yarns. Good quality wool serge is made of fine fiber, two-ply worsted yarns, and has a high thread count. Serge comes in various weights.

Twill flannel is similar to serge in construction but differs in appearance. Flannel has a napped surface, which gives it a soft fuzzy texture. The filling yarns are low-twist, larger yarns specially made for napping. Some flannels have a 2/1 construction. Flannels may be either woolen or worsted. Worsted flannels, frequently used in tailored suits, are easy to press and will take and hold a sharp crease. They usually have less nap than woolen flannels and are less apt to show wear at the edges of sleeves and at elbows. Low-count flannels will tend to get "baggy" in areas of stress because there are fewer points of contact between fibers in low-twist yarns. The fibers tend to pull past one another when there is tension on the fabric.

Surah is a printed filament twill fabric of 2/2 construction, which is used in silk-like dresses, linings, ties, and scarves.

Warp-Faced Twills. Warp-faced twills have a predominance of warp yarns on the right side of the cloth. Since warp yarns are made with higher twist, they are stronger and more resistant to abrasion; thus, they should be more durable than comparable filling-faced fabrics. (See Figure 16–14.) They are widely used in utility garments.

Fig. 16–14. Twill 2/1—warp-faced.

EXAMPLES OF WARP-FACED TWILLS

Fabric	Thread Count	Range in Warp	Yarn Size Filling
Drill	60 × 36 to 80 × 48	12s to 20s	10s to 22s
Jean	84 × 56 to 100 × 64	21s to 24s	24s to 30s
Denim (work)	60 × 36 to 72 × 44	7s to 16s	8s to 23s
Gabardine	110 × 76 to 130 × 80	15s to 39/2	15s to 26s

Drill is a fairly heavy cotton fabric used for work clothing, uniforms, and ticking. It is piece-dyed. It also has many uses in the unfinished, gray-goods state. For example, it makes good ironing board covers.

Jean is lighter in weight than drill. It is used for children's play clothes, draperies, slipcovers, and work shirts. Jean is not heavy enough for work pants.

Denim is a yarn-dyed fabric that comes in two weights. Overall denim is made of heavier yarns than drill and usually has blue yarns in the warp and natural yarns in the filling. Sportswear denim is similar to drill in weight and may have stripes, plaids, or appear to be a solid color. It is used in sportswear, slipcovers, and the like. Blue jeans, levis, dungarees, and overalls are all made of denim; the name refers to the cut of the trousers. Fashion fabrics in denim may be napped, overprinted, or figured.

Gabardine is a warp-faced *steep* twill with a very prominent, distinct wale. It has a 63° angle or greater and always has many more warp than filling. Cotton gabardine is made with 11, 13, or 15 harnesses. Long floats, which make the diagonal lines, are combined with short floats between the wales. Cotton gabardine is used for slacks and shorts, wind-repellent jackets, and raincoats. Rayon and wool gabardine are sometimes made with a three-harness arrangement in which the warp yarns are crowded close together, giving a steep twill.

Herringbone Fabrics. Herringbone fabrics have the twill line reversed at regular intervals to give design that resembles the backbone of a fish. These may be steep or regular twills and the twill lines may be equally prominent or one side may be more subdued.

Satin Weave

Satin weave is one in which each warp yarn floats over four filling yarns (4/1) and interlaces with the fifth filling yarn with a progression of interlacings by two to the right or the left. (Or each filling yarn floats over four warp and interlaces with the fifth warp [1/4] with a progression of interlacings by two to the right or left.) In certain fabrics such as double damask and slipper satin, each yarn floats across seven yarns and interlaces with the eighth yarn. Satin weave is the third basic weave that can be made on the simple loom and the basic fabrics made with this weave are *satin* and *sateen*.

Satin weave fabrics are characterized by luster because of the long floats that cover the surface. Note in the checkerboard designs that (1) there are few interlacings; thus, the yarns can be packed close together to produce a very high-count fabric; and (2) no two interlacings are adjacent to one another so no twill effect results from the progression of interlacings unless the thread count is low.

When warp yarns cover the surface, the fabric is a warp-faced fabric—satin—and the warp count is high. When filling floats cover the surface, the fabric is a filling-faced fabric—sateen—and the filling count is high. These fabrics are, therefore, unbalanced; but the high count compensates for the lack of balance.

All these fabrics have a right and wrong side. A high yarn count gives them strength, durability, body, firmness, and wind repellency. Fewer interlacings give pliability and resistance to wrinkling but may permit yarn slippage and raveling.

Designs may be achieved with satin weave by changing the direction of floats (from warp to filling floats) to make figures, stripes, or checks. Satin weaves may be used in combination with other weaves to produce woven designs.

Warp-Faced Satin Weave Fabrics

TYPICAL SATIN FABRICS

| Fabric | Count | Kind of Yarn | |
		Warp	Filling
Satin	200 × 64	100-denier rayon	100-denier rayon
Nylon satin	320 × 140		
Slipper satin	300 × 74	75-denier acetate	300-denier acetate
Crepe-backed satin	128 × 68	100-denier acetate	100-denier rayon crepe

Satin fabrics are usually made of bright filament yarns with very low twist. Warp floats completely cover the surface. Because of the bright fibers, low twist, and long floats, satin is one of the most lustrous fabrics made. It is made in many weights (see table) for use in dresses, linings, lingerie, draperies, and upholstery. It seldom has printed designs. It is especially good for linings because the high count makes it very durable and the smooth surface makes the garment easy to slip on and off. Satin makes a more pliable lining than taffeta and thus does not split as readily at the hem edges of coats and suits. Quality is particularly important in linings. The higher the count, the better the quality. Low-count satins will pull at the seams, rough up in wear, and the floats will shift in position to make bubbly areas and wrinkled effects on the surface of the cloth. Satin upholstery should be applied so one "sits with" the floats. (See Figure 16–15.)

In crepe-back satin, the crepe yarns are used in the filling and the low-twist warp floats give the

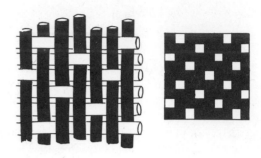

Fig. 16–15. Satin weave 4/1, warp-faced. Top, diagram. Bottom, fabric.

smooth satiny surface to the fabric. The crepe yarns give softness and drapability.

Care of satin fabrics should be directed toward maintenance of luster and prevention of distortion of floats. Wash or dry clean as indicated by the fiber content and press on the wrong side or iron with the direction of the floats.

Filling-Faced Satin Weave Fabrics

TYPICAL SATEEN FABRICS

| Fabric | Count | Kind of Yarn | |
		Warp	Filling
Filling sateen	60 × 104 carded	32s	38s
	84 × 136 carded	40s	50s
	96 × 108 combed	40s	60s
Warp sateen	84 × 64 carded	12s	11s
	160 × 96 carded	52s	44s

Sateen is a highly lustrous fabric made of staple fiber. In order to achieve luster with staple fibers, low twist must be used in the yarns forming the float surface. These yarns are the *filling* yarns because if warp yarns were made with twist that is low enough to produce luster, they would not be strong enough to resist the tensions of weaving. A resin finish is used also on the woven cloth to enhance the luster and make it durable. (See Figure 16–16.)

Filling sateen is a smooth lustrous cotton fabric used for draperies and dress fabrics. It is often made with carded yarns with a high filling thread count. Yarns are similar in size to those used in print cloth, but the filling yarns have a low twist and are larger in size than the warp yarns. (This factor can be used to help identify the warp and filling direction of the fabric.)

Luster is obtained by the Schreiner finish. (See page 183.) Schreinering is a mechanical finish in which fine lines, visible only under a hand lens, are embossed on the surface. Unless a resin finish is applied at the same time, the finish is only temporary. Carded sateens are Schreinered only, because short fibers are used; mercerization would not produce enough luster to justify the cost. Combed sateens are usually mercerized as well as Schreinered.

Warp sateens are cotton fabrics made with warp floats in 4/1 interlacing pattern. They have a rounded wale effect that makes them resemble a twill fabric. They are stronger and heavier than filling sateens because of the high warp count. They are less lustrous than filling sateen and are used where dur-

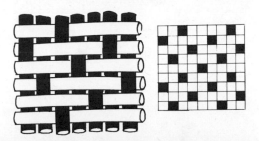

Fig. 16–16.   Satin-weave sateen fabric 1/4—filling faced.   Top, diagram. Bottom, fabric.

ability is more important than luster. Large amounts of warp sateens are used in pillow and bed tickings.

17 Leno, Piqué, and Other Figured Weaves

Leno, piqué and figured weaves are made on special looms or on a simple loom with special attachments.

Leno Weave

Leno is a weave in which the warp yarns do not lie parallel to each other but one yarn of each pair is

Fig. 17–1. Leno weave.

crossed over the other before the filling yarn is inserted, as shown in Figure 17–1.

Leno is made with a *doup attachment*, which may be used with a plain or a dobby loom. The attachment consists of a thin hairpin-like needle supported by two heddles. One yarn of each pair is threaded through an eye at the upper end of the needle, and the other yarn is drawn between the two heddles. Both yarns are drawn through the same dent in the reed. During weaving, when one of the two heddles is raised, the doup warp yarn that is threaded through the doup needle is drawn across to the left. When the other heddle is raised, the same doup warp yarn is drawn across to the right.

By glancing at a leno fabric, one might think that the yarns were twisted fully around each other, but this is not true. Careful examination shows that they are *crossed* and that one yarn of the pair is always above the other.[1] The fabrics made with leno weave are lace-like in character. The word "leno" comes from the French word *linon*, which means flax. At one time this weave was called *gauze* weave, meaning fine peculiar weave originating in Gaza, Asia. Today the word "gauze" refers to a low-count plain weave used for bandages, while leno refers to the lace-like weave.

[1] Alfred G. Duerst, "Designing and Weaving Leno Fabrics," *Modern Textiles Magazine* **43**:38 (March, 1962).

Fabrics made by leno weave are *marquisette* (see Figure 17–2), mosquito netting, bags for laundry, fruit, and vegetables. Acetate and polyester marquisette are widely used for glass curtains. Thermal blankets are sometimes made of leno weave. All these fabrics are characterized by sheerness or open spaces between the yarns. The crossed yarn arrangement gives greater firmness and strength than plain weave fabrics of the same low thread count and also gives resistance to slippage of yarns. Care is determined by the fiber content.

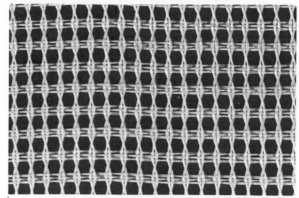

Fig. 17–2. Marquisette.

Piqué Weave

Piqué (or cord) weave is made on a loom with a dobby attachment that provides for 20 or 30 different interlacing arrangements of the warp yarns. This means that the figure must be completed with the insertion of 20 to 30 filling yarns. Figure 17–3 shows the punched plastic tape that controls the warp; Figure 17–4 illustrates the dobby attachment.

Piqué weave is characterized by ridges called wales or cords that are held up by floats on the back of the fabric. The wales vary in width. *Widewale piqué* ($\frac{1}{4}$ inch) is woven with 20 or more warp yarns in the face of the wale and then two warps in between. *Pinwale piqué* ($\frac{1}{20}$ inch) is a six-warp wale with two consecutive filling yarns floating across the back of

Fig. 17–3. Plastic punched tape that controls the warp shedding. (Courtesy of Crompton & Knowles Corporation.)

Fig. 17–4. A loom with dobby attachment. (Courtesy of Crompton & Knowles Corporation.)

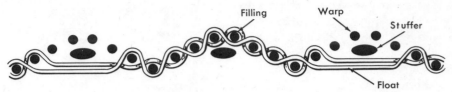

Fig. 17–5. Six-warp pinwale piqué.

the odd-numbered wales and then woven in the face of the even-numbered wales. The next two consecutive picks alternate with the first two by floating across the back of the even-numbered wales. Figure 17–5 shows a six-warp pinwale piqué.

Stuffer yarns are laid under the ridges in the better quality fabrics to emphasize the roundness or quilted effect and their presence or absence is one way of determining quality. The stuffer yarns are not woven in the main part of the fabric and may be easily removed when analyzing a swatch of fabric.

Characteristics of Cord and Piqué Fabrics

The word "piqué" comes from the French word meaning "quilted" and the raised effect in these fabrics is similar to that in quilts. Cords or wales usually run in the *lengthwise* direction with the exception of birdseye and bullseye piqués in which the cords run crosswise. Cord fabrics have a definite right and wrong side. The fabric tears more easily in the lengthwise direction. If there are stuffer yarns, it is especially difficult to tear the fabric crosswise. In wear, the floats on the wrong side usually wear out first.

Piqué fabrics are more resistant to wrinkling and have more body than flat fabrics, and for these reasons they have less need to be given a resin finish for wash-and-wear. Piqué fabrics should be ironed on the wrong side because the beauty of the fabric is in the roundness of the cord and pressing on the right side will flatten it.

Fabric Descriptions

Fabrics in this group are called piqué with the exception of a wide-wale fabric called Bedford cord. Cord weave may be combined with other weaves to produce such fabrics as seersucker piqué, crepe piqué, and novelty piqué.

Bedford cord is a heavy fabric with warp cords. It is used for slacks, trousers, uniforms, and upholstery. It is made with carded cotton yarns, woolen or worsted yarns, rayon or acetate, or com-

binations. The wales are wide and stuffer yarns are usually present.

Piqué is lighter in weight than Bedford cord and has a narrower wale. The better quality fabrics are made with long-staple, combed, mercerized yarns and have one stuffer yarn. The carded yarn piqués are made without the stuffer and are sometimes printed.

Birdseye piqué has a tiny "eye-shaped" design formed by the wavy arrangement of the cords and by use of stuffer yarns. *Bullseye piqué* is made like birdseye but has a much larger design. Both these fabrics have crosswise rather than lengthwise cords. They are used for collars and cuffs, hats, and dresses.

Some fabrics that are called piqué such as waffle piqué, embossed piqué, and dimity piqué are *not* made by the piqué weave. Also the birdseye design in diaper cloth is not made by the piqué weave but is made by satin floats.

Figured Fabrics

Figures *in* fabrics are made by knitting or weaving, while figures *on* fabrics are made by various finishes such as printing, embossing, and flocking. Woven or knitted figures are permanent and are always "on-grain." Figures made by finish vary in permanence depending on the techniques and chemicals used and the care with which they are applied. These figures are often "off-grain" in the filling or crosswise direction.

Woven Figures

Woven figures are made by changing the weave pattern in the figure to make the figure stand out from the background or by using yarns of different color, twist, or size. A combination of these two construction variations may be used. Either method requires a special loom or loom attachments. Woven figures are described below as large figures, small figures, and figures made with extra yarns.

Large Figures. Large figures require more than 25 different arrangements of the warp yarns to make the pattern. They are made on a Jacquard loom (shown in Figure 17–6) in which each warp is controlled independently. For each arrangement of the warp yarns, a card is punched. The cards are laced together, and as they move over the loom, all the warp yarns are raised by rods attached to them. When the rods hit the cards, some will go through the holes and thus raise the warp yarns, while others will remain down. In this manner the shed is formed for the passage of the filling yarn. Figure 17–7 shows a picture woven with fine silk yarns on a Jacquard loom. Notice that there is no repeat of the pattern from top to bottom or from side to side. The repeat would be another picture. Figure 17–8 was made by a textile engineering student as a class exercise. It has a repeat both crosswise and lengthwise.

Fabrics made on a Jacquard loom are damask, brocade, and tapestry. *Damask* has satin floats on a satin background, the floats in the design being in the opposite direction from those in the background. It is made from all kinds of fibers and in many different weights for apparel and home

Fig. 17–6. Jacquard loom for weaving large figure fabrics. (Courtesy of Crompton & Knowles Corporation.)

Fig. 17–7. Woven tapestry picture.

Fig. 17–8. Exercise in threading Jacquard loom.

furnishings. Quality and durability are dependent on high count. Low-count damask is not durable because the long floats rough up, snag, and shift during use. *Brocade* has satin floats on a plain, ribbed, or satin background. Brocade with a satin ground differs from damask in that the floats in the design are more varied in length and are often of several colors. Originally, *tapestry* was an intricate hand-woven picture, usually a wall hanging that took years to weave. The Jacquard tapestry is mass-produced for upholstery, handbags, and the like. It is a complicated structure consisting of two or more sets of warp and two or more sets of filling interlaced so that the face warp is never woven into the back and the back filling does not show on the face. Upholstery tapestry is durable if warp and filling yarns are comparable. Very often, however, fine yarns are combined with coarse yarns, and when these wear off, they release the floats as long loose strings. *Brocatelle* is a tapestry-type upholstery fabric similar to matelassé (see crepe fabrics) but made with heavy regular-twist yarns. Wilton rugs are figured pile fabrics made on a Jacquard loom. These rugs, once considered imitations of Oriental rugs, are so expensive to weave that the tufting industry is trying to find ways to create similar figures by tufting.

Small Figures. Small figures require less than 25 different arrangements of the warp yarns to make the pattern. They are made on a dobby loom. (See page 151.) *Birdseye* has a small diamond-shaped filling-float design with a dot in the center that resembles the eye of a bird. This design was originally used in costly white silk fabric for ecclesiastical vestments. At one time it was widely used for towels and diapers. *Huck* or *huck-a-back* has a pebbly surface made by filling floats. It is used primarily in face towels. *Shirting madras* has small satin float designs on a ribbed or plain ground. See Glossary for descriptions of other fabrics called madras.

Extra-Yarn Figures. Figures made with extra yarns usually have warp or filling floats in the design area and cut ends at the extremities of the design. Extra warp yarns are wound on a separate beam and threaded into separate heddles. The extra yarns

interlace with the regular filling yarns to form a design and float above the fabric until needed for the repeat. The floats are then clipped close to the design or clipped long enough to give an eyelash effect. Figure 17–9 shows a fabric before and after clipping.

Extra filling yarns are inserted in several ways. Clipped spots are made with low-twist filling yarns inserted by separate shuttles. The shedding is done so that the extra yarns interlace with some warp and float across the back of others. Clipped spots are woven on a box loom that has a wire along the edge to hold the extra yarns so that they need not be woven in the selvage. Figure 17–10 shows a clipped spot dotted swiss before and after clipping. Swivel dots are made on a loom that has an attachment holding tiny shuttles. The fabric is woven face down to keep the shuttles and extra yarns above the ground fabric. Each shuttle carrying the extra yarn goes four times around the warp yarns in the ground fabric and then the yarn is carried along the surface to the next spot. The yarn is sheared off between the spots.

Dotted swiss is made with either clipped or swivel dots on a sheer cotton ground. The name is rather loosely used today to refer to any dotted fabric. Figures 17–11a and 17–11b show three fabrics called dotted swiss. Notice in the clipped spot that the filling yarns are spread apart by the thick extra yarns and that there is no spreading with the swivel dot. The paste dot in the lower part of the picture is still called dotted swiss even though it is made by a

Fig. 17–9. Fabric made with extra warp yarns. Left, right side of fabric. Right, wrong side of fabric before and after clipping.

Fig. 17–10. Clipped spot dotted swiss: before and after clipping.

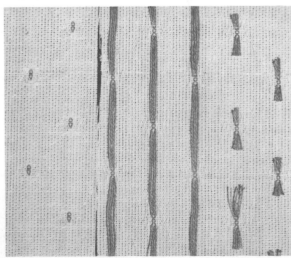

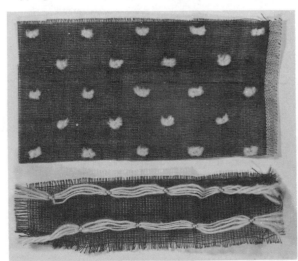

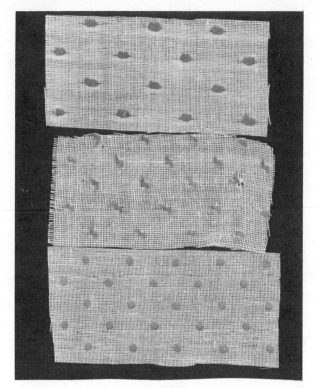 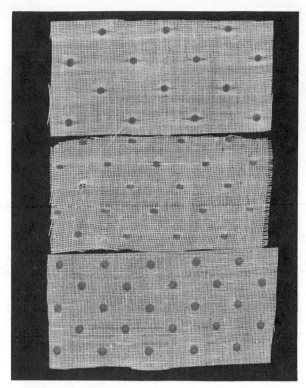

Fig. 17–11. Dotted swiss. Left, top to bottom: wrong side—clipped dots, swivel dots, and paste dots. Right, top to bottom: right side—clipped dots, swivel dots, and paste dots.

finish rather than a weave. Paste dots are often used on nylon or polyester sheers, which require little or no ironing. There is no right or wrong side to dotted swiss even though it does not look alike on both sides. It is a matter of opinion which side should be worn outside.

Figures by Finish

Figures by finish are usually cheaper than woven figures because decisions about the figures need not be made so early in the production process and orders for cloth can be filled more quickly.

Embroidered fabrics are made on a Schiffli machine, which consists of a frame 10 to 15 yards long, many needles, and many shuttles containing bobbins. The operation is similar to making fancy stitches on a sewing machine except that 648 needles and bobbins are employed. The machine is programmed by punching Jacquard-type cards. All kinds and qualities of fabrics are embroidered. The process is fairly expensive but designs are usually very durable.

Other figures by finish are discussed elsewhere:

Color printing, page 211   Burnt-out, page 189
Flocking, page 168   Plissé, page 160
Embossing, page 183   Parchmentized, page 189

18 Crepe Fabrics

A crepe crinkle can be obtained in several ways. This chapter, unlike the previous chapters on weaving, therefore deals with a family of crepe fabrics including those made by crepe weave.

"Crepe" is a French word meaning "crinkle." Crepe fabrics are classified according to the way the crinkle is obtained. *True crepes* have a crinkle resulting from high-twist yarns. (See page 99.) *Crepe-effect* fabrics are those in which the crinkle is achieved by the weave, the finish, or by textured yarns. True crepes and crepe effects are compared in the table on page 157.

True Crepe

True crepe fabrics are made with plain weaves and high twist crepe yarns. (See page 99.) They are made on a loom with a box attachment that can insert alternating groups of S- and Z-twist yarns to enhance the amount of crinkle. Rayon, cotton, flax, wool, and silk are the fibers that are used for the high-twist yarns because the liveliness of the high twist can be controlled or "set" by wetting and drying before weaving. Thermoplastic fibers will not take such a set. They must be set with heat, which kills the liveliness. Acetate fiber is often used for the low-twist warp yarns.

Gray-goods crepe fabric is smooth as it comes from the loom. It is woven wide and then shrunk to develop the crinkle. Immersion in water causes the crepe-twist yarns to regain their liveliness and contract or shrink. For example, the fabric is 47 inches wide on the loom, contracts to 30–32 inches in boil-off, and is finished at 39 inches. This explains why a crepe fabric will shrink when it gets wet and why garment size is so much more easily controlled by dry cleaning than by washing.

True crepe fabrics are classified by the position of the crepe yarn as: filling crepes, warp crepes, balanced crepes, and variations.

Filling Crepe Fabrics

These fabrics have high-twist crepe yarns in the *filling* direction and low-twist yarns in the warp direction. (See Figure 18–1.)

Multifilament and *French crepe* are the smoothest and most lustrous of the true crepe family. Because they are smooth, they are washable and are used in lingerie and sometimes in blouses. They contain crepe yarns of the lowest twist.

COMPARISON OF CREPE FABRICS

True Crepe by High-Twist Yarns	Crepe Effect By Weaving	By Finish
Permanent crinkle. Will flatten during use. Moisture will restore it	Crinkle does not flatten in use	Crinkle may sit out or be less prominent after washing
High potential shrinkage	Lower potential shrinkage	Lower potential shrinkage
Good drapability	Less drapable	Less drapable
Stretches	Low stretch	Low stretch
Resilient, recovers from wrinkles	Wrinkles do not show because of rough surface	Wrinkles do not show because of the rough surface
Dry cleaning preferable	Washable unless fiber content requires dry cleaning	Washable unless fiber content requires dry cleaning
Typical fabrics* French crepe Flat crepe Wool crepe Crepe de chine Matelassé Chiffon Georgette	Typical fabrics Sand crepe Granite cloth Seersucker	Typical fabrics Plissé Embossed crepe

* Some of the less commonly used crepes are described in the Glossary.

TYPICAL FILLING CREPE FABRICS

Kind of Crepe	Thread Count	Denier Warp	Filling	t.p.i.
Multifilament	250 × 104	55*	75	30
French	150 × 94	75	75	38 S- and Z-twist
Flat	150 × 76	75	75	50 S- and Z-twist

* Yarn has 50 filaments. High number of filaments gives softness.

Flat crepe is the most widely used filling crepe. It has a dull crepy surface. A rayon/acetate fiber combination is frequently used. The acetate is very low-twist filament *warp* and the rayon is the crepe yarn filling. The rayon crepe yarns alternate with S- and Z-twist or with 2S- and 2Z-twist. A high warp count and low filling count give a crosswise *rib* effect. Low count in the filling gives the crepe yarns room to contract so that the amount of crinkle will be greater. Figure 18–1 shows a filling crepe. Analysis of a filling crepe fabric will show that it is easy to distinguish between the warp and filling yarns.

Fig. 18–1. Flat crepe. Notice crimp on regular yarn due to pressure of crepe yarns when fabric was pressed. These are not crepe yarns.

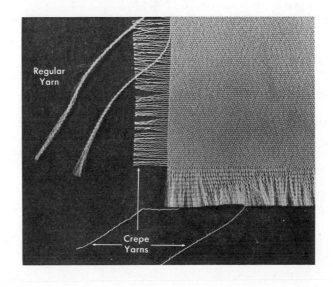

Regular Yarn

Crepe Yarns

When sewing crepe it is *not advisable to preshrink* the cloth with the hope that it will then be completely relaxed. If crepes are completely relaxed, they will stretch too much during pressing and use. True crepes present some problems in pressing, but the secret is to work quickly with as little pressure and moisture as is necessary to obtain good results. It is best to dry-clean crepes that have enough crinkle to present pressing or shrinkage problems.

Warp Crepe Fabrics

Warp crepe fabrics are made with crepe yarns in the warp and regular yarns in the filling direction. There are very few warp crepes on the market, possibly because they tend to shrink more in the warp direction and it is, therefore, difficult to keep an even hemline in washable fabrics. Bemberg sheer and some wool crepes belong in this group. (See Figure 18–2.)

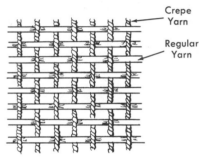

Fig. 18–2. Diagram of warp crepe.

Balanced Crepe Fabrics

Balanced crepe fabrics have crepe yarns in both directions and are usually balanced in thread count. They are often made in sheers and the crepiness of the yarns in both directions helps prevent yarn slippage. Figure 18–3 is a diagram of a balanced crepe.

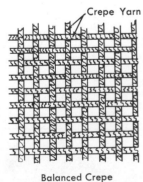

Balanced Crepe

Fig. 18–3. Diagram of balanced crepe.

Fig. 18–4. Rayon crepe seersucker.

Variations

Other forms of true crepes are the crepe seersuckers and the double-cloth crepes.

Puckered rayons (seersucker) are made in plain weave with alternating groups of regular yarns and crepe yarns in the filling direction. Warp yarns are regular yarns. When the fabric is wet in finishing, the crepe yarns shrink causing crosswise puckers in the regular yarn stripe. (See Figure 18–4.)

Matelassé is a double-cloth construction with either three or four sets of yarns. Two of the sets are always the regular warp and filling yarns and the others are crepe yarns. They are woven together so that the two sets criss-cross as shown in Figure 18–5. It is as if two fabrics are interlaced with each other. The crepe yarns shrink during wet finishing and create puffy areas in the regular-yarn part of the fabric. Matelassé is usually a rayon/acetate combination.

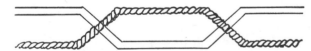

Fig. 18–5. Matelassé double cloth construction showing crepe and regular yarns crisscrossing.

Crepe-Effect Fabrics

The crinkled effect of a true crepe can be simulated by use of textured polyester yarns in the filling direction of the fabric, by weave, and by finishes.

Crepe Effect by Textured Yarns

Filament polyester yarns textured by the false-twist process (page 107) are woven as the filling yarns in a plain weave fabric with standard filament yarns in the warp.[1] These textured filament yarns are *low-twist*. The warp yarns are low-twist polyester or triacetate filament fibers. The crepe effect forms during the wet finishing of the cloth when the textured polyester shrinks. The finished fabric has a high level of crinkle, good hand, and exceptional performance for the consumer. One of the first textured yarn crepes on the market was "Whipped Cream" by the Klopman Co.

Crepe Effect by Weaving

Two kinds of weaves are used: the crepe weave and slack tension weave.

Crepe Weave. Crepe is the name given to a class of weaves that present no twilled or other distinct weave effect but give the cloth the appearance of being sprinkled with small spots or seeds. The effect is an imitation of true crepe, which is developed from yarns of high twist. They are made on a loom with a dobby attachment. Some are variations of satin weave with filling yarns forming the *irregular* floats. Some are even-sided and some have a decided warp effect. Crepe weave is also called *granite* or *momie weave*. Fibers that do not lend themselves to true crepe techniques are often used in making crepe weave fabrics. Wool and cotton fibers are also used frequently because the crepe-effect fabric is easier to care for than the true crepes. For a comparison of characteristics refer to the table on page 157. The irregular interlacing pattern of crepe weave is shown in Figure 18–6.

Sand crepe is one of the most common crepe weave fabrics. It has a repeat pattern of 16 warp and 16 filling and requires 16 harnesses. No float is greater than two yarns in length. It is woven of either spun or filament yarns. The silk-like acetate sand crepe (Magic Crepe, etc.) is widely used.

Granite cloth is made with granite weave, based on the satin weave, and is an even-sided fabric with no long floats and no twilled effect. It is used in ginghams, draperies, etc.

Moss crepe is a combination of true crepe yarns and crepe weave. The fiber content is usually rayon

[1] R. W. Jackle, "Properties and Uses of Polyester Fibers," *American Dyestuff Reporter* **54**:17 (December 6, 1965).

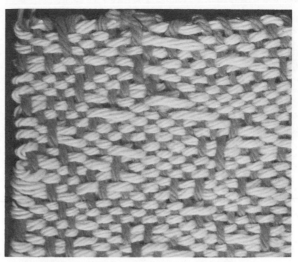

Fig. 18–6. Crepe weave; irregular interlacings.

and acetate. The yarns are ply yarns with one ply made of crepe twist rayon fiber. Regular yarns may be alternated with the ply yarns or they may be used in one direction while the ply yarns are used in the other direction. This fabric should be treated as a true crepe fabric. Moss crepe is used in dresses and blouses.

Slack Tension Weave. In slack tension weaving, two warp beams are used. The yarns on one beam are held at regular tension and those on the other beam are held at slack tension. As the reed beats the filling yarn into place, the slack yarns crinkle or buckle to form the puckered stripe and the regular tensioned yarns form the flat stripe. (Loop pile fabrics are made by a similar weave; see page 164.) *Seersucker* is the fabric made by slack tension weave. (See Figure 18–7.) The yarns are wound onto the two warp beams in groups of 10 to 16. The crinkle stripe may have slightly larger yarns to enhance the crinkle stripe and this stripe may also have a 2 × 1 basket weave. The stripes are always in the warp direction. Seersucker is produced by a limited number of manufacturers. It is a low-profit, high-cost item to produce because of slow weaving. Most seersuckers are made in 45-inch widths in plain colors, stripes, plaids, and checks. Cotton, polyester, acetate, and triacetate fibers are used singly or in blends. Seersucker is used in large amounts in the men's wear trade for suitings and for women's and children's dresses and sportswear.

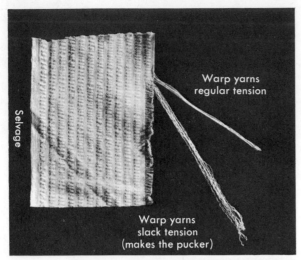

Fig. 18–7. Seersucker showing the difference in length of slack and regular tension yarns.

Fig. 18–8. Plissé crepe.

Crepe Effect by Finish

This effect is usually achieved by plisséing or embossing a plain woven fabric. The pucker is permanent or durable.

Plissé is converted from either lawn or print cloth gray goods by printing sodium hydroxide (caustic soda) on the cloth in the form of stripes or designs. The chemical causes the fabric to shrink in the treated areas. As the treated stripe shrinks, it causes the untreated stripe to pucker. Shrinkage causes a slight difference in thread count between the two stripes. The untreated or plain stripe in-

creases in thread count as it shrinks. The upper portion of the cloth in Figure 18–8 shows how the cloth looks before finishing and the lower portion shows the crinkle produced by the caustic soda treatment. This piece of goods was found on a remnant counter and was defective because the roller failed to print the chemical in the unpuckered area.

Embossed crepe is made by pressing a crinkled design onto the surface of the cloth. Cotton cloth must be given a resin finish also to make the design durable. Thermoplastic fibers can be heat-set to make the design permanent.

19 *Pile Fabrics*

Pile fabrics are three-dimensional fabrics that have yarns or fibers forming a dense cover of the ground fabric. Pile fabric can be both functional and beautiful. In apparel fabrics, a high pile is used to give warmth in coats and jackets as either the shell or the liner and as the liner for gloves and boots. In household uses, high-count fabrics give durability and beauty in carpets, upholstery, and bedspreads. In towels and washcloths, low-twist yarns give absorbency. Other uses for pile fabrics are stuffed toys, wigs, paint rollers, buffing and polishing cloths, and decubicare pads for bed-ridden patients.

Interesting fabric effects can be achieved by use of cut and uncut pile combinations, pile of various heights, high- and low-twist yarn combinations, areas of pile on a flat surface; printing, curling, crushing, or forcing pile into a position other than upright.

In pile fabrics, the pile wears out first but a durable base structure is necessary in order to have a satisfactory pile. Close weave increases the resistance of a looped-pile to snagging and of a cut-pile to shedding and pulling out. A dense pile will stand erect, resist crushing, and give better cover. Care must be taken in washing and ironing to keep the pile erect. Cut-pile fabrics usually look better if dry-cleaned, but they can be washed if the laundry procedures are suited to the fiber content. All pile fabrics are softer and less wrinkled if tumble-dried or line-dried on a breezy day. Minimum or no pressure and a steam iron should be used in removing wrinkles. Flattening of the pile causes the fabric to appear lighter in color. Many pile fabrics are pressed in finishing so the pile slants to give an *up and down.* Garments should be cut so that the pile is directed *up.* (See Figure 19–1.) The fabric looks

Fig. 19–1. Pile should be directed up.

richer and deeper in color as one looks into the pile. However, it is not as important that the pile be directed up as it is that the pieces of a garment all be cut with the pile going in the same direction. Otherwise, light is reflected differently and it looks as if

METHODS OF MAKING PILE FABRICS

Method	Uses	Characteristics	Identification
Weaving (page 162)	Dresses and suits Terry towels Rugs and carpets Fur-like fabrics	Very versatile	Can ravel adjacent sides
Weaving chenille yarns (page 165)	Rugs and carpets Upholstery fabrics Decorative fabrics	Dense pile possible Can be any size or shape	Caterpillar-like yarn looks like pipe cleaner
Tufting (page 165)	Rugs and carpets Bedspread, robes Blankets	Loosely twisted yarn punched into previously woven cloth	Look on reverse side for straight rows of thick areas
Knitting (page 166)	Fur-like fabric Industrial polishing cloth	Less expensive than weaving	Look for interlocking loops on the wrong side
Flocking (finish) (page 168)	Belts, jackets, toys, bookbacks	Short fibers	Fuzzy designs rather stiff in design area
Other	Kraftamatic Machine, English invention (page 169) Mali and Arachne machines (page 178)		

two different colors were used in the garment. Direction of the pile can be determined by running the hand over the fabric.

Pile fabrics can be made by several different methods. These are presented and compared briefly in the above table.

Woven Pile Fabrics

Woven pile fabrics are three-dimensional fabrics made by weaving into the basic structure an extra set of warp or filling yarns to make loops or cut ends on the surface. Pile fabrics are classified by the set of yarns used to form the pile, as filling pile and warp pile fabrics. (See Figure 19–2.)

Filling Pile Fabric

This fabric is made with three sets of yarns. An extra set of filling yarns forms the pile. During weaving, extra yarns float across the ground weave. In *corduroy*, the floats are arranged in lengthwise rows; in *velveteen*, they are scattered over the base fabric. The floats are cut by a special machine consisting of guides that lift the individual floating yarns from the ground fabric and of revolving knives that cut the floats. (See Figures 19–3 and 19–4.) Figure 19–5 shows a corduroy gray goods in

Loop Pile

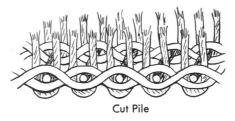
Cut Pile

Fig. 19–2. Woven pile fabric.

Fig. 19–3. Filling pile. Floats are cut.

which some of the floats have been cut. For wide-wale corduroy, guides and knives can be set to cut all floats in one operation. For pinwale corduroy and velveteen, alternate rows are cut and the cloth must be run through the machine twice. The little cutting

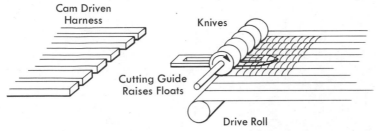

Fig. 19–4. Diagram of a machine for cutting corduroy.

discs are dulled very quickly by nylon yarn, and this has presented one of the technical difficulties in the development of a nylon corduroy.

Both velveteen and corduroy are made with long-staple, combed, mercerized cotton used for the pile. In good quality fabrics, long-staple cotton is used for the ground as well. The ground may be a plain or a twill weave. With a twill weave, it is possible to have a higher count and, therefore, a denser pile. Corduroy can be recognized by lengthwise wales, which vary from wide wale, 5–8 wales per inch, to pinwale, 16–21 wales per inch. Pinwale corduroy has a shallower pile and is more pliable. It is warm, washable, durable, inexpensive, and needs no ironing. Velveteen has more body and less drapability than velvet. The pile is not over $\frac{1}{8}$ inch high. Turn to page 164 for a discussion of ways to tell the warp from the filling in velveteen and in velvet.

Filling pile fabrics are finished by scouring, brushing many times, singeing, and waxing. The final pressing lays the pile at a slight slant giving the fabric an up and down. The back of both velveteen and corduroy is given a slight nap.

Warp Pile Fabrics

These fabrics are made with two sets of warp and one set of filling yarns, the extra set of warp yarns making the pile. Several techniques are used:

Double-Cloth Method. Two fabrics are woven, one above the other, with the extra set of yarns interlacing with both fabrics. There are two sheds, one above the other, and two shuttles are thrown with each pick. The fabrics are cut apart while still on the loom by a traveling knife that passes back and forth across the breast beam. With this method of weaving, the depth of the pile is determined by the space between the two fabrics. (See Figure 19–6.)

Velvet was originally made of silk and was a compact, heavy fabric. Today, velvet is made of

Fig. 19–5. Corduroy gray goods showing some floats cut.

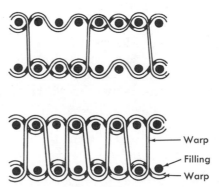

Fig. 19–6. Warp pile—double cloth method. Top, W-interlacing, Bottom, V-interlacing.

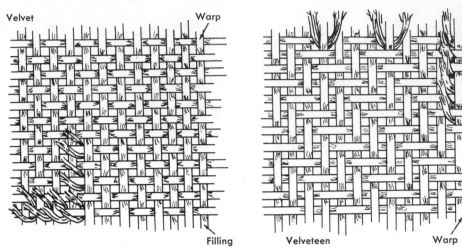

Fig. 19–7. Left, pile yarns in velvet. Right, pile yarns in velveteen.

rayon, nylon, or silk filaments with a pile $\frac{1}{16}$ inch high or shorter. (See Glossary for types.) Velvet is not wound on bolts as are other fabrics, but it is attached to hooks at the top and bottom of a special bolt so that there are no folds and creases in the fabric.

Velvet and velveteen, the hard-to-tell-apart fabrics, can be distinguished by fiber content, since velvet is usually made with filaments and velveteen of staple. To tell warp direction in these fabrics, ravel adjacent sides. In velvet, the tufts will be interlaced with a filling yarn; in velveteen, they will be interlaced with a warp yarn. (See Figure 19–7.) Another way to tell warp direction is to bend the fabric. In velveteen, the pile "breaks" into lengthwise rows, since the filling tufts are around the warp threads. In velvet, the pile breaks in crosswise rows, since the warp tufts are around the ground filling yarns. This technique works best with medium to poor quality fabrics.

Velour is a cotton fabric used primarily for upholstery and draperies. It has a much deeper pile than velveteen and is heavier in weight.

Plush is a cut-pile fabric; it may be cotton, wool, silk, or rayon. It has a deeper pile than velvet or velour, usually greater than $\frac{1}{4}$ inch. Plush is used for coats, capes, upholstery, and powder puffs.

Fur-like fabrics may be finished by curling, shearing, sculpturing, or printing to resemble different kinds of real fur.

Over-Wire Method. A single cloth is woven with wires placed across the width of the loom over the ground warp and under the pile warp. Each wire

has a knife edge, which cuts all the yarns looped over it as it is withdrawn. Uncut pile can be made over wires without knives or over waste picks of filling yarns. The wires are removed before the cloth is off the loom, while the waste picks are removed after the fabric is off the loom. Friezé and mohair-pile plush are made in this way.

Friezé, an uncut pile fabric, is an upholstery fabric usually made of mohair with a cotton back. Durability of friezé depends on the closeness of the weave. (See Figure 19–8.)

Fig. 19–8. Friezé is woven over wires.

Slack-Tension Method. The pile is formed by a special weaving arrangement in which three picks are put through and beaten up with one motion of the reed. After the second pick in a set is inserted, there is a let-off motion which causes the threads on the warp-pile beam to slacken, while the threads on the ground pile beam are held at tension. The third pick is inserted and the reed moves forward all the way and all three picks are beaten up firmly into the fell of the cloth. (See Figure 19–9.) These picks move

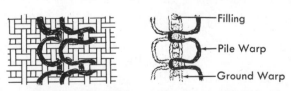

Fig. 19–9. Warp pile, slack tension method.

along the ground warp and push the pile warp yarns into loops. The loops can be on one side only or on both sides. The height of the loops is determined by the distance the first two picks are left back from the fell of the cloth.

Terry cloth and some friezés are made by this method. *Shag-bark gingham*, which is a combination of plain weave with scattered loops, is also made in this way.

Terry cloth is a highly absorbent cotton fabric used for bath towels, beach robes, and sportswear. Each loop acts as a tiny sponge. The fabric does not have an up and down.

Chenille Yarn Pile Fabrics (Woven)

Chenille yarn is made by cutting a specially woven ladder-like fabric into warpwise strips. (See Figures 19–10 and 19–11.) The cut ends of the softly

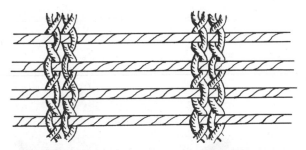

Fig. 19–10. Fabric from which chenille yarn is made.

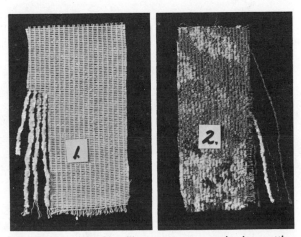

Fig. 19–11. (1) Chenille yarns are made by cutting specially woven fabric. (2) Fabric made from chenille yarn.

twisted yarns loosen and form a pile-like fringe. This fringed yarn may be woven to make a fabric with pile on one or both sides. If the pile is on one side only, the yarn must be folded before it is woven. The yarn is sometimes referred to as a "caterpillar" yarn.

Tufted Pile Fabrics

Tufting is a process of making pile fabrics by punching extra yarns into an already woven fabric. The ground fabric ranges from thin cotton sheeting to heavy burlap and the pile yarns can be of any fiber content.

Tufting is a less costly method of making pile fabrics, because it is an extremely fast process and involves less labor and time to create new designs. A tufted bed-size blanket can be made in two minutes. A tufting machine can produce approximately 645 square yards of carpeting per hour compared to an Axminster loom, which can weave about 14 square yards per hour.

Tufting developed in the southeastern United States as a handcraft. It is said that the early settlers trimmed off wicks from their homemade candles and carefully worked them into bedspreads to create interesting textures and designs. Later, a needle was used to insert the thick yarn and the making of candlewick bedspreads grew into a cottage industry. Hooked rugs were also made by hand in the same way. In the 1930's, machinery was developed to convert the hand technique to mass production. Cotton rugs, bedspreads, and robes were produced in many patterns and colors at low cost. In 1950, the first room-width carpeting was made; by 1966, 85 per cent of the broadloom carpeting was made by tufting.

In 1960, Barwich Mills, Inc., started pilot plant operations on tufted blankets. This end-use *combines pile construction with napped finish*. It has the advantage over traditional blanket fabric of maintaining a strong, firm ground fabric, since the fibers are teased from the pile yarns to create the nap. Also the thickness of the blanket is determined by the height of the pile rather than by the thickness of the yarn. Tufted blankets have not been successful in the United States but are being produced in Europe.

Tufting is done by a series of needles, each carrying a yarn from a series of spools held in a creel. (See Figures 19–12 and 19–13.) The backing fabric is held in a horizontal position, the needles all come down at once and go through the fabric at a predetermined distance, much as a sewing machine needle goes through cloth. Under each needle is a hook that moves forward to hold the loop as the needle is retracted. For cut-loop pile, a knife is attached to the hook and it moves forward as the needles are retracted to cut the loop. The fabric moves forward at a predetermined rate, and the needles move downward again to form another row of tufts.

The tufts are held in place by the blooming (untwisting) of the yarn and by shrinkage of the ground fabric in finishing. In carpeting, a latex coating is put on the back to help hold the tufts in place.

Variations in texture can be made by loops of different heights. Cut and uncut tufts can be combined. Tweedy textures are made by the use of different-colored plys in the tufting yarns. New techniques of dyeing have been developed to produce colored patterns or figures in which the color penetrates the tufts completely.

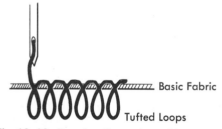

Fig. 19–12. Drawing illustrating tufting process.

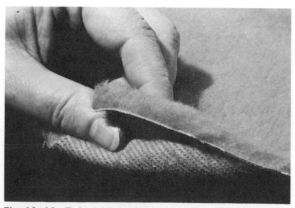

Fig. 19–13. Tufted fabric. Notice machine-like stitches on wrong side.

Knit-Pile Fabrics

Pile knits look like woven pile fabrics, but they are more pliable and stretchy. Knitted pile fabrics are classified as circular knit or sliver knit.

Circular knits usually have cotton backing yarns comparable in size to those used in mediumweight fabrics and low twist, larger-sized, face yarns. The fabrics are terry cloth and velour.

Knitted terry cloth is often used for baby towels and wash cloths because it is absorbent but softer than woven terry. Because it does not conform to shape as well and, thus, does not look good on the rack, towels and washcloths for adults are seldom made of knitted terry.

Velour, a fashion fabric in men's apparel in the 1960's, is a cut-pile knit.

Sliver knits are used to produce imitation fur fabrics. The knitted back makes the fabric more pliable with better draping characteristics. It has only been since 1955 that fabrics with a true fur-like appearance and texture have been available. They have the luxurious hand and dense face of the furs but are much lighter in weight and require no special storage. Until recently, special care in cleaning was necessary because the heat-sensitivity of the fibers caused shrinkage and fabric distortion when fabrics were cleaned in the normal manner. By using a cold tumble dryer and combing the pile rather than steam pressing, the fabrics can be successfully dry-cleaned.

High-pile knits are made from acrylic, modacrylic, or olefin fibers or blends or combinations of these fibers. The back is knit from fibers (Dynel) that will shrink during the finishing operation to make the pile surface more compact. There is a trend to use cotton for the back to reduce the cost.

The background is knit with yarns but the pile is made from a *sliver*. Fibers from the sliver are picked up by the needles along with the ground yarn and are locked into place as the stitch is formed.

The steps used in finishing these fabrics are: (1) heat-setting, which shrinks the ground fabric and shrinks and expands the diameter of the individual face fibers; (2) tigaring—a brushing operation which removes surplus fiber from the face of the fabric; (3) shearing; and (4) electrofying, a process that combs the fibers first in one direction and then in another by grooved heated cylinders that rotate

COMPARISON OF FUR-LIKE FABRICS*

Apparel	Pile Height, in.	Total Weight oz./sq. yd.	Pile, oz./sq. yd.	Back, oz./sq. yd.
Shell-beaver type	0.38–0.5	15–19	10–12	5–7
Shell-mink type	0.56–0.63	19–22	14–15	5–7
Liner-sliver knit	0.32–0.60	8.5–12.5	5.0–8.0	3.5–5.0
Liner-tufted	0.38–0.44	8.0–11.5	5.0–7.0	3.0–4.5

* *Textile Industries* **128**:98 (December, 1964).

at high speed. This process imparts high luster to the pile. The electrofying process may be repeated many times to develop the required finish.

Fur-like fabrics are used for shells (the outer surface) or liners (the inner surface) of coats and jackets. The table above shows the difference between shells and liners that are made by sliver knitting, weaving, and tufting.

Notice in the above table that the difference is mainly one of weight, the shells being heavier than the liners. In actual use the dividing line is less distinct because shell fabrics are used as liners in expensive garments and liner fabrics are used as shells in low-priced items.

In sliver knits, the fibers from the sliver are already loose on the surface, while in the tufted and woven constructions, the fibers must be opened or teased from the yarns. A denser pile can be obtained because the amount of face fiber is not limited by yarn size or distance between the yarns as it is in tufting and weaving.

In tufting 5/64-gauge machines are used for apparel pile fabrics. This gauge is the distance in inches between the tufting needles. Normal tufting specifications on this gauge call for 10 to 11 stitches per inch and a pile height of $\frac{1}{8}$ inch.[1]

Woven fabrics are usually $\frac{1}{2}$ inch or less in pile height. They are less pliable than knits or tufted fabrics and rows of tufts sometimes cause the fabric to "grin" (the back shows) when fabric is folded at the edges.

Flocked Pile Fabrics: A Finish

Flock are very short fibers attached to the surface of the fabric by an adhesive to make a pile-like design or fabric.

[1] Stanley P. Leffler, "Pile Fabrics: How They Are Made and Marketed," *Modern Textiles Magazine* **127**:12 (December, 1963).

In the 1920's, white cotton and colored rayon flock dots were used on dress and curtain fabrics and some overall flocking was done on industrial fabrics. A renewed interest in flocking began in 1960 with the development of new adhesives, new improved substrates, and the availability of new precision-cut fibers.

In apparel, flock is used for velvet and suede-like fabrics as well as for pile designs on fabrics. In the automotive industry, there has been interest in flocked fabrics for floor coverings, head liners, trunk liners, and weather stripping.

Flock may be made from any fiber. Rayon is the most widely used because it is cheap and easy to cut. Nylon, which has excellent abrasion resistance and durability, is tough and requires special cutting knives. Polyester, acrylic, and olefin fibers are used. Fibers for flocking must be straight and, therefore, the length and denier are important. As the fiber length is increased, the denier also must be increased so that the fiber will stand up straight in the fabric. Fibers that are cut square at the ends will anchor more firmly in the adhesive. (See Figure 19–14.) The adhesive is a latex dissolved in a solvent that evaporates.

The base fabric can be of any type. For overall flocking, woven fabrics present some problems because of surface irregularities and a heavy filler coating must be used. Some of the newer and cheaper base materials are nonwovens of various types, urethane, and vinyl foams. Flock also can be

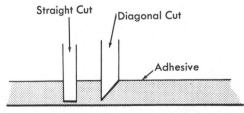

Fig. 19–14. Flock with square-cut ends is anchored on wrong side.

Mechanical Flocking	*Electrostatic Flocking*
	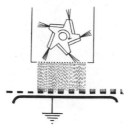

Fig. 19–15. Diagrams showing flocking process. Left, mechanical flocking. Right, electrostatic flocking. (Courtesy of the Monsanto Company and *Modern Textile Magazine*.)

1. Flock is sifted onto the adhesive coated fabric. Vibration of beater bars causes those fibers which do not fall flat against the adhesive to stand erect and once erect, the fibers penetrate fully into the adhesive. The erect fibers help the free fibers to align themselves and to work down to the adhesive.
2. Most units consist of 6 to 20 beater bars and one or more sifting hoppers and run as high as 10 or more yards per minute.
3. Simpler in design, usually less expensive and most widely used in the United States.

1. Flock passes through an electrostatic field which orients the fibers. In coating irregular surfaces, the lines of force are always perpendicular to the substrate so that this method is best for three-dimensional surfaces.
2. Most units operate at speeds of 3 to 5 yards per minute.
3. Can "up-flock" as well so that both sides of a fabric can be flocked.
4. Requires generators, proper insulation, gives better end-on-end fiber orientation, and higher densities are possible.

applied to an adhesive film, which can be peeled off and laminated to a base fabric.[2]

The two basic methods of applying the flocking are mechanical and electrostatic.[3] (See Figure 19–15.) In both processes, the flock is placed in an erect position and after flocking, the fabric is sent to an oven for drying the adhesive. In the above chart, a comparison of the two methods is given. Overall flocking or space flocking can be done by either method.

The potential for flocked fabrics is great. T. W. Qualman says,

We can impart a pleasing flannel surface to a rubber bed sheet, make burlap with a hand like the most luxurious suede, or transform a whole boat deck into one continuous, soft, cool, sure-footed carpet. We impart beauty and styling to foundation garments for the ladies and at the same time engineer the adhesive and design areas to add control where desired.[4]

Chenille-type yarns have been made by flocking. Fleece-type fabrics utilizing two pile heights for outer wear are possibilities.

Other Pile Construction Processes

Techniques involving new machines are being investigated in the United States as possibilities for making pile fabrics more economically than by traditional methods.

[2] David I. Walsh, "Flock Application: New Tools Reshape an old Art," *Dyestuff Reporter* **55**:9 (April 25, 1966).

[3] Kenneth K. Griffin, "Today's Improved Flocking Technique," *Modern Textiles Magazine* **45**:8 (August, 1964).

[4] T. W. Qualman, "The Expanding Potential for Flocked Fabrics," *Modern Textiles Magazine* **45**:8 (August, 1964).

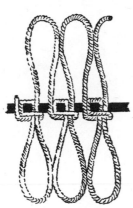

Fig. 19–16. Kraftamatic machine makes loops on both sides.

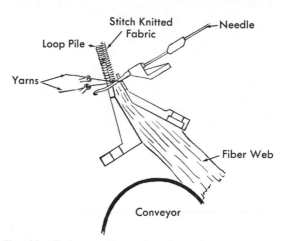

Fig. 19–17. Loop pile produced on Arachne machine. (Courtesy of Stellamcor, Inc.)

In England a Kraftamatic machine has been invented which combines tufting and knitting. It is said to be a sewing machine above the backing fabric and a knitting machine below. The difference between this technique and tufting is that the loops are locked firmly in the backing. Loops can be produced on both sides of the fabric. (See Figure 19–16.) It is being used to make terry cloth for towels. Other end-uses are diapers, blankets, and carpets. The Kraftamatic can produce fabrics ten times faster than a loom.

The Mali and Arachne machines (described on page 178) can produce pile fabrics through a non-woven fiber web. (See Figure 19–17.)

20 *Napped Fabrics*

The average consumer—as well as some writers who may not be well grounded in textile information—confuse the terms "nap" and "pile." These are two very different fabric effects. Chapter 19 explained how pile fabrics are made. This chapter explains how napped fabrics are made.

Process of Napping

Nap consists of a layer of fiber ends, on the surface of the cloth, that are raised from the ground weave by a mechanical brushing action. Thus napped fabrics are literally "made" by a finishing process. Figure 20–1 shows a fabric before and after napping.

Napping was originally a hand operation in which the napper tied together several teasels (dried thistle-like vegetable burs, shown in Figure 20–4) and swept them with a plucking motion across the surface of the cloth to raise fibers from the ground weave. The teasels had a gentle action and the barbs would break off before causing any damage to the cloth. The raised fibers formed a nap that completely changed the appearance and texture.

Before napping   After napping

Fig. 20–1. Fabric before and after napping.

Teasels are still used in the machine finishing of fine wool fabrics such as duvetyn. For machine processing (gigging) they are mounted on rollers and as the barbs wear off or break off, the worn teasels are replaced by new ones. The fabric may be either wet or dry.

Most napping is now done by rollers covered by a heavy fabric in which bent wires are embedded. (See Figure 20–2.)

Napping machines may be either single-action or double-action.

Fewer rollers are used in the single-action machine. They are all alike and travel at the same speed. They are called pile-rolls and the bent ends

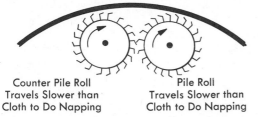

Counter Pile Roll
Travels Slower than
Cloth to Do Napping

Pile Roll
Travels Slower than
Cloth to Do Napping

Fig. 20–2. Napping rolls. Left, counter pile. Right, pile roll.

of the wires point in the direction in which the cloth travels but the rollers rotate in the opposite direction. These rollers are all mounted on a large drum or cylinder which rotates in the same direction as the cloth. The pile-rolls must travel faster than the cloth in order to do any napping.

In the double-action napping machine every other roll is a counter-pile roll. This roll has wires which point in the direction opposite to those of the pile-roll. The counter-pile roll must travel slower than the cloth in order to produce a nap. When the speed of the rolls is reversed (pile-rolls at slower speed and counterpile rolls at faster speed), a "tucking" action occurs. Tucking pushes the raised fibers back into the cloth and makes a smooth surface.

Reasons for Napping

1. *Warmth*. A napped surface and the soft twist of the filling yarns increase the dead air space. Still air is one of the best insulators.
2. *Softness*. This characteristic is especially important in baby clothes.
3. *Beauty*. Napping adds much to fabric attractiveness.
4. *Water and stain repellence*. Fiber ends on the surface cut down on the rapidity with which the fabric gets wet.

Quality, Characteristics, and Care

The amount of nap does not indicate the quality of the fabric. The amount may vary from the slight fuzz of Viyella flannel to the very thick nap of imitation fur. Short compact nap on a fabric with firm yarns and a closely woven ground will give the best wear. Stick a pin in the nap and lift the fabric. A good durable nap will hold the weight of the fabric. Hold the fabric up to the light and examine it. Press the nap aside and examine the ground weave. A napped surface may be used to cover

Fig. 20–3. Pilling on a wool sweater.

defects or a sleazy construction. Rub the fabric between the fingers and then shake it to see if short fibers drop out. Thick nap may contain flock (very short wool fibers). Rub the surface of the nap to see if it is loose and will rub up in little balls (pilling). Notice the extreme pilling on the sweater in Figure 20–3.

Some napped fabrics have an up and down. To test this, brush the surface of the fabric. Brushing against the nap roughs it up and causes it to look darker because more light is absorbed. This is the "up" direction of the fabric. When the nap is smoothed down, the reflection of light from the surface gives a lighter shade of color. Napped fabrics should be made with the nap "down" so garments will be easier to brush. However, the direction of the nap is not as important as the fact that the same direction of nap is used in all parts of a garment.

Low-count fabrics usually have low-twist yarns; and when strain is applied, the fibers slip past one another and do not return to their original position. Thus garments tend to "bag" in the seat and elbow areas. Tightly twisted yarns are more resistant to bagging. It is best to line low-count napped fabrics or to make the garment with gored or flared skirts.

Wear on the edges of sleeves, collars, buttonholes, and so forth, causes an unsightly contrast to unworn areas. Very little can be done to it except that a vigorous brushing will give a fuzzier appearance. *Price is no indication of resistance to wear*, since the more expensive wool fibers are finer and less resistant to abrasion. Wear will flatten the nap but if nap is still present on the fabric it can be raised by brushing or steaming. Loosely napped fabrics will shed short fibers on other garments or surfaces. They also shed lint in the wash water so should be washed separately or after other articles are washed. Napped fabrics are fluffier if dried on a breezy day or dried in a dryer.

Construction

Napped fabrics must be made from especially constructed gray goods in which the filling yarns are made of *low-twist* staple (not filament) fibers. Turn back to page 99 and reread the information about yarn twist. The difference in yarn structure makes it easy to identify the lengthwise and crosswise grain of the fabric. Figure 20–4 shows the warp and filling yarns from a camel's hair coat fabric, before and after napping.

Fabrics can be napped on either or both sides. The nap may have an upright position or it may be "laid down" or "brushed." When a heavy nap is raised on the surface, the yarns are sometimes weakened. Wool fabrics are fulled or shrunk to bring the yarns closer together and increase fabric strength.

Yarns of either long- or short-staple fibers may be used in napped fabrics. Worsted flannels, for example, are made of long-staple wool. The short-staple fiber yarns used in woolen flannels have more fiber ends per inch, and thus can have a heavier nap. In blankets, which are heavily napped for maximum fluffiness, a fine cotton (core) ply is sometimes used in the yarn to give strength.

Although napped fabrics can be made of any staple fiber, they are most frequently made of cotton, rayon, wool, or the acrylic fibers. Pilling and attraction of lint due to electrostatic properties are problems with the nylons and polyesters.

Napped fabrics may be plain weave, twill weave, or knit. More filling yarn is exposed on the surface in a 2/2 twill or a filling-faced twill, therefore a heavier nap can be raised on twill fabrics. The knit construction in napped fabrics is often used for articles for the baby. Some brands of coats are always made of napped knit fabrics.

Napping is less expensive than pile weave as a way of producing a three-dimensional fabric.

NAPPED FABRICS

Wool		Rayon	Cotton
Flannel	Suede*	Rayon	Flannelette
Fleece	Duvetyn*	flannel	Duvetyn*
Broadcloth*	Kasha*	Brushed	Suede*
Melton*	Chinchilla*	rayon*	Outing
Kersey*	Zibiline*	Suede*	flannel
			Canton
			flannel*

* See Glossary (page 229) for fabric descriptions.

The name flannel is almost synonymous with the word "napped." When the name is used alone it implies wool fiber content. If the fabric is made of fiber other than wool, a descriptive adjective is used with the word *flannel*—for example, *cotton* flannel.

Flannel is an all-wool napped fabric made in dress, suit, or coat weights. It may be made with either worsted or woolen yarns. They may be yarn-dyed.

Worsted flannels are important in men's suits and coats and are used to a lesser extent in women's suits and coats. They are firmly woven and have a very short nap. They wear well, are easy to press, and hold a press well.

Woolen flannels are fuzzier, less firmly woven fabrics. Many have been given a shrinkage control

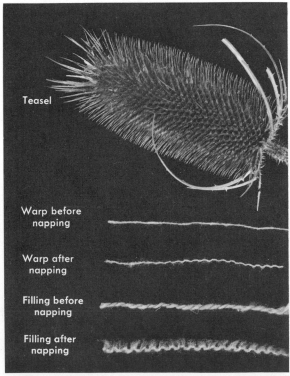

Fig. 20–4. A teasel; yarn before and after napping.

Labels in figure: Teasel; Warp before napping; Warp after napping; Filling before napping; Filling after napping

treatment which alters the scale structure of the fiber. Because this causes some weakening of the fabric, 15 to 20 per cent nylon is blended with the wool to improve the strength. These fabrics do not take or hold sharp creases so are best when used in less tailored garments.

Fleece is a coat-weight fabric with long brushed nap or a short clipped nap. Quality is very difficult to determine.

Cotton flannels flatten under pressure and give less insulating value than wool because cotton fibers are less resilient. The fibers are also shorter, thus there is more shedding of lint from cotton flannels. The direction of nap (up and down) is relatively unimportant in these fabrics because in many, the nap is very short, and also because their chief uses are robes, nightwear, baby clothes, and sweat shirts.

Flannelette is a plain-weave fabric which is converted from a gray-goods fabric called soft-filled sheeting. It is napped on one side only, has a short nap and a printed design, unless it is white. The nap will form small pills and is subject to abrasion. Suede and duvetyn are also converted from the same gray goods but are sheared close to the ground to make a smooth, flat surface. Duvetyn is the lighter weight of the two.

Outing flannel is a yarn-dyed fabric (or white) which is similar in fabric weight and length of nap to flannelette but is napped on both sides.

As the warp yarns in both fabrics are standard weaving yarns, it is easy to identify the grain of the fabric.

Rayon flannel is widely used in dresses and suits. It is similar in appearance to worsted flannel but is much less expensive. It is usually a blend of rayon and acetate.

Napped Fabrics: Blankets [1]

Blankets are a specialized end-use group of fabrics, which are used primarily for warmth. The maximum amount of nap is desired, since the effectiveness of the blanket depends on the amount of dead air space in it.

With the modern heated house and the electric blanket now in use, fewer blankets are needed than

[1] See page 165 for "Tufted Blankets."

were needed years ago. There is also a trend toward the use of the thinner "sheet" blanket.

Fiber content is an important factor in the selection of the blanket because fibers differ in their ability to maintain dead air spaces. Other fiber properties are also important considerations.

Wool has been widely used because of its excellent springiness. Mohair is even fluffier but is more expensive and seldom on the market in this country. Wool is the most expensive of the commonly used fibers. Its nonflammability is of value, since many fires are started by people who fall asleep while smoking in bed. Its drawbacks, other than price, are: it shrinks easily and becomes boardy when shrunk, and it is also subject to moth damage and must be stored in sealed containers with a sprinkling of moth crystals.

Cotton and rayon are low in cost but lack the resiliency necessary to keep the blanket fluffy. Cotton, however, is very washable, and is a good choice if frequent washing or sterilization is necessary.

Acrylics and modacrylics excel in softness, light weight, and bulk. They are washable and not subject to moth damage. The acrylics, however, burn like cotton. Modacrylics melt but do not burn. Good quality acrylic blankets are comparable to wool in price.

Blends containing wool are just as subject to moth damage as are 100 per cent wool blankets.

Olefins are the lightest weight and low in cost. *Polyesters* are used in the "skinny" blankets.[2]

Construction

The warp yarn twist is usually low in blanket fabrics and some of the nap comes from the warp yarn. See the chart for a typical Orlon blanket construction.[3]

Loom count 36 ends 41 picks
3 × 1 double woven
Warp Z-twist, 12.5 t.p.i.
Type 42 $2\frac{1}{2}$-inch staple
Filling Z-twist, 7 t.p.i.
Type 39 Orlon

The Type 39 Orlon filling yarn is a blend of staple lengths ranging from $1\frac{1}{4}$ to 3 inches and with deniers of 2 to 6.

[2] Chatham's nonwoven, low-nap blanket.
[3] K. D. Houser and L. Bidgood, Jr., "How to Finish Orlon Blankets," *Modern Textiles Magazine* **38**:50 (November, 1957).

Fig. 20–5. Double-faced blanket construction.

Fig. 20–6. Blanket of single-cloth construction in twill weave.

A double woven blanket construction is shown in Figure 20–5. Single-cloth construction in either a plain or twill weave is shown in Figure 20–6. As mentioned previously, yarns in highly napped fabrics may be made with a cotton core for strength.

Thermal Blankets

A blanket that could be sterilized, but would not shrink, nor lose its loftiness was needed for hospital use. The first development, called *thermal* blanket, was made of low-twist plied cotton yarns in a fancy leno weave resulting in a fabric with waffle-like depressions and ridges. When used with a sheet above and below the blanket, it held in sufficient body heat for warmth. As thermal blankets were adapted for home use, other weaves and fibers were used. To improve their appearance and warmth, some were napped.

For a discussion of nonwoven blankets, see page 120.

Care

Most blankets can be washed. Wool blankets must be washed in warm water with as little agitation as possible to prevent shrinkage.

Electric blankets should not be dry-cleaned because of damage to the insulation of the wiring. Be sure to read the directions that come with the blanket.

In order to reduce the frequency with which a blanket must be cleaned, protect it by turning down a length of the end of the sheet over the upper part of the blanket.

21 Double Cloth, Multicomponent, and Knit-Sew Fabrics

Woven double cloth is made with four or five sets of yarns usually interlaced so that the back and face of the fabric are different in appearance. *Double knits* are those in which two yarns are knitted as one or as one in some parts and separately in the same fabric. *Multicomponent* fabrics consist of two or more fabrics stitched or pressed together to make one usable fabric. Although the construction techniques vary, these fabrics are discussed together because they have similar properties. *Knit-sew* fabrics are made by the Mali aud Arachne processes. Sheets of yarn or fiber batts are "sewn" together by a chain stitch.

Double Cloth

Woven double cloth is composed of two separate cloths woven on the same loom, one above the other with two distinct systems of both warp and filling yarns. Warp and/or filling of one fabric often exchange positions and appear in the other cloth. *True double cloth* has a fifth set of yarns (warp), which interlace with both fabrics. True double cloth can be separated by pulling out the yarns holding the two cloths together. (See Figure 21–1.) True double cloth is expensive to make, but it is more pliable than the same weight fabric using two sets of heavy yarns. On reversible garments, the edges can be turned in and stitched together. The edges of regular double cloth or double-faced fabrics must be hemmed, bound, or finished with facings.

Double-faced fabrics are made with three sets of yarns; two warp and one filling or two sets of filling and one set of warp. Blankets and satin ribbon are often made using this process.

Fig. 21–1. True double cloth, made with five sets of yarns.

Pile fabrics are made with three sets of yarns but they are not considered double cloths, since they have a definite right and wrong side. However, some warp pile fabrics are made as true double cloths and cut apart. See page 163.

Double Cloth Fabrics

1. *True double cloth:* coating fabric, melton, kersey, beaver, saxony, whitney, montagnac
2. *Double cloth:* matelassé, brocatelle
3. *Double-faced:* blanket cloth, double satin ribbon, Sun-bak (a rayon, acetate, or silk filament warp and filling and low-twist staple filling)

Multicomponent Fabrics

Multicomponent fabrics differ from double cloths in that already constructed fabrics, foams, or webs, are joined together in various ways. It is somewhat like finishing rather than fabric construction. Multicomponent fabrics are made from two or more elements stitched or pressed together. The elements can be separated by the consumer.

Bonded Fabrics

Bonded or laminated fabrics consist of two fabrics made to adhere together by an adhesive or a flame-foam process, shown in Figure 21–2.

In the wet-adhesive method, the adhesive is applied to the underside of the face fabric; and the liner fabric is joined by passing through rollers. It is heated twice, once to drive out solvents and to give a preliminary cure, and second to effect a permanent bond. In the foam-flame process, polyurethane foam acts as the adhesive. The foam is made tacky first on one side and then on the other by passing the foam under a gas flame. The final thickness of the foam is about 15/1000 of an inch. This method gives more body but reduces the drapability of the fabric.

THERE ARE TWO BASIC METHODS for PRODUCING BONDED TEXTILES

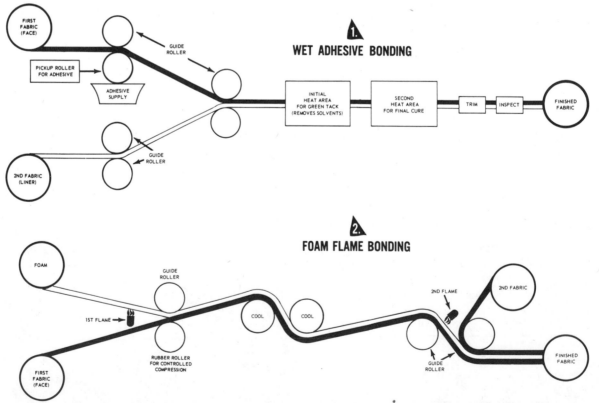

Fig. 21–2. Two basic methods for producing bonded textiles. (From *American Fabrics*, No. 68, Summer, 1965.)

The use of bonded fabric started about 1961 with an inexpensive wool flannel bonded with an adhesive to an acetate jersey. In spite of delamination problems today all kinds of combinations are used. Woven fabrics are bonded to knits, woven fabrics to woven fabrics, knits to knits, knit-sew fabrics to knits, and lace to knits. It is possible to buy companion fabrics, bonded and unbonded in the same fabric.

The advantages of bonded fabrics are:

1. Inexpensive fabrics have better appearance and body when bonded and they can be used for outer wear more satisfactorily. For example, a sleazy wool jersey bonded to an inexpensive acetate tricot has the body and weight of a double-knit wool jersey.
2. In mass-production or home sewing of apparel, separate linings usually are not used, which reduces cutting and sewing time. Bonded fabrics are easier to seam together than face and lining fabrics. No seam finishes are necessary. Interfacings usually are not needed.

The disadvantages of bonded fabrics are:

1. The backing fabric does not prevent bagging in skirts and slacks, since it often is a knit or cheesecloth, which is quite pliable.
2. Fabrics often are bonded off grain, which detracts from the beauty of a finished garment. Before purchasing bonded fabric, the home sewer should examine the fabric, particularly along the fold line.
3. Bonded fabrics may delaminate during washing or dry cleaning.

If delamination occurs, there usually is shrinkage of one component causing bubbles or a rough appearance to the fabric. Standards have been proposed for bonded fabrics but until these are accepted by various segments of the industry, the consumer must rely on trade names[1] and examination of fabric and/or garments. The National Institute of Dry Cleaning has recommended the following test to determine durability of the laminate: Soak fabric for 10 minutes in perchloroethylene. If the face and back do not separate, the fabric should withstand normal dry cleaning.[2]

[1] Certifab is a trade mark of Collins & Aikman used on fabrics that have peel-bond strength of 16 oz. dry.
[2] *Textile Industries* 131:2 (February, 1967), p. 52.

Foam Laminates

Foam laminates consist of a layer of foam covered by another fabric or between two fabrics. Foam laminates were first visualized as thermal garments for outdoor workers because they are light in weight but warm. Foams were quilted to lining fabrics for a lining, interlining combination. In 1958, they were introduced in inexpensive fabrics primarily as a way to use up undesired fabric (yardage that did not sell). The first fabric to sell in volume was a dress-weight jersey laminated to foam and made up in spring coats. This was so successful that coats were made for all-purpose uses. This is the only instance in textiles in which a new development was introduced in cheap lines and then adopted and upgraded into expensive merchandise. Foam laminates today are made using all kinds and qualities of fabric with many different thicknesses of foam.

The advantages of foam laminates are:

1. Fabrics have body and good drapability.
2. Unlike stiffened fabric, foams do not hold yarn stiff and rigid. Therefore, durability is good.
3. Foams are weak, but the combination of foam and fabric is quite satisfactory.
4. Foams tend to stabilize fabrics.
5. Warmth is directly proportional to the thickness of the foam and independent of fiber or fabric of outer shell.

Lamination is done in three ways:

1. An adhesive that adheres to foam and fabric was the first method used. It is not too satisfactory because the adhesive adds stiffness, and often is not durable to cleaning.
2. The most commonly used method is to run the foam over a gas flame so that it becomes sticky or tacky and then to apply the fabric. This technique burns off $\frac{1}{32}$ inch of the foam but is no more expensive than the cost of the adhesive. It is usually satisfactory in laundry and dry cleaning.
3. Generating the foam at the time it is to be applied, flowing it onto the cloth, and curing on the cloth is thought to be the method of the future.

Foam laminates have had and still have some disadvantages. Getting the foam and fabric to be firmly welded together depends somewhat on the fabric. Filaments do not stick as well as staple fibers; smooth fabrics are better if napped slightly before laminating. Fabrics are often applied "off grain," which affects their esthetic appeal. The character of the fabric somewhat limits styling.

Quilted Fabrics

Quilted fabrics are multicomponent fabrics consisting of two fabrics above and below a layer of wadding or batting held together by machine stitching or by fusion. Any fabric can be used for the shell or covering. A fashion fabric is always used on one side. If the article is reversible or needs to be durable or beautiful on both sides, two fashion fabrics are used. If the fabric is to be lined or used as a chair covering or bed spread, the under layer is often white or black cheesecloth. Beauty of fabric is important for all end-uses. For ski jackets and snow suits, a closely woven water- and wind-repellent fabric is desirable; for comforters, resistance to slipping off the bed is important; for upholstery, durability and resistance to soil are important.

The three layers must be held together both for construction and for care. Quilting is sewing with regular or chain stitch in lines or patterns. The disadvantage of quilting is that threads break when one sits in the garment or on the bed or from abrasion. Broken threads are unsightly and with cotton, wool, or acetate fiberfills, the loose fiber is

Fig. 21–3. Nylon taffeta and polyurethane foam; stitchless quilting. Notice the adhesive on the foam.

no longer held in place. (See page 122 for comparison of battings.)

A new technique—stitchless quilting—consists of pressing fabric to polyurethane foam using an embossing technique. Chem-Stitch, a trade name, resembles quilted fabrics both in appearance and purpose. (See Figure 21–3.)

Knit-Sew or Stitched-Through Fabrics

Newly invented machines, which are neither looms nor knitting frames, can produce fabrics that look like woven or knitted fabrics more quickly and with less labor than the traditional techniques. Chain stitches are made through fiber webs or around crosswise yarns to make drapable fabrics. It is estimated that one machine can replace 30 conventional looms in output. Because there is less tension on the yarns, lower twist yarns can be used and, if warp threads are used, they do not need to be sized.

Malimo, Maliwatt, and Malipol were invented in East Germany in 1958, and in 1965 the first American fabrics were introduced. The *Malimo* process consists of filling yarns laid as a sheet, warp yarns coming down from a creel, and a third set of yarns employing a chain stitch binds the yarns together. (See Figure 21–4.) The warp yarns can be omitted in the process. Notice in Figure 21–5 that the filling yarns are stitched with a tricot-type warp knit. *Maliwatt* is a nonwoven process in which a chain stitch sews through a fiber batt. *Malipol* is similar to tufting in that a loop pile is stitched through a base fabric.

The *Arachne* process consists of stitching through a web of fibers. The fiber web is made by laying one layer of carded fibers across another layer and chain stitching with filament yarns by a series of needles placed about $\frac{1}{4}$ inch apart. The warp strength comes from the chain stitches, and the crosswise strength comes from the fibers in the web. Fabrics made on this machine, thus far, are a bit stiff for dress fabrics, but suitable for jackets and coats and for base fabrics. *Araloop* is a variation for making loop-pile fabrics for use as towels, coatings, and floor coverings.

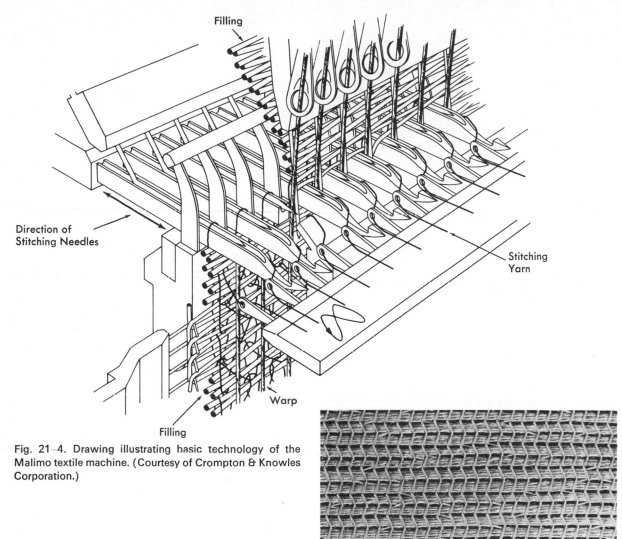

Filling

Direction of
Stitching Needles

Stitching
Yarn

Warp

Filling

Fig. 21–4. Drawing illustrating basic technology of the Malimo textile machine. (Courtesy of Crompton & Knowles Corporation.)

Fig. 21–5. Section of napkin made by knit-sew method.

22 *Finishes: Introduction and Mechanical Finishes*

A *finish* is defined as anything that is done to fiber, yarn, or fabric either before or after weaving or knitting to change the *appearance* (what you see), the *hand* (what you feel), and the *performance* (what the fabric does).

Fabrics have always been finished. Early finishing was done to improve the appearance and hand only. Natural dyes applied by laborious hand processes were used to color fabrics. To make sleazy fabric into salable merchandise, china clay and starch were added to fill up the spaces between the yarns. Various mechanical finishes were applied to make fabrics smoother, more lustrous, and better looking. These finishes were temporary and were lost during the first washing. Two important durable finishes, which have been used for over 50 years, are *mercerization* and *tin weighting* of silk. The uses of mercerization have increased while weighting of silk has almost ceased.

The arts and techniques of finishing have developed to the extent that the finish is as important and in some cases more important than the fiber content. The properties of a fiber can be so completely changed by a finish that the finished product bears little resemblance to the original.

The consumer needs to recognize visible finishes and to recognize the *need* for nonvisible finishes. He needs to know how good the finish is in terms of serviceability. A *permanent or durable finish* lasts the life of the garment. *Durable* also refers to a finish that lasts longer than a temporary finish but that may be unsatisfactory in appearance while still present in the fabric. A temporary finish lasts until the garment is washed or dry-cleaned. A *renewable* finish can be applied by the homemaker with no special equipment, or it may be applied by the dry cleaner.

Finishing may be done in the mill where the fabric is constructed or it may be done in a separate establishment by a highly specialized group called *converters*. Most mills, especially cotton weaving mills, are not equipped to do finishing. Converters operate in two ways: They perform a service for a mill by finishing goods to order, in which case they are paid for their services and never own the fabric; or they buy the fabric from a mill, finish it according to their own needs, and sell it to the cutting trade or as yard goods under their own trade name.

In 1960, there were over 1,800 finishing plants, 50 per cent of them were located in the Southeastern U.S. Cotton accounted for 78 per cent of the fabric finished.

Fig. 22–1. Fabrics converted from the gray-goods print cloth. Top: left, print cloth; right, chinz. Middle: left, percale; right, embossed cotton. Bottom: plissé.

All fabric finishing adds to the cost of the fabric. Since it is relatively easy to prepare man-made fiber fabrics for finishing, these plants have lower costs.

When a finish is new and in demand, the con-verter can realize a greater profit, for example, the wash-and-wear finish.

Many factory finishing processes are similar to operations done in the home. In the study of this unit, observe these similarities.

Gray goods (grey, greige, or loom state) are fabrics, regardless of color, which have been woven on a loom and have received no wet or dry finishing operations. Some gray goods fabrics have names, such as print cloth, soft-filled sheeting, and so forth, which are used only for the gray goods. Other gray goods names such as lawn, broadcloth, and sateen, are also used for the finished cloth.

Mill-finished fabrics can be sold and used without converting, although they may be sized or Sanfor-ized before they are sold.

Converted or finished goods have received wet or dry finishing treatments such as bleaching, dyeing, or embossing. Some converted goods retain the gray goods name. Others, such as madras gingham, are named for the place of origin; and still others, such as silence cloth, are named for the end-use. Figure 22–1 depicts some of the fabrics that can be converted from a single gray goods.

All gray goods must be cleaned and made ready for the acceptance of the finish. Gray goods contain a warp sizing, which makes the fabric stiff and inter-feres with the absorption of liquids. This sizing must be removed before further finishing can be done. Also, fabrics are often soiled during weaving and must be cleaned for that reason.

Initial Fabric Cleaning

Desizing is the process of removing the sizing on the warp yarns. A desizing substance, sulfuric acid or an enzyme, solubilizes the starch, which is then completely removed by washing. *Degumming or boil-off* are terms used to describe the desizing of silk. Silk is woven "in the gum" with the sericin forming the protective covering for the silk fila-ments. Boiling-off consists of washing in a caustic solution. Boil-off is also used as a desizing operation for the man-made fibers.

Washing removes the sizing, dirt, and oil spots. *Kier boiling* of cotton in an alkaline solution, some-times combined with bleaching, is done in a pressure kier, which resembles a large pressure cooker. The boil is done from 2 to 14 hours depending on the type of goods, results desired, and the strength of the alkaline solution. After boiling, cold water is pumped in and the goods are rinsed until cool. *Scouring* of wool fabric is necessary to remove warp sizing, oils used in spinning, and dirt or grease acquired in weaving. Heavy and mediumweight woolens are washed as a continuous rope of cloth in a continuous piece washer. Lightweight fabrics and clear finished worsted (those in which the weave shows clearly) are washed full width in a broad washer. These fabrics are liable to crease when washed in rope form.

Singeing is the burning of free projecting fiber ends from the surface of the cloth. These protruding ends cause roughness, dullness, pilling, and interfere with finishing. Singeing is the first finishing operation for all smooth finished cotton fabrics and for clear finished wool fabrics. Fabrics containing heat-sensitive fibers such as polyester/cotton blends are often singed after dyeing because the little melted balls on the ends of the fibers may cause unevenness in the color. Singeing is one of the best remedies for the problem of pilling. Singeing is usually done by a gas-flame singer. The fabric is first run open width over a heated roll to dry it, after which it is run at high speed through a gas flame and into a water bath to extinguish any sparks. The water bath may contain the desizing agent.

When the fabrics are cleaned and ready for further finishing, the order of application and the kind of finish applied varies with the fiber content of the fabric. In the discussion that follows, finishes are grouped together as : *Mechanical:* finishes that cause a physical change only. *Additive:* finishes in which a compound or substance is held mechanically on the fiber or fabric. *Chemical:* finishes in which a chemical reaction causes a permanent change in the fiber. (Additive and chemical finishes are discussed in Chapter 23.)

Mechanical Finishes

Calendering

Calendering is a mechanical finishing operation performed by a "stack" of rollers through which the cloth passes. There are several types: the simple

calender, the friction calender, the moiré calender, the Schreiner calender, and the embossing calender. Each produces a different finish.

Most calender machines have three rollers. (Others have two, five, or seven.) Hard metal rollers alternate with softer cloth wrapped rollers or with solid paper rollers. Two metal rollers never run against each other.

The *simple calender* corresponds to the household ironer and gives a smooth ironed finish to the fabric. The cloth is slightly damp before it enters the calender. The metal roll is heated. The cloth travels through the calender at the surface speed of the rollers so the rollers simply exert pressure to smooth out the wrinkles and give a slight sheen.

The *friction calender* is used to give a highly glazed surface to the cloth. If the fabric is first saturated with starch and waxes, the finish is only temporary; but if the resin finishes are used, the glaze will be durable. (See Figure 22–2.)

The cloth is first passed through the finishing solution and then dried to a certain degree of dryness. It is then threaded into the calender. The speed of the metal roller is greater than the speed of the cloth and the roller polishes the surface just as the sliding motion of the hand iron polishes the fabric. If the metal roll is hot, a higher glaze is obtained.

The *moiré calender* has been used for more than 200 years to produce a "water-marked" design on ribbed silk and wool fabrics. When acetate came on the market, it was possible to have a permanent moiré pattern.

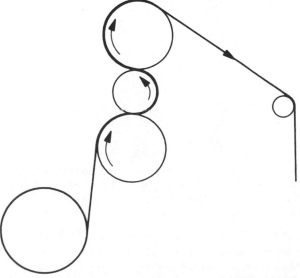

Fig. 22–2. Calender machine.

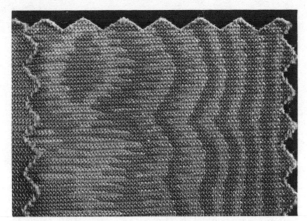

Fig. 22–3. Moiré finish on knitted automobile upholstery.

True moiré is applied to ribbed fabrics such as taffeta and faille. The rib is essential in producing the pattern, since the rolls of the calender are smooth. An embossed moiré design is made on a calender with an engraved roll.

True moiré is made by placing two layers of ribbed fabric, one on top of the other, so the ribs of the top layer are slightly "off-grain" in relation to the under layer. The two layers are stitched or held together along the selvage and are then fed into the smooth, heated, metal roll calender. Pressure of eight to ten tons causes the rib pattern of the top layer to be pressed into the bottom layer and vice versa. Flattened areas in the ribs reflect more light and create a contrast to unflattened areas. This procedure can be modified to produce patterned moiré designs other than the water-marked one. (See Figure 22–3.)

The *Schreiner calender* has a metal roller engraved with 200 to 300 fine diagonal lines visible only under a hand lens. (The lines should not be confused with yarn twist.) Until the advent of the resins and the thermoplastic fibers, this finish was temporary and was removed by the first washing. The primary purpose of this finish is to produce a *deep-seated luster*, rather than a shine, by breaking up reflectance of light rays. It also *flattens* the yarns to reduce the openness between them, and give *smoothness* and *cover*.

It can upgrade a sleazy material. This finish was originally used with cotton sateen and table damask to make them more lustrous and more salable. It was later used on polished resinated cottons and sateens as a durable finish. In 1957, it was first used to produce the *Satinette* finish on nylon and polyester tricot jersey. It has upgraded tricot and aroused increased interest in its use for the following reasons: the Satinette finish is permanent in laundry, thin fabrics are more opaque, smoothness gives a better base for printing color on the fabric. There is less tendency for tricot garments to sag at the hemline.

The diagram in Figure 22–4 shows a Schreiner calender for tricot fabrics. To avoid stretching the knit construction, the fabric is delivered to the calender in a tensionless state.

The *embossing calender* produces either flat or raised designs on the fabric. Embossing became a much more important finish after the heat-sensitive fibers were developed because it was possible to produce a durable, washable, embossed pattern. Nylon, acrylics, acetate, polyesters, and fabrics made of nylon and metallic yarns are used. If the fabrics are made of solution-dyed fibers, they can be embossed directly off the loom and are then ready for sale. Embossed satins are used in high-style

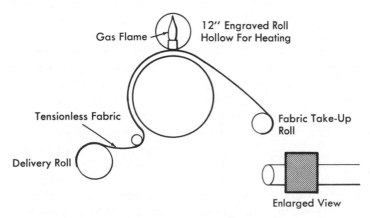

Fig. 22–4. Schreiner calender machine for tricot.

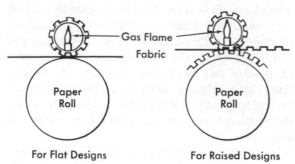

For Flat Designs   For Raised Designs

Fig. 22–5. Embossing rolls.

garments and can be sold for a much higher price than the unembossed fabric.

The embossing calender consists of two rolls, one of which is a hollow engraved metal roll heated from the inside by a gas flame. The other is a solid paper roll exactly twice the size of the engraved roll.

The process differs for the production of flat and raised designs.

1. *Flat designs* are the simplest to produce. A copper roll, engraved in deep relief, revolves against a smooth paper roll. (See Figure 22–5.) The hot engraved areas of the roll produce a glazed pattern on the fabric. Embossed brocades are an example of this type of design.
2. *Raised* or *relief* designs require a more complicated routine. The paper roll is soaked in water and then revolved against the steel engraved roll (without fabric) until the pattern of engraving is pressed into the paper roll. The temperature is adjusted to suit the fabric, which is then passed between the rolls.

Pleating

Pleating is really a variation of embossing. It is an ancient art that dates back to the Egyptians who used hot stones to make the pleats. Colonial women in the United States used heavy pleating irons to press in fancy pleats and fluting. Today pleating methods are highly specialized operations done by either the paper pattern technique or by the machine process.

The *paper pattern method* is a hand process and, therefore, more costly; but it produces a wider variety of pleated designs. Garments in partly completed condition, such as hemmed skirt panels, are placed in a pleated paper pattern mold. The fabric is placed in the paper mold by hand and another pattern mold is placed on top so that the fabric is pleated between the two pleating papers. The whole thing is rolled into a cone shape, sealed, and put in a large curing oven for heat-setting.

The *machine pleating method* is less expensive. The machine has two heated rolls. The fabric is inserted between the rolls as high-precision blades put the pleats in place. A paper backing is used under the pleated fabric and the pleats are held in place by paper tape. After leaving the heated roll machine, the pleats are *set* in an aging unit. Durability of pleats differs in the eyes of the producer and the consumer. If the pleat line is still evident after wear or washing, the producer considers this permanent and satisfactory. The consumer, however, is interested in having the pleats hang perfectly flat as if they had just been pressed. Permanence depends on the fiber content.

Beetling

Beetling is a finish that is used on linen and a few fabrics resembling linen. As the cloth revolves slowly over a huge wooden drum, it is pounded with wooden block hammers. This pounding may continue for a period of 30 to 60 hours. It flattens the yarns and makes the weave appear less open than it really is. The increased surface area gives more luster, greater absorbency, and smoothness to the fabric.

Decatizing

Decatizing produces a smooth, wrinkle-free finish and lofty hand on woolen and worsted fabrics and on blends of wool and man-made fibers. The process is comparable to steam ironing. A high degree of luster can be developed by the decating process because of the smoothness of the surface. The dry cloth is wound under tension on a perforated cylinder. Steam is forced through the fabric. The moisture and heat cause the wool to become plastic and tensions relax and wrinkles are removed. The yarns become set in the shape of the weave and are fixed in this position by the cooling-off, which is done with cold air. For a more permanent set, dry decating is done in a pressure boiler.

Wet decating often precedes napping or other face finishes to remove wrinkles that have been acquired in scouring. Wet decating as a final finish gives a more permanent set to the yarns than does dry decating.

Tentering

Tentering, one of the final finishing operations, performs the double process of straightening and drying fabrics. If the fabric is started into the tenter frame in a crooked position, it will be dried in an "off-grain" shape. The crosswise grain or threads are on the diagonal or pulled into a curved shape rather than being at right angles to the yarns in the lengthwise direction. Today many fabrics are of either heat-set synthetic fibers or have a durable-press finish, so that it is *impossible* to straighten them. Heat setting of man-made fiber fabrics is often combined with tentering.

The use of electronic monitors on the tenter frame will control the speed of the two sides of the tenter and keep the filling yarns at right angles to the lengthwise yarns. These straightening devices are called "weft straighteners."

Tenter machines are similar to a curtain stretcher in principle. They are of two types; the pin tenter and the clip tenter. The diagram in Figure 22–6 shows a pin tenter and dryer. The pin device on the sides moves around like a caterpillar tractor wheel. The clip tenter operates in the same way except that the fabric is gripped by a series of clips. More tension can be exerted by the clip tenter, but it may also damage some fabrics, in which case the pin tenter is used. The marks of the pins or the clips are often evident along the selvage.

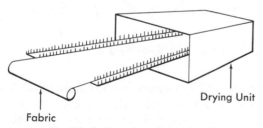

Fabric

Drying Unit

Fig. 22–6. Drawing of a tenter-dryer.

Loop Dryer

Fabrics with a soft finish, towels, and stretchy fabrics such as knits, are not dried on the tenter frame but are dried on a loop dryer, where the drying can be done without tension. Many rayon fabrics are dried on loop dryers.

Shearing

Shearing is a finishing process done by a machine similar to a lawn mower. Gray goods fabrics are sheared to remove loose fiber or yarn ends, knots, etc. Napped and pile fabrics are sheared to control the length of the pile or nap surface and to create a design or a smooth surface. *Sculptured* effects are made by flattening portions of the pile with an engraved roller and then shearing off the areas that are still erect. Steaming the fabric raises the flattened portions. Straightline designs in either the warp or filling directions or diagonally on the cloth are made by lifting the cutter blade at regular predetermined intervals.

Brushing

Brushing follows shearing to clean the surface of clear-face fabrics. When combined with steaming, it will lay nap or pile in one direction and fix it in that position thus giving the "up-and-down" direction of pile and nap fabrics.

Inspecting

Fabrics are inspected by pulling or running them over an inverted frame in good light. Broken threads are clipped off, snagged threads are worked back into the cloth, and defects are marked so that adjustments can be made when fabrics are sold. The fabric is then wound on bolts or cylinders ready for shipment.

23 *Additive and Chemical Finishes*

The *pad machine*, often called the "work horse" of the textile industry, is used to apply dyes, chemicals, and additive finishes. It will apply them in either liquid or paste form, on one or both sides, by immersion or by transfer from a roller which revolves in the finishing solution. A simple pad machine is shown in Figure 23–1.

Padding is done by passing the fabric through the finishing solution, under a guide roll and between two padding rolls. The rolls are metal or rubber, depending on the finish to be applied. The rolls exert tons of pressure on the fabric to squeeze the finish into the fiber or fabric in order to assure good penetration. Excess liquid is squeezed off. The fabric then travels into the steaming or washing and drying machine.

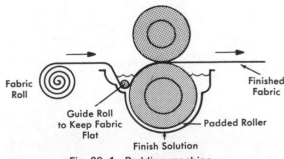

Fig. 23–1. Padding machine.

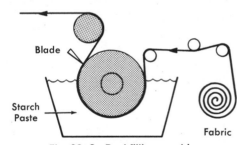

Fig. 23–2. Backfilling machine.

The backfilling machine is a variation of the pad machine. It applies the finish to one side only, usually to the wrong side of the fabric. The fabric is held tightly against the large roll which revolves in the finishing paste and a blade scrapes off the excess. (See Figure 23–2.)

Additive Finishes

Additive finishes are applied to give texture (body, stiffness, softness), luster, embossed designs, and abrasion resistance to the fabric. They are held on the surface mechanically and their permanence depends on the efficiency of the finish and the type of finish itself.

Sizings

Also called dressings, sizings are used to give body, stiffness, strength, weight, and/or smoothness to the fabric. The following chart lists the commonly used sizings.

SIZINGS

Temporary	Durable
Starch	Resins
Gelatin	Cellulose solutions
Softeners	

Starching at the mill is similar to starching at home except that the starch mixture contains waxes, oils, glycerine, and similar compounds, which act as softeners. For added weight, talc, clay, and chalk are used. Starches come from wheat, corn, potatoes, sago, and other plants. Each starch has individual properties that determine its use.

Gelatin is used on the rayons because it is a clear substance that does not detract from the natural luster of the fibers but enhances it. Many rayon fabrics are sold in the loom state and the gelatin is lost in washing. It can be restored by the following home process:

Dissolve 2 tablespoons of gelatin in 1 gallon of water. Rinse the garment in the solution and remove excess liquid to prevent its draining to the lower edge and stiffening it.

Cellulose solutions are dissolved cellulose similar to the solution from which rayon fibers are spun; carboxy methyl cellulose is commonly used.

Surface Coatings

These are made of rubber latex, thermoplastics and resins to increase abrasion resistance, serve as a binder, give luster, or give water profing.

USES

Uses
Coat individual warp yarns in denim
Backing for carpets
hold tufts
nonslip finish
Binder for pigment colors
Binder for flock
Glaze
Rainwear

Glazed Effects. The thermosetting resins (see page 199), urea and melamine formaldehyde, were first used in 1940, when a process was developed for polymerizing them on the surface of the fabric. The fabric is kept under tension and the resin remains on the surface where it is dried, polished, embossed, and cured. These resins are held to the surface by a *chemico-mechanical* action.

Glazed effects produced by this means are of two kinds. *Glazed chintz* is often a plain color but may be printed. It has a heavy, rubbery layer of resin on the surface. *Polished cotton* is similar but has a much thinner layer of resin on the surface and is much more apt to wrinkle during washing.

Embossed designs are similar to the glazed fabrics except that an engraved roller presses a raised pattern into the cloth.

If these fabrics have a resin applied as a continuous coating, they are uncomfortable for summer wear because they prevent the passage of moisture vapor. (See Figure 23–3a.) If they are applied as a discontinuous coating, the fabric can "breathe" and is more comfortable. (See Figure 23–3b.)

Resin on the Surface and on the Yarns

Resin on the Surface Only

Fig. 23–3. Glazed fabrics. Left, continuous resin coating. Right, discontinuous resin coating.

Chemical Finishes

Chemical finishes are some of the oldest finishes used. Natural dyes, iron rust dyeing, caustic from ashes and urine, and bleaching by sunlight are examples. Chemical finishes are usually permanent; and unlike the additive finishes, they do not add weight to the fabric.

Some of the following chemicals are now used in large quantities by the textile industry:

1. Caustic soda (alkali)
2. Sodium phosphate
3. Soda ash
4. Chlorine
5. Sulfuric acid
6. Sodium sulfate
7. Hydrogen peroxide

Bleaching

Most bleaches are oxidizing agents. The actual bleaching is done by *active oxygen*. A few bleaches are reducing agents. These are used to strip color from dyed fabrics. Bleaches may be either acid or alkaline in nature. They are usually unstable, especially in the presence of moisture. Bleaches that are old or have been improperly stored will lose their oxidizing power.

Any bleach will cause some damage, and since damage occurs more rapidly at higher temperatures and concentrations, these factors should be carefully controlled.

The same bleach is not suitable to all kinds of fibers. Because fibers vary in their chemical reaction, bleaches must be chosen with regard to fiber content. The anklets in Figure 23–4 had been all white, but when bleached with a chlorine bleach, the wool-ribbed cuff section became discolored, while the cotton feet remained white.

The consumer uses bleaches to remove stains,[1] and off-white "tattle-tale" gray caused by the soil and soap curds from wash water should be removed by reconditioning treatments rather than by a bleach. Better still, wash often and use correct washing procedures from the start. Reconditioning is done by soaking the article in a solution made with a nonprecipitating water softner[2] and then washing it in hot, sudsy, *softened* water. This must be repeated several times. Mild bleaches may be used on fabric to remove stains without damage to the original color of the fabric. Garments that have a resin finish should not be bleached with chlorine since yellowing will result.

The *finisher* uses bleaches to clean and whiten gray goods. The natural fibers are an off-white color because of the impurities they contain. Since these impurities are easily removed from cotton, most cotton gray goods are bleached without damage. The bleaching step is often omitted with wool because it has good affinity for dyes and other finishes even if not bleached.

Liquid chlorine bleaches were, for many years, the common household bleaches. They are efficient bactericidal agents, and as such can be used for sterilizing fabrics. They are cheap and efficient bleaches for cotton and rayon. The bleaching is done by the

[1] A good reference is "Stain Removal from Fabrics—Home Methods," *Farmers Bulletin* 1474, United States Department of Agriculture, 1959.

[2] Calgon, Phosphotex, and Noctil are trade names.

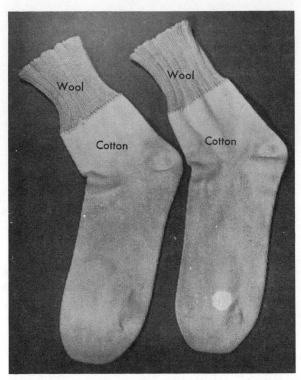

Fig. 23–4. White anklets of cotton and wool after bleaching in chlorine bleach.

hypochlorous acid liberated during the bleaching process. This *tenders* cellulose fibers and the bleach must be thoroughly rinsed out or an antichlor (sodium thiosulfate) should be used. Chlorine bleaches, other than sodium chlorite, are of no value on the protein and thermoplastic fibers and if used will cause yellowing. Man-made fibers are often damaged or are unaffected by the household chlorine bleaches. The weekly wash also contains many fabrics with crease-recovery and embossed finishes, which should *not* be bleached with chlorine.

Peroxide bleaches are common factory bleaches for cellulose and protein fibers and fabrics. *Hydrogen peroxide* is an oxidizing bleach. A 3 per cent solution is relatively stable at room temperature and is safe to use. Peroxide will bleach best at a temperature of 180 to 200° F in an alkaline solution. These bleaching conditions make it possible to do peroxide bleaching of cellulose gray goods as the final step in the kier boil.

In the *peroxide cold bleach* procedure, the fabric is soaked overnight or for a period of eight hours. This procedure is often used on cotton knit goods and wool to preserve a soft hand. Peroxide is good for removing light scorch stains.

Sodium perborate is a powder bleach[3] which becomes hydrogen peroxide when it combines with water. It is a safe bleach for home use with all kinds of fibers. Satisfactory results have also been obtained with the thermoplastic fibers by use of the cold bleach process. Powder bleaches are recommended for regular use in the wash water to maintain the original whiteness of the fabric rather than as a *whitener* for discolored fabrics.

Acid bleaches such as oxalic acid and potassium permanganate have limited use. Citric acid and lemon juice are also acid bleaches which are good rust spot removers.

Reducing bleaches are good for stripping color from dyed fabrics. Sodium hydrosulfite is available at drug stores.

Optical brighteners are also used to whiten off-white fabrics. They are fluorescent white compounds, not bleaches. The fluorescent white compounds are absorbed into the fiber and emit a bluish fluorescence that covers up yellowish tinges. At the mill, optical brighteners give best results when used in combination with the bleach rather than as a substitute for it. These new fluorescent whites are often incorporated in soaps and detergents as "whiter than new" ingredients. They also are added to the spinning solution of some man-made fibers.

Acid Finishes

Transparent (or parchment) effects in cotton cloth are produced by treatment with strong sulfuric acid. One of the oldest finishes is a Swiss or organdy finish produced by the Heberlein process. Since acid damages cotton, the process must be very carefully controlled, and "split-second" (five to six seconds) timing is necessary to prevent *tendering* or weakening of the fabric. These effects are possible: all-over parchmentization, localized parchmentization, and plissé effect on either of the first two.

Since all-over parchmentizing is for the purpose of producing a transparent effect, a sheer fabric of combed lawn is used. The goods are singed, desized, bleached, and mercerized. Mercerization is such an important part of the process that the fabric is mercerized again after the acid treatment in order to improve the transparency. The fabric is then dyed or printed with colors that will resist acid

[3] Trade names: Dexol, Snowy, Vans, Safety.

damage. The cloth is immersed in the acid solution and partial solution of the surface of the cellulose takes place. Upon drying, this surface rehardens as a cellulose film and gives permanent crispness and transparency. After the acid treatment, the cloth is neutralized in weak alkali, washed, and then calendered to give more gloss to the surface. This all-over treatment produces *organdy* fabric.

In localized parchmentizing, if the design is a small figure with a large transparent area, an acid-resist substance is printed on the figures and the fabric is run through the acid bath. The acid-resistant areas retain their original opacity and contrast sharply with the transparent background. (See Figure 23–5.) If a small transparent design is

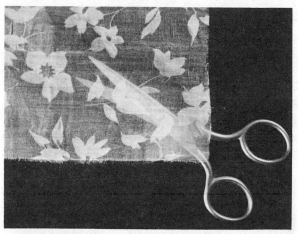

Fig. 23–5. Localized parchmentizing—acid finish—gives transparent background.

desired, the acid is printed on and then quickly washed off.

The three-dimensional plissé effect is achieved by printing caustic soda on the parchmentized fabric. The untreated areas pucker as the caustic soda causes the printed areas to shrink. The plissé effect can also be made on fabric with local parchmentization.

Burnt-out or etched effects are produced by printing sulfuric acid on a fabric made of fibers from different fiber groups, rayon and silk, for example. (See Figure 23–6.) The rayon will be "eaten" away leaving sheer silk areas.

Carbonizing, which is the treatment of wool yarns or fabrics with sulfuric acid, destroys vegetable matter in the fabric and more level dyeing can be obtained. Carbonizing is also done on reused and reprocessed wool to remove any cellulose that may

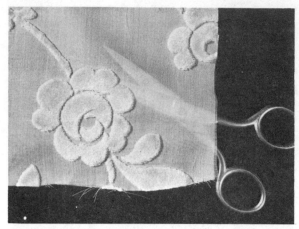

Fig. 23–6. Burnt-out design or etched effect by acid. Acid has eaten away pile in the velvet cloth leaving a transparent background.

have been used in the original fabric. Carbonizing gives better texture to all-wool fabrics.

Puckered surfaces are created by partial solution of the surface of a nylon or polyester fabric. Plissé, sculptured, and "damasque" effects are made by printing a chemical on the fabric to partially dissolve it. Shrinking occurs as it dries, thus creating a puckered surface. (See Figure 23–7.)

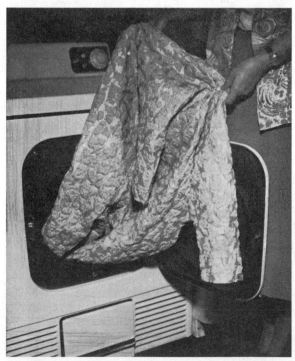

Fig. 23–7. Removing a nylon "damasque" housecoat from an automatic dryer after washing.

Mercerization

Mercerization is the action of an alkali (caustic soda) on a fabric. Mercerizing was a revolutionary development discovered in 1853 by John Mercer, a calico printer. He noticed that his cotton filter cloth shrank, became stronger, more lustrous, and more absorbent after filtering the caustic soda used in the dye process. Little use was made of mercerization at that time because the shrinkage caused a 20 to 25 per cent yardage loss, and the increased durability caused mill men to fear that less fabric would be used. In 1897, Lowe discovered that if the fabric were held under tension, it did not shrink but became very lustrous and silk-like.

Mercerization is used on cotton and linen for many different reasons. It increases the luster and softness, gives greater strength, and improves the affinity for dyes and water-borne finishes. Plissé effects can be achieved in cotton fabrics. (See page 160.) "Mercerized cotton" on a label is associated with luster. Cotton is mercerized for luster in both yarn and fabric form.

Yarn mercerization is a continuous process in which the yarn under tension passes from a warp beam through a series of boxes with guide rolls and squeeze rolls, through a boil-out wash, and a final wash. (See Figure 23–8.)

Fabric mercerization is done on a frame that contains mangles for saturating the cloth, a tenter

Fig. 23–8. Mercerization of warp yarn. (Courtesy of Coats & Clark, Inc., New York, N. Y.)

frame for tensioning the fabric both crosswise and lengthwise while wet, and boxes for washing, neutralizing with dilute sulfuric acid, scouring, and rinsing. Turn to page 32 for a discussion of the changes that occur in the cotton fiber. In rayon, the amount of improvement in luster corresponds to the difference in luster between dull and bright fibers.

Greater absorbency results from mercerization because the caustic soda causes a rearrangement of the molecules, thus making the hydroxyl groups available to absorb more water and water-borne substances. Thus dyes can enter the fiber more readily, and when they can be fixed inside the fiber, they are more fast. (Caustic soda is also used in vat dyeing to keep the vat dye soluble until it penetrates the fiber.) Mercerized cotton and linen take resin finishes better for the same reason.

Increased strength is an important value from mercerization. Mercerized cotton fibers are stronger because in the swollen fiber, the molecules are more nearly parallel to the fiber axis. When stress is applied, the attraction, which is an end-to-end molecular attraction, is harder to rupture than in the more spiral fibril arrangement.

Stretch is achieved in 100 per cent cotton by *slack mercerization*. It gives comfort in fabrics. (See page 113.)

Waterproof and Water-Repellent Fabrics

A waterproof fabric is one that no water can penetrate. A water-repellent fabric is resistant to wetting, but if the water comes with enough force, it will penetrate the fabric.

The Federal Trade Commission has suggested the use of the terms "durable" and "renewable" in describing water-repellent fabrics.

Water repellency is dependent on surface tension and fabric penetrability and is achieved by (1) finish and (2) cloth construction.

Water-Repellent Finishes

Finishes that can be applied to a fabric to make it repellent are wax emulsions, metallic soaps, and surface active agents. They are applied to fabrics such as tackle twill, poplin, and rayon and cotton

Waterproof Fabrics	*Water-Repellent Fabrics*
Fabrics are plastic films or low-count fabrics with a film coating.	High-count fabrics with a finish that coats the yarn but does not fill up the interstices of the fabric.

Characteristics

No water can penetrate.	Heavy rain will penetrate.
Most plastic fabrics stiffen in cold weather.	Fabric is pliable, and is no different from untreated fabric.
Cheaper to produce	Fabric can "breathe," is comfortable for raincoats.
Permanent	Durable or renewable finish

satin, all of which have a very high warp count and are made with fine yarns.

Wax emulsions and *metallic soaps* coat the yarns but do not fill the interstices between the yarns. These finishes are not permanent but tend to come out when the fabric is washed or dry-cleaned. They can be renewed.

Surface active agents[4] have molecules with one end that is water-repellent and one end that will react with the hydroxyl (OH) groups of cellulose. After they are applied, heat is used to seal the finish to the fabric. This finish is permanent to washing and dry cleaning.

Cloth Construction

Cloth construction can be water-repellent without a finish. *Shirley cloth* developed at the Shirley Institute in England is similar in construction to the canvas bags found in Egyptian tombs. They were plain weave with two warp threads woven as one. They were always made of flax. Studies showed that cotton and flax swell about the same amount. It was decided that twist made the difference between cotton and the flax. Shirley cloth is made of long, fine cotton fibers, three-ply yarns of very low twist, and oxford weave. It is a nearly waterproof fabric. It is cool and porous when dry, but moisture causes the yarns to swell and close the interstices between them.

It is more difficult to select a water-repellent coat than a waterproof coat because the finish is not obvious and one must depend on the label for information. However, the consumer can recognize

---

[4] Zelan is one example.

some guides for buying. *The cloth construction is far more important than the finish.* The closer the weave, the greater the resistance to water penetration. The kind of finish used is important in selection because it influences the cost of upkeep. The use of two layers of fabric across the shoulders gives increased protection, but the inner layer must also have a water-repellent finish or it will act as a blotter and cause more water to penetrate.

Care is important in water-repellent fabrics. The greater the soil on the coat, the less water-repellent it is.

Water-repellent finishes render fabrics spot and stain-resistant. Some of the finishes are resistant to water-borne stains, some are resistant to oil-borne stains, and some to both. Durable water-repellent finishes often hold greasy stains more tenaciously than untreated fabrics. Unisec, Scotch-gard, and Zepel are trade names for finishes that give resistance to both oily and water-borne stains. Hydro-Pruf and Syl-mer are silicone finishes that give resistance to water-borne stains.

Flammability and Fire-Retardant Finishes

The Flammable Fabrics Act became effective on July 1, 1954. The terms "flammable" and "inflammable" both mean "will burn." "Nonflammable" means "will not burn." "Fire retardant" means "burns slowly."

The mineral fibers are *flameproof.* The protein and some of the thermoplastic fibers melt as they burn and may stick to the skin, resulting in an even deeper burn.

Cellulose fibers burn easily and completely but leave an afterglow, a continued slow burning that can be as dangerous as the flame itself.

The construction of the fabric determines the degree to which oxygen is made available to the fiber. Thick heavy fabrics burn slowly, thin open fabrics burn very rapidly. Fabrics with a fuzzy surface burn along the surface before the base fabric catches fire.

Fabrics are divided into three groups according to their flammability.

1. *Safe* fabrics that do not burn—Fiberglas, wool, etc.

2. *Borderline* fabrics that should be tested for flammability are sheer fabrics such as organdy, lawn, and voile, and napped fabrics with short nap.
3. *Dangerously flammable* fabrics—very sheer fabrics and nets, long and/or irregular napped and pile fabrics with loose base construction, and fabrics with certain flammable finishes.

Brushed rayons are easier to ignite than other napped fabrics and burn with greater speed and intensity.

Blending fire-resistant fibers with cellulose fibers will lower the flammability of cellulose fabrics.

According to existing theories, fire-retardant compounds either cut off the supply of oxygen to the fabric by forming a coating or by producing a noncombustible gas, or chemically alter the fiber so that it forms a nonvolatile charred residue rather than the usual flammable tarry products.

Mothproofing

It has been estimated that $100 million is lost annually from damage of textiles by moths and carpet beetles. Most of this damage occurs where storehouses store raw wool, manufacturers store fabrics, and stores carry over suits and coats from one season to another. Moth damage is an equally serious problem for consumers.

Both moths and carpet beetles attack not only 100 per cent wool, but also blends of wool and other fibers. Although they can digest only the wool, they eat through the other fibers. The damage is done by the larvae and not the adult moth. Clothes moths are about ¼ inch long; they are not the large moths that we may occasionally see about the house. Larvae shun bright sunlight and do their work in the dark. For this reason, it is necessary to clean often under sofas, under sofa cushions, in creases of chairs and garments, and dark closets. Larvae are supposed to be killed by direct sunlight, so it is a good practice to hang garments in the sun occasionally.

Means of controlling moth damage are as follows:

1. Cold storage.
2. Odors that repel. Paradichlorobenzene and naphthalene (moth balls) used during storage.

3. Stomach poisons. Fluorides and silicofluorides are finishes for dry-cleanable wool.
4. Contact poisons. DDT is very effective but requires frequent application.
5. Chemicals, added to the dyebath, permanently change the fiber making it unpalatable to the larvae.

Molds and Mildew

Molds and mildew will grow on and damage both cellulose and protein textiles. They will grow on but not damage the thermoplastic fibers. Losses are estimated in the millions of dollars.

Prevention is the best solution to the problem in apparel since cures are often impossible. To prevent mold or mildew, keep textiles clean and dry. Soiled clothes should be kept dry and washed as soon as possible. Sunning and airing should be done frequently during periods of high humidity. An electric light can be used in dark humid storage places. Dehumidifiers in homes are very helpful.

If mildew occurs, wash the article immediately. Mild stains can be removed by bleaching.

Other Finishes

Antiseptic finishes are used to inhibit the growth of bacteria and other odor-causing germs and to prevent decay and damage from perspiration. These finishes are important in skin-contact clothing, shoe linings, and especially hospital linens. The chemicals used are surface reactants, mostly quaternary ammonia compounds. Those substances can be added to the spinning solution of rayon and acetate fibers. Most diaper service establishments add the finish during each laundering. Eversan and Sanitized are two trade names.

Soil-retardant finishes are used on cellulosic fabrics that cannot be laundered easily. The first attempt was made on rayon carpeting. Upholstery fabrics of cotton and rayon soil readily and need this kind of finish. Mixes containing colloidal silica or alumina have given good results. The submicroscopic particles fill surface pores, which are the main gathering places for soil. Other finishes reduce positive charges on the fibers, so they will no longer attract negatively charged soil.

Soil-release finishes became important when consumers became more critical of oil-staining of durable-press garments. Soil-release finishes are said to be effective usually with one "warm water" wash. For stubborn stains, one or two washes in hot water may be necessary. One technique called *alpha radiation* is due to new technology by Deering-Milliken. The process of how soil is released has not been reported, but "It is probable that a suitable chemical or monomer is grafted onto the polyester component to form a protective coating thus preventing deep penetration of stain."[5] Visa is the trade name for this fabric finish. Fybrite, a nonsoil-retentive finish by Celanese, is a chemical additive that deposits a hydrophilic chemical charge that resists staining and redeposition of soil. Come Clean and Zip Clean are other trade names for soil release finishes.

[5] Stanley M. Suchecki, "Durable Press, Phase 2," *Textile Industries* 130:9 (September, 1966).

24 Special-Purpose Finishes: Stabilization and Durable Press

A fabric is stabilized when it retains its original size and shape during use and care. Unstable fabrics shrink or stretch. Of these, shrinkage is the more serious problem. *Shrinkage* is the reduction in size of a fabric or garment.

The shrinkage problem with cotton began when spinning, weaving, and finishing were mechanized. Fabrics are under tension on the loom, and in wet finishing, fabrics are pulled through machines in long continuous pieces and finally set under excessive warpwise tension that leaves the fabric with high residual shrinkage. This shrinkage will take place when tensions are released by laundering or steam pressing.

Shrinkage is used to advantage in the manufacture of some fabrics. For example, *fulling* of wool cloth closes up the weave and makes a firmer fabric and shrinkage of the high-twist yarns in crepes creates the surface crinkle. Shrinkage is a disadvantage to the consumer when it changes the length or size of a garment. Shrinkage of 5 per cent in a size 15 shirt can shorten the sleeve length ¾ inch and reduce the chest size by 2 or 3 inches. A washable garment should not shrink more than 2 per cent. Before the 1930's, washable cotton garments were often purchased one size too large and then shrunk down to fit. Then the compressive shrinkage

control process was invented and garments bearing the label Sanforized could be purchased in the correct size with the assurance that they would not shrink more than 1 per cent (unless tumble dried).

There are two types of shrinkage: *relaxation* (or fabric) shrinkage that occurs in the first wash, and *progressive* (or fiber) shrinkage that occurs during subsequent washes. Mechanical control methods or heat are used to eliminate relaxation shrinkage, and chemical control methods are used to prevent progress shrinkage.

1. *Cotton, linen, and high-wet-modulus rayon:*
   exhibit relaxation shrinkage,
   and no progressive shrinkage.
2. *Regular rayon:*
   exhibits high relaxation shrinkage,
   and moderate progressive shrinkage.
3. *Wool:*
   exhibits moderate relaxation shrinkage,
   and high progressive shrinkage.

Relaxation Shrinkage and Methods of Control

Knit Fabrics. Knit fabrics shrink because the loops are elongated 10 to 35 per cent lengthwise in knitting and in wet finishing, as shown in Figure

Before Redmanizing   After Redmanizing

Fig. 24–1. Knit stitches. Left, before orientation. Right, after orientation.

24–1, thus making the fabric longer and narrower than it should be. During home laundering, the stitches will reorient themselves to their normal shape, and the garment will become shorter and wider. Mechanical methods of shrinkage control for knit fabrics consist of using a spreader to stretch the fabric crosswise to reorient the stitches. The fabrics is then dried on a special tensionless calender or it may be tumble-dried. Completed garments may also be tumble-dried to give them controlled shrinkage. At the present time, mechanical relaxation shrinkage control treatments are usually done in conjunction with a resin finish. A large percentage of cotton knit goods is sold as white shirts and underwear, so that the resin must be of the nonyellowing type.

Woven Fabrics All woven fabrics shrink when the strains of weaving, warp yarn sizing, and wet finishing are released when the fabric gets wet in laundering. The warp yarns are stretched out straight while they are on the loom, and the filling is inserted in a straight line. The filling takes on crimp as it is beaten back into the cloth, but the warp stays straight. When the fabric is thoroughly wet and allowed to relax, the yarns readjust themselves and the warp yarns move to a crimped position also. (See Figure 24–2.) This crimp shortens the fabric in the warp direction. With the exception of crepe fabrics, less change occurs in the filling direction.

Compressive shrinkage processes are used on woven fabrics of cotton, linen, and high-wet-modulus rayon. Regular rayons will not hold a compressive shrinkage treatment because of the high swelling and wet elongation of the rayon fibers.

Sanforize and Rigmel are trade names for compressive shrinkage processes used on woven cloth. The principles involved can be demonstrated by placing a piece of fabric over the clenched fist, then placing a rubber band over the cloth. When the fist is opened and the band is released, the cloth will be squeezed or compressed.

In the factory process, a woolen felt blanket is the medium that shrinks the cloth. A thick blanket will shrink the cloth more than a thin one. The blanket, with the moist cloth adhering to its surface, is passed around a feed-in roll. In this curved position, the outer surface stretches and the inner surface contracts. The blanket then reverses its direction around a heated drum. The outer curve becomes the shorter inner surface and the fabric adhering to it is compressed. The fabric, which is now against the drum, is dried and set with a smooth finish. The number of yarns per square inch will increase, and the cloth will actually be improved after compressing. (See Figures 24–3 and 24–4.)

Research has shown that faulty laundering will cause compressively shrunk fabrics to shrink as much as 6 per cent. Tumble-drying may also compress the yarns beyond their normal shrinkage.

Fig. 24–2. Left, position of the fabric on the loom. Right, after the fabric relaxes when it becomes wet.

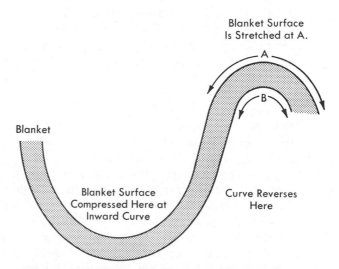

Fig. 24–3. Diagram shows how the reversal of curves can cause change in size, which compresses the fabric.

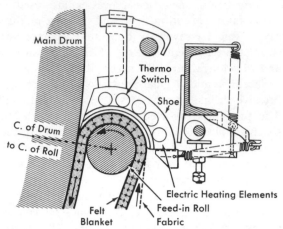

Fig. 24–4. Enlarged cross-sectional diagram of the point in the compressive shrinkage process where length shrinkage is obtained. The electrically heated shoe holds the fabric firmly on the outside of the blanket so that when the blanket collapses in straightening out, the fabric is shrunk accordingly. (Courtesy of "Sanforized" division of Cluett, Peabody & Co., Inc.)

The trade name *Sanforized Plus* may be used on wash-and-wear and durable-press garments that meet specified standards of shrinkage control, wrinkle resistance, smoothness after washing, tensile strength, and tear strength.

London shrunk is a 200-year old relaxation finish for wool fabrics, which removes strains caused by spinning, weaving, and finishing. At first, the wool was laid out in the fields of the city of London and the dew soothed away the stresses and improved the hand of the fabric. While techniques have been modernized, there is still much hand labor involved. A wet blanket, wool or cotton, is placed on a long platform, a layer of cloth is then spread on it, and alternate layers of blankets and cloth built up. Sufficient weight is placed on top to force the moisture from the blankets into the wool. The cloth is left in the pile for about 12 hours. The cloth is then dried in natural room air by hanging it over sticks. When dry, the cloth is subjected to hydraulic pressing by building up layers of cloth and specially made press boards with a preheated metal plate inserted at intervals. A preheated plate is also placed on the top and bottom. This set-up of cloth, boards, and plates is kept under 3,000 pounds pressure for 10 to 12 hours. London shrinking is done for men's wear fine worsteds—not for woolens or women's wear.

Fig. 24–5. The London Shrunk Label.

Today, the right to use the label "Genuine London Process" or something similar is licensed by the Parrott group of companies, Clothworkers of London, Leeds, and Huddersfield to garment makers all over the world. A label from a suit is shown in Figure 24–5.

The permanent set finish Si-Ro-set, which produces washable, wrinkle-free wool fabrics, is now applied to some fabrics during the London Shrunk processing.

A similar method for home use is that of rolling wool cloth in a wet sheet, allowing it to stand for six hours, and then placing it flat on a table or floor to dry. If it is straightened while wet, pressing may be unnecessary. This is the best means for straightening wool which has been tentered or decated "off-grain." It should not be used on wool crepe. Fabrics that have a napped surface, such as wool broadcloth or some wool flannels, may be changed in appearance. Wool fabrics should always be tested for shrinkage prior to cutting. A simple method of testing is to draw a right angle on the ironing board, place the warp edge along one side and the filling edge along the other side, and hold the steam iron over the fabric. If either edge draws away from the pencil line, the fabric will shrink during steam pressing and it should be shrunk.

Progressive Shrinkage and Methods of Control

Thermoplastic Fibers. Thermoplastic fibers are stabilized by heat-setting. (See page 43 on "Heat-Setting.") If properly heat-set, fabrics will exhibit no progressive shrinkage and relaxation shrinkage will have been controlled also.

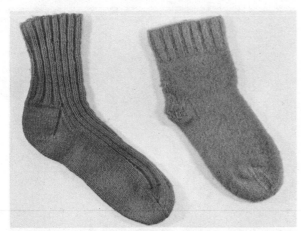

Fig. 24–6. These socks were the same size when knitted. Left, nylon sock. Right, wool sock.

Wool Fibers. Washable wool is important in children's clothing, in skin-contact clothing, and in blends with washable fibers. If wool fabrics are to maintain their position in the competitive market with fabrics made from wool-like fibers that have easy-care characteristics, they must be finished to keep their original size and surface texture with home cleaning methods. It might be assumed that people who can afford professional care will not be interested in washing wools. Another assumption might be that washable wools (those given a felting shrinkage control treatment) are the poor-to-medium quality wools. Whether or not these assumptions are true, felting shrinkage is important today, as evidenced by the fact that 250 patents for feltproofing wool were issued prior to 1957 and more have been issued since. (See page 18 for discussion of wool felting.)

To prevent felting shrinkage, the finish must alter the scale structure by "smoothing off" the free edges and thus reduce the differential friction effect that prevents wool fibers from returning to their original position in the cloth. The effectiveness of felting shrinkage treatments depends on the kind and amount of finish used, and on the yarn and fabric construction. Worsteds need less finish than woolens. Low-count fabrics and low-twist yarns need more finish to give good washability. Treated wool fabrics are usually considered machine washable, but care should be taken to use warm, not hot, water and a short agitation period. Hand washing is preferable, since soil is easy to remove from the fiber and the hand washing process ensures lower temperature and less agitation. Machine washing may cause more loosening of fibers, which results in a fuzzy or slightly pilled surface.

Two methods are used to smooth off the free edges of the scales; halogenation treatments and surface coatings:

Halogenation treatments are the most widely used—primarily chlorine. They are low in cost, can be applied to large batches of small items such as wool socks, do not require padding or curing equipment, and are fairly effective. The processes are quite delicate and if not carefully done, are apt to damage the fibers. The scales are more resistant to damage than the interior of the fiber, and should not be completely removed or there will be considerable reduction in wearing properties, there will be loss of weight, and change in hand. The fabric will feel harsh and rough. To maintain the strength of the fabric, 18 per cent nylon fiber is blended with the wool before weaving.

Surface coatings of a polyamide-type solution are applied to mask the scales. This is a very thin, microscopic film on the outside of the fiber. In addition to controlling shrinkage, the coating tends to minimize pilling and fuzzing (one of the greatest problems in wash-and-wear wools), gives the fabrics better wash-and-wear properties, and increases resistance to abrasion. This process carries the trade name Wurlan. It was developed at the Department of Agriculture Laboratory in Albany, California.

Rayon Fibers. The shrinkage of regular rayon varies with the handling of the fabric when wet. While it is wet, it can be stretched and it is difficult to keep from overstretching it during processing. If it is dried in this stretched condition, it will have high potential shrinkage and shrink when wet again and dried without tension. Unfortunately, it is difficult to dry it without tension because the moisture in the fabric adds enough weight to stretch it.

Shrinkage control treatments for rayon reduce the swelling property of the fiber and make it resistant to distortion. Resins are impregnated inside the fiber to form cross-links that prevent swelling and keep the fiber from stretching. The resin also fills up spaces in the amorphous areas of the fiber, making it less absorbent. The non-nitrogenous resins (the aldehydes) are superior to the other resins because they do not weaken the fabric and are nonchlorine retentive and have excellent wash fastness. Treated rayons are machine washable, but the wash cycle should be short. High-wet-modulus rayon is also resin treated, primarily for wash-and-wear purposes, since its shrinkage can be controlled by the relaxation shrinkage control method of Sanforization.

Durable Press and Wash-and-Wear Finishes

Surveys have shown that ironing is the household task that women dislike the most. Durable press and wash-and-wear finishes for cotton, linen, and rayon fabrics have greatly reduced the amount of time spent in ironing. The cellulose fibers have always been low in resiliency and fabrics made from them have had very poor recovery from wrinkles. *Wrinkles* are undesirable mussiness and puckering in fabrics caused by wear and washing. They are formed under a wide range of pressures, times, temperatures, and humidities and they take various times to recover. This makes finishing of the fabric to improve its behavior a complicated affair. *Creases* are sharp folds added to a fabric deliberately by pressing—pleats and the like for purposes of styling.

The introduction of the first *finish* by Tootal, Broadhurst, Lee of England for improvement of wrinkle recovery, coincided with the development in the United States of the first *wash-and-wear synthetic fibers*—about 1940. The finishing substance was a *resin*. Urea formaldehyde, the first resin finish, was used on linen and rayon; but because of poor chlorine resistance and loss of strength, its use on cotton was limited. Regular rayon fibers have always had poor washability and the resin treatments further reduced rayon's wet abrasion resistance, so the finish was limited to dry-cleanable rayon fabrics, which were sold as "crease-resistant" materials. In 1940, melamine formaldehyde resins were developed for use on cotton and the wash-and-wear finishes got their start. The polyester/cotton blends were introduced in 1954 about a year after the first polyester—Dacron—was made. Only the cotton component of the blend required a resin finish. Dacron was a higher-priced fiber and was not used in low-cost items, whereas 100 per cent cotton was used at all price levels.

Fig. 24–7. Durable-press shirt. (Courtesy of E. I. du Pont de Nemours & Company.)

The idea of setting *permanent shape*—durable press—in a garment began in 1955 when Korot of California asked their suppliers to apply and dry the resin monomer on the cotton cloth but *not* cure it. Korot then cut and pleated the fabric and oven-cured the garment to set the pleats. The wash-and-wear industry took little interest in this change in the conventional process until 1964 when Levi Strauss introduced "Oven-Baked" pants of 100 per cent cotton under the Korot trade name of Koratron. They were a tremendous and instantaneous success even though the first pants split at the creases and cuff edges frayed after two or three washings. Men's shirts were next given the durable-press finish shown in Figures 24–7 and 24–8, and within two years dresses, blouses, rainwear, jackets, sheets, and pillow cases were being made with a durable-press finish. It is said that each garment has a certain drama. For example, in slacks the focal point is the crease; and if it is a good sharp crease, some puckering or wrinkling does not dissatisfy the consumer. This may account for the immediate acceptance of the durable-press concept.

To overcome the high strength loss and the lowering of abrasion resistance caused by the resin and the high heat of curing, manufacturers gradually shifted to the use of "reinforcing" synthetic fibers blended with cotton (Nylon 420, Tough Stuff Vycron, etc.). Research in 100 per cent cotton fabrics was intensified to find a durable-press finish that would leave the cotton fiber with most or all of its natural good wearing qualities but that would give the additional durable-press performance.

Wash-and-Wear Versus Durable Press

The conventional wash-and-wear finish was designed to *set flat fabric* so that it would retain a smooth unwrinkled condition. The diagram (Figure 24–9) shows the steps in the process. Durable press has been described as the mature, more sophisticated heir to wash-and-wear garments. It was designed to *set the shape of the garment*. Figure 24–10 is a diagram of the general durable press procedure. Specific information for all commercial procedures is given in the section that follows.

There have been two theories concerning the function of the resins in the fiber. The *deposition theory* was that the resin filled up space within the fiber to prevent the penetration of moisture and keep the fiber from swelling when it became wet. The *cross-linking theory*, accepted about 1948, was that the resin or reactant formed cross-links between the molecular chains to tie them together and limit chain slippage.

Finishing Agents

A continuing research program by industry—particularly the cotton industry—has resulted in the development of many (1) new resins and reactants and (2) better processes to improve continually the performance of the wash-and-wear finishes available to the consumer.

The finish usually contains more than the resin or reactant. Some of the other substances are: catalysts, silicone emulsion softeners, optical whiteners, and thermoplastic polymers.

Resins are a family of chemicals that can be applied to cotton, rayon, and linen fabrics *in monomer form*. They will polymerize when heat-cured to form *cross-links* between the molecular chains of the cellulose. The formaldehyde resins have been known for 60 years and used for about 30. (The newest method—the vapor phase method—

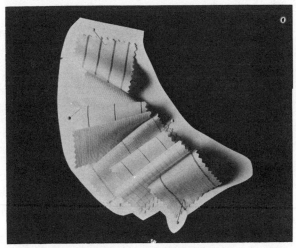

Fig. 24–8. Durable-press shirting fabrics. (Courtesy of E. I. du Pont de Nemours & Company.)

uses formaldehyde resins.) Phenol formaldehyde was the first to be used but it was discarded because it discolored the cloth. Urea formaldehyde for rayon and melamine formaldehyde for cotton were the first to be used successfully. Many resins have been tried and discarded because of poor resistance to conditions of use or for lack of permanence to washing. The nitrogen-containing resins could not be used on white fabrics because of yellowing when bleached with chlorine.

Cellulose reactants are nonresinous chemicals that have a definite chemical reaction with the cellulose fiber polymer. The aldehydes and sulfones are examples of these. Cellulose reactants have been described as: ". . . an effective way to impart crease recovery to cellulose fabrics by establishing covalent bonds between the molecule and the individual fiber."[1]

COMPARISON OF RESINS AND REACTANTS

Resins	Reactants
Durability depends on processing	Good durability
May contain nitrogen	Free of nitrogen
Adds weight and body	Adds little weight to fabric
May stiffen	Softer hand
Reduces fabric strength	Less strength loss

[1] Richard Steele, "The Cross-linking of Cellulose," *American Dyestuff Reporter* **54**: 19 (January 4, 1965).

METHODS OF ACHIEVING WASH-AND-WEAR AND DURABLE PRESS

I. WASH-AND-WEAR WITH THERMOPLASTIC FIBERS (NO CHEMICAL FINISH IS NEEDED)
   Flat fabric or garments are *heat-set* by dry or moist heat

II. WASH-AND-WEAR FINISH OF FLAT FABRIC
   Conventional method
   Saturate the fabric with the resin cross-linking solution and dry
   Cure in a curing oven (cross-links form between molecular chains)
   Cut and sew garment. Press with iron
   Figure 24–9 shows the steps in the process

Advantages	*Disadvantages*
Fabric had good wrinkle recovery (when properly finished) if good laundry procedures were used	Fabric resisted being shaped into garment; creases were difficult to press, seams puckered, etc.
Less loss of strength and abrasion resistance than durable-press	Exhibited other problems common to durable-press (see discussion of problems)

Some trade names:
   Disciplined cotton (Bates)
   Regulated cotton (Penney's)
   Belfast (Deering-Millikin)
      If Sanforized, the fabrics were labeled Sanforized Plus

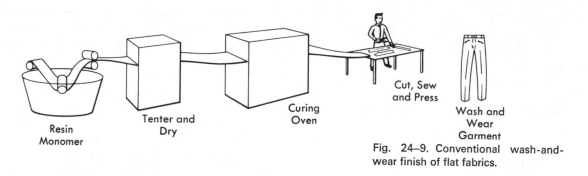

Fig. 24–9. Conventional wash-and-wear finish of flat fabrics.

III. DURABLE-PRESS FINISH FOR GARMENT
   Postcure Process
   Saturate the cloth with a resin cross-linking solution and dry
   Cut and sew garment and press shape with hot-head press
   Cure by putting pressed garment into a curing oven at 325 to 250° F
   Figure 24–10 shows the steps in the process

Advantages	*Disadvantages*
Garment retains shape and smoothness	Higher level of resins needed
Wide range of blends may be processed	Garment alteration is difficult
	Some garment shrinkage occurs so garments need to be cut oversize (see discussion of problems)

Some trade names:
   Koratron (Korot of California)
   Dan-Press (Dan River Mills)
   Reeve-set (Reeves Bros.)

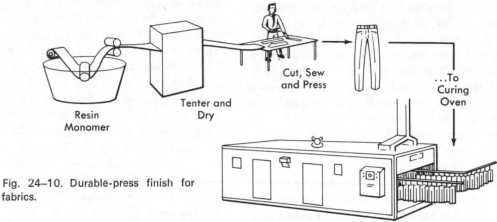

Fig. 24–10. Durable-press finish for fabrics.

IV. DURABLE-PRESS FINISH FOR GARMENT

Precured Process. (Recured process)
Treat fabric with cross-linking resin (sulfone) solutions and dry
Cure in the flat state
Cut and sew the garment
Set or recure the garment shape in hot-head press. (This setting temperature must be higher than the flat fabric curing temperature. Its purpose is chiefly to set the shape of the thermoplastic fibers in the blend)

Fig. 24–11. Hot head press for precure (recure).

Some trade names:
  Coneprest (Cone Mills)
  Burmi-crease (Burlington Mills)

V. DURABLE-PRESS FINISH ON THE GARMENT

Vapor Phase Process
For 100% cotton
Garment, preimpregnated with cross-linking agents is put in a reaction chamber which is then closed
A gas (nitrogen, air, or carbon dioxide) is passed through the vapor reagent and on into the chamber
Reaction with the impregnated garment takes place

Advantages	*Disadvantages*
No baking at high temperature	Too new to tell; not on market in 1967
Higher overall strength	
Resistant to chlorine	
Durable to laundering	
Softer Fabric	
Low add-on (2 to 3 per cent)	

Commercialized by Dubin-Haskell-Jacobson

Theory of Wrinkle Recovery

Several terms are used to describe the wrinkling characteristics of a fabric. *Wrinkle* or *crease resistance* means that a fabric resists bending, twisting, and other deformation. *Wrinkle recovery* means that the fabric can bend and twist and then recover from this deformation. A fabric that resists bending when the body bends is less comfortable than one that "gives" and then recovers its original smoothness. Therefore, wrinkle recovery describes the performance that the consumer desires in a fabric.

Fabric wrinkle recovery is dependent on the resiliency of the *fibers*. Fiber resiliency is dependent on the strength of the bonds and/or cross-links that hold the molecular chains together or that pull them back into position after the cloth is bent, thus preventing the formation of a wrinkle. Wool fibers have natural cross-links. All cellulose fibers can be

given cross-links. Rayon can be cross-linked in two ways: (1) add the cross-linking agent to the fiber spinning solution before extrusion as in the fiber modification Corval; or (2) add a cross-linking agent to the woven or knitted cloth. Cotton and linen are only cross-linked by applying a finish to the cloth.

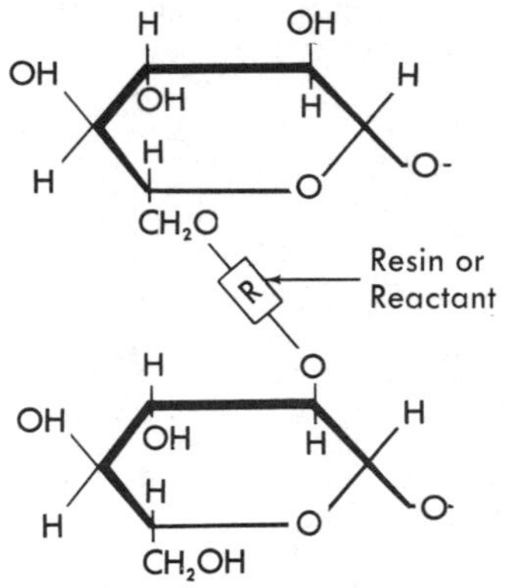

Although cellulose fibers do not naturally have cross-links, the molecular chains are held together by hydrogen bonds that operate like the attraction of a magnet for a nail. The hydrogen bonds of cellulose break with the stress of bending and new bonds form to hold the fiber in this bent position thus making a wrinkle. (See Figure 24–12 and 24–13a and b.)

Problems

There have been and still are problems for both the consumer and the manufacturer in all methods of achieving a "no-iron" fabric. In the delayed-cure process, for example, the sensitized cloth may tend to self-cure if it is stored very long before being made up into garments and it will then tend to resist shaping during the garment-curing step.

Strength Loss. Strength loss of the cellulose fibers is one of the most serious problems for the consumer. The high level of resin needed to give durability to the durable press and the heat necessary to shape-set the garment have weakened the garment as much as 50 per cent, causing the manufacturers to shift to the use of blends with polyesters and Nylon 420. Strength loss is due to a change in the mechanical properties of the cellu-

Fig. 24–12. A resin cross-link between two glucose units.

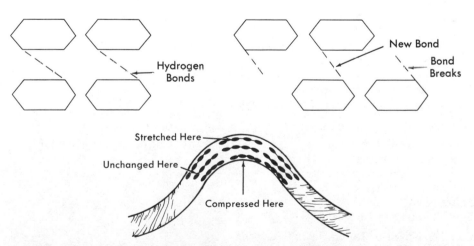

Fig. 24–13. Top, slippage of molecule causes breaking of molecular bonds between molecular chains. Bottom, effect of bending on the molecular chains of the cellulose fiber.

lose fibers and is not due to any chemical tendering of the cloth, since stripping the resin will restore the tensile strength to its original value. The physical position of the cross-links seems to be more important than the exact chemical nature of the cross-links.

If the fabric becomes stiff, there is a loss in tear strength. Wear resulting from lack of abrasion resistance is usually shown first in the edges of cuffs, pockets, closures, and in the roll of the collar. Fabric construction can be adjusted somewhat to compensate for strength loss and to improve abrasion resistance. Weaves with *long floats*, such as sateen, and *basket weaves*, such as Oxford, are more flexible and tend to resist abrasive wear better than the firmer weaves. Slightly coarser filling yarns will improve the strength of broadcloth. Balancing the weave crimp in both the warp and the filling is helpful also.

Color Loss. "Frosting" is a term widely used in the textile industry to refer to the loss of color from durable-press and wash-and-wear fabrics. It is caused by localized wear. In single fiber constructions, frosting occurs where there is variation due to incomplete penetration of dyestuffs. In fiber blends, differential wear produces frosting where the fibers do not match in shade. Color that wears away is permanently lost from the garment.

Soiling. Soiling is a problem that became more acute when the polyester/cotton blends began to replace the 100 per cent cotton in durable press. Soil did not wash out easily. The introduction of *soil release* finishes in 1966 gave great impetus to the use of the blends. The soil release finish consists of a suitable chemical grafted, cured, or polymerized on the surface of the cloth. Visa by Deering-Millikin, Come-Clean by Burlington and X-it by Graniteville were the first three introduced. The use of soil release finishes are particularly important in white shirts, blouses, uniforms, and sheets.

Resin finishes, like the synthetic fibers, have an affinity for oily soil and need special cold-spotting treatments before the garment is laundered.

Chlorine Damage. Chlorine bleaches will cause yellowing and tendering of the cellulose. The nitrogen groups (NH) pick up the chlorine and hang on to it during rinsing and dry storage. The heat of ironing releases the chlorine in the form of hydrochloric acid (HCL) and the acid weakens the fabric causing strength loss. If there is no hot ironing there is no damage. Rinsing with an antichlor, such as sodium thiosulfate, will remove the chlorine. The amount of chlorine retained need not be high to cause damage. More chlorine is retained with urea formaldehyde than with melamine. In the cyclic ureas, the amine groups are not free to pick up chlorine, and the aldehydes do not contain nitrogen, thus they are nonchlorine-retentive.

Odors. The fishy amine odor is produced during the curing step and is held in the fabric as an amine salt. When articles are stored or when clothing is worn during hot, humid weather, the amines combine with the moisture and a fish odor results. The odor is due to the formation of free formaldehyde.

Sewing Problems. Resin-treated fabrics create problems for the home sewer. Fabrics can seldom be straightened if they are "off-grain." In plaid gingham, this makes matching impossible. It is difficult to ease-in excess fabric. Creases will not lie flat. Collars and cuffs must be edge stitched if a flat effect is desired. Pin marks show, and if machine stitching must be ripped, the needle holes show and the fabric may tear easily.

The alteration of durable-press garments created a big problem. Garments could not be lengthened or seams let out because the original crease could not be pressed out and would show. Alter-Ease, a spray product by J. P. Stevens, was developed to remove the original creases and to permit new ones to be pressed in the cloth.

Care

Durable-press garments should be laundered before the fabrics become heavily soiled and as soon as possible after soiling. Turn the garment inside out to reduce "frosting" and to prevent wear on the creases. Launder in the coolest water that will remove the soil. For heavily soiled spots, apply a liquid detergent full strength to the spot. Soak in hot water, let water cool, and agitate for six to eight minutes. (USDA recommended procedure, Leaflet 993–67.) Agitation time should be as short as possible to remove soil. Rinse in cool water. Use of a fabric softener will reduce the build-up of static, which attracts soil and which causes garments to cling.

For drying, keep loads small and set the heat at wash-and-wear. At the end of the period, let garments tumble for a cool-down period of five to ten minutes. Remove the garments as soon as the dryer stops.

25 Color

Color is one of the most important aspects in fabric. In many cases, it is the primary reason for purchase. In all cases (except perhaps blue jeans or bleeding madras) one wants to keep the original color for the life of the textile.

Color Problems

Many color problems occur with fabrics. Color loss occurs through bleeding, crocking, and migration. *Bleeding* is color loss in water. *Crocking* is color loss from rubbing or abrasion while wearing the garment. (See page 67.) *Migration* is shifting of color in printed fabric.

If the color is not fast in the fabric as purchased, it is not possible to make it fast. Salt and vinegar are used as exhausting agents for household dyes, but there is no available research to support the theory that they will "set" color.

Change of color from fume fading (see page 54), perspiration, and light results when a chemical change occurs in the dye. Perspiration may cause either acid or alkaline damage. Light fading is caused by oxidation of color. Color damage of this type is sometimes accompanied by fabric damage.

Fig. 25–1. Tendering of cotton draperies caused by sulfur dye, atmospheric moisture, and heat.

The dye itself may tender cotton (Figure 25–1) and rayon fabrics. Sulfur in a dye may combine with moisture in the air to form sulfuric acid, which is harmful to the cellulose.

Today, the problems of fabric degradation and color changes are quite critical in draperies, because so many people have picture windows and have invested considerable money to dress their windows. So much fabric is necessary to cover the window that it no longer is possible to care for the draperies in the home. The added cost of care has in many cases meant that the draperies are not cleaned as

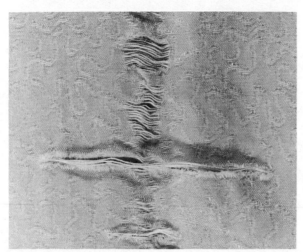

Fig. 25–2. Cotton and rayon drapery fabric. After dry-cleaning yellowish streaks were obvious; after washing splits occurred.

often as they should be. The problem results when the draperies are apparently in good shape when sent to the cleaner, but come back with color changes and splits. (See Figure 25–2.) Research has shown that all fibers with the exception of glass, are subject to degradation by sunlight, smog, and also from acidic gases present in homes using central heating.

Lining draperies will increase their resistance to degradation and to color change. Frequent cleaning to remove the acidic condition of the draperies should lengthen their life. It has been estimated that draperies should be cleaned every nine months.[1]

Wear may remove the surface color of heavy fabrics. (See Figure 25–3.) Movement of yarns in bending causes undyed fibers to work out to the surface. Color streaks may result from uneven removal of warp sizing before the dye is applied. These fabrics may be labeled "fast color" and no doubt they are, but the portions of the fabric that did not come in contact with the dye were not even dyed! Some resin-treated fabrics show this sort of color change because the dye either was applied with the resin and did not penetrate sufficiently, or the fabric was dyed after being resin-treated, in which case there were not enough places for the dye to be anchored. The best way to check the dye penetration in heavy fabrics is to examine the fabric. In yard goods, ravel off a yarn to see if it is the same color throughout.

[1] George W. Sands, "The Dry Cleaning and Laundering of Textile Materials," *Canadian Textile Journal* **78**:52–53 (January, 1961).

In ready-to-wear, look at the edge of seams. In heavy prints, look at the reverse side. The more color on the wrong side, the better the dye penetration.

Off-grain prints (see page 141) create problems in draperies, slipcovers, and apparel because the fabric cannot be both straight with the print and cut "on grain." If cut "off grain," the fabric tends to assume its normal position when washed causing twisted seams and uneven hemlines. If cut "on grain," the print will not be straight and will be unpleasing esthetically.

A new problem has developed with durable-press apparel. The high curing temperatures needed do unprecedented things to dyes. Some of them change hues, some sublimate or migrate out of the fiber, and if fibers are yellowed because of heat, the colors will be muddy rather than clear. In polyester/cotton blends two different, but color-matched, dyes are used. During wear, as the cotton wears off, it becomes lighter in color, while the unabraded polyester keeps its color. This causes a "frosting" effect.

The producer must select a dye or pigment suited to the fiber and the end-use of the fabric, apply the color so that it penetrates each fiber and is held in the fiber, and inform the purchaser (garment

Fig. 25–3. Denim jeans—loss of surface color.

manufacturer or retailer) of the fastness properties. Difficulties are encountered because of the innate properties of some of the man-made fibers, of dye limitations, and because conventional techniques of applying color may not work well with the new or modified fibers. In some cases, the desired hue is not available with the satisfactory fastness properties at the price the purchaser is willing to pay, or the technique for application is too costly if the fabric is to be competitive in price. The emphasis on wash-and-wear and durable-press garments has created a demand for better dye performance.

The consumer should know what he expects from the textile, read labels for guarantees of fastness and suggested care, and report to the retailer if fabrics do not give satisfactory performance.

No one dye is fast to everything, and *the dyes within a group are not equally fast.* A complete range of shades is not available in each of the dye groups. The dyer chooses a dye suited to the fiber content and the end-use of the fabric. Occasionally the garment manufacturer or the consumer select fabrics for uses that are different than the fabric manufacturer intended. For example, a lining fabric used for draperies may not be fast to sunlight.

One cannot tell by looking at a fabric the kind of dye that has been used, or how fast the color is. It is very important, therefore, to look for labels that guarantee fastness of color and suggest how to care for the fabric.

Principles of Dyeing

Color has always been important in textiles. Until 1856, natural dyes and pigments were used as coloring agents. These dyes and pigments were obtained from plants and insects. When Perkin, a young chemist, discovered mauve, the first synthetic dye, a whole new industry came into being. All over Europe chemists started to develop synthetic dyes. Germany became the foremost center for synthetic dyes and it was not until World War I, when our trade with Germany was cut off, that a dye industry was developed in the United States. Since that time, many dyes and pigments have been developed so that today there are hundreds of colors from which to choose.

Kinds of Color

The chart shows the differences between two coloring substances, pigments and dyes. (See Figure 25–4.)

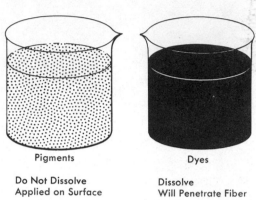

Pigments   Dyes

Do Not Dissolve   Dissolve
Applied on Surface   Will Penetrate Fiber

Fig. 25–4. Pigments and dyes.

Pigments	Dyes
Insoluble in water	Soluble substances
Held mechanically on the surface by resins	Penetrate into the fiber and are fixed by chemical action, heat, or other treatment

Pigments are insoluble color particles that are held on the surface of a fabric by a binding agent. Their application is quick, simple, and economical. Any color can be used on any fiber, since the pigments are held on mechanically. Stiffening of the fabrics, crocking, and fading are some of the problems encountered. Pigments are also mixed with the spinning solution for man-made fibers. Fluorescent colors are pigments that glow when exposed to ultraviolet light. They have been increasingly useful in safety clothing and furnishings.

Dye must be in small particles that can be thoroughly dissolved in water or some other carrier in order to penetrate the fiber. Undissolved particles stay on the outside and the colors then have poor fastness to crocking and bleeding.

Dyeing of Fabrics

Dyeing of fabrics is extremely complicated. The dye manufacturers and the machinery manufacturers are doing more research and development than ever before to produce better dyes and improve dyeing processes. Fibers have an affinity for

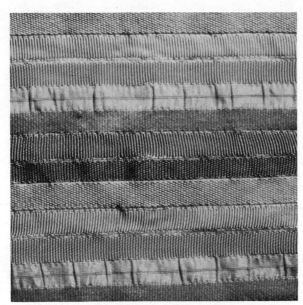

Fig. 25–5. Six-fiber test cloth showing difference in color absorbed from Texchrome, a mixture of several dyes.

certain dyes, but not for others. The thermoplastic fibers are difficult to dye because their absorbency is so low. The six-fiber test fabric in Figure 25–5 was piece-dyed with Texchrome, a mixture of several dyes. The wool is deep yellow, the cotton is blue, rayon is lavender, nylon and acetate are light yellow.

In order for a fabric to be colored, the dye must penetrate the fiber and either combine chemically with it or be locked inside the fiber. Fibers that dye easily are those that are absorbent and that have dye sites in their molecules, which will react with the dye molecules.

Dyeing consists of:

1. Wetting out the fibers.
2. Applying dye in acid, alkaline, or other media.
3. After-treatments to remove the media and set the dye.

The dye reacts with the surface molecules first. Moisture and/or heat swell the fibers, causing the molecule chains to move farther apart so that more reactive groups are exposed to react with the dye. During drying, the chains move back together, trapping the dye in the fiber.

The dyeing of wool with acid dyes is a good example of dyeing fibers that are both absorbent and have many dye sites. In wool, the salt linkages give the fiber its tinctorial properties. The acid in the bath activates the salt linkages and becomes fixed at the amino sites. The dye then reacts with and displaces the acid. Wool is dyed with basic dyes in a similar manner except that the dye attaches to the carboxyl groups.

Nylon resembles wool in dyeing properties except that it has fewer dye sites—one amino group for every 30 in wool. Nylon is more oriented and crystalline than wool and thus is less absorbent.

Cellulosic fibers are absorbent because of the many hydroxyl groups, but most dyes do not combine chemically with them. With direct dyes, the dye particles move into the amorphous areas of the fibers and form large aggregations that are too large to move back out of the fiber. The addition of salt gives better dye absorption. Other dyes are developed on or in the fibers. Fiber Reactive Dyes[2] were introduced in 1956 and are the first dyes that actually combine with the hydroxyl groups of cellulose. These dyes contain a color-producing group, a solubilizing group, and a fiber-reactive group. In the future they may replace older forms of dyes such as vats, naphthol, and developed dyes because it is easier to get shade continuity and they are somewhat cheaper because of production savings.

Many of the acrylic fibers have anionic dye sites that react with cationic dye stuffs. The acrylics have low moisture absorption; but when heat is applied during dyeing, the kinetic motion of the polymer chains creates spaces large enough for dye to enter.

The hydrophobic fibers, polyester and olefins, are the most difficult to dye because they have no dye sites and they are practically nonabsorbent. Disperse dyes (developed to dye acetate in the early 1930's) are the most widely used, usually with carriers, for these fibers. The carrier is forced inside the fibers by heat, causing the fibers to swell so that dyes can be diffused through the fiber.

The following chart gives a list of commonly used dyestuffs with their fastness properties. The consumer is seldom informed about the kind of dye used. Fastness properties may or may not be given on labels, but care instructions often are based on dye fastness.

2 V. S. Ryan, "Recent Advances in Fiber Reactive Dyes," *American Dyestuff Reporter* **54**:8 (April 12, 1965).

Classification of Dyes

Dye	Characteristics	Fiber
Acid dyes (dye liquor is acidic) or pre-metalized acid	Vary in fastness to light and washing. Bright colors	Wool, silk, nylon, acrylic, spandex
Azoic dyes, also called naphthol (developed on fiber). Insoluble color precipitates made by adding a solution of diazo compound to an alkaline solution of naphthol.	Good fastness surpassed only by vat dyes. Have tendency to crock	Widely used on cotton prints. Polyester, acetate, olefin, rayon
Basic dyes (contain amino dyes).	Brilliant colors. Many are not fast to washing, light, or rubbing	Wool, silk, nylon, modacrylic
Cationic dyes—some as basic dyes	Wet fastness is excellent. Light fastness is fair to very good	Acrylics
Developed direct dyes (similar to direct cotton dyes, but must be developed on the fiber).	Good wash fastness. Fair light fastness	Cotton, rayon, silk, linen
Direct cotton dyes	Wide color range. No brilliant colors. Used where fastness is not necessary	Protein, cellulose
Disperse dyes, including insoluble azo, or anthraquinone dyes kept in colloidal suspension by sulfonated oils.	Good fastness to light, washing, and perspiration. Subject to fume fading	Acetate, nylon, acrylic, modacrylic, olefin
Fiber reactive dyes	Bright shades with excellent fastness	Cotton, linen, rayon, wool
Mordant and chrome dyes (can be made to combine with metallic salts)	Excellent fastness to wet processing and dyes	Wool, acrylic, cotton
Sulfur dyes (made by reaction of sulfur with organic compounds)	Wide range of rather dull colors. Fast to washing. Fair fastness to light Cheap and easy to apply	Cotton, rayon
Vat dyes: Pigments reduced to leuco compounds, which are soluble in alkali. Pigments are reoxidized by air or oxidizing agent.	Most satisfactory of all dyestuffs. Generally fast to light, washing, bleaching	Cotton, rayon, acrylic, modacrylic, nylon

Dyeing Processes

A dye process is the environment created for the introduction of dyes to fibers. It includes even application of dye by hot water, steam, or dry heat. Accelerants and regulators are used to regulate penetration of the dye. Dyeing processes have developed from hand to machine processes, from simple techniques to complex ranges which give better results in less time.

Stages of Applying Color

The stage at which color is applied has little to do with fastness, but has a great deal to do with dye penetration and is governed by fabric design. Some color problems are due to poor dye penetration. A

knowledge of equipment and methods used may give the consumer a better understanding of these problems.

I. *Dyed Before Yarn Spinning*

1. *Solution* (spun or dope) dyeing consists of adding colored pigments or dyes to the spinning solution; thus, each fiber is colored as it is spun.
2. *Stock or fiber dye* is used when mottled or heather effects are desired. Dye is added to loose fibers before yarn spinning. Good dye penetration is obtained but the process is fairly expensive. (See Figure 25–6.)
3. *Top dyeing* gives results similar to stock dye and is more commonly used. Tops, the

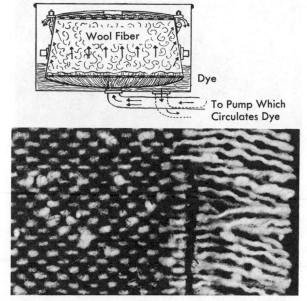

Fig. 25–6. Stock or fiber dye. Top, diagram. Bottom, tweed stock dye example.

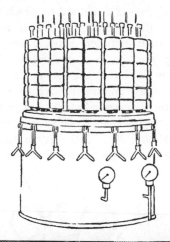

Fig. 25–7. Top, yarn dye machine. Bottom, gingham yarn-dyed fabric. Notice that fabric has same intensity of color on both sides.

loose ropes of wool from the combing machine, are wound into balls, placed on perforated spindles and enclosed in a tank. The dye is pumped back and forth through the wool. Continuous processes on loose fiber and wool tops are also used using a pad-steam technique.

II. *Yarn Dyed After Spinning: Before Weaving or Knitting*. Yarns are dyed in skeins or packages. Packages containing one to two pounds of yarn are wound on perforated spools or tubes. Some warp yarns are dyed on perforated warp beams. Rayon is usually dyed in the cakes in which it is laid after spinning. It is difficult to wind the rayon in packages and have the correct tension to allow for the swelling of the fibers when they become wet. The packages are placed on carriers, put in the dyeing machine, and fastened in place. A lid is clamped on and the dye is circulated around the packages in a two-way motion. Yarn dyeing is less costly than raw stock dyeing. (See Figure 25–7.)

III. *Piece Dyeing After Weaving or Knitting*. Piece dyeing usually produces solid-color fabrics. It generally costs less to dye fabric than to dye loose fiber or yarns. One other advantage is that decisions on color can be delayed so that fashion trends can be followed more closely.

Piece dyeing is done with various kinds of equipment.

1. *Jig dyeing* consists of a stationary dye bath with two rolls above the bath. The cloth is wrapped around the rolls in open width and is rolled back and forth through the dye bath once every 20 minutes or so and is on rollers the remaining time. There are some problems of level dyeing. Acetate, rayon, and nylon are usually jig dyed. (See Figure 25–8.)

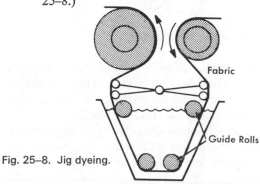

Fig. 25–8. Jig dyeing.

2. *Pad dyeing* is a method in which the fabric is run through the dye bath in open width and then between squeeze rollers which force the dye into the fabric. Notice in Figure 25–9 that the pad box holds only a very small amount of dye liquor, making this an economical method of piece dyeing. The cloth runs through the machine at a rapid rate, 30 to 300 yards a minute. Pad-steam processes are the most widely used.

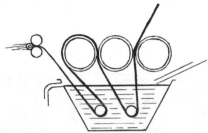

Fig. 25–9. Pad dyeing.

3. *Winch, reel, or beck dyeing* is the oldest type of piece dyeing. (See Figure 25–10.) The fabric, in a loose rope sewed together at the ends, is lifted in and out of the dye bath by a reel. The fabric is kept immersed in the dye bath except for the few yards around the reel. Penetration of dye is obtained by continued immersion in slack condition rather than by pressure on the wet goods under tension. This method is used on light-weight fabrics which cannot withstand the tension of the other methods and on heavy goods, especially woolens. Reels are of various shapes—oval, round, octagonal.

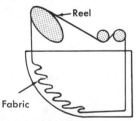

Fig. 25–10. Winch or reel dyeing.

4. *Continuous machines* called *ranges* are used for large lots of goods. They consist of compartments for wetting-out, dyeing, after treatments, washing, and rinsing.
5. *Cross-dyeing* is piece dyeing of fabrics made of fibers from different groups such as protein and cellulose or cellulose and ace-

Fig. 25–11. Cross-dyed fabric. White is acetate; dark is rayon.

tate. Man-made fibers are often modified so they will accept different classes of dyestuffs; 100 per cent acrylics, for example, can be piece dyed and still have two colors in the fabric. (See Figure 25–11.)

6. *Union dyeing* is piece dyeing of fabrics made of fibers from different groups; but unlike cross-dyeing, the finished fabric is a solid color. Dyes of the same hue, but of composition suited to the fibers to be dyed, are mixed together in the same dye bath.

IV. *High-Temperature Processes.* High-temperature dyeing is necessary to get good dye penetration on the thermoplastic fibers (except acetate and Dynel). The following methods have given satisfactory results.

1. *Molten-Metal Process.* Fabrics are dyed with vat colors, passed through a U-shaped tank in which a molten metal alloy is maintained at 200 to 250° F. As the cloth passes through the molten metal, the dye is reduced under pressure. The metal is rinsed out and the fabric oxidized, scoured, and rinsed. This method is used to obtain level dyeings in dense fabrics, in slubby yarn type constructions, and for embroidered fabrics in which it is difficult to obtain the same shade on the ground and embroidery.

2. *Thermosol Process.* Fabrics are dyed at normal temperatures on regular equipment, dried, and then heat-set for 30 seconds to 1 minute at 350° F. Colors are fast to machine washing. Dacron responds best to this treatment.

Printing

Printed fabrics are often printed off-grain. (See page 141.) In an all-over design, this is not important, but in large checks and plaids or designs with crosswise lines, matching at seam lines is impossible and slanting lines across the fabric are seldom desirable. The reason for off-grain prints is that the fabric is started into the machine crooked or the mechanism for moving the fabric does not work properly. It is a problem that can easily be corrected at the mill. If consumers will refuse to buy off-grain prints and let retailers know why they are not buying them, better prints will be on the market.

Direct Prints

Block printing and stencil printing are the earliest forms of decorating textiles. The former is a hand process, which is seldom done commercially because it is costly and slow. A design is carved on a linoleum block, the blocks are dipped in a shallow pan of dye, and stamped on the fabric. Uniform pressure is needed to transfer the color to the fabric. (See Figure 25–12.)

Stencil printing has more depth or texture than other prints. The roller that is used is a hollow copper cylinder, which is perforated in the form of a design. The printing paste is in a trough inside the cylinder and flows through the perforations on to the cloth as it is pressed against the roller. As the material leaves the cylinder, it is dusted with rayon flock. *Lacquer*

Fig. 25–13. Screen printing—machine can be operated by one man. (Courtesy of *Textile World*.)

Fig. 25–12. Block print—carved wooden block and the cloth printed from it.

printing is like flock printing except that colored enamel or opaque ink is used.

Screen printing is done commercially for small yardages, 500 to 5,000 yards. The cloth to be printed is pinned or pasted to a long flat table that has been covered with a thick wool felt pad, an oil cloth that protects the wool felt, and a cotton cloth that must be changed quite often as it takes up color from the dyed fabric. The screens consist of wooden or metal frames over which silk, nylon, or Vinyon gauze has been stretched. The design is applied to the screen by a photographic method in which the screen is covered with sensitized gelatin film and a plate of the original design is reproduced on the film. All but the design is painted out with caustic-resistant paint and the unpainted gelatin is washed out in warm water. A special screen is prepared for each color in the design. Along the sides of the table, a metal straight edge with adjustable stops makes it easy to set each screen correctly. After the screen is set, the color in paste form is poured on the screen and is forced through the screen by moving a squeegee across the screen. A screen printing machine that can be operated by one man is shown in Figure 25–13. Screen printing is used extensively for designs larger than the circumference of the rolls used for roller printing.

Direct roller printing was developed in 1785, about

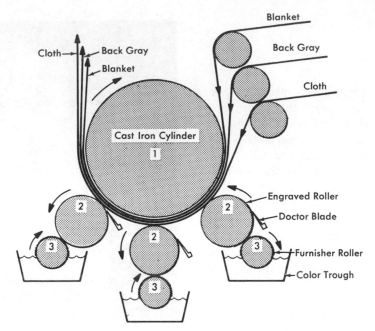

Fig. 25–14. Direct roller printing machine.

the time all textile operations were becoming mechanized. Figure 25–14 shows the essential parts of the printing machine.

A cast iron cylinder (1 in Figure 25–14) is the roller around which the cloth is drawn as it is printed. The copper printing roller (2 in Figure 25–14) is etched with the design. There are as many different rollers as there are colors in the fabric. In the diagram, three engraved rollers are used. Furnisher rollers are covered with hard rubber or brushes made of nylon, Orlon, or hard rubber bristles. They revolve in a small color trough, pick up the color, and deposit it on the copper rollers. A doctor blade scrapes off excess color so that only the engraved portions of the copper roller are filled with dye when it comes in contact with the cloth. The cloth to be printed, a rubberized blanket, and a back gray cloth pass between the cylinder and the engraved rollers. The blanket gives a good surface for sharp printing; the gray goods protect the blanket and absorb excess dye.

Rayon and knitted fabrics are usually lightly coated with a gum sizing on the back to keep them from stretching or swelling as they go through the printing machine. After printing, the cloth is dried, steamed, or treated to set the dye.

Duplex printing is roller printing that prints on both sides of the fabric with the same or different patterns. This process is seldom used today.

Warp printing is done on the warp yarns prior to weaving. This technique gives an interesting, rather hazy pattern, softer than other prints. To identify, ravel adjacent sides. Color in the form of the design will be on the warp yarns. Filling yarns are white or solid color. Imitations have splotchy color on both warp and filling yarns. Warp printing is usually done on taffeta, satin ribbons or fabric, and on upholstery or drapery fabric. (See Figure 25–15.)

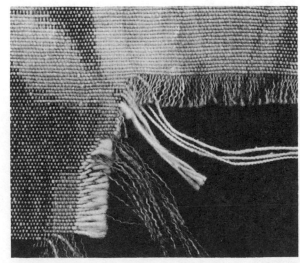

Fig. 25–15. Warp-printed cretonne. Notice color on warp yarn only.

Resist or Discharge Prints

Resist or discharge prints are piece-dyed fabrics. The designs are effected by the following methods:

1. *Batik* is a hand process in which hot wax is poured on a fabric in the form of a design. When the wax is set, the fabric is piece-dyed. The wax prevents penetration of color into the wax-covered portions. Colors are built up by piece-dyeing, light colors first, covering portions and redyeing until the design is complete. The wax is later removed by a solvent. (See Figure 25–16.)
2. *Tie and dye* is a hand process in which yarn or fabric is wrapped in certain areas with fine thread or string. The yarn or fabric is then piece dyed and the string is removed, leaving undyed areas. (See Figure 25–17.)
3. *Discharge printing* is usually done on dark backgrounds. The fabric is first piece dyed in any of the usual methods. A discharge paste, which contains chemicals to remove the color, is then printed on the fabric. Dyes that are not harmed by the discharging materials can be mixed with printing solution if color is desired in the discharge areas. The fabric is then steamed to develop the design either as a white or colored area. Better dye penetration is obtained with piece dyeing than with printing, and it is hard to get good dark colors except by piece dyeing.

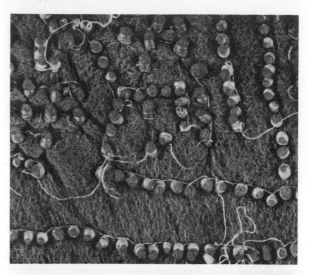

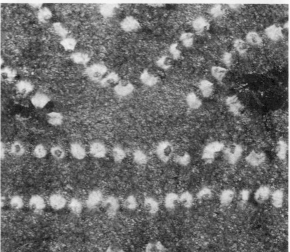

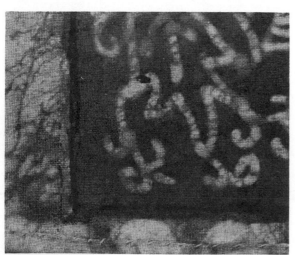

Fig. 25–16. Batik. Veins of color are due to cracks in the wax during the piece yarn.

Fig. 25–17. Top, tie and dye showing thread used to tie design. Middle, design after thread is removed. Bottom, Tie and dye fabric is rolled up on the bias, tied, and dyed. Then the fabric is untied, rolled on the opposite bias, and dyed again.

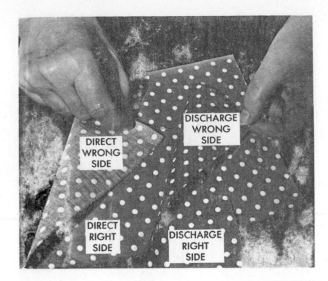

Discharge prints can be detected by looking at the wrong side of the fabric. In the design area, the color is often not completely removed and one can see evidences of the background colors especially around the edges of the design. Background colors must be colors that can be removed by strong alkali. Discharge prints are usually satisfactory. (See Figure 25–18.)

4. *Resist printing* is the opposite of discharge printing. A resist paste is printed on a white fabric, which is then piece-dyed. This method is used only with dyes that cannot be discharged, such as aniline black.

Fig. 25–18. Discharge print vs. direct print.

Appendix A

Fiber Property Charts

The data used are from *Textile World*, "Man-Made Fiber Chart 1966." Variables are due to different fiber types and fibers from different companies. The starred information is from Burlington Industries Inc., *Textile Fibers and Their Properties 1965*.

DENSITY AND SPECIFIC GRAVITY

Fibers	Density (Grams per cc)
Glass	2.45–2.55
Saran	1.71–1.1
Cotton	1.54
Rayon	1.54–1.50
Flax	1.50
Polyester	1.38–1.22
Modacrylic	1.37–1.30
Vinyon	1.34
Acetate	1.32
Wool	1.32
Silk	1.30
Spandex	1.21
Acrylic	1.18–1.16
Nylon	1.14
Olefin	0.91

BREAKING ELONGATION

(Standard conditions: 65% relative humidity, 70° F.)

Fiber	Elongation at Break in Per Cent Std	Wet
Spandex	500–700	Same
Acetate	25–45	30–50
Wool	25–35	25–50
Nylon (rug)	23–65	28–70
Nylon (HT)	16–28	18–32
Acrylic	20–55	26–72
Silk	20	
Polyester (reg)	18–50	Same
Polyester (HT)	9–13	Same
V. rayon (reg)	15–30	20–40
Cupra rayon	7–26	16–42
Rayon (HWM)	6.5–18	7.0–22
Modacrylic	14–35	Same
Cotton	3–7	
Glass	3.1–5.2	Same
Flax	2.0	

ABSORBENCY

Moisture Regain (70° F, 65% relative humidity)			
Hydrophilic		*Hydrophobic*	
Wool	16	Nylon	3.5–5.0
Viscose	13	Triacetate	3.2
Cuprammonium	12.5	Acrylic	1.0–2.5
Rayon HWM	11.5–13	Modacrylic	0.4–3.0
Silk	10	Polyester	0.6–0.4
Cotton	7	Saran	0.1–1.0
Diacetate	6.5	Spandex	0–1.3
		Olefin	0.01–0.1
		Glass	0

FIBER STRENGTH

Fiber	Tenacity—Grams per Denier	
	Dry	*Wet*
Glass	15.3–9.6	Same
Nylon	9.5–3.0	8.2–2.6
Polyester	9.5–2.2	Same
Flax	6.6	8.4
Olefin	8.0–3.0	Same
Silk	4.5	3.9
Cotton	4.9–3.0	6.37–3.3
Modacrylic	4.2–2.5	Same
Acrylic	4.2–2.0	3.6–1.6
Rayon	5.5–0.73	4.0–0.7
Wool	1.7–1.0	1.63–0.76
Acetate	1.4–1.1	1.0–0.8

EFFECT OF HEAT

Fiber	Melting Point, ° F	Sticking Point, ° F	Softens, ° F	Safe Ironing Temperature, ° F *
Glass	———	———	1350	
Triacetate	572	450		400
Diacetate	500	350–375	400–445	350
Polyester	455–554	446–455		300–350, depending on type
Spandex	446–518	347–446	Above 300	250–300, depending on type
Nylon	420–482	445		300–350
Acrylic	Indeterminate	420–490		300–350
Modacrylic	371	390–400		225–275
Saran	340–335	210–220	240–320	150
Olefin	325–350	320	285–330	250

* SOURCE: Burlington Industries Inc.

Fiber	Decomposes, ° F	Burns	Safe Ironing Temperature, ° F
Flax	500	Yes	450
Cotton	464	Yes	425
Rayon	464	Yes	375–400
Wool	266–400	No	300

FIBER TOUGHNESS

Spandex	2.00
Nylon	1.00–0.50
Polyester	1.00–0.32
Olefin	0.90–0.75
Acrylic	0.70–0.4
Rayon (HT)	0.65–0.22
Modacrylic	0.60–0.46
Rayon (HWM)	0.48–0.18
Glass	0.37–0.15
Rayon (Viscose)	0.32–0.04
Acetate	0.30–0.17
Saran	0.26–0.16
Wool	0.25
Cotton	0.15
Rayon (cupra)	0.14

SOURCE: From "Textile World Chart, 1966," by Noreen Heimbolt, *Textile World Magazine*, Vol. 116 (1966).

FIBER STIFFNESS

	Grams per Denier
Glass	310–380
Cotton	57–60
Rayon (HWM)	28–75
Nylon 6	29–48
Nylon 6,6	5–58
Olefin	18–60
Polyester	6–80
Rayon (reg.)	6–50
Saran	5–10
Acetate	3.5–5.5
Wool	3.9
Acrylic	4–18
Spandex	0.11–0.16

RESISTANCE TO ABRASION*

Excellent	Good	Fair	Poor
Nylon	Cotton	Acrylic	Acetate
Olefin	Polyester	Rayon	Glass
	Spandex	Flax	
	Saran	Silk	
		Wool	

* SOURCE: Burlington Industries Inc.

RESISTANCE TO SUNLIGHT

Excellent	Good
Glass	Saran
Acrylic	Polyester
Modacrylic	Linen
	Rayon
	Cotton
	Olefin (to indirect)
	Acetate

ELASTIC RECOVERY

Fiber	Recovery from 5–10% Stretch, in Per Cent
Spandex	99
Nylon	99–100
Olefin	95–100
Saran	86–94
Wool	63
Modacrylic	55–98
Acetate	48–65
Cotton	45
Acrylic	40–58
Polyester	35–93
Rayon	30–74

Appendix B

Historical Development of
Man-Made Fibers in the United States

This chart shows the development of man-made fibers. It will be more meaningful if the student traces the development by making separate charts for (1) introduction of each fiber family; (2) companies producing each fiber and/or more than one fiber; (3) fiber types and modification showing how each type or modification started with one fiber and was later used with other fibers.

Asian and European Background

Prior to 8000 B.C.   *Flax*

Prior to 3000 B.C.   *Wool*

      2640 B.C.   *Silk*

Prior to 1300 B.C.   *Cotton*

1664   Idea that man could make fibers—Robert Hooke

1857   *Rayon*
      Cuprammonium process, Germany

1869   *Triacetate*
      Germany

1884   *Rayon*
      Nitrocellulose process, Chardonnet in France

1892   *Rayon*
      Viscose process, Cross and Bevan in England

1893   *Glass*
      First fabric displayed at Columbia Exhibition, Chicago, Ill.

1894   *Azlon*
      Italy

1903   Diacetate process

American Background

1910   *Rayon*
      Filament—American Viscose Corp.

1916   *Rayon*
      Industrial Rayon Corp.

1919   *Acetate*
      Filament—Lustron Corp.

1921 *Rayon*
         Du Pont
1924 Rayon adopted as name for cellulose-base
         fibers
1925 *Acetate*
         Celanese Corp.
1926 *Rayon*
         Delaware Rayon Corp.
         Skenandoa Rayon Corp.
         Beaunit Mills—cuprammonium
         Delustering of bright viscose
         High tenacity
1927 *Rayon*
         Crepe yarn technique

         Acetate
         Celanese—Lustron merge
1929 *Rayon*
         New Bedford Rayon Co.
         Celanese Corp.
         North American Rayon Corp.
         American Enka Rayon Corp.
         Fair Haven Mills

         Acetate
         Tubize Rayon Corp.
         American Chatillon Corp.
         Du Pont Co.
1930 *Rayon*
         Resin finishes for crease resistance
         Acetate
         Tubize—American Chatillon merge
         American Viscose Corp.
1931 *Rayon*
         Staple fiber
         Acetate
         Tennessee Eastman Co.
         Delustered filament
1934 *Rayon*
         Nitrocellulose process discontinued
1935 *Rayon*
         High-tenacity
         Acetate
         Crimped staple
1937 *Rayon*
         Tire cord
         Cuprammonium staple
         Thick and thin yarns
         Crimped carpet fiber
1938 *Rayon*
         Fortisan

         Nylon
         Du Pont—nylon 6,6
         Filament
         Azlon
         Aralac—milk protein
         Glass
         Owens-Corning Fiberglas Corp.
         Filament
1939 *Vinyon*
         American Viscose Corp.
1940 *Saran*
         Dow Chemical Co.
1941 *Rayon*
         Fair Haven Mills
         Continuous spinning process
1946 *Acetate*
         Celanese and Tubize merger
         Nylon
         Tire cord
         Staple fiber
1948 *Azlon*
         Aralac—discontinued
         Vicara—corn protein, Virginia Carolina
         Corporation
1949 *Rayon*
         Beaunit Mills Inc.—Viscose
1950 *Acrylic*
         Du Pont—Orlon
         Filament
         Staple
1951 *Rayon*
         Latent crimp—Fiber E
         Mohawk buys New Bedford and Dela-
         ware Companies
         Bigelow—Sanford buys Hartford Co.

         Acetate
         Solution dye
         Nylon
         Chemstrand—nylon 6,6
         Modacrylic
         Carbide and Carbon Co. Dynel
1952 *Acrylic*
         Chemstrand—Acrilan staple
         Acetate
         Separated from rayon as fiber group
1953 *Rayon*
         Courtaulds Inc. merge with North Amer-
         ican Rayon Corp.
         Carpet fiber

Nylon
    Delustered

Polyester
    Du Pont—Dacron

1954 *Rayon*
    Solution dye

    Acetate
        Crystal acetate
        Latent crimp

    Nylon
        Allied Chemical Corp. nylon 6
        Industrial Rayon Corp.
        Enka Rayon Corp.
        Textured filament—stretch, Taslan

1955 *Acetate*
    Textured filament yarns

    Nylon
        Carpet fiber

    Nytril
        B. F. Goodrich—Darlan

1956 *Nylon*
    Solution dye

    Acrylic
        Acrilan fiberfill

    Polyester
        Dacron fiberfill

    Nytril
        Name changed to Darvan

1957 *Rayon*
    Textured filament

    Acetate
        Fiberfill—Celacloud, Celafil
        Hollow—filament
        Y cross section

    Nylon
        Low elongation—Type 420 for blends with cotton

    Acrylic
        Filament Orlon discontinued

    Modacrylic
        Eastman Kodak Co.—Verel

1958 *Rayon*
    Cross-linked—Corval, Topel

    Acrylic
        Dow Chemical Corp.—Zefran staple
        Acrilan carpet fiber

Polyester
    Tennessee Eastman—Kodel
    Fiber Industries Inc.—Teron
    Dacron 65 for blends with wool

Azlon
    Vicara—discontinued

1959 *Rayon*
    Hollow filament
    Slubbed filament
    Flat filament—Strawn

    Acetate
        Textured filament—Celaloft

    Nylon
        Trilobal—Antron
        Fluorescent whiteners—Blanc de blanc, Type 91
        Carpet fiber—textured filament, trilobal—Type 501; Cumuloft

    Acrylic
        American Cyanamid Corp.—Creslan staple
        Bicomponent filament—Orlon Cantrece
        Bicomponent staple—Orlon Sayelle

    Polyester
        Beaunit Mills Inc.—Vycron
        Trilobal—Dacron 62

1960 *Rayon*
    Hi-wet-modulus—Zantrel, Fiber 40—Avril, SM-27-Lirelle
    Multicellular—Avlin
    Hi-strength—Avron

    Nylon
        Industrial Rayon Plant sold to Hercules Powder Co. for production of olefin

    Acrylic
        Solution dyed—Acrilan

    Spandex
        Du Pont—Lycra
        U.S. Rubber—Vyrene

    Nytril
        Celanese acquires world rights to produce

1961 *Rayon*
    Solution dye—Avicolor
    Improved hi-wet-modulus

    Nylon
        High temperature resistant HT-1
        Carpet fiber—Nylon 6—Nyloft

Acrylic
Textured filament for carpets
Nonacid dyeable Creslan
Improved Zefran

Modacrylic
Filament—Aeress
Textured carpet fiber—Verel
—Dynel

Nytril
Production discontinued

1962 *Rayon*
Du Pont phases out

Nylon
Pill-resistant—Enkaloft

Acrylic
Orlon Cantrece discontinued

Polyester
Pill-resistant—Dacron Type 64

Spandex
Globe Manufacturing Co.—Glospan
Firestone Tire and Rubber—Spandelle
International Latex—Stretchever

Olefin
Hercules Powder Co.—Herculon
—Prolene

Glass
Very fine filament—Beta Fiberglas
Hollow filament—Pittsburg Plate Glass

1963 *Rayon*
Composite fiber
Bacteriostatic staple

Acetate
Sunlight-resistant dull fiber—SLR Estron
Triangular-shaped fiber
Random luster

Nylon
Bicomponent—nylon Cantrece
Nomex—trade name for HT-1
Hollow-core
Thick and thin—undrawn nubs—Speck-elon
Ultra deep dye—Cumuloft

Acrylic
Solution dye—Zefkrome
Bicomponent staple carpet fiber
Continuous filament—Glacé

1963 *Polyester*
Fluorescent whiteners—Kodel IV, Kodel III

Spandex
Orofil—not a true spandex

Olefin
Vectra
Reevon

1964 *Rayon*
Modulized rayon—Nupron
Medical—surgical—Purilon
Conjugate filaments
Stronger hi-wet-modulus

Acetate
Three-dimensional crimp
Four-leaf clover cross-section

Nylon
Multi-lobal—Enkalene
Sewing thread—500° F. Melting point—Hyten

Acrylic
Flame-resistant

Spandex
Chemstrand Corp.—Blue C
Corespun yarn

1965 *Rayon*
Acid-dyeable—Enkrome

Nylon
Multilobular—Enkalure

Acrylic
Filament—Creslan 63
High shrinkage—Orlon 38, Acrilan Hi-shrunk

Polyester
Slub filament—Dacron 69
High bulk—Dacron 65
High strength—Vycron Xtra Tuf for durable-press
Pill-resistant—Kodel II
Self-crimping

Spandex
American Cyanamid—Numa
Fluorescent whiteners—Lycra 125

Olefin
Marvess
Polycrest

1966 *Polyester*
    High strength–low elongation for durable press—Celanese Type 310

1967 *Rayon*
    Celanese—phased out of rayon and Fortisan
    Higher strength polynosic—Vincel
    Heat-resistant—Avceram
    Flame-retardant

    Nylon
    Random denier fluctuation—Variline
    Cationic dyeable
    Phillips—nylon 6, 6
    Rohm & Haas—Arlyn

    Acrylic
    Creslan filament discontinued
    Basic—dyeable—Acrilan 70
    Pill resistant

Polyester
    Fibercoil fiberfill
    American Enka Corp.—Enkron
    American Viscose Corp.—Avlen
    Tire cord—Vita cord
    Phillips—Quintess
    Hystron—Trevira

Olefin
    Bicomponent

Saran
    Rovana discontinued

Spandex
    Blue C
    Spandelle   } discontinued
    Stretchever

Appendix C

Fiber Trade Marks of
Members of Man-Made Fiber Producers Association, Inc.

Fiber Trade Mark	Generic Name	Member Company
A.C.E.	nylon	Allied Chemical Corporation, Fibers Division
Acele	acetate	E. I. du Pont de Nemours & Company, Inc.
A-Acrilan	acrylic	Monsanto Company, Textiles Division
Acrilan	acrylic	Monsanto Company, Textiles Division
Acrilan-Spectran	acrylic	Monsanto Company, Textiles Division
American Bemberg	rayon (cuprammonium)	Beaunit Corporation, Beaunit Fibers Division
Antron	nylon	E. I. du Pont de Nemours & Company, Inc.
Arnel	triacetate	Celanese Corporation
Avicolor	rayon and acetate	FMC Corporation, American Viscose Division
Avicord	rayon	FMC Corporation, American Viscose Division
Avicron	rayon	FMC Corporation, American Viscose Division
Aviloc	rayon	FMC Corporation, American Viscose Division
Avlin	polyester	FMC Corporation, American Viscose Division
Avril	rayon (high-wet-modulus)	FMC Corporation, American Viscose Division
Avron	rayon	FMC Corporation, American Viscose Division
Bembella	rayon (cuprammonium)	Beaunit Corporation, Beaunit Fibers Division
Blue-C	polyester	Monsanto Company, Textiles Division
Briglo	rayon	American Enka Corporation
C-Cadon Nylon	nylon	Monsanto Company, Textiles Division
C-Chemstrand Nylon	nylon	Monsanto Company, Textiles Division

SOURCE: Courtesy Man-Made Fiber Producers Association, Inc.

Fiber Trade Mark	Generic Name	Member Company
		(continued)
C-Cumuloft Nylon	nylon	Monsanto Company, Textiles Division
C-Nylon	nylon	Monsanto Company, Textiles Division
C-Polyester	polyester	Monsanto Company, Textiles Division
Cadon	nylon	Monsanto Company, Textiles Division
Cantrece	nylon	E. I. du Pont de Nemours & Company, Inc.
Caprolan	nylon	Allied Chemical Corporation, Fibers Division
Celacloud	acetate	Celanese Corporation
Celacrimp	acetate	Celanese Corporation
Celafil	acetate	Celanese Corporation
Celaloft	acetate	Celanese Corporation
Celanese Nylon	nylon	Fiber Industries, Inc., marketed by Celanese Fibers Marketing Company, a division of Celanese Corporation
Celaperm	acetate	Celanese Corporation
Celara	acetate	Celanese Corporation
Celarandom	acetate	Celanese Corporation
Celatow	acetate	Celanese Corporation
Celatress	acetate	Celanese Corporation
Celaweb	acetate	Celanese Corporation
Chromspun	acetate	Eastman Kodak Company, Tennessee Eastman Company Division
Coloray	rayon	Courtaulds North America Inc.
Comiso	rayon	Beaunit Corporation, Beaunit Fibers Division
Cordura	nylon	E. I. du Pont de Nemours & Company, Inc.
Courtaulds Nylon	nylon	Courtaulds North America Inc.
Crepeset	nylon	American Enka Corporation
Creslan	acrylic	American Cyanamid Company
Cumuloft	nylon	Monsanto Company, Textiles Division
Cupioni	rayon (cuprammonium)	Beaunit Corporation, Beaunit Fibers Division
Cupracolor	rayon (cuprammonium)	Beaunit Corporation, Beaunit Fibers Division
Cuprel	rayon (cuprammonium)	Beaunit Corporation, Beaunit Fibers Division
Cuprussah	rayon	Beaunit Corporation, Beaunit Fibers Division
Dacron	polyester	E. I. du Pont de Nemours & Company, Inc.
Drapespun	rayon	Midland-Ross Corporation, IRC Fibers Division
Dream Slub	rayon	Beaunit Corporation, Beaunit Fibers Division
Dul-Tone	rayon	Midland-Ross Corporation, IRC Fibers Division
Dy-Lok	rayon	Midland-Ross Corporation, IRC Fibers Division
Dynel	modacrylic	Union Carbide Corporation, Fibers and Fabrics Division
Encron	polyester	American Enka Corporation
Englo	rayon	American Enka Corporation
Enkalene	nylon	American Enka Corporation
Enkaloft	nylon	American Enka Corporation
Enkalure	nylon	American Enka Corporation
Enkasheer	nylon	American Enka Corporation
Enkatron	nylon	American Enka Corporation
Enkrome	rayon	American Enka Corporation
Estron	acetate	Eastman Kodak Company, Tennessee Eastman Company Division
Fiber-HM	rayon (high-wet-modulus)	American Enka Corporation
Fiber 24	rayon	Midland-Ross Corporation, IRC Fibers Division
Fiber 40	rayon (high-wet-modulus)	FMC Corporation, American Viscose Division
Fiber 700	rayon (high-wet-modulus)	American Enka Corporation
Fibro	rayon	Courtaulds North America Inc.

Fiber Trade Mark	Generic Name	Member Company
		(continued)
Flaikona	rayon (cuprammonium)	Beaunit Corporation, Beaunit Fibers Division
Fortisan	rayon	Celanese Corporation
Fortrel	polyester	Fiber Industries, Inc., marketed by Celanese Fibers Marketing Company, a division of Celanese Corporation
Fortrel 7	polyester	Fiber Industries, Inc., marketed by Celanese Fibers Marketing Company, a division of Celanese Corporation
Herculon	olefin	Hercules Incorporated, Fibers & Film Department
Hi-Narco	rayon	Beaunit Corporation, Beaunit Fibers Division
I.T.	rayon	American Enka Corporation
Jetspun	rayon	American Enka Corporation
Kodel	polyester	Eastman Kodak Company, Tennessee Eastman Company Division
Kolorbon	rayon	American Enka Corporation
Krispglo	rayon	American Enka Corporation
Lirelle	rayon (high-wet-modulus)	Courtaulds North America Inc.
Loftura	acetate	Eastman Kodak Company, Tennessee Eastman Company Division
Lurex	metallic	Dow Badische Company
Lycra	spandex	E. I. du Pont de Nemours & Company, Inc.
Marvess	olefin	Alamo Industries, Inc., a subsidiary of Phillips Petroleum Company
Monosheer	nylon	American Enka Corporation
Multi-Cupioni	rayon	Beaunit Corporation, Beaunit Fibers Division
Multi-Strata	rayon	Beaunit Corporation, Beaunit Fibers Division
Narco	rayon	Beaunit Corporation, Beaunit Fibers Division
Narcon	rayon	Beaunit Corporation, Beaunit Fibers Division
Newbray	rayon	Mohasco Industries, Inc., New Bedford Rayon Division
New Color	rayon	Mohasco Industries, Inc., New Bedford Rayon Division
New-Dull	rayon	Mohasco Industries, Inc., New Bedford Rayon Division
New-Low	rayon	Mohasco Industries, Inc., New Bedford Rayon Division
Nomex	nylon	E. I. du Pont de Nemours & Company, Inc.
Nub•Lite	rayon (cuprammonium)	Beaunit Corporation, Beaunit Fibers Division
Numa	spandex	American Cyanamid Company
Nupron	rayon	Midland-Ross Corporation, IRC Fibers Division
Ondelette	rayon (cuprammonium)	Beaunit Corporation, Beaunit Fibers Division
Orlon	acrylic	E. I. du Pont de Nemours & Company, Inc.
Orlon	acrylic	E. I. du Pont de Nemours & Company, Inc.
Parfé	rayon (cuprammonium)	Beaunit Corporation, Beaunit Fibers Division
Polycrest	olefin	UNIROYAL FIBER AND TEXTILE, Division of UNIROYAL, Inc.
Polynosic	rayon (high-wet-modulus)	American Enka Corporation
Purilon	rayon	FMC Corporation, American Viscose Division
Qulon	nylon	Beaunit Corporation, Beaunit Fibers Division
Rayflex	rayon	FMC Corporation, American Viscose Division
Rovana	saran	Dow Badische Company
Skybloom	rayon	American Enka Corporation
Skyloft	rayon	American Enka Corporation
Softglo	rayon	American Enka Corporation
Strata	rayon (cuprammonium)	Beaunit Corporation, Beaunit Fibers Division
Stratella	rayon (cuprammonium)	Beaunit Corporation, Beaunit Fibers Division
Strawn	rayon	Midland-Ross Corporation, IRC Fibers Division
Super L	rayon	FMC Corporation, American Viscose Division

Fiber Trade Mark	Generic Name	Member Company
		(continued)
Super Narco	rayon	Beaunit Corporation, Beaunit Fibers Division
Super Rayflex	rayon	FMC Corporation, American Viscose Division
Suprenka	rayon	American Enka Corporation
Suprenka Hi Mod	rayon	American Enka Corporation
Teflon	fluorocarbon	E. I. du Pont de Nemours & Company, Inc.
Tusson	rayon	Beaunit Corporation, Beaunit Fibers Division
Type F	acetate	Celanese Corporation
Type K	acetate	Celanese Corporation
Tyron	rayon	Midland-Ross Corporation, IRC Fibers Division
Tyweld	rayon	Midland-Ross Corporation, IRC Fibers Division
Unel	spandex	Union Carbide Corporation, Fibers and Fabrics Division
Variline	nylon	American Enka Corporation
Verel	modacrylic	Eastman Kodak Company, Tennessee Eastman Company Division
Villwyte	rayon	Midland-Ross Corporation, IRC Fibers Division
Vycron	polyester	Beaunit Corporation, Beaunit Fibers Division
Vycron Tough Stuff	polyester	Beaunit Corporation, Beaunit Fibers Division
Vyrene	spandex	UNIROYAL FIBER AND TEXTILE, Division of UNIROYAL, Inc.
Xena	rayon	Beaunit Corporation, Beaunit Fibers Division
Xtra-Tuf	polyester	Beaunit Corporation, Beaunit Fibers Division
Zantrel	rayon (high-wet-modulus)	American Enka Corporation
Zantrel 700	rayon (high-wet-modulus)	American Enka Corporation
Zefkrome	acrylic	Dow Badische Company
Zefran	acrylic	Dow Badische Company

Appendix **D**

Members of Man-Made Fiber Producers Association, Inc.

Allied Chemical Corporation
Fibers Division
One Times Square
New York, New York 10036

American Cyanamid Company
111 West 40th Street
New York, New York 10018

American Enka Corporation
Enka, North Carolina 28728

Beaunit Corporation
Beaunit Fibers Division
261 Madison Avenue
New York, New York 10016

Celanese Corporation
Celanese Fibers Company Division
522 Fifth Avenue
New York, New York 10036

Courtaulds North America Inc.
104 West 40th Street
New York, New York 10018

Dow Badische Company
Williamsburg, Virginia 23185

E. I. du Pont de Nemours & Company, Inc.
Textile Fibers Department
Wilmington, Delaware 19898

Eastman Kodak Company
Tennessee Eastman Company Division
Marketed by Eastman Chemical Products, Inc.
Kingsport, Tennessee 37662

FMC Corporation
American Viscose Division
1617 John F. Kennedy Boulevard
Philadelphia, Pennsylvania 19103

Fiber Industries, Inc.
Box 10038
Charlotte, North Carolina 28201

Hercules Incorporated
Fibers & Film Department
910 Market Street
Wilmington, Delaware 19899

Midland-Ross Corporation
IRC Fibers Division
55 Public Square
Cleveland, Ohio 44113

Mohasco Industries, Inc.
New Bedford Rayon Division
P.O. Box 908
New Bedford, Massachusetts 02742

Monsanto Company
Textiles Division
350 Fifth Avenue
New York, New York 10001

Phillips Fibers Corporation
A subsidiary of
Phillips Petroleum Company
P.O. Box 66
Greenville, South Carolina 29602

Union Carbide Corporation
Fibers and Fabrics Division
270 Park Avenue
New York, New York 10017

UNIROYAL FIBER AND TEXTILE—
Division of UNIROYAL, Inc.
350 Columbia Road
Winnsboro, South Carolina 29180

Fabric Glossary

Alpaca is a flat, dull fabric with the appearance of wool. It contains two-ply yarns, one ply a crepe viscose and the other ply a larger, regular twist acetate (grenai yarns). Crepiness is obtained from the viscose ply and body is obtained from the acetate ply. (Alpaca is also a speciality hair fiber used to make pile weave coating fabric.)

Balbriggan is a plain knit cotton fabric used for lingerie.

Balloon cloth is a fine yarn cotton fabric in balanced plain weave. It is used for dresses, blouses, coverings for balloon gas cells, airplane coverings, and typewriter ribbons.

Barathea is a ribbed fabric with a broken-surface effect due to weave. It has filament yarn in the warp and filament or staple in the filling. It may be silk, rayon, or acetate.

Batiste, wool, is a smooth, balanced fabric which is white or light in color. It is not as sheer as wool voile, but is very lightweight for a wool fabric.

Broadcloth is a lustrous woolen fabric which is highly napped and then pressed flat. The weave is not visible. Broadcloth has an up and down, and will reflect light differently if all pieces of a pattern are not cut going in the same direction.

Buckram is similar to crinoline except that it has a stiffer finish. Often two layers of crinoline are glued together to make a very heavy and stiff fabric. It is converted from cheesecloth gray goods.

Burlap is a coarse, heavy plain weave fabric made of jute. It is used primarily as carpet backing and furniture webbing, but can also be used for decorative textiles.

Butcher rayon is a crash-like fabric that is made in various weights. All kinds of names are given to this fabric. In heavier weights it looks like linen suiting. Butcher rayon may be an acetate and rayon blend or it may be 100 per cent rayon. It is often given a crease resistant finish. A Federal Trade Commission ruling prohibits the use of the word "linen" in this type of fabric.

Cambric is a fine, firm, plain weave balanced fabric finished with starch and has a slight luster on one side. It is difficult to distinguish from percale, nainsook, or longcloth.

Canvas is a heavy, firm, rather stiff fabric made of cotton or linen and is used for awnings, slipcovers, shoes, etc.

Hair canvas is a woven interfacing material in various weights. Coarse goat hair combined with wool, cotton, or rayon is used in the filling direction. Armo and Hymo are trade names.

Casement cloth is any lightweight, plain weave fabric used for glass curtains.

Cavalry twill is a smooth surfaced twill with a pronounced double twill line.

Challis (pronounced shal′i) is a lightweight, plain weave balanced fabric with a soft finish. Originally of wool, it is now made of any staple fiber or blend of fibers. Cotton challis has a slight nap to achieve softness. Challis has been used for lingerie, blouses, and dresses and is usually printed.

China silk is a soft, sheer, plain weave fabric used in sheath linings and scarves.

Chinchilla is a heavy, twill-weave wool coating which has a napped surface that is rolled into little balls. It is one of the most durable coating fabrics.

Covert was first made in England, where there was a demand for a fabric which would not catch on brambles or branches during fox hunts. To make this tightly woven fabric, a two-ply yarn, one cotton and one wool, was used. Because the cotton and wool did not take the same dye, the fabric had a mottled appearance.

Cotton covert is always mottled and it may be made with ply yarns, one ply white and the other colored, or it may be fiber dyed white and a color. It is a 2 × 1 twill of the same weight as denim and is used primarily for work pants, overalls, and service coats.

Rayon covert looks like wool covert. It is made with a blend of rayon and acetate in dress weight.

Wool covert is made from woolen or worsted yarns. It may be mottled or solid color and may be suit or coat weight. It may be napped slightly or have a clear finish. The mottled effect is obtained by using two different colored plys or by blending different colored fibers.

Crepe refers to any fabric made with crepe yarns (true crepe) or with a puckered surface (crepe effects).

Canton crepe is a filling crepe made with coarse yarns of alternate S and Z twist (2S and 2Z); (4S and 4Z); (6S and 6Z). It has a low count and is rough looking. There is much crosswise stretch in the fabric. It is used for dresses and suit dresses. Dry cleaning is preferable.

Chiffron is a smooth, plain weave, balanced fabric. It is a soft, filmy fabric with fine yarns.

Crepe-backed satin is a satin weave with crepe filling yarns.

Crepe de Chine was originally a washable silk crepe woven in the gum. Now it refers to a lightweight flat crepe.

Crepe Romaine, triple sheer and semi-sheer, is a heavier fabric than georgette and not as transparent. It is a 2/1 basket weave.

Crepon and bark crepe are heavy crepes with a rough appearance. Bark crepe has the appearance of tree bark. Crepon has wavy lines in the warp direction caused by high twist filling yarns. Dry cleaning is preferable.

Georgette has a duller texture than chiffon, with a texture similar to voile.

Dimity is a Greek word which means "double thread." Dimity cord has warp-wise cords made by weaving two or more yarns as one and separating them by areas of plain weave. Dimity is sheer with a crisp finish.

Barred dimity has cords in both warp and filling.

Duvetyn is similar to suede, but is lighter in weight and is more drapable. It has a soft, velvet-like surface made by napping, shearing, and brushing.

Flannel refers to any napped fabric.

Canton flannel is a twill weave cotton fabric napped on one side. It has a long nap. It is used for work mittens and pocket linings.

Tarnish-resistant flannel is a solid-color cotton fabric, which is impregnated with chemicals to absorb sulfur fumes. It is used for silverware cases and chest linings.

Viyella flannel is part wool, part cotton flannel similar to outing flannel, but with a twill weave. The cotton content makes it more washable than an all-wool flannel. It is used for shirts and baby clothes. The fabric is imported from England.

Foulard is a printed lightweight twill weave fabric of silk, cotton, rayon, or wool. Silk surah is a similar fabric.

Gauze is a low, plain weave balanced fabric used for bandages.

Theatrical gauze is made from linen fiber which has more body and luster than cotton. It may be yarn dyed or plain color. Its chief use is for curtains.

Gingham is a yarn dyed, plain weave fabric which varies in weight from tissue to suiting. It may be balanced or ribbed. Usually it is made of cotton, but silk, rayon, and blends are called ginghams.

Shagbark gingham has slack tension loops scattered over the surface.

Herringbone fabrics have warp stripes which are made by changing the direction of the twill line. The chevron-like stripes may be of equal prominence, or one may be prominent and the other subdued. These fabrics are made in all weights, of all fiber contents, and in many types of interlacings.

Homespun is a coarse, balanced, plain weave fabric with a hand-woven look. It is used for coats, suits, and dresses.

Hopsacking is a suiting weight fabric made with a basket weave.

Interfacing is a woven or nonwoven fabric used to give body to a garment. Any fabric may be used. Choice depends upon weight of fabric and proper cleaning method. Specially prepared interfacings are:
Nonwoven: Pellon, Keybak, Textryl, Pelonite, Remay
Woven: hair-canvas, Armo, Hymo, Siri, Wigan, Lamicel

Jaspé cloth is a plain weave suiting weight cloth made with multicolored warp yarns and plain filling yarns. It is used for slipcovers and draperies.

Kasha is a type of flannel which has black and colored fibers in the filling yarns.
Kersey is a very heavy, thick, boardy wool coating fabric which has been fulled and felted.

Lamé is a fabric containing metallic yarns.
Linen[1] is the only fabric which can be called by the fiber name. Linen usually means a plain weave, suiting weight fabric.

Crebasi linen refers to a dress weight, plain weave linen fabric.
Handkerchief linen is similar in luster and count to batiste, and like batiste it wrinkles badly. Linen yarns are more uneven than cotton yarns. This helps in identifying the fabric. Cotton and rayon yarns are sometimes made to resemble linen yarns by being purposely spun with irregularities.
Lining refers to any fabric used on the back of a shell.
Metal coated or reflective linings are lining fabrics that have a finish of metallic particles sprayed on the inner side. Aluminum is used because it is economical and lightweight, but any metal that flakes could be used. The metal can be applied to any type of fiber.
Sheath lining is a medium weight, plain weave, balanced fabric which resembles China silk.
Longcloth is a plain weave, balanced white cotton fabric used for handkerchiefs, lingerie, and blouses.

Melton is similar to kersey, but is heavier in weight.
Mousseline de soie is French for "silk muslin." It is a plain weave, balanced sheer fabric with a crisp finish.

Nainsook is a soft-finished and sometimes mercerized, plain weave, balanced cotton fabric. It may be white, pastel-colored, or printed. Nainsook is similar to batiste, but it is less transparent. It is used for

[1] *Linen* and *flax* are terms which are used interchangeably.

lingerie, handkerchiefs, interfacings, and infant's wear.
Ninon is a plain weave, sheer fabric made of acetate or polyester filaments and used for glass curtains.

Organza is rayon or silk organdy.
Osnaburg is a coarse, suiting-weight cotton fabric characterized by uneven yarns which have bits of cellulosic waste. It is used for slipcovers, draperies, and sportswear.
Ottoman is a ribbed fabric with alternate large and small ribs made by adjacent filling yarns of different sizes.

Pajama check is similar to dimity in construction, but it is made with carded yarns and is not as sheer. It has a soft finish and grouped yarns in both directions.
Peau de soie is French for "skin of silk." It is a very smooth semi-dull satin construction which has satin floats on both sides of the fabric. It is a fairly heavy fabric made in silk, acetate, or in mixtures.
Piqué. (*See* page 151.)
Dimity piqué is neither like piqué nor like dimity. It has the sheerness of dimity, but not the double thread. It has the appearance of a piqué cord, but is not a cord weave. Dimity piqué is made with combed, cotton yarns and spaces are left at regular intervals between the warp threads (skipped dents).
Embossed piqué is a plain weave, balanced fabric which is treated with a resin, and then embossed in a piqué stripe. The resin finish is cured to make it durable.
Novelty piqué is any fabric which has a combination of piqué weave with another weave. Often the piqué stripe does not go the entire length of the fabric.
Picolay (trade name) is an embossed fabric which resembles birdseye piqué. Proper care must be given if the design is to last satisfactorily.
Seersucker piqué is made with slack tension weaving in which the tight stripe is a piqué weave. Wales and crinkle stripes are in the warp directions. Like all piqué, and unlike seersucker, the fabrics have a right and wrong side.
Waffle cloth is sometimes incorrectly called waffle piqué. Waffle cloth has a honeycomb or waffle design which is woven in. A dobby loom is used. It looks the same on the right and wrong sides. Waffle cloth is made in the same weight as pinwale piqué with carded or combed cotton, and is made in a heavier drapery fabric which has large waffle squares. Baby blankets with wool yarns are sometimes made with this weave.
Pongee is a wild-silk, plain weave fabric. It is also the name of a ribbed fabric comparable to broadcloth in weight which is made with acetate filament warp and cotton filling yarns.

Sailcloth is a suiting-weight cotton fabric in a 2/1 basket weave.

Sharkskin is a woolen or worsted 2/2 twill made with yarns of two different colors and having a smooth, flat appearance. The twill line, unlike most of the wool twill fabrics, goes up to the left. Acetate or Arnel sharkskin is a plain weave, solid-color fabric, but it has the smooth, flat appearance of the wool fabric. It is used primarily for women's summer suits.

Suede is a plain weave or twill weave fabric which is napped and then sheared to resemble leather. Suedes for jackets and ski wear are often napped on both sides. Any suitable fiber can be used.

Taffeta refers to any plain weave, balanced, or ribbed fabric made with filament yarns.

Faille taffeta has a crosswise rib made by using many more warp yarns than filling yarns. All ribbed taffetas have crispness.

Paper taffeta is a very lightweight, stiff, transparent fabric.

Pigment taffeta is woven with delustered rayon filaments with little or no twist, into a plain weave, balanced fabric. It is not crisp.

Tarlatan is a low count, plain weave, cotton cheese-cloth with a starched finish.

Ticking is made in plain, twill, satin, or figure weave of cotton. Fabrics are used for mattress covers, slip-covers, and upholstery. A lighter weight fabric is used for sportswear.

Tricotine is a clear-finish twill weave fabric in cotton, wool, or man-made fibers. It has a double twill line.

Tufted fabric is one in which the pile is made by inserting the extra yarns into an already woven backing fabric. The yarns are punched through the fabric by needles and are locked in the fabric by the blooming or untwisting action of the yarn plus the shrinkage of the backing fabric. They are not held in by weaving as are the pile yarns in other pile fabrics. In carpeting, the back is given a coat of lastex to give stiffness and skid resistance to the carpet. Chenille bedspreads and robes are made with cotton yarns on a heavy muslin background. All kinds of fibers are used in carpeting on a canvas-base fabric.

Velvet comes from the Latin "vellus" meaning a fleece or tufted hair. It is not known where or when it originated, but it was made the official fabric for both the court and the church during the Middle Ages. In France, blue velvet was reserved exclusively for the King's family. As people attained wealth and power, the use of velvet became more widespread.

Brocade velvet has a pile of different heights cut to form a design.

Chiffon velvet is very durable, lightweight, and is made with a rayon pile and a silk back. Faconné velvet is patterned by burnt out designs.

Embossed velvet has certain areas pressed flat.

Lyons velvet is a closely woven fabric with a deep pile which sometimes has a cotton pile and a silk back. It is used for coat collars, suits and coats, and for millinery.

Nacré velvet is a changeable fabric with the back of one color and the pile of another.

Panne velvet has the pile pressed flat and is a smooth, lustrous fabric.

Wool plaids and checks are often made with a 2/2 twill weave. They may be made with woolen or worsted yarns; they may be napped or smooth; they are always yarn dyed. They are named according to the arrangement of the colored yarns; for example, shepherd's check, hound's tooth check, Glen plaid.

Zibilene is a heavy coating fabric with a long, shaggy nap laid in one direction. The fabrics sometimes have crosswise ridges caused by a longer nap in those areas.

Index